LB
1028
.3
S38
2006

D1302031

Self, Peer, and Group Assessment in E-Learning

Tim S. Roberts
Central Queensland University, Bundaberg, Australia

LIBRARY
NSCC, KINGSTEC CAMPUS
236 BELCHER ST.
KENTVILLE, NS B4N 3X3 CANADA

WITHDRAWN

 Information Science Publishing

Hershey • London • Melbourne • Singapore

Acquisitions Editor: Michelle Potter
Development Editor: Kristin Roth
Senior Managing Editor: Amanda Appicello
Managing Editor: Jennifer Neidig
Copy Editor: Chuck Pizar
Typesetter: Diane Huskinson
Cover Design: Lisa Tosheff
Printed at: Yurchak Printing Inc.

Published in the United States of America by
    Information Science Publishing (an imprint of Idea Group Inc.)
    701 E. Chocolate Avenue
    Hershey PA 17033
    Tel: 717-533-8845
    Fax: 717-533-8661
    E-mail: cust@idea-group.com
    Web site: http://www.idea-group.com

and in the United Kingdom by
    Information Science Publishing (an imprint of Idea Group Inc.)
    3 Henrietta Street
    Covent Garden
    London WC2E 8LU
    Tel: 44 20 7240 0856
    Fax: 44 20 7379 0609
    Web site: http://www.eurospanonline.com

Copyright © 2006 by Idea Group Inc. All rights reserved. No part of this book may be reproduced, stored or distributed in any form or by any means, electronic or mechanical, including photocopying, without written permission from the publisher.

Product or company names used in this book are for identification purposes only. Inclusion of the names of the products or companies does not indicate a claim of ownership by IGI of the trademark or registered trademark.

Library of Congress Cataloging-in-Publication Data

Self, peer, and group assessment in e-learning / Tim S. Roberts, editor.
      p. cm.
   Summary: "This book encourages the development of higher-quality learning and assess-
ment practices and describes the principal characteristics of self-assessment, peer assessment,
and group assessment with guidelines for effective implementation"--Provided by publisher.
   Includes bibliographical references and index.
   ISBN 1-59140-965-9 (hardcover) -- ISBN 1-59140-966-7 (softcover) -- ISBN 1-59140-
967-5 (ebook)
   1. Computer-assisted instruction--Evaluation. 2. Web-based instruction--Evaluation. 3.
Group work in education. 4. Peer review. I. Roberts, Tim S., 1955-
   LB1028.3.S38885 2006
   378.1'66--dc22
                                 2005027416

British Cataloguing in Publication Data
A Cataloguing in Publication record for this book is available from the British Library.

All work contributed to this book is new, previously-unpublished material. The views expressed in this book are those of the authors, but not necessarily of the publisher.

Dedication

This book is dedicated to my mother, Roma Roberts. As someone who moved from one side of the world to the other, on her own, she is an inspiration to all of us to not be afraid of new adventures.

Self, Peer, and Group Assessment in E-Learning

Table of Contents

Preface

How can assessment practices be used to assist and improve the learning process? This book attempts to answer this question by bringing together 13 contributions from prominent researchers and practitioners actively involved in all aspects of self, peer, and group assessment.

Two factors—the rapidly increasing use of computers in education in general and the provision of courses online via the Web in particular—have caused a resurgence of interest amongst educators in nontraditional methods of course design and delivery. In addition, greater curiosity than ever before is being shown in more student-centered methods of teaching and learning, as evidenced by the number of books, journal articles, and conference papers devoted to topics such as problem-based learning, collaborative and cooperative learning, and CSCL (which originally stood for computer-supported collaborative learning, but now seems to be an acronym used in its own right).

We might call this an example of *convergence*, the coming together of two or more disparate disciplines or technologies, or, perhaps more properly, *synergism*, where two apparently disparate factors combine for increased effect. In this case, the greater use of online technologies would seem to provide an ideal environment for students to become more actively involved in their own learning. One of the ways that this greater involvement can be encouraged is by the more widespread use of self, peer, and group assessment.

There is a growing emphasis on students helping each other with their learning. The use of both group and collaborative work, especially as they can be employed in an online *Web-based* environment, has been the central theme of two earlier books (Roberts, 2003, 2004). This current book concentrates on the different forms of noninstructor-based assessment that can be usefully employed in an online environment.

As with much educational literature, there are significant problems with the definition of key terms. Does the term *assessment* mean the same as *evaluation*? Are there significant differences? Do both terms relate solely to student learning, or are they equally applicable to the instructors, the materials, and the course delivery? Is *assessment* only really assessment if marks counting towards final grades are involved? What if peer feedback provides qualitative guidance, but not quantitative scores, to the instructor, who nevertheless decides upon the final grade based at least partly on such feedback? Is *e-learning* the same as *online learning*? How much of a course must be online before it can be considered to be Web-based? Can on-campus students sometimes be *e-learners*, too?

This book takes a liberal attitude to such matters, recognizing that definitions are liable to change from culture to culture and with the passage of time. Hopefully, though, the wide variety of experiences and case studies reported here will serve to benefit readers eager to explore the possibilities provided by non-traditional methods of assessment in the still relatively new world of e-learning.

As is inevitably the case in any book resulting from the contributions of multiple authors, the alert reader will find some duplication: There are two chapters about the LENTEC project, for example, and many of the authors draw similar conclusions about the benefits and problems of peer assessment. There are also significant differences, however, in terms of course content and audience, and how self, peer, and group assessment techniques are used and administered.

Much of the interest in alternative forms of assessment has tended to be concentrated in fields ranging from the arts to the softer sciences, such as the studies of creative writing, language learning, and education. It would be wrong to overgeneralize from this, however, and conclude that such methods cannot be applied in the harder sciences—one of the case studies included here describes the use of peer and group assessment in an engineering course, for example.

Chapter I, *Self, Peer, and Group Assessment in E-Learning: An Introduction*, has a modest aim: to explain what is meant by each of the terms, list some of the commonly experienced advantages and disadvantages of each, and provide some guidelines for effective implementation, based on both research and practice. Many references are provided for readers interested in some of the more recently published books and articles in this area.

In Chapter II, *A Case Study in Peer Evaluation for Second Language Teachers in Training*, Pamela L. Anderson-Mejías, of the University of Texas - Pan American, describes a case study of master's-level second language teachers in training who used self and peer evaluation within a capstone course in their program. Various instruments for students to evaluate their peers are described, including online quiz instruments, immediate chat feedback quizzes, and peer evaluation rubrics. A significant component of each final grade in the course was determined by peer evaluation.

One particularly interesting finding reported by the author was that greater honesty was elicited by the use of quizzes and surveys submitted online, rather than paper-based ones submitted directly to the instructor in a face-to-face setting.

In Chapter III, *Peer and SelfAssessment in Portuguese Engineering Education*, Natascha van Hattum-Janssen and Pedro Pimenta, both from the University of Minho in Portugal, describe the implementation of peer and selfassessment in two first-year engineering courses. The first section of the chapter pays particular attention to learning and the influences of peer and selfassessment, while the second describes the case study and illustrates how students assumed responsibility in their own assessment processes. The chapter discusses some of the advantages and disadvantages of peer and selfassessment and concludes by highlighting some of the lessons learned from the case study.

While lending weight to the belief that the move to more student-centered assessment can work well, van Hattum-Janssen and Pimenta stress the need for clear and transparent criteria to enable a fair and unambiguous interpretation and grading process and say that ill-defined criteria can lead to significant difficulties when trying to attribute a fair grade.

In Chapter IV, *Learning and Assessment: A Case Study—Going the Full Monty,* Mary Panko, of Unitec New Zealand, reflects on the lessons learned by the developers of a course about self, peer and group assessment for adult educators, in which online discussion forums played an integral and essential role. The chapter examines the ways in which the learners used online discussion forums and also looks at particular exchanges to show how the group projects were developed in an e-learning environment.

As the author notes, there is always a potential for relationships to become destructive and for learning opportunities to be lost, but, as is commonly found to be the situation, the groups in this case study tended to be very supportive of one another, thus effectively becoming productive learning communities.

In Chapter V, *A Case Study of the Integration of Self, Peer and Group Assessment in a Core First-Year Educational Psychology Unit through Flexible Delivery Implementation,* Rozz Albon, from Curtin University of Technology in Perth, Australia, provides a case study of one lecturer's approach to innovative assessment in a first-year unit of university study of 188 students. Many insights are provided into the training, preparation, and assessment experiences of self, peer, group, and lecturer assessments bound together by technology for flexible delivery.

By contrast, the target audience for Margaret Riel, from Pepperdine University, in California, and her colleagues James Rhoads, from Citrus College in

California, and Eric Ellis, from Treasure Valley Community College in Oregon, could hardly be more different: In Chapter VI, *Culture of Critique: Online Learning Circles and Peer Review in Graduate Education,* they explore a strategy for helping graduate students develop their own authority and trust in evaluating research and a respect for the authority of their peers. The chapter evaluates the use of learning circles for group work in graduate online education, explores the type and form of peer feedback from within this collaborative structure, and poses the question: Under what conditions are students willing to be critical, and to accept criticism from their peers as legitimate?

Two chapters follow on a particularly noteworthy example of involving students in their own learning and assessment—the European Leonardo Project LENTEC, carried out from 2001 through 2003. The project involved upper secondary vocational school students from six different European countries and used problem-based learning (PBL) methods to improve their English language skills in an online environment.

In Chapter VII, *Learning English for Technical Purposes: The LENTEC Project,* Anne Dragemark, from Göteborg University in Sweden, describes the project, and finds that moving the responsibility for assessment to the students themselves not only motivated the students but also gave them added time for actual language learning.

One finding reinforces what has been found in other research: More advanced students tended to underestimate their ability somewhat, while those with lesser skills tended to overestimate.

In Chapter VIII, *Self and Peer Assessment in a Problem-Based Learning Environment: Learning English by Solving a Technical Problem–A Case Study,* Bernarda Kosel, of the University of Ljubljana in Slovenia, uses the project to offer some suggestions on assessing student-centered groups, and shows how self and peer assessment can complement teachers' assessments. Many readers new to student-centered methods of assessment might find the "Tips for the Teacher" at the end of Kosel's chapter particularly valuable.

In Chapter IX, *Evaluating Designs for Web-Assisted Peer and Group Assessment,* Paul Lam and Carmel McNaught, both from The Chinese University of Hong Kong, look at the use of e-resources, e-display, and e-communication in the context of six cases of teachers using peer and group assessment. The chapter provides an analysis of evaluation data gathered from student surveys, focus-group interviews, teacher surveys, analysis of forum postings, and counter site logs within the various designs of these courses, and concludes—while at the same time stressing the need for careful planning—that Web-enabled peer and group assessment activities can produce positive results.

In Chapter X, *How's My Writing? Using Online Peer Feedback to Improve Performance in the Composition Classroom,* Vanessa Paz Dennen, of Florida State University, and Gabriel Jones, of the University of California in San Diego, present a case study showing how online peer feedback was used as a formative learning and assessment activity in a required, university-level composition course. The authors argue that such activities, if designed effectively, contribute significantly toward a student's sense of audience, authority, and empowerment as a productive member of a larger discourse community.

Particularly worthy of note is that the online e-learning environment provided students with the time to think and reflect as they engaged in asynchronous critiques and also enabled permanent documentation of their efforts.

In Chapter XI, *Interpersonal Assessment: Evaluating Others in Online Learning Environments*, Aditya Johri, of Stanford University, introduces and discusses the concept of *interpersonal assessment*—that is, the act of assessing what other participants in an online learning environment know and how they behave. Lack of face-to-face interaction, mediated cues, and unshared contexts mean that such assessment is often difficult in an online environment, and in collaborative groups students need to know what others in a group know and how they act to be able to work them; but, is this difficulty critical for successful learning outcomes?

In Chapter XII, *A Framework for Assessing Self, Peer and Group Performance in E-Learning,* Thanasis Daradoumis, Fatos Xhafa, and Ángel Alejandro Juan Pérez, all from the Open University of Catalonia in Barcelona, Spain, propose a framework to support the analysis and assessment of collaborative learning of student groups working on complex tasks in a real Web-based, distance learning context. The aim of their work is to provide a better understanding of group interaction, and to determine some practical steps to best support the collaborative learning process.

Finally, in Chapter XIII, *E-Assessment: The Demise of Exams and the Rise of Generic Attribute Assessment for Improved Student Learning,* Darrall Thompson, from the University of Technology in Sydney, Australia, takes us out with the provocative suggestion that examinations may be on the way out. He provides five reasons for a reduced focus on exams, suggests that exam grades cannot provide accruing developmental information about the students' attributes and qualities vital for a changing world and workplace, and argues for the integrated assessment of generic attributes. Two e-assessment tools to facilitate this approach are described.

Hopefully, this collection of chapters from international authors working on four continents will prove to be, at the very least, intellectually challenging and thought provoking. If so, then this book will have fulfilled part of its aim. The other part, perhaps more important still, is that some or all of the chapters will provide the stimuli not just for thoughts but also for actions—the introduction of higher-quality learning and assessment practices, ones in which the learners themselves assume a greater responsibility for, and play a more active role in, their own learning.

The editor would welcome feedback. Agreements, disagreements, comments, criticisms, and complaints (of course) can be sent to the address below.

Tim S. Roberts
Central Queensland University
Bundaberg, Queensland, Australia
t.roberts@cqu.edu.au

References

Roberts, T. S. (2003). *Online collaborative learning: Theory and practice.* Hershey, PA: InfoSci.

Roberts, T. S. (2004). *Computer-supported collaborative learning in higher education.* Hershey, PA: Idea Group Publishing.

Acknowledgments

It goes without saying that any book such as this is inevitably the result of a lot of hard work by a large group of people. First and foremost, I would like to thank all of the authors of the individual chapters. Without exception, their contributions to this book have provided unique and thought-provoking insights into the increasingly important world of self-, peer, and group assessment in e-learning. This book is a testament to their conscientiousness and expertise.

Many thanks also to all of those who served as reviewers, without whose critical, but always constructive, comments this book would never have seen the light of day. Special mention in this regard must go to Azza Arif, Rommel Barbosa, Michael Barbour, Debbie Hopgood, Wendy Marley, Shannon McNair, June Mogensen, Bryan Morgan, Mark Nichols, Elena Raileanu, and Ladislav Samuelis.

Extra special thanks must be extended to Joanne McInnerney, who assisted in the review process, read draft forms of almost all of the chapters on several occasions, suggested many corrections, and played a very significant role in ensuring that the finished book was of a high standard throughout.

I would also like to express my gratitude to Central Queensland University, which provided me with the very necessary time and resources to see the book through to completion, and to the very helpful and professional staff at Idea Group Inc., whose patience and assistance throughout the whole process has been of the highest order. In particular my thanks go to Mehdi Khosrow-Pour, who initially accepted the worth of such an undertaking; to Jan Travers, who continually provided assistance where needed; to Michele Rossi and Kristin Roth, who kept me on track throughout the editing process; and to Amanda Appicello, who oversaw the proofing and production of the book in exemplary fashion.

Last but not least, I would like to thank you, the readers of this book. Hopefully *Self-, Peer, and Group Assessment in E-Learning* will help you towards the view that student-centered forms of assessment can greatly assist the learning process. If you would like to write to me with your comments or feedback, good or bad, please do so. My e-mail address is t.roberts@cqu.edu.au

Tim S. Roberts

Chapter I

Self, Peer, and Group Assessment in E-Learning:
An Introduction

Tim S. Roberts
Central Queensland University, Bundaberg, Australia

Abstract

This chapter provides an informal introduction to self, peer, and group assessment, especially as they may be applied within an online, or e-learning, environment. What is self assessment? What is peer assessment? What is group assessment? In what ways are they similar, and what distinguishes one from another? The principal characteristics of each are described. An assumption, made explicit from the start, is that assessment should not just be about grading, but about assisting the process of learning itself. References are made throughout to the thoughts and experiences of many researchers and practitioners currently working in the field.

Copyright © 2006, Idea Group Inc. Copying or distributing in print or electronic forms without written permission of Idea Group Inc. is prohibited.

Introduction

And what is good, Phaedrus,And what is not good—Need we ask anyone to tell us these things?

Robert Pirsig, Zen and the Art of Motorcycle Maintenance

The traditional view has always been something along the following lines: assessment is about grading. One or more instructors assess the work of the students, with the primary—and perhaps sole—aim of assigning fair and appropriate grades to each of the students at the end of the course.

An alternative view, and one that has claimed a large number of adherents in recent years, is that assessment can and should also play a vital part in the learning process itself. The most radical form of this alternative view is that the primary role of assessment is not about grading at all, but about learning, and that assessment practices should be developed and refined so that they assist the learner to learn effectively and efficiently.

This would have been an extremely radical thesis not too long ago, but these days an ever-increasing interest is being shown in nontraditional methods of teaching, and most particularly, in methods that involve learners in a more active way in their own learning. Partly, this has been brought about because of a concern that many traditional methods, such as lectures and tutorials, perhaps do not perform as well as might be hoped in some circumstances, particularly in what might be termed generic skills. Bligh (2000), for example, says, "Use lectures to teach information. Do not rely on them to promote thought, change attitudes, or develop behavioral skills if you can help it" (p. 20).

There is also a growing interest in methods where students help each other, in the form of group or collaborative learning. Two earlier books by the current author (Roberts, 2003, 2004) have dealt with collaborative learning in the context of online courses.

Any discussion of the use of self, peer, and group assessment in e-learning is therefore both important and timely. The ability to assess one's own and others' work is clearly a vital skill in the real world. For this reason alone, such methods should be worthy of further study. When one combines this with other identified benefits, such as: assisting learners to quickly identify areas requiring further study, improving communication skills, and increasing self reliance, the importance of such methods should be apparent to all.

Copyright © 2006, Idea Group Inc. Copying or distributing in print or electronic forms without written permission of Idea Group Inc. is prohibited.

Self Assessment

Self assessment means the process of having the learners critically reflect upon, record the progress of, and perhaps suggest grades for, their own learning. *Critical reflection* has been shown to positively enhance the learning process; *recording of progress* can act as a stimulus to focus learning in appropriate directions; and *suggested grades*, while in no way diminishing the responsibility of the instructor for the final marks and grades awarded, can act as guides to assist the instructor in making appropriate judgements as to the real level of learning that has occurred.

Active Learning

The very act of self assessment can be a force pushing students to engage more actively in their own learning. Buchanan (2004) summarizes the feelings of many other researchers when she says that, "self assessment can promote more active engagement with the course than simply sitting back and awaiting a grade from one's instructor" (p. 169), and she quotes Schunk (2000, p. 379) as saying that "developing self evaluation strategies helps students gain control over their learning … [and] allows them to focus more effort in studying those areas where they need more time."

"Self assessment is a means—to what end?" asks Wiggins (1998), who then immediately supplies one possible answer—"Self adjustment and eventual expertise" (p. 162). Similar sentiments are expressed by Hanna, Glowacki-Dudka, and Conceicao-Runlee (2000), who also suggest that self assessment serves to aid not only the learner but also the instructor, because it "gives learners the opportunity to reflect on their own learning.…it's a great way to uncover the internal journey of each learner … [this] may be much more significant than you can observe from the outside" (p. 44).

This sounds well and good, but it has been shown by a number of researchers that students, particularly those just starting out on tertiary study, may not be naturally skilled at self assessment, and their self assessed grades may have little correlation with those assigned by the instructor (Falchikov & Boud, 1989). This should not be unduly surprising—like many other skills, self assessment improves with guidance and practice. And the same researchers have shown that correlations do indeed improve significantly if specific guidelines for self assessment are provided, and if such techniques are utilized within the context of upper-level undergraduate or graduate courses. More recently, other work has confirmed the ability of upper-level students to self assess appropriately (Kardash, 2000).

Copyright © 2006, Idea Group Inc. Copying or distributing in print or electronic forms without written permission of Idea Group Inc. is prohibited.

Reflection

Reflection is an essential component of self assessment, providing students with an opportunity to consider not only their own learning, but also how they have learned, including any problems encountered along the way. Such reflection aids in self awareness and can provide invaluable feedback to guide future learning. Frequently, course schedules are devised without any time specifically set aside for reflection; this is a pity, because it forces students from one topic to the next, without the time necessary to realize their maximum learning potential. The inclusion of self assessment practices necessarily introduces such periods as integral parts of the course.

Portfolios

The keeping of portfolios is a practice largely encouraged within some subject areas, particularly the creative arts, but hardly practiced at all within others, such as the physical sciences. Portfolios can act as showcases for a student's best work, and can provide evidence of learning accomplishments, and of growth throughout a course. They can also act as integral components of the process of self assessment, by providing the basic raw materials by which students are enabled to reflect upon, and assess, their own learning.

Excellent discussions of the whys and wherefores of using portfolios to promote, support, and evaluate learning, and their advantages and disadvantages, are to be found in many places; amongst the best treatments of the use of portfolios are those provided by Huba and Freed (2000, pp. 233-268) and Wiggins (1998, pp. 189-203).

Rubrics and Guidelines

In order to self assess appropriately, students need two things: a clear set of guidelines and practice.

Many authors suggest that the provision of a set of guidelines, perhaps in the form of a rubric or menu of questions to be asked, is of high importance. Race (2001) suggests a menu of questions that can be used for self assessment, including:

- *What do you ... consider will be a fair score or grade ...?*
- *What ... was the thing you did best in this assignment?*

Copyright © 2006, Idea Group Inc. Copying or distributing in print or electronic forms without written permission of Idea Group Inc. is prohibited.

- *What did you find the hardest part of this assignment?*
- *What was the most important thing you learnt about the subject through doing this assignment?*
- *How has doing this assignment changed your opinions?* (pp. 101-102).

Race again makes the important point that self assessment forces students to reflect on what they have done.

The previous menu of questions is clearly generic; more specific questions might well be appropriate in many contexts. Some excellent advice on the design, scoring, and use of rubrics and templates for assessment of all kinds, including self assessment, is given by Wiggins (1998, pp. 153-185).

Like any other skill, self assessment can be improved with practice. McKeachie (2002) asserts, "if one of our goals is continued learning, students need practice in self assessment", and that "like other skills, self evaluation is learned by practice with feedback. Thus students need many opportunities for self evaluation with feedback about their evaluation as well as about the work being evaluated" (p. 71).

Summary

In appropriate contexts, self assessment can also be used for the purpose of deciding when to sit for formal evaluation. Cucchiarelli, Panti, and Valenti (2000) say that "the search for assessment methods able to reach an objective judgement of student's knowledge is a crucial goal for both teachers and educational institutions", and that "self assessment may be viewed as a mix of formative and diagnostic assessment, that may be used by the student to monitor the level of acquired knowledge in order to decide how and when to face summative evaluation" (p. 176). Such examples are commonplace outside of formal educational institutions (think of learning to drive or applying for a promotion, for example) but still comparatively rare within it.

A good summary of the advantages of self assessment can be found in Buchanan (2004): a greater autonomy and sense of control exerted by the student, an ability to see where one needs to improve, and a facilitation of dialogue between the student and the instructor. Amongst the disadvantages listed are that students may be more concerned with the grade than the learning process, that they may not know what they do not know, and that the instructor must provide guidelines or a rubric. Listed amongst both advantages and disadvantages is that self assessment forces the instructor to be clear in articulating goals and objectives (p. 174).

Copyright © 2006, Idea Group Inc. Copying or distributing in print or electronic forms without written permission of Idea Group Inc. is prohibited.

Davis (1993) expressing one of the principal reservations about the use of self assessment, states that it "... takes away from faculty one of their chief responsibilities: to make professional judgements about students' learning, and tell students how well they are performing" (p. 291). It need not, of course; if self assessment is used appropriately, it can serve as a valuable assistant and guide to the students' learning, rather than as a dictatorial process somehow imposed on the instructor.

Peer Assessment

The term *peer assessment* refers to the process of having the learners critically reflect upon, and perhaps suggest grades for, the learning of their peers. Peer assessment is distinguished from group assessment in that students assess each other's learning, even though the learning may have occurred individually, or at least outside of any formal collaborative groups.

Authenticity

As with self assessment, this more active role can have a very positive effect on the process of learning. McConnell (2000) says that:

... if learners are actively involved in decisions about how to learn, what to learn and why they are learning, and are also actively involved in decisions about criteria for assessment and the process of judging their own and other's work, then their relationship to their studies will be qualitatively different to those learners who are treated as recipients of teaching and who are the object of others', unilateral, assessment. (p. 127)

Quite so. It has been clearly shown in many contexts that a more active and responsible role can lead to greater engagement. He also makes the point that peer assessors "will have also gone through a similar learning experience. They will be in a position to relate their own experiences to that of the assignment writer, ask relevant questions and take part in the assessment from a closer 'learner's' perspective than the tutor" (p. 127).

A similar point is made by Kearsley (2000) that "feedback from fellow students is often quite helpful because it comes from their perspective rather than an expert's" (p. 81). However, he says, it is necessary to "remind students to be constructive in their comments; students tend to assume that evaluation needs to

Copyright © 2006, Idea Group Inc. Copying or distributing in print or electronic forms without written permission of Idea Group Inc. is prohibited.

be negative" (p. 81). As regrettably do many instructors! It is almost common-place, for example, for essays and reports to be returned with comments alongside only those passages that need correction—and no comment at all besides passages that may range from acceptable to excellent. Some research (e.g., Falchikov, 1996) has in fact suggested that, overall, feedback from fellow students may be more positive than that received from instructors.

Benefits

Race (2001), talking about how to involve students in their own assessment, says "Introducing peer assessment can seem a daunting and hazardous prospect, if you are surrounded by an assessment culture where lecturers undertake all of the assessing. There are, however, several good reasons why the prospect should not seem so formidable ...", and then proceeds to give seven reasons why we should be brave in this respect:

- Students are doing it already (students are continually peer-assessing: they look at other's work, judge against their own or other's, and may or may not get a chance to state their views publicly)
- Students find out more about assessment cultures (getting involved in peer assessment makes the assessment culture much more transparent)
- We cannot do as much assessing as we used to (more students, heavier teaching loads, shorter timescales ...)
- Students learn more deeply when they have a sense of ownership of the agenda (of course: a sense of ownership always increases involvement)
- The act of assessing is one of the deepest learning experiences (applying criteria to someone else's work is one of the most productive ways of developing and deepening understanding of the subject matter involved in the process. Measuring and judging are far more rigorous processes than simply reading, listening, and watching.
- Peer assessment allows students to learn from each other's successes, and
- Peer assessment allows students to learn from each other's weaknesses. (Race, 2001, pp. 94-95)

Guidelines

Most researchers and practitioners are in agreement that for peer assessment to work well, it is important for the instructor to provide clear and concise

Copyright © 2006, Idea Group Inc. Copying or distributing in print or electronic forms without written permission of Idea Group Inc. is prohibited.

guidelines, and for the instructor to maintain the ultimate responsibility for the final grades. Kearsley (2000, p. 91) says that when peer assessment is used, "… the guidelines that students are to use in evaluating each other's work must be clearly defined. Checklists that list each of the points to assessed … are very useful. Although students may generate the grades, the teacher should … reserve the right to make adjustments if necessary." Templates for peer assessment can be found in many places; two basic but excellent templates that can be used for peer assessment can be found in Race (2001, pp. 99-100).

A standard template should have, as a general rule, a list of the criteria to be used when carrying out the assessment; a maximum mark or weighting for each of the criteria listed; and then small spaces for the assessor to fill in a quantitative mark against each criterion, and larger spaces to provide qualitative comments. Assessors should be advised to make the comments as constructive as possible: single words such as "Fair" or "Poor," if used at all, should be supplemented with reasons to justify such comments, and suggestions for improvement.

Reservations

Students can exhibit strong reservations about the use of group or peer assessment. Such reservations come in two varieties. The first relates to the student's own ability to assess others—*am I sufficiently skilled to assess someone else's work?*—and any reverberations that might be encountered from less-than-happy fellow students. The second relates to fears that one's peers might provide damning assessments, perhaps based on invalid criteria—*after all, isn't assessment the teacher's job?*

Buchanan (2004, p. 170) says that peer assessment "… usually raises fear among students, who are afraid of facing their friends the next week in class after issuing someone a bad grade …" and that, even in an online environment, there is the possibility of inflated grades, because "… no-one wants to be known as the guy who gives harsh grades to his online friends…so a higher-than-deserved grade may be issued."

McConnell (2000) says that collaborative assessment "can initially produce strong feelings of antipathy. There is often a general feeling of uncertainty about participants assessing themselves, and more strongly about assessing each other" (p. 128), but that the initial fears held by the students "usually give way to very positive feelings once participants take part in the task. With few exceptions, learners find this is a most worthwhile use of time …" (p. 128).

Copyright © 2006, Idea Group Inc. Copying or distributing in print or electronic forms without written permission of Idea Group Inc. is prohibited.

Workload

One valid question concerns the additional workload brought about by the introduction of peer assessment. Many educators believe that there is a direct correlation between interaction (of all forms) and the levels of learning achieved. However, making a course highly interactive can create a higher workload for instructors, who may have previously assumed their role to consist principally of "delivering the content." One way to reduce—not increase—the workload brought about by the need for greater interaction is to rely more heavily on peer assessment. Of course, added time may be needed at the beginning of the course, in the form of preparing students adequately, and the provision of guidelines and templates; but this is usually more than compensated for by the increased amount of learning that takes place via student-to-student interaction, rather than by student-to-instructor interaction.

Group Assessment

The term *group assessment* can mean several different things, from the assessment of groups as a whole, to the assessment of individuals within a group, to the group members assessing other group members' contributions to the group. The last meaning is generally the one referred to here, but a brief comment about assessing group work in general would perhaps not be out of order.

Free-Riders

The problems of allocating a uniform mark to all members of a group are well-known and well-documented; see, for example, Roberts (2004). The most frequently encountered problem is that of the free-rider—the group member who sits back and contributes little, secure in the knowledge that they will benefit from a shared group mark in the end. This and other similar problems can best be countered by ensuring that all group members do not share the same mark.

But this raises a problem: if the assessment items have been submitted by groups as a whole, how does one distinguish the individual contributions? Many ways have been suggested, such as that each member of the group keep a journal of their contributions, or that, in an e-learning environment, statistics be kept as to number of postings, and so on. But the most reliable and fair schemes would seem to include a high-level of peer assessment within the groups themselves.

Copyright © 2006, Idea Group Inc. Copying or distributing in print or electronic forms without written permission of Idea Group Inc. is prohibited.

Excellent advice for instructors contemplating the introduction of, or greater emphasis on, learning in groups can be found in many places, for example Davis (1993), Felder and Brent (2001), Kemery (2000), and McConnell (2000).

Templates

Buchanan (2004) suggests a basic sample template for group assessment:

1.   _____ *participated actively in our group planning. YES / NO*
2.   _____ *was willing to offer suggestions for group work. YES / NO*
3.   _____ *was prepared for our group's working session. YES / NO*
4.   _____ *did his/her share of the work (typing, taking notes, etc.) YES / NO*
5.   *I feel* _____ *contributed poorly / adequately / superiorly [sic] to my group.*
6.   *On a scale of 1 to 5, with 1 being lowest and 5 highest,* _____ *deserves a* _____ *for his/her work in the group.*
7.   *Think of a pie. You must slice up the pie based on the contributions of each member, with the biggest contributor getting the most pie. List each group member with a percentage of the pie. Be sure to include yourself in the slices.* (p. 171)

Many other researchers and practitioners suggest something similar. For example McKeachie (2002, p. 94) asks each student "... to turn in a slip of paper listing the members of his or her group and dividing 100 points in proportion to each member's contribution."

Such suggested divisions of marks may be made either public or private. In most cases, though, the latter will be more appropriate; that is, that each assessment made by each group member, of each group member, be considered confidential between the student providing the assessment, and the instructor. This confidentiality prevents any fears of possible retribution, whether real or imagined, and students generally feel freer to provide honest opinions. However, it is of vital importance, as with any other form of self, peer, or group assessment, that the methods to be used, and the rules concerning them, be provided to all students at the very start of the course, in as open and transparent a manner as possible, and that any reservations expressed be addressed fairly and honestly, perhaps by making students aware of the benefits of such forms of assessment referred to in the literature.

Copyright © 2006, Idea Group Inc. Copying or distributing in print or electronic forms without written permission of Idea Group Inc. is prohibited.

Advantages and Disadvantages

Amongst the advantages listed by Buchanan (2004, p. 174) of group assessment—that is, peer assessment used specifically within the context of group work—are that it may encourage students to work harder to "face" their peers, it can create a more collegial environment, and that it enables the instructor to facilitate and oversee the learning process. Amongst the disadvantages listed is the possibility of grade inflation, or, on the contrary, the possibility of harsher grading, and that group assessment can create a more hostile environment. However, there is a greater possibility of unfair and inequitable distribution of work and tasks if peer grading on group work is *not* used.

E-Learning

Many guides to *e-learning*, or online learning, or Web-based learning, devote little or no space to assessment, preferring instead to concentrate on aspects of course delivery. Still others mention assessment almost as an aside, concentrating on conventional methods such as multiple-choice quizzes (often marked electronically) and essays (almost always marked by the instructor).

Talking about assessment methods in general, McCormack and Jones (1998) suggest that using online systems can improve face-to-face methods in various ways, including saving time, reducing turnaround time, reducing the resources needed, keeping records, increasing convenience, and increasing the ease with which the data can be used (pp. 236-237).

These are all very valid and important points, to which most online instructors will wholeheartedly agree. Beyond these, however, there are specific advantages for self, peer, and group assessment techniques in e-learning because of the characteristics of the online environment.

Examples of work to be assessed are much more easily copied and communicated in an e-learning environment; no longer is it a reasonable excuse to not have handouts for everyone because the photocopier has jammed at the last minute! In suitable cases, work can be easily distributed and assessed from initial draft form right up to the finished product, and communication can take place via e-mail, blogs, discussion lists, and so on.

Templates and rubrics for assessment, often essential aids as described earlier, can easily be provided online, made available to all for inspection, and amended and updated as required, perhaps as a result of student feedback. Old versions can be stored for record-keeping purposes.

Copyright © 2006, Idea Group Inc. Copying or distributing in print or electronic forms without written permission of Idea Group Inc. is prohibited.

Once completed, templates and rubrics can be easily submitted, stored, and sorted; and comparisons made across age groups, genders, or any other criteria required, including perhaps previous course offerings.

The advantages of using some form of self, peer, and group assessment within an e-learning environment are not confined to ease of distribution, however. Buchanan (2004) makes the point that self assessment "… opens the door to a more fluid teaching and learning environment, which coincides nicely with the structure of online environments" (p. 170).

From the point of view of the instructor in an e-learning environment, without the advantages that are naturally provided by face-to-face contact and body language, it can be more difficult to gain an accurate assessment of the learning achieved. In such circumstances the instructor may see it as more appropriate for the learners themselves to gauge their learning, and, in cases where group or collaborative learning is being employed, the learning of other members within their online groups.

Students may feel less inhibited about providing positive or negative feedback about themselves or others in an online environment, though the danger of flaming, or deliberately making spiteful—as opposed to insightful—comments may occur if not adequately warned against and controlled. Certainly there is less of a risk of bullying, in the sense of one or more students coercing others to recommend good grades, or to disclose recommended grades intended for viewing only by the instructor (what might be appropriately coined the "you show me yours and I'll show you mine" phenomenon). And in cases where students wish to revise their comments, perhaps based on further reflection, they can do so easily without the minor embarrassment of having to ask for another form.

But perhaps the most important advantage of using some form of self, peer, or group assessment within an e-learning environment is that it can help to foster the building of a learning community. One very important point about e-learning environments that has been stressed by many researchers (e.g., McInnerney & Roberts, 2004; Palloff & Pratt, 1999) is the sense of isolation that can be experienced by the online learner, and the discouragement to learning that may result. While not a problem exclusive to online learners—it can be common for students in a 300-seat lecture hall to feel isolated, too—it can be particularly acute in the e-learning environment, where students may be at a considerable geographic distance not only from their instructors, but also from their fellow students.

Wegerif (1998) makes an interesting distinction between *insiders*, students who enjoy and successfully complete a course, and *outsiders*, who do not, and says that often "this threshold is essentially a social one; it is the line between feeling part of a community and feeling that one is outside that community looking in."

Copyright © 2006, Idea Group Inc. Copying or distributing in print or electronic forms without written permission of Idea Group Inc. is prohibited.

Clearly, any increased interaction with other students, particularly if that interaction is of sufficient quality and quantity as that required for assessment of others' work, is likely to substantially reduce such feelings of being alone, and help to build a true community of learners.

Concluding Remarks

At the heart of Robert Pirsig's 1974 bestseller *Zen and The Art of Motorcycle Maintenance* is one man's search for the meaning of quality. What do we mean, exactly, when we say that a work of art, or a student essay, or an acting performance in a motion picture, is good, or bad, or indifferent? How can we rate such things in comparison to others that may be similar in shape or form? Are we all equally qualified to pass such judgments? And what gives such judgments any validity?

Professional educators spend a fair portion of their working lives passing judgments on their students' works, and thereby, indirectly, on the students themselves. It would seem to be reasonably important, therefore, that answers to these questions, and others like them, be readily forthcoming, lest the whole edifice of assessment in education be discovered to be without any firm foundation, and thereby risk collapsing in a heap.

One answer immediately suggests itself: *experience*. The more experience we have in a field, so the argument would go, the more we are qualified to pass judgement, to recognize quality when we see it. Alas, though this may have some element of truth, it is far from the whole truth. Bain (2004, p. 162) says that the best teachers tend to be very humble when it comes to grading, and quotes one unnamed professor as saying that "… I recognize the enormous difficulty of understanding someone's intellectual growth…part of my intellectual mission [is] to help students try to understand their own learning. In the end, I simply make the best judgment I can."

We often try to hide away from this truth, of course. Many very authoritative works on the processes of teaching and learning shy away from consideration of alternative models of assessment altogether, perhaps because they are still seen as controversial and unproven. There are still others that are in most respects quite excellent and highly recommended, but that include only a passing reference, or perhaps a few paragraphs at best, to self and peer assessment.

There are also many that recognize the growing importance of self, peer, and group assessment. For example Race (2001), in a chapter entitled "Designing Assessment and Feedback to Enhance Learning," makes the point that:

Copyright © 2006, Idea Group Inc. Copying or distributing in print or electronic forms without written permission of Idea Group Inc. is prohibited.

... one of the most significant problems with assessment is that just about all the people who do it have already survived having had it done to them. This can make us somewhat resistant to confronting whether it was...valid, fair and transparent, and explains why so many outdated forms of assessment still permeate higher education practice today. (p. 31)

McConnell (2000, p. 129) does not mince words when he makes the interesting observation that collaborative assessment is inherently subversive. "In carrying it out, we are implicitly questioning the status quo of education and training ... [it] opens up issues to do with....democracy in the learning process and the position of the learner ..."

Boud (1995) suggests that there needs to be a balance between, on the one hand, a traditionally conservative system where student involvement in assessment is nonexistent, and on the other extreme, one in which instructor's responsibility is completely abdicated (p. 175). Some middle path would seem to be clearly indicated. Where exactly the optimal path between the two extremes is located is likely to vary enormously depending upon a range of factors including, but not limited to, the nature of the course, the background of the students, and the feelings of the instructor.

But as has been made clear in this article, assessment should not just be about— or perhaps even be primarily about—grading. It should also be about assisting the learners to learn. Bain (2004) has admitted that like many other teachers, he "...failed to understand that testing and grading are not incidental acts that come at the end of teaching but powerful aspects of education that have an enormous influence on the entire enterprise of helping and encouraging students to learn" (p. 150) and that "... [t]he outstanding teachers used assessment to help students learn, not just to rate and rank their efforts" (p. 151).

It would seem that there are some compelling reasons for giving serious consideration to a far greater use of self, peer, and group assessment, especially within the modern world of e-learning. Any change from tradition is always a risky business, of course, but sometimes the benefits are worth the risks.

References

Bain, K. (2004). *What the best college teachers do.* Cambridge, MA: Harvard University Press.

Bligh, D. A. (2000). *What's the use of lectures?* San Francisco: Jossey-Bass.

Copyright © 2006, Idea Group Inc. Copying or distributing in print or electronic forms without written permission of Idea Group Inc. is prohibited.

Boud, D. (1995). The role of assessment in student grading. In *Enhancing learning through self assessment* (pp. 167-175). London: Kogan Page.

Buchanan, E. A. (2004). Online assessment in higher education: Strategies to systematically evaluate student learning. In C. Howard, K. Schenk & R. Discenza (Eds.), *Distance learning and university effectiveness: Changing educational paradigms for online learning.* Hershey, PA: Information Science Publishing.

Cucchiarelli, A., Panti, M., & Valenti, S. (2000). Web-based assessment in student learning. In A. Aggarwal (Ed.), *Web-based learning and teaching technologies: Opportunities and challenges.* Hershey, PA: Idea Group Publishing.

Davis, B. G. (1993). *Tools for teaching.* San Francisco: Jossey-Bass.

Falchikov, N. (1996, July 8-12). Improving learning through critical peer feedback and reflection. In Different approaches: Theory and practice in higher education. *Proceedings of the HERDSA Conference,* Perth, Western Australia.

Falchikov, N., & Boud, D. (1989). Student self-assessment in higher education: A meta-analysis. *Review of Higher Education Research, 59*(4), 395-430.

Felder, R. M., & Brent, R. (2001). *Effective strategies for cooperative cearning.* Retrieved from http://www2.ncsu.edu/unity/lockers/users/f/felder/public/Papers/CLStrategies(JCCCT).pdf

Hanna, D., Glowacki-Dudka, M., & Conceicao-Runlee, S. (2000). *147 practical tips for teaching online groups.* Madison, WI: Atwood Publishing.

Huba, M. E., & Freed, J. E. (2000). *Learner-centered assessment on college campuses: Shifting the focus from teaching to learning.* Needham Heights, MA: Allyn and Bacon.

Kardash, C. M. (2000). Evaluation of an undergraduate research experience: Perceptions of interns and their faculty members. *Journal of Educational Psychology, 92*(1), 191-201.

Kearsley, G. (2000). *Online education: Learning and teaching in cyberspace.* Belmont, CA: Wadsworth.

Kemery, E. R. (2000). Developing online collaboration. In A. Aggarwal (Ed.), *Web-based learning and teaching technologies: Opportunities and challenges.* Hershey, PA: Idea Group Publishing.

McConnell, D. (2000). *Implementing computer supported cooperative learning.* London: Kogan Page.

McCormack, C., & Jones, D. (1998). *Building a Web-based education system.* New York: John Wiley & Sons.

Copyright © 2006, Idea Group Inc. Copying or distributing in print or electronic forms without written permission of Idea Group Inc. is prohibited.

McInnerney, J., & Roberts, T. S. (2004). Online learning: Social interaction and the creation of a sense of community, *Educational Technology & Society, 7*(3), 73-81.

McKeachie, W. J. (2002). *McKeachi's teaching tips: Strategies, research, and theory for college and university teachers.* Boston: Houghton Mifflin Company.

Palloff, R. M., & Pratt, K. (1999). *Building learning communities in cyberspace.* San Francisco: Jossey-Bass.

Pirsig, R. M. (1974). *Zen and the art of motorcycle maintenance.* London: Transworld Publishers.

Race, P. (2001). *The lecturer's toolkit* (2nd ed.). London: Kogan Page.

Roberts, T. S. (2003). *Online collaborative learning: Theory and practice.* Hershey, PA: InfoSci.

Roberts, T. S. (2004). *Computer-supported collaborative learning in higher education.* Hershey, PA: Idea Group Publishing.

Schunk, D. (2000). *Learning theories: An educational perspective.* Upper Saddle River, NJ: Prentice Hall.

Wegerif, R. (1998). The social dimension of asynchronous learning networks, *Journal of Asynchronous Learning Networks, 2*(1). Retrieved from http://www.aln.org/alnweb/journal/vol2_issue1/wegerif.htm

Wiggins, G. (1998). *Educative assessment: Designing assessments to inform and improve student performance.* San Francisco: Jossey-Bass.

Copyright © 2006, Idea Group Inc. Copying or distributing in print or electronic forms without written permission of Idea Group Inc. is prohibited.

Chapter II

A Case Study in Peer Evaluation for Second Language Teachers in Training

Pamela L. Anderson-Mejías
University of Texas-Pan American, USA

Abstract

This chapter provides a case study of master's level second-language teachers in training who used self and peer evaluation within a capstone course in their program. Two differing sections are reported; one was conducted entirely online, and the second was conducted face-to-face with a significant portion of online collaboration required. The author was a participant observer conducting this action research. Both courses required students to evaluate peers using various techniques including online quiz instruments, immediate chat-feedback quizzes, and peer evaluation rubrics. In addition, participants evaluated themselves both on the skills of teaching demonstrated and on their participation within the community. At least one fourth of each course grade was determined by peer evaluation. E-assessment strategies are detailed, and suggestions for future online peer assessment are given from this case to guide tertiary-level colleagues'

Copyright © 2006, Idea Group Inc. Copying or distributing in print or electronic forms without written permission of Idea Group Inc. is prohibited.

future peer evaluation efforts in the best sense of online collaborative discourse.

Introduction

This chapter is a case study report based on action research conducted by the instructor in two sections of a practical application/teaching course for graduate students studying to be teachers of English to speakers of other languages (TESOL). One course was conducted entirely online while the second was conducted in a face-to-face (f2f) classroom but with a significant portion of online requirements. For this case study, the key changes were in participant assessment and course grading. Through use of on-going discussion of procedures and summative post-course assessment in both sections, student and instructor analysis of the self and peer evaluation strategies will be presented.

The chapter has three key goals for the reader. First, in the best sense of collaborative online discourse, it seeks to describe the positive as well as negative details of the case so that others may benefit from the experiences of the author/ investigator. A second goal is to present sufficient information regarding all aspects of the participants, courses, and various assessment strategies so that others may replicate the peer evaluation strategies within their own communities with expectations of success because they understand the context of the case. Finally, the chapter verifies the usefulness, indeed importance, of including peer evaluation in any e-learning assessment context.

Overview

An overview of this chapter will allow readers to decide which sections are particularly pertinent to their interests, so I will begin with such an outline. In the first section, "Case Study Setting," I will describe the pertinent specifics of the case in order to give as much information about the program, course, students, participant-observer, and so forth for readers to determine similarities and differences to their own contexts. In the second section, I describe the *self evaluation strategies* used in the case study. This is for those whose interest may be in self evaluation at the tertiary level. In the final section of the chapter, I will describe the *peer evaluation techniques* used both in online and f2f contexts.

This case study is grounded in the work of Vygotsky (1978) whose cognitive studies emphasized the importance of the social nature of learning and language

Copyright © 2006, Idea Group Inc. Copying or distributing in print or electronic forms without written permission of Idea Group Inc. is prohibited.

learning, as well as how cognition develops through the individual's "readiness" for the next stage of information in her or his "zone of proximal development" (Vygotsky, 1978). This leads to a paradigm where students work together bringing their varied experiences to the whole group as a means to scaffold from the experiences of their peers. In addition to the work of Vygotsky, those of Freire (1972, 1973)—where learning is seen as a social construct in which students dialog with one another and must take responsibility for their inquiry— led to use of a collaborative learning framework as articulated by Johnson and Johnson (2000) among others. It is from these perspectives that the course evaluation procedures were determined, although much of the literature of sociolinguistics, sociology of language, and second language teaching method-ologies also played a significant role as will be indicated in the description of the setting for this case.

Key issues which surfaced during the case and reflection on it include the importance of clearly articulated deadlines and organization for e-learning contexts, potential need for training of tertiary students for collaborative work online, importance of the relationship between type of online assignment and its assessment, and assessment strategies that encourage greater levels of honesty.

Case Study Setting

Definitions

As this case study is based on a course in applied linguistics, where a number of acronyms are used to shorten lengthy titles, I will begin with some key definitions. Those who learn or teach English within an English-using environment are referred to as ESL learners or teachers, while those learning or teaching English in a non-English using environment, like Mexico where English is a foreign language in the educational curriculum, are EFL learners or teachers. The general usage of TESOL, teachers of English to speakers of other languages, encompasses both as well as those who work with learners from differing dialectal varieties. L1 indicates the first language, while L2 indicates a second (or subsequent) language and both are used consistently as such in the literature.

Theoretical Background

In the late 1970s, while work on learning by Vygotsky began to circulate in the TESOL literature, Hymes (1974) and others somewhat on the edges of the great

Copyright © 2006, Idea Group Inc. Copying or distributing in print or electronic forms without written permission of Idea Group Inc. is prohibited.

Chomskian syntactic leap forward within U.S. linguistic circles, were considering language as a social phenomena that could not be divorced from its usage to encode messages for and from specific groups of people. Communicative competence was needed in language learning, not merely linguistic competence, in order to send and receive messages among real people. Labov (1966) had studied language as indicative of social stratification in early sociolinguistics, while Fishman (1968) explored issues of attitudes toward languages, maintenance/shift possibilities, and other social constructs found in language. As TESOLers struggled to make learning communicative, they tried numerous methodologies from Gattegno's (1972) *Teaching Foreign Languanges in Schools: The Silent Way* to Curran's (1976) *Counseling Learning in Secondary Languages* and Lozanov's (1978) *Suggestopedia and Outlines of Suggestopedy*. But no one method seemed to work for all students. Thus, practitioners moved from that level to the less generalized areas of trying specific techniques, among which was the use of cooperative group work. As information became more available to practitioners, cooperative learning and group work began to impact the ESL/EFL classroom. Cooperative groups were seen to facilitate development of interpersonal skills, increase retention of information, and generate higher achievement among students overall (Johnson & Johnson, 1987). In getting groups to "work" in language acquisition and learning, teachers found it necessary to use activities known as "communication gap" tasks, where each person within the group would be given differing pieces of information which she or he must effectively communicate to the others in order to solve a problem. This type of interdependence and the importance of the social interaction moved the earlier cooperative groups of Johnson and Johnson (1987) toward collaborative learning as articulated somewhat later by Johnson and Johnson (2000). Teacher's textbooks, such as *The Tapestry of Language Learning* (Scarcella & Oxford, 1992) began to incorporate the principles of group learning.

Yet, the area of assessment in ESL/EFL education lagged behind. Testing and evaluation of student learning was still based on demonstrating competence on discrete portions of language in a highly controlled, usually "objective" exam setting. Only recently has the importance of "authentic assessment indices" become of greater importance in the field in particular within criterion referenced testing as exemplified by textbooks for teachers like Brown and Hudson (2002).

It was into this arena that "computer assisted language learning" emerged for EFL/ESL students and the possibility of distance education for TESOLers became a reality which would permit EFL teachers to remain in their homelands, with their families and income from their jobs, while adding to their professional education by attending the major training programs in the United States, the United Kingdom, Canada, Australia, and New Zealand.

Copyright © 2006, Idea Group Inc. Copying or distributing in print or electronic forms without written permission of Idea Group Inc. is prohibited.

Case Study Parameters

The Program

Master of Arts in English as a Second Language (MAESL) trains those who wish to become teachers of English to speakers of other languages. The MAESL at the University of Texas—Pan American (UTPA) is comprised of 36 credit hours or 12 three-hour courses each. Along with three potential electives from various disciplines, there are two required classes which consider the English language itself, two which consider second language/culture issues, and three required courses which address pedagogical issues such as ESL testing and assessment, methods of teaching, or curricular designs. Finally there is the capstone course, which requires actual teaching in an ESL or EFL classroom while being guided and observed by the faculty and peers. It is this course, Practicum in ESL, which is described within this chapter.

Practicum Goals

The goal of the Practicum in ESL is to help teachers practice a means to continue their professional growth beyond the MAESL through use of a reflection model as advocated by Wallace (1991). The means to this goal is through direct observation of their teaching, to ensure that they will have the tools of planning, organizing, creating lessons, and guiding and evaluating their pupils' work that are needed in accordance with standards as established by various state and/or national governing bodies. An additional goal of the course is to assist the students in the MAESL program to review the issues of second language acquisition, culture, testing, curriculum design, methodology, and English language and unify their personal approach to the field. In short, it is a capstone course intended to provide both guided experience and summation of the program before graduation.

Assignments

Key assignments have been developed over many years, but always include the reflection journal—a guided, weekly journal that is then summarized for a grade—an action research (Nunan, 1990) within the practicum teaching assignment graded by the instructor, and at least one teaching demonstration—observed directly or via videotape by the faculty and peers. Additional assignments are geared to encourage collaborative learning, since many of the "students" have been teachers in a variety of fields, some even in EFL or ESL

Copyright © 2006, Idea Group Inc. Copying or distributing in print or electronic forms without written permission of Idea Group Inc. is prohibited.

through the Peace Corps or other agency. It is imperative that these experiences be shared, explored, and used as means of improving both the individual's teaching and that of the peers. Thus, collaborative learning groups work well with these students.

Assessment

Student assessment has likewise been varied over the years developing this course. In many cases, self evaluation has been used particularly in terms of the reflection journal and one section of the demonstration paper that requires the demonstrator to "grade" his or her teaching based on group-discovered principles. These principles tend to be in three areas: one, the management of the materials and the class time; two, the allowance or encouragement of varying cognitive styles, affective variables, and language learning strategies (Oxford, 1990); and three, the physical appearance, voice usage, clarity of directions, movement around the classroom, and so forth.

In addition to the self evaluation, peers have evaluated the demonstrations as well. Some of these evaluations were anonymously presented via a rubric immediately following the presentation, some were explicitly given orally immediately following (and could thus be taken into consideration for the self evaluation), and some were submitted to the instructor, but graded for the submitter rather than applied to the demonstration itself or the teacher.

A useful technique of evaluation in the f2f setting was to have impromptu minilessons based on one facet of the original demonstration but which approached that issue from another perspective. The teacher trainee would provide his or her lesson plan immediately following the video, and all students, including the demonstrator, would brainstorm individually ways to "reteach" some part of the lesson. Then random names were drawn to reteach a minilesson. Such reteaches allowed the whole group to participate in the lessons, and all learned from the very creative ideas of their peers. The "evaluation" of the demonstration by peers was thus given in terms more of additional ideas for teaching some component part rather than as a "critique" of those parts.

In short, in the f2f setting, a variety of techniques had been used to assess the students. For the most part, the decision as to how these evaluations were carried out and graded was left to the participants in the given course.

The Case Study Participants

For this case study, two groups of students and their self and peer evaluation assignments, as well as their reflections on these procedures, will be described.

Copyright © 2006, Idea Group Inc. Copying or distributing in print or electronic forms without written permission of Idea Group Inc. is prohibited.

Table 1.

2002			ONLINE	N=9		
Student #	Physical Location	Cultural heritage		Teaching assmt.	Gender	
A02	Edinburg TX	US Anglo Swedish		Univ. developmental	F	
B02	Pharr TX	Mexican-American		Private institute	F	
C02	McAllen TX	Korean		Volunteer adult ed	F	
C02	Monterrey Mexico	Mexican		Public university	F	
E02	Montemorelos Mex.	US Anglo		Private university	F	
F02	Montemorelos Mex.	Mexican		Private university	F	
G02	San Miguel Mexico	US Anglo		Private institute	F	
H02	Pharr TX	Mexican-American		US public high school	F	
I02	McAllen TX	Mexican-American		Public university	M	dropped
2004			HYBRID F2F	N=10		
A04	Does not apply	Canadian		US public high school	F	
B04	to this group	Mexican		Volunteer US public HS	F	
C04		Indian		Volunteer univ. developm.	F	
D04		Mexican-American		Commun. col. developm.	M	
E04		US Anglo		Univ. developmental	M	
F04		US Anglo		Private institute	M	
G04		US Anglo		US public high school	M	
H04		US Anglo		US public high school	F	
I04		Mexican-American		US public high school	F	
J04		US Anglo		Univ. developmental	F	

Both included a large e-learning component. The 2002 course was entirely conducted online, while the 2004 course was both f2f and online. Both groups were small and contained highly motivated professionals at the master's level of study. Nearly all had already or were teaching language professionally in some context. Additional information on the participants is found in Table 1.

2002 Students

This group consisted of nine students enrolled in the completely online practicum. Five lived in the local area, and four were truly remote students living in three different areas of Mexico: Monterrey, Montemorelos, and San Miguel de Allende. Among the students were three local Mexican Americans, one local Korean, two Mexican nationals, and three Anglo Americans. One student, and the only male, dropped out due to family obligations. All remaining students were female. In Mexico, two taught EFL in a private university, one in a public

Copyright © 2006, Idea Group Inc. Copying or distributing in print or electronic forms without written permission of Idea Group Inc. is prohibited.

university, and one in a private institute. One local student taught as a volunteer in the adult education program at a local library, one in a private institute, and one taught in public high school. One taught at UTPA in the developmental English program and tutored in the writing center.

2004 Students

In the 2004 group, there were two Mexican American local RGV students, one Canadian, one Indian, one Mexican national, and five Anglo American students from various locations (four of whom were Spanish L2 speakers). Six were female; four were male. Among these students, four taught in RGV public schools grades 9 through 12, three were teaching assistants in the developmental English program at UTPA and/or the community college, one was teaching at a private institute, and two were not yet teaching. The two who were not yet teaching had found volunteer positions with peers to fulfill the course require-ments of the ten-week teaching journal, action research, and teaching demon-strations. Both were offered a position for the following academic year in the school systems where they volunteered.

Participant-Observer

As the sole instructor of the Practicum in ESL for UTPA during the case study reported, I believe a bit of my background may be helpful to readers. I studied as an undergraduate student in an exchange program in Germany where I first explored my interest in language and different cultures. When I entered my master's level work, in Urban and Overseas English (TESOL), I worked within the Project Options for Student Teachers office as director of the American Indian Project. In that capacity, under the direction of Dr. James Mahan at Indiana University, I presented multicultural activities to sensitize undergraduate students to differing cultural norms of people groups where they would be student teaching. In addition, I taught English as an associate instructor in the Center for English Language Training in a variety of classes for ESL students from the Middle East, Asia, and South and Central America. My doctoral work centered on a syntactic and discourse analysis of the oral and written narrative of students from a variety of native languages and cultures. Since that time, I have participated in teacher training in the United States and Argentina, have researched primarily in the areas of applied- and sociolinguistics, and have lived in the bilingual/bicultural Rio Grande Valley of south Texas—17 miles from the border with Mexico—for nearly 25 years.

In 1998, I was dragged, more or less kicking and screaming, into an online exchange program whereby the faculty of UTPA would use Interactive Telecast

Copyright © 2006, Idea Group Inc. Copying or distributing in print or electronic forms without written permission of Idea Group Inc. is prohibited.

(ITV) to train teachers simultaneously at five sites in Mexico. As the program materialized and my courses came up for ITV delivery, the center for distance learning had expanded and it was suggested that I add a WebCT discussion board and perhaps chat sessions to the Tuesday evening course delivery. I did and have been hooked on online delivery ever since! All of my courses now contain a significant online portion; this is the future, and our students must become familiar with using technology in their studies and worksites.

As a teacher trainer, I have always believed that the key courses in pedagogy as delivered by faculty must incorporate current issues presented with variety and excellence as a model for the students. This places a major burden on the teacher trainer to keep up with the field in not only the terms of theory and methods of teaching, but also in methods of evaluating students in f2f and online delivery settings.

Self Evaluation Strategies

This case study considers both self evaluation strategies and peer evaluation techniques. The self evaluation strategies were essentially the same for both the 2002 and 2004 groups within the case. In both courses, the major strategy was the teaching journal, a reflection on practice via guided prompts, which was "graded" by each student and worth 25% of the entire course grade. The second self evaluation strategy is one-third of a paper that follows the teaching demonstration. The whole paper was teacher graded, but the reflection section was evaluated by the student himself or herself and this grade was added into the teacher's assessment.

Journal Assignment

Wallace (1991) discusses the importance of reflection as part of any professional training program. Most programs currently offered for teacher education are based on what he calls the applied science model where separate courses cover differing aspects of a field. The previous model, the craft model, was based on long-term apprenticeship programs where preservice teachers would be assigned to "master teachers" and learn the basics through observation and participation under their guidance. Both models have advantages and disadvantages; reflective models assist preservice and in-service teachers to review their progress and the strengths and weaknesses of their own teaching and analyze the incorporation of changes in a systematic manner. It is particularly important

Copyright © 2006, Idea Group Inc. Copying or distributing in print or electronic forms without written permission of Idea Group Inc. is prohibited.

in our action-packed world to take the required time to reflect upon one's practice in order to learn from and advance beyond the status quo.

The key reflective assignment in the practicum is a 10-week guided journal. Participants may choose any 10 weeks from the 16-week semester. They follow a guideline prepared by the instructor from student input over many years. It may be found in Appendix A. Following the 10-week collection, students are required to review their teaching in each of the areas of the guideline and summarize with appropriate critique the overall picture. They then discuss their own assessment of their teaching—did it change, how, was there improvement, specifically what happened, and so forth. These issues are discussed during the 11th or 12th week of class and correspond with the chapter in Shurm and Glisan (2000) on assessing language performance in context. A group discussion (online via discussion board and f2f in a portion of one class) reviews the "good, the bad, and the ugly" aspects of teaching during their semester assignment, and the class members consider how they wish to address their own performance. The online 2002 section conducted this via the WebCT discussion board topic. The 2004 students discussed the journal summaries in class. Neither group wished to create a rubric for self evaluation; both believed that the context should be paramount and therefore the assessment as flexible as possible.

Online Discussion Results

The discussion on how to evaluate one's own teaching was via WebCT and was heavily controlled by three participants. From the eight who continued in the online course, I considered three measures to determine how the topic was approached: one, number of posts from each in that discussion topic; two, length of post by word count, and finally, content as to (a) new idea, (b) restatement of previous idea with suggested change, (c) restatement of previous idea without change, (d) acceptance of idea(s) of others, (e) rejection of other's idea(s) with addition of a new idea, and (f) rejection of other's idea(s) without new idea.

Students were randomly given letters from A to H in the analysis. Students A02, D02, and G02 controlled the discussion. These three posted a total of 36 messages with an average of 95.5 words. Two of these people were native speakers of English; one remote and one local. The other was a remote student whose first language was Spanish. The combined total of the other five students' messages was 13 with average of 21.8 words. Thus, the total number of posts for the topic was 49, and the overall word average was just over 77.

In terms of discourse, A02, D02, E02, and G02 generated all of the new ideas. One restatement with suggested change was given by B02, and four restatements without change were given by B02, D02, E02, and F02. There were no rejections with or without additions; the other responses were generally all

Copyright © 2006, Idea Group Inc. Copying or distributing in print or electronic forms without written permission of Idea Group Inc. is prohibited.

acceptances. Thus, the discussion on how one could go about self evaluation of their teaching through the journal assignment was very agreeable, if somewhat controlled by the three major players in this group. One caveat seems in order here: In a group of eight people, for there to be three active participants while the other five are less so may not be particularly unusual or positive or negative regardless of the delivery system online or f2f. I have not located any research information regarding norms in this type of discourse, but am simply describing what occurred among these participants.

In-Class Discussion Results

The in-class discussion (2004) was more open-ended; and, although two students did not actively participate verbally, they were present and indicated agreement through kinesics. The whole group of 10 students was seated in a circle, following review of issues covered in the language assessment chapter. As instructor, I started the discussion by asking what had been found in their "three positive teaching experiences" and then we continued through the varying sections of the guide sheet. None had written their summaries at the time of the discussion, and the group then moved naturally into a consideration of how to self evaluate their teaching experiences. Hash marks were used by each student's name when she or he made a contribution, and I tried to remain outside of active participation. Hindsight is 20/20; I wish that I had taped this class to be able to analyze more similarly to that online, but I did not.

Of the 10 students, those who participated most were B04 (14 marks), G04 (11), E04 (9), and A04 (6). B04 was a nonnative English speaker while A04 (non-US), E04, and G04 were native speakers. Two others, both native speakers from the United States, did not comment directly at all (J04 and F04). All others commented ranging from C04, with one mark only, to H04 with five marks. Throughout the semester, students C04, E04, F04, I04, and J04 were usually quiet, although when it came to his own work, E04 would actively support and defend his points.

As can be seen from the previous analysis of the in-class decision-making process on how to use the journal for self evaluation, neither native language nor country of origin was clearly indicative of more participation. Again, norms for discussion by 10 participants may be similar or different from these described results.

Teaching Demonstration Reflection

The secondary self evaluation assignment in the course is one-third of the paper that follows each teaching demonstration. The complete assignment is as

Copyright © 2006, Idea Group Inc. Copying or distributing in print or electronic forms without written permission of Idea Group Inc. is prohibited.

follows. Students prepare to teach a "normal" class with their group and arrange to be videotaped while doing so. In order to minimize nervousness and/or special-feature performance factors, the demonstration is *not* graded on the video, but rather on a paper due the week following our viewing of the video as a group (whether in-class or via the streamed media online). The components are first, a review of the theoretical background underpinning the lesson (information reviewed from previous coursework), the lesson plan, and the reflection following the teaching demonstration and peer comments. This third section of the paper is self evaluative in nature. For the 2002 group, it was simply a part of the grade. For the 2004 group, this self evaluation was included separately as a grade by the student on her or his actual performance. The first two parts of the paper were instructor graded.

Online Class

Among the online group, the demonstration was sent via videotape to the instructor, who then segmented it into sections in order to ease the time frame for uploading streaming media. The technical wizards in the Center for Distance Learning then converted the video to streamed segments. These were released to participants on specified days at a given time and followed by peer comments as will be described later as part of peer evaluation. In the week following release of the teaching streamed media, the teacher/demonstrator was responsible for e-mailing the paper component to the instructor. One third of the grade was based on individual reflection over the teaching, which could include comments from peers with rebuttal, but did not necessarily need to do so.

All students in this group were able to evaluate their own teaching demonstration. Most were harsher on themselves than their peers had been in the chats or discussions following the demonstration. All received complete credit for the reflection portion of the paper; that is, all received 100% for that one-third of the paper grade.

In-Class Reflections

In the f2f setting, students brought their videotaped lessons to class as scheduled. Each tape was viewed by the group, the demonstrator was then asked to comment on anything he or she wanted to share with the group regarding the circumstances (such as the intrusion of a student from another group or unexpected change to the lesson because of a student's question), and to comment on what he or she saw as the strengths and then weaknesses of the lesson as viewed now. During the individual's comments on strengths, the whole

Copyright © 2006, Idea Group Inc. Copying or distributing in print or electronic forms without written permission of Idea Group Inc. is prohibited.

class group would become involved in agreeing or adding to these. A similar pattern occurred during the individual's self analysis of weaknesses, where peers would agree occasionally, but usually were more likely to see other areas for improvement. Interestingly, most of these comments were couched with great care as "in my context…I would need to do X rather than what you did…." Following the class discussion, the demonstrator would have one week to complete and hand in (or e-mail) his or her paper component.

To evaluate these papers, I viewed the theory and lesson plan components and assigned a grade based on the accuracy of these applications of theory to the lesson. In the third section of the paper, I recorded the student's self evaluation as a separate grade, and then averaged that as one third of the paper.

Summary of Reflections

For both cases, the online group and the f2f group, on the one third of the paper for self evaluation students graded themselves highly. Most gave themselves between 90 and 100 for the preparation of the lesson, the demonstration lesson itself, and their teaching skills. Two participants in the online group (C02 and E02) and one in the f2f group (C04) considered that their demonstration lesson was within the 80 to 89 bracket. One person in the online group (D02) graded her teaching in the 90s but commented that it was more for her efforts rather than how she felt the lesson itself turned out. No student evaluated his or her performance below 80% (a B or 3.0 on a 4.0 scale).

Summary of Self Evaluation Strategies

In both groups, a comprehensive summative assignment required students to discuss all of the different evaluations. The following considers self evaluation strategies.

Both self evaluation strategies were positively viewed by the students from the online and the f2f groups. Although the journal assignment gathered a number of complaints during the semester for its repetitiveness and ubiquity, following the entire assignment, students all believed that it was not only useful, but had helped them recall important aspects to their teaching which would have been lost in the "shuffle" had they not been keeping the journal. Fourteen of these 18 individuals (78%) stated in class or in a discussion forum online that they would continue keeping some form of written record for both their positive and the negative experiences, although it was generally conceded that they would not use the extensive format required in the course.

Copyright © 2006, Idea Group Inc. Copying or distributing in print or electronic forms without written permission of Idea Group Inc. is prohibited.

Of the 10 f2f students in 2004 whose one third of the demonstration paper was self evaluated, all but one commented positively. That one stated he believed he was just "giving myself a bump" in the grade. He seemed to believe that an outside expert's opinion was more valid than his own despite that person's not being present in the actual lesson and not really knowing the students or the context. When asked whether he believed he could review his own performance accurately, he was still unsure. Freire (1973) seems to point to this type of "passive" learner who has been treated as an object of education so long that he or she refuses the responsibility for his or her own inquiry.

Both sections reported in this case study used self evaluation for a portion of the final course grade. In both, all students took the self evaluation via the reflective journal seriously and evaluated it positively. Unlike the self evaluations used, the peer evaluations used in the 2002 group (entirely online) differed from those in the 2004 group (one half online and one half f2f).

Peer Evaluation Techniques

Peer evaluation is an essential component of collaborative learning, whether f2f or online. It is in this area where the case study includes a variety of e-learning assessment techniques. To begin discussion, two different types of activities will be considered, both of which were peer evaluated, but differently, between the 2002 and 2004 sections of the course. One of these is peer evaluation for performance—in our case study, the teaching performance seen online via streaming media and in the f2f class via videotape. The second is peer assessment for participation; in this study, we include moderating or leading a group and working within groups as participation. The key distinction is whether one's personal performance is viewed or one's ideas are seen via the written language.

Performance Peer Evaluation

In both sections of the practicum, a major assignment is to videotape and present oneself teaching a group of real students. Because appearing in front of one's peers is socially different from appearing in front of one's students or unknown audiences, performances such as theatre scenes or teaching demonstrations seem to call for different types of peer evaluation than when one is leading a discussion or chat session. Many articles considering rubrics for such evaluation of teaching may be found online and in the professional literature. Most of these are for faculty colleagues, like those of Middendorf and Kalish (1995) or

Copyright © 2006, Idea Group Inc. Copying or distributing in print or electronic forms without written permission of Idea Group Inc. is prohibited.

Prideaux (2002). A key point recommended is immediate feedback given by the evaluator to the demonstrator. Another important consideration is use for improvement in teaching but not for promotion, tenure, or hiring (and presumably grades).

For the assessment of teaching conducted in the two sections of Practicum, the 2002 peer evaluations were used for student evaluation worth 10% of the whole course grade, while those in the 2004 group were used as feedback, but were not considered as part of a grade.

2002 Peer Evaluation of Teaching

Chats

The 2002 course began with the goal of incorporating the immediacy of minilessons as peer evaluation following the streamed teaching demonstrations. In previous f2f settings, these minilessons, which retaught a portion of the lesson, were rated strongest for professional development by students of those courses. To generate the immediacy, the streamed videos were released on a schedule that students knew from the onset of the course, a randomly grouped chat session was required within six hours of the release, and following the chat, participants were to evaluate their peer moderator and would be likewise evaluated by that person.

Prior to the chats, a conditional quiz was available to the moderators. This gave them a series of suggested prompts based on the demonstration lesson. Some of these were general, such as "You may want to start by asking the chat members what they believed was the strongest part of this lesson, then follow with what was weaker. Be sure to ask participants to state why they believe as they do." Other prompts were specifically oriented to the lesson itself, such as "In the introductory remarks, X used the overhead to orient her students. Is this an effective way to start? Does anyone have another suggestion for this type of activity based on your experience?" Only the moderators received this via selective release, and they were not required to use the prompts; these suggestions were made in order to help them get started in the chat sessions.

The first demonstration-chat-peer-evaluation sequence was a disaster! This was not from lack of planning nor student sincerity at the attempt. In fact, the Center for Distance Learning had provided CD ROM WebCT information, computer and browser configuration requirements, downloads for using the online media, and so forth to the students; all had viewed these and believed their computers were appropriately configured. The challenges were due to the normal vagaries of Web browsers, Internet providers, phone lines, and so forth.

Copyright © 2006, Idea Group Inc. Copying or distributing in print or electronic forms without written permission of Idea Group Inc. is prohibited.

Of the eight women who stayed with the course, three were able to view the streamed media without a problem. One of these was in Mexico, and the other two were local students. All were from off-campus sites. Among the rest, one had so many difficulties accessing and trying to download the streamed media, she changed Internet providers three times during the first two months of the course. Two others in remote sites had difficulties gaining access through their Internet providers at the scheduled times of the chats. One local woman entered the chat room, waited just over a minute, and then left before anyone else had entered. Had she waited longer, she would actually have been part of the chat session from this first round. One "sort-of chat" took place; it included mostly questions like "Are we in the right room? Who else is supposed to be here?" and so forth.

To fix this situation, these first chat sessions were held two days later than scheduled. For one group, a chat time earlier in the day made Internet access (via phone line) more feasible. However, some members of that original group could not participate at the time selected by the group because they were teaching. So, these members were moved to a late-night chat session. After rescheduling the chats around peak Internet usage hours, scheduling so that remote students could use their work access rather than home computers, and arranging new providers, the next two demonstration sequences worked out. The initial plan to reconfigure each chat group, however, was not possible since now time constraints had entered into the picture. So the same groups were kept for the first three sessions, although the moderators varied.

Analysis of Chats

From the six chat groups, which did use peer evaluation for the demonstration seen via streaming media, moderators dominated the discourse. Nonetheless, there was general participation by all who were involved and that participation included positive, as well as negative, critique. Negative remarks were prefaced with "softening comments" such as "It was difficult to see what you were writing on the chalkboard, but ..." Chats moved along rapidly, where one topic would change to another before some slower typing students could comment, which led to an erratic "discussion," but eventually all participants generally had their say about the demonstration. It was interesting to note that moderators would often begin by following the prompts which they had received just prior to the session, but then were very capable of using peer comments to generate the next issue for consideration, thus they abandoned the prompts within the first 10 to 15 minutes of the chat.

After numerous complaints, particularly from one remote student, I reviewed the course up to that point and concluded that technology issues were

Copyright © 2006, Idea Group Inc. Copying or distributing in print or electronic forms without written permission of Idea Group Inc. is prohibited.

interfering with the educational objectives. I asked the students if they would prefer to shift to discussion boards and all indicated they would. Thus, the move from synchronous to asynchronous started with the fourth demonstration. This change had unforeseen consequences in the level of honesty for online peer evaluation.

Discussion Boards

Following this decision, we used one discussion area to consider each teaching demonstration. Comments and questions were to be uploaded within three days, so that the demonstrator could use them in her reflection for the paper component if she wished. Although the moderator's job was continued for the fourth and fifth demonstrations, for the final three it was disbanded. In this manner, each student had been moderator once, reviewed two of her peers once, and was reviewed by her peers at least once. Although not entirely satisfactory, this allowed the group to complete the course on time and with less frustration. Additional details and recommendations regarding this change in the middle of the course may be found in Anderson-Mejías (2005).

The discussion boards did permit the entire group to interact with one another but at a price. As one might expect, some students participated more often and with more words than others. Interestingly, the local student (C02) who was a nonnative speaker of English, prepared much longer discussion messages than any of her other work in the discussion boards or in chat. This was also true of one of the remote students, E02, who accessed the Internet using the same computer as F02. E02 is a native English speaker, working in EFL in a remote site. F02, who is more "verbal" online, is a nonnative English speaker, working in EFL in the remote site. Because Internet access was a challenge from their location, they would access the discussions together and then identify themselves by name when commenting or responding.

For the peer reviews of teaching via discussion board, responses by the eight students were far more similar in length, word count, and discourse than had been the discussion of how to evaluate one's reflection on teaching. The comments made were nearly all positive, with very few discussion comments or even questions for the demonstrator/teacher. The medium of online response for peer evaluation clearly affected usefulness of the comments and perhaps honesty in response. In fact, as was seen in the summative evaluation of the peer reviews, most students felt that changing from chat to the discussion board was not a good decision in the final analysis.

Copyright © 2006, Idea Group Inc. Copying or distributing in print or electronic forms without written permission of Idea Group Inc. is prohibited.

2004 Peer Evaluations of Teaching

Based on many of the summative comments as well as the difficulties encountered with chat and discussion-board peer evaluation, the 2004 course was revised. Yet, the vital importance of peer evaluation in a group of variously experienced professional adults was deemed imperative. Thus, peer evaluation was restructured for this second group.

In-Class Peer Evaluation

Teaching demonstrations for the 2004 course were viewed via videotape in the classroom setting, and the self evaluation following led to oral peer review. The students decided that their review of the lessons should not be for a "grade" but rather as feedback to the teacher. Thus, following each video, the demonstrator/teacher would talk about what he or she believed were the strong points in the lesson. The peers would ask questions, make comments, and generally evaluate the performance.

In terms of peer evaluation in class, all students felt that the f2f evaluations of the teaching demonstrations were excellent. None expressed a preference for having a written component for these, although suggestions for a rubric were presented both in the textbook and by the instructor. Even though the peer evaluation of teaching was informal, serious critique did take place.

From the 10 student demonstration lessons, 6 were given all positive critique while 4 were given both positive and some quite seriously negative critique by their peers. Of course, not all gave negative critique, but since most were seasoned teachers, both negative and positive comments were given and received. In only one case did a demonstrator/teacher try to rebut the negative critique of his or her peers. Nonetheless, these oral reviews were considered one of the best parts of the course in the summative evaluations.

Participation Peer Evaluations

Peer Evaluation Via Quiz/Survey of Chats/Discussions

Overview 2002

Peer evaluations worked as follows during the first section of the course, which was entirely online. Each group leader (moderator) evaluated the participants in her group and each participant evaluated the moderator. Both were due within

Copyright © 2006, Idea Group Inc. Copying or distributing in print or electronic forms without written permission of Idea Group Inc. is prohibited.

one week of the chat/discussion via the WebCT quiz/survey function. These evaluations were then averaged for each person as the participation grade.

The quizzes used may be seen in Appendices B and C. They included multiple-choice items, which could have more than one answer marked, as well as open-ended questions to which the evaluator could respond regarding her peer's contributions. Chats were in rooms where transcripts were available to the instructor should the need arise to decide whether the assigned grades were reasonable. In actual practice, the transcripts were unnecessary as all students took the peer evaluation seriously.

2004 Peer Evaluations

Changes from 2002

Due to the chat difficulties and student summative evaluation of the chat/discussion peer evaluations in the 2002 course, I found changes were required for 2004. Thus, in the 2004 course, we disbanded the chats and discussion-board peer evaluation of teaching, followed by quiz/survey peer evaluation, and instead used a series of case-study analyses and discussions, which were entirely group directed and evaluated. Not only did we use online collaborative groups for the case studies, but we also used essentially the same procedures within the f2f preparation and in-class discussion for other case studies. All cases were contained within the course textbook, *The Teacher's Handbook: Contextualized Language Instruction* (Shrum & Glisan, 2000). Following each of the 12 chapters of the textbook, two case studies are presented with suggested background readings. One of these was assigned for the online delivery medium while the other was assigned for f2f preparation and in-class discussion. (One was used as a sample with the whole group in class and three were unused).

Each of the 10 students was then assigned to be a group leader for one online and one f2f case study. In addition, each student was a participant in two online and two f2f groups. They were randomly divided into case study groups with each total group having three persons—the leader and two members. As the assignments were given, students were asked to consider their two "treatments" as if it were research and to carefully distinguish between the delivery methods of the two types of work.

Online Case Study Parameters

The online case study groups were assigned a group presentation area, a group-only-preparation-discussion-board forum, and a case-study-whole-group-discussion-board area. The working presentation site and preparation forum were available only to the group members until the due date, by which time the others

Copyright © 2006, Idea Group Inc. Copying or distributing in print or electronic forms without written permission of Idea Group Inc. is prohibited.

were then allowed to read through the case. Students were asked to limit *all* preparation to online means—via e-mail, presentation site updates, their group–discussion-board forum, chat, or whatever they desired *but entirely online*. No f2f interaction about their assigned case study was to occur. Each group would then post a finalized version of the issues they had prepared for their case in the presentation area and notify the instructor to announce on the home page that the case was posted and open for discussion via the bulletin board. Then the groups would lead an entirely online discussion with their nongroup peers in the class. Questions and comments from the whole group were to be solicited and summarized over a two-week period following the posting of the case. According to the summative evaluations at the end of the course, everyone complied totally with this request.

This collaboration was evaluated as follows: an online quiz/survey was to be submitted by the group leader assessing each of the two members while each participant also submitted another quiz/survey assessing the group leader. All students therefore were required to submit four online evaluations: one for each of their two group leaders and two for the two group members when they were leader. The grade of each individual for online participation was the average of the two member grades. The grade for leading the online group was the average of the two grades for leadership. The instructor did not grade the online participation or leadership at all, although did constantly monitor what was going on and was able to match the peer grades with her own assessment.

F2F Case Study Parameters

The f2f, in-class case-study groups were similarly assigned a working area and time following instruction during the first four weeks of class. These groups were asked to limit their preparation of the case to nononline means, although short e-mail to confirm meetings or answer questions was considered alright since phone areas were long distance for some participants. Then they were given in-class time to lead a discussion of the case with the whole group.

These case studies conducted in the f2f setting were assessed by peers in a process similar to that of the online quizzes; however, the quiz/survey forms were distributed in class and were to be returned to the instructor by the following class. Again, each participant evaluated the group leader, and each group leader evaluated the two group members. Again, there were four assessments from each individual and these were averaged for one grade as a participant and a separate grade as a group leader.

Summary of 2004 Peer Evaluation

Thus, following the case study preparation and presentation for discussion to the whole group, whether online or in class, each member of each group was to

Copyright © 2006, Idea Group Inc. Copying or distributing in print or electronic forms without written permission of Idea Group Inc. is prohibited.

evaluate his or her peers. This assessment was conducted via the WebCT quiz features for the online groups and via a hard-copy rubric passed out to the class members following their in-class discussion. Group leader evaluations of participants (GL→P) quiz and rubric are found in Appendices D and E and those of participants for their two group leaders (P→GL) online quiz and in-class rubric are found in Appendices F and G.

All of these peer evaluated assignments comprised one fourth of the course grade. In the final analysis, the instructor's graded portion of the course was about 40% of the course grade.

Group Leader Evaluation Results

2002 Group-Online-Leader Evaluation

Assessment of the group leaders or moderators by their peers proceeded smoothly after the first chat session was revised. Each moderator of a chat was evaluated by only three participants while the two who moderated in the discussion boards were evaluated by seven peers. All moderators were given very high scores by their participants. A letter grade or its numeric equivalent was not given directly by the peers. Therefore, to calculate each moderator's peer grade, the instructor awarded a 1 to all responses of strongly agree, a 2 to agree responses, a 3 to all disagree and a 4 to all strongly disagree responses then averaged the items and divided by the total number of people who submitted a score.

Although one person noted in the summative remarks that it was unfair to nonnative typists during the chats and subsequent peer evaluations, the fear that these students were negatively viewed due to their typing abilities was unfounded. The participants who assessed the nonnative typing moderators did not differ in their scoring from those who evaluated native typing moderators.

2004 Group-Online-Leader Evaluation

Unlike the 2002 assessments, each peer evaluator was asked to give a numerical grade to her or his group leaders. Once all of the results were received from the online participants (who had to evaluate both group leaders in the same quiz/ survey), completed grades ranged from 75-100%. The average grade was 92% and the median was 95. Two group leaders were rated 100%, two were between 70% and 80%, and the other six were in the 90-100% range. The two who received 100% from their peers were the first online group leader and the eighth group leader. The two who received between 70-80% were the fourth and ninth group leaders. Comments on the two who were 100% were that they spent time beyond the call of duty getting prepared and organizing the online discussions.

Copyright © 2006, Idea Group Inc. Copying or distributing in print or electronic forms without written permission of Idea Group Inc. is prohibited.

Comments on those in the 70-80% range were that they lacked organization in the preparation and in the online whole-group discussion. It appears that, as a group leader of an online discussion, organization skills are paramount—at least for these students.

In-Class Leader Evaluation

Among the peer evaluations for in-class group leaders, the range was from 91-96% (on a 100% scale). The average was 94.6% and the median 95%. The student with the lowest peer grade (91%) was considered "too quiet" but the second lowest (92%) was "too talkative." There were virtually no comments about organization for these group leaders, unlike the overwhelming number of such for the online group leaders. Organization may well be a key component to e-learning assessment as it was for these students; it is not as critical in f2f settings.

Peer Evaluation of Group Member Results

2002 Group

Like the group leader/moderator evaluations for this class, the evaluations of the participants were not given a numeric or letter grade and thus cannot be summarized on a percentage scale. The same rating was used by the instructor in figuring overall peer grades as noted for the group leader/moderator grading. All eight students were rated very highly for their participation by their moderators.

However, one moderator, a native English speaker living in a remote location, refused to evaluate one of her peers who was a nonnative speaker of English and accessing from the local site for the first chat. This moderator believed that a fair assessment would have to include some negative critique, which was unjust as this person's typing and possibly nonnative reading abilities were the cause of her limited and disjointed participation in the chat. The other moderators had no such qualms and this participant's final grade was as high as the native speakers'.

2004 Online Participant's Evaluations

Among the online participants, scores ranged from 70-95% (on a scale of 100%). Two participants were in the 70-80% range, one in the 80 to 90 range, and the remaining seven in the 90-100% range. The average was 89.4% but the median was 95%. Comments for those participants who received lowest participant evaluations by their peers differed greatly. For one, the comments were that she

Copyright © 2006, Idea Group Inc. Copying or distributing in print or electronic forms without written permission of Idea Group Inc. is prohibited.

or he was not available, did not contribute at all, and one group leader actually evaluated this person with a 0 overall, then seemed to reconsider and simply put 50%. For the other, she or he did not participate at all in one group but in the other she or he was "knowledgeable, but always late" with the work. The leader felt that the participant always had to make a special effort to get her contributions and got very tired of being the police for this student.

For those seven who were in the top group, consistently the comments indicated that they were organized, checked online often, and contributed quality information in a timely manner.

In-Class Participant's Evaluations

Among the peer evaluations by group leaders on the participants in their case studies, scores ranged from 93-98%. The average was 95.5% and the median was 96%. Interestingly, the same two students who were deemed low (yet still in the highest grade bracket since 90-100% is an A in the United States) as group leaders were evaluated as low when participating f2f and for essentially the same reasons.

Summary

A brief review of the online versus f2f peer evaluations shows that the group leaders and participants online both appeared to be more honest, particularly with negative commentary, than did the same people when handing in their assessments directly to the instructor. This was true even though none of the peer remarks were seen by the person being evaluated until he or she received the composite score of all online participation, online leadership, in-class participation, and in-class leadership grades.

Summative Evaluation of Peer Evaluation Strategies Used

Finally, each class member evaluated the usefulness (or value) of peer assessment through the online medium and in the f2f setting for both sections, 2002 and 2004. These were summative evaluations with guided but open-ended prompts; they were not used in determining grades but rather for reflection on the usefulness of peer evaluation through the different means used in the course. These comments were in addition to the university required "course evaluations."

Copyright © 2006, Idea Group Inc. Copying or distributing in print or electronic forms without written permission of Idea Group Inc. is prohibited.

2002 Online Summative Comments

After completing the course, each student wrote a summative evaluation of all aspects of the course. Four students believed that peer evaluation was a positive experience and should be incorporated into any teaching situation. Three students believed that it would have value in some teaching situations, but did not like it in the online context. One student did not believe that peer evaluation had any use in any context.

Of the four who thought peer evaluation was positive, all believed that considering another's teaching and formulating a serious critique, delivering this in a kind and helpful manner, and receiving another's critique was not only valuable in the course, but also a key component of educational practice. All of these four were teaching in public educational programs; one was in Mexico, and three were in or had taught in the United States.

Criticism of the process within our online course was centered on the change over from chat to discussion board which meant that serious peer critique could be read by everyone, including the demonstrator, and all four felt that this medium stifled useful, true, and potentially all negative comments. In the chat sessions, it was generally believed that negative, or "helpful suggestions" were given more often (which was true), and that participants and moderators were more likely to respond accurately. One student commented that she felt there was no useful critique in the "bulletin board discussion of the demonstrations, which were a waste of time, since everyone was so positive." She believed her own lesson was rated highly despite many flaws. As to using the quiz feature for the peer review of the chats or discussions, most felt that these were helpful and all liked the idea of peer grading in this way. Nonetheless, all felt that they wanted to write more but did not want to do so online. They also felt that it would have benefited them had there been one single quiz completed by the moderator for her two or three participants, rather than separate quizzes for each; and likewise for the participants evaluating moderators, if we had gone ahead and each had needed to evaluate two moderators. Finally, this group of positive four, liked the quickness of the multiple-choice items, but only one had realized she could select multiple answers to the questions despite the directions given at the top.

From the three who believed that peer evaluation was useful, but did not like it in our online course, all noted that it was "unfair" to those whose evaluations were given during the chats rather than the discussion board sessions. Two of these participants thought that the critique was "better" during the chat sessions themselves but felt that doing the peer assessment after the chats was likely to generate lower grades due to the special difficulties of the chat format. One in particular reflected that the nonnative English users who were less proficient in writing English were penalized in the chat sessions but could be evaluated higher

Copyright © 2006, Idea Group Inc. Copying or distributing in print or electronic forms without written permission of Idea Group Inc. is prohibited.

Library, Nova Scotia Community College

in the discussion boards. The facts were actually different, as those who assessed the nonnative English users during their chat participation tended to compensate for the time lags and writing difficulties of their peers more than was done for these students during the discussion board peer evaluations. However, this fact was unknown to the participant who made the comment.

Another important summative comment from this group of three, was that peer evaluation was generally good, but it is better in f2f settings since feelings can be considered by visual cues that cannot be seen online. Apparently, all of these students were referring to nonwritten performance peer assessment.

A final suggestion from two of the three members of this group was that the case studies included with the textbook were underutilized in the course and could become a better venue for group work with peer evaluation than the chat on teaching demonstrations. This difference in comfort with online peer evaluation for performance activities, as opposed to written activities, may be indicative of the importance of correlating certain types of e-assessment with the assignments. It appears that these tertiary students were more comfortable and honest with short, immediate, and fleeting online assessment of performance activities and, perhaps, would have preferred using peer assessment with written activities only.

Finally, from the one who did not believe peer evaluation was useful, she felt that people are generally "too nice" or "too mean" to their peers based on personality. In the online environment, where f2f contact is not possible, this participant believed it would be easy to be "mean" since the people would never meet. Thus, this student felt she went to the extreme to be "nice." In addition, having to evaluate her peers seemed to contradict some internal "right of the teacher." She did not think she would use peer evaluation in her classes.

2004 Summative Comments

As previously noted, many of the comments by members of the 2002 online-only students were taken into consideration in the planning of the 2004 course. To summarize, these were to use the case studies in the textbook, to peer evaluate teaching demonstrations in a f2f setting where feedback could be more than "pats on the back" but a serious critique since the kinesics would be available and a "written record" would not be seen, to use chat only as a tool for communication but not as a means of peer evaluation, and to keep the online quiz/survey but to consolidate these into a single quiz per person for all participants and all group leaders.

Copyright © 2006, Idea Group Inc. Copying or distributing in print or electronic forms without written permission of Idea Group Inc. is prohibited.

Online

The summative evaluations of online practices in the 2004 course noted that this method of quiz/survey was very effective and efficient. Students liked working in groups without instructor input and with the ability to grade themselves. Only one student noted that it is very difficult to work in a group with some adults and suggested that maybe we include a training session on collaboration before doing any online group work again.

All student comments were positive regarding the e-learning experience with the course although one student did state that the course really seemed like *two* courses—the online case study version and then the in-class course. This participant believed that there was simply too much material covered by the course and recommended that it be expanded to cover two semesters rather than only one.

The quiz/survey for evaluation of the group work by peers, and the use of peer evaluation overall in the course were likewise positively viewed. Three student comments are of particular note here. First, two students noted the logistics of keeping track of which group they were working in at a given time was easier online than in the f2f setting because all groups were working simultaneously in the classroom, and they were involved as leader for one case study, but also participant in another which was meeting at the same time. On the Web they could separate out groups and positions within these more clearly.

A second pertinent comment about the peer evaluations in the 2004 course was that f2f work gave more visibility to the quieter members of the groups. In the case of one particular student who did not participate actively whether in-class or online, the f2f setting allowed her/his peers to see contributions that the online setting did not. Finally, six students were very concerned that peer evaluations for the first three online discussions were probably "harsher" than those for the last and for the in-class discussions because of a learning curve in the e-discussion format. Several of these students noted that the whole class f2f discussions that occurred at the beginning were better formulated and conducted than the first three e-discussions. One noted that a significant change occurred when online groups realized "not to say everything [about the case] in the presentation but keep some ideas in reserve for the discussion prompts." The first group leader stated that s/he learned by the "seat of the pants" and would have conducted the online discussion very differently had s/he been later in the semester. (But note, s/he was graded as perfect by peers with a 100% average!)

In-Class

The 2004 group rated the in-class activities, which were peer evaluated, very highly but 8 of 10 students mentioned that the WebCT quiz format for submitting peer evaluation was much easier than the paper-and-pen format used. It is

Copyright © 2006, Idea Group Inc. Copying or distributing in print or electronic forms without written permission of Idea Group Inc. is prohibited.

interesting to note that, one of the 2002 students hypothesized that students would have written more if the peer evaluations were not online. Her hypothesis was not confirmed by the 2004 group, as there were no additional comments written on the forms whatsoever.

The responses on the summative evaluation indicated two other important issues. All issues referred to timing. Since the 2002 group had recommended putting all peer evaluations into a single document, this was done for the 2004 group. Yet, students were rushed toward the end of the course when preparing their peer evaluations, and the length of the paper-and-pen document was daunting. Seven students independently suggested that the group leader evaluation be separated so that a more immediate response could be given. A related issue was that many students had forgotten the negatives of in-class discussion and f2f preparation of the case because they did not complete the peer evaluations in a timely manner. It was suggested that the instructor needed to enforce the deadline to turn in f2f peer evaluations the week following the in-class case study discussion.

Conclusion

Peer evaluation is an essential part of true collaboration and its use is ever increasing within "real world" contexts such as the school setting, business, and perhaps industry. Thus, it must be a part of the university training experience. As the online environment permits asynchronous communication, strategies for contributing to useful working relationships online must become a part of life at the university or we will not be true to our calling to prepare leaders for tomorrow.

Challenges in Peer Evaluation

Summary of Results

In e-learning, as seen among these 18 participants in two different sections of the same course as previously described, more honest and potentially negative evaluation is elicited via chat, where a written record is not generally available, rather than on bulletin boards. Likewise greater honesty is elicited by quizzes/surveys submitted via online rather than paper quizzes/surveys submitted directly to the instructor in a f2f setting. This was true despite the fact that all quiz/surveys were seen only by the instructor and not the peer who was being assessed unless the individuals involved shared these on their own.

Copyright © 2006, Idea Group Inc. Copying or distributing in print or electronic forms without written permission of Idea Group Inc. is prohibited.

As seen among these participants, online peer evaluations result in more comments and more negative responses when students do not participate at all or are late. These were the key focal points in lower evaluations of online peers. In the f2f peer evaluations, students made no negative comments and all were assessed as "good" or a "B" grade. The lateness and lack of participation in the f2f setting either: one, does not matter to peers or, two, is not noted because of the interactions with those who are participating and available. More important in the f2f setting appears to be contribution amount and manner, as neither quality nor organization/timing were commented upon.

I would suggest that these findings indicate current tertiary students are still more comfortable with collaborative work and peer evaluation in a f2f setting when their peers are aware of their assessment, while these same students are more likely to be more critical, perhaps more honest, in an online survey/quiz peer evaluation. Actual ability for tertiary students to collaborate in the online setting seems to vary greatly among individuals, but those things that matter most to their peers in the e-environment are timeliness and organized participation.

Addressing the Challenges

One challenge of the online environment is the type of activity that is being assessed by peers. In the "performance" activities, such as teaching demonstrations or other tasks where students are seen potentially via streaming media or another method, peer feedback may need to be different in type, timing, and amount from activities where written text is the primary focus, such as in the case study preparations and eventual discussions. Performance feedback needs to be less permanent and more immediate, via chat perhaps, and shorter in amount than similar peer evaluation when written text is primarily the focus. It was not until organizing this report that I realized the key differences between peer assessments of these two types.

In a f2f setting, contextual cues such as voice quality, style of discourse, facial expression, gesture and so forth give peers sufficient information that they seem more comfortable with evaluating one another on performance, like a teaching demonstration, than in the online format where these cues are (currently) absent. In the near future, technology will undoubtedly make this observation obsolete, but in the meantime, context cues seem important when assessing performance in order to get the same level of honesty as found when peers evaluate written participation where greater honesty may be seen online than in the paper-and-pen surveys.

Whether for performance or participation, peer evaluation, as part of collaborative learning, still appears to be different for students of differing age groups or personalities. Perhaps training in how to work in collaboration with others (who

Copyright © 2006, Idea Group Inc. Copying or distributing in print or electronic forms without written permission of Idea Group Inc. is prohibited.

will be assessing that collaborative performance) may need to be implemented for e-learning groups. Adults in general are not accustomed to collaborative groups in education and peer evaluation in general. To help everyone benefit, sample introductory collaborative groups may be needed whether in the f2f classroom or online.

When collaborative efforts will be conducted online, it is imperative that all participants recognize the need for clear organization of tasks and definition of deadlines by the group leader, as well as attention to time management, prompt responses to online messages and other key issues of online management. These must be articulated explicitly in order to ensure positive interactions online. When being evaluated by peers in e-learning, these issues seem to take the forefront of negatives.

Call for Research

In light of the preceding work, I believe there are many issues that can benefit by empirical investigation. Research like that of Meyer (2003) into higher order thought in discussions online versus in-class could be a model for work considering several topics found through the previously described case study. Those which seem most clearly in need of controlled study are division of performance vs. written participation peer evaluation strategies, willingness to give negative critique to peers via online quizzes vs. pencil-and-paper surveys, refining the rubrics for peer assessment, and benefit of preparatory exercises vs. lack thereof when using collaborative groups and peer feedback. Certainly there are others suggested by this work as well.

In the final analysis, however, this work shows the usefulness of peer evaluation in e-learning. This case study of TESOL in training illustrates the great benefit of collaborative learning and peer evaluation through e-learning particularly well. Among the 18 students enrolled in these two sections of the practicum course, contexts of public education in the United States were compared to public education in Mexico; private education was compared to public education in both countries as well as Korea, Canada, and India. Native speakers teaching EFL compared experiences with nonnative speakers teaching ESL and vice versa. Age, gender, location, native language, second languages, learning through school programs, acquiring bilingually in the preschool environment, or through immersion in second language environment, ease and comfort with computers and even with the online environment, plus other topics too numerous to list were all discussed, analyzed, and seen through streamed or direct video. Then, after seeing the variety of contexts in which colleagues were working on a daily basis, these teachers learned to evaluate one another not based on some "perfect form" for teaching, but rather by viewing principles in practice within

Copyright © 2006, Idea Group Inc. Copying or distributing in print or electronic forms without written permission of Idea Group Inc. is prohibited.

contexts far different from their own experiences. Evaluation of their students, and their colleagues of the future, will benefit all because of these shared experiences in peer evaluation.

E-quiz rubrics have major advantages in efficiency and perhaps honesty over traditional pen-and-paper style peer rubrics. The electronic environment fosters a variety of means for assessment available to any group of learners. And collaboration in online groups permits those experienced adults, who both favor e-learning and benefit from its asynchronous nature, to exchange their experiences, challenges, and pitfalls with one another from environments beyond those available in any one locale.

References

Anderson-Mejías, P. L. (2005). Online training for English as a second/foreign language teachers. In M.O. Thirunarayanan & A. Perez-Prado (Eds.), *Integrating technology in higher education*. Lanham, MD: University Press of America, Inc., Rowman & Littlefield Publishing Group.

Brown, J. D., & Hudson, T. (2002). *Criterion-referenced language testing*. Cambridge,UK: Cambridge University Press.

Curran, C. (1976). *Counseling-learning in second languages*. Apple River, IL: Apple River Press.

Fishman, J. A. (1968). *Readings in the sociology of language*. The Hague, The Netherlands: Mouton.

Freire, P. (1972). *Pedagogy of the oppressed*. Harmondsworth, UK: Penguin.

Freire, P. (1973). *Education: The practice of freedom*. London: Writers and Readers Publishing Cooperative.

Gattegno, C. (1972). *Teaching foreign languages in schools: The silent way* (2nd ed.). New York: Educational Solutions.

Hymes, D. (1974). *Foundations in sociolinguistics: An ethnographic approach*. Philadelphia: University of Pennsylvania Press.

Johnson, D. D., & Johnson, R. T. (1987). *Learning together and alone: Cooperation, competition, and individualization*. Englewood Cliffs, NJ: Prentice Hall.

Johnson, D. W., & Johnson, F. P. (2000). *Joining together: Group theory and group skills* (7th ed.). Needham Heights, MA: Pearson Education.

Labov, W. (1966). *Social stratification of English in New York city*. Washington, DC: Center for Applied Linguistics.

Copyright © 2006, Idea Group Inc. Copying or distributing in print or electronic forms without written permission of Idea Group Inc. is prohibited.

Lozanov, G. (1978). *Suggestology and outlines of suggestopedy*. New York: Gordon and Breach.

Meyer, K. A. (2003). Face-to-face versus threaded discussions: The role of time and higher-order thinking. *Journal of Asynchronous Learning Networks, 7*(3).

Middendorf, J., & Kalish, A. (1995). Peer evaluation of teaching. *Teaching Resources Center Newsletter, 6*(2). Retrieved September 13, 2004, from http://www.indiana.edu/~teaching/peer.html

Nunan, D. (1990). Action research in the language classroom. In J. Richards & D. Nunan (Eds.), *Second language teacher education* (pp. 62-81). Cambridge, UK: Cambridge University Press.

Oxford, R. L. (1990). *Language learning strategies: What every teacher should know*. Boston: Heinle & Heinle.

Prideaux, D. (2002). *Suggestions for peer review of teaching*. Retrieved September 18, 2004, from http://www.flinders.edu.au/teach/evaluate/prideaux.htm

Scarcella, R. C., & Oxford, R. L. (1992). *The tapestry of language learning*. Boston: Heinle & Heinle.

Shurm, J. L., & Glisan, E. W. (2000). *Teacher's handbook: Contextualized language instruction* (2nd ed.). Boston: Heinle & Heinle.

Vygotsky, L. (1978). *Mind in society: The development of higher psychological processes*. Cambridge, MA: Harvard University Press.

Wallace, M. J. (1991). *Training foreign language teachers: A reflective approach*. New York: Cambridge University Press.

Appendix A

Journal Guidelines
(Self Evaluation 25% of Course Grade)

Following are a list of eight guidelines which you MUST follow each week as you reflect on your own teaching. You must answer each of these each and every week. Sometimes that will require a s – t – r – e – t – c – h in our thoughts over teaching ... That's the purpose! At the end of the ten weeks of reflection, you will summarize your findings—what types of comments surfaced over and over in each area and why you think this is so. You will submit all ten weeks of the weekly journal and this summary, but you will grade your teaching experience

Copyright © 2006, Idea Group Inc. Copying or distributing in print or electronic forms without written permission of Idea Group Inc. is prohibited.

yourself. Your evaluation should reflect what you have learned, not how great you were from the beginning. Our goal is to grow as teachers and human beings, so don't think you must be perfect for every lesson. You just should reflect on what worked and why plus what did not work and why. Then learn...

1. What are the THREE (3) most positive experiences I had teaching this week? Explain.

2. What are the THREE (3) most negative experiences I had teaching this week? Explain.

3. What is ONE theory of language or learning which I implemented or saw in action during this week (recall information from ENG 6328).

4. What is ONE procedural or methodological concern (management, discipline, administration, teaching technique, etc) that I needed to deal with during this week? How did I handle this situation?

5. What is ONE thing that I learned about myself as a teacher during this week?

6. What would I change in my teaching after reviewing my week? Why?

7. My reaction to my teaching this week is:

8. My reaction to reflecting on my teaching this week is:

9. Other comments I want to make:

Appendix B

Chat Quiz for Participants to Evaluate the Moderator (Leader)

Enter your chat group number:

Enter the chat date:

Enter the time of chat:

What kind of chat was this (official chat or unofficial/additonal chat)?

Enter the moderator's name:

Enter your name:

Copyright © 2006, Idea Group Inc. Copying or distributing in print or electronic forms without written permission of Idea Group Inc. is prohibited.

1. *The moderator gave a clear introduction to get the chat started.*
    Strongly Agree

    Agree

    Disagree

    Strongly Disagree

2. *The moderator encouraged each member to participate.*
    Strongly Agree

    Agree

    Disagree

    Strongly Disagree

3. *The moderator asked thought-provoking questions/stems.*
    Strongly Agree

    Agree

    Disagree

    Strongly Disagree

4. *The moderator summarized periodically before moving on.*
    Strongly Agree

    Agree

    Disagree

    Strongly Disagree

5. *The moderator added her or his own critique to discussion.*
    Strongly Agree

    Agree

    Disagree

    Strongly Disagree

6. *The moderator kept the discussion on task to creatively modify or improve the lesson seen at the beginning of chat.*
    Strongly Agree

    Agree

    Disagree

    Strongly Disagree

Copyright © 2006, Idea Group Inc. Copying or distributing in print or electronic forms without written permission of Idea Group Inc. is prohibited.

7.   *Inappropriate remarks or criticism rather than critique were handled in a professional manner.*

Strongly Agree

Agree

Disagree

Strongly Disagree

8.   *Particularly insightful or creative comments and suggestions were appropriately and effectively brought out/summarized.*

Strongly Agree

Agree

Disagree

Strongly Disagree

9.   *Additional comments on this moderator:*

Appendix C

Chat Quiz for Moderator to Evaluate Participants

Enter the chat group:

Enter the date of chat:

Enter the time:

Enter the participant's name:

Enter your name:

1.   *The quantity of participation was: (may choose multiple answers)*

Excellent

Good

Average

Poor

Too much

Too little

None

Copyright © 2006, Idea Group Inc. Copying or distributing in print or electronic forms without written permission of Idea Group Inc. is prohibited.

2. *The quality of participation was:*

    Excellent

    Good

    Average

    Poor

3. *The type of participation was: (may choose multiple answers)*

    Creative

    Innovative

    Average

    Mundane

    Trite

    Useless

4. *Overall, this participant:*

    Greatly enhanced the chat discussion

    Added to the chat discussion appropriately

    Could have more actively participated

    Was having a really bad day

5. *The strongest addition/variation/commentary made by this participant was:*

6. *The weakest addition/variation/commentary made by this participant was:*

7. *Other comments regarding this participant:*

Appendix D

GL → Participant ONLINE Quiz

In this "quiz," GROUP LEADER, you will EVALUATE the two participants with whom you worked in your group. You will do one then the other on the same quiz. Please submit within a week of your online discussion's closing. NOTE: questions with * may have multiple selections if you wish.

Copyright © 2006, Idea Group Inc. Copying or distributing in print or electronic forms without written permission of Idea Group Inc. is prohibited.

Enter your name:
Enter the participant's name:

1. *The quantity of participation was*:*
    Excellent
    Good
    Average
    Poor
    Too much
    Too little
    None

2. *The quality of participation was:*
    Excellent
    Good
    Average
    Poor

3. *The type of participation was*:*
    Creative
    Innovative
    Average
    Mundane
    Trite
    Useless

4. *Overall, this participant:*
    Greatly enhanced the group work
    Added to the group work appropriately
    Could have more actively participated in group activities
    Was having a really bad day/week/semester

5. *The amount of this individual's participation in the online discussion with the whole class was:*
    Beyond the call of duty
    Excellent as expected
    Very good

Copyright © 2006, Idea Group Inc. Copying or distributing in print or electronic forms without written permission of Idea Group Inc. is prohibited.

About average

Poor

Really disappointing

Non-existent...she or he pulled a disappearing act

6. *The quality of this person's participantion in the online discussion with the whole class was:*

Excellent

Good

Average

Poor

She or he did not add anything significant to the class discussion online

7. *The type of participation by this person in the online discussion was*:*

Creative

Innovative

Average

Mundane

Trite

Useless

8. *In the online discussion with the whole class, this participant's record overall:*

Greatly enhanced the class discussion

Added to the discussion appropriately

Could have more actively participated in class discussion

Did not add anything of significance to the class discussion

9. *The strongest addition/variation/commentary made by this participant was:*

10. *The weakest addition/variation/commentary made by this participant was:*

11. *Other comments regarding this participant:*

12. *Overall grade for this participant:*

Copyright © 2006, Idea Group Inc. Copying or distributing in print or electronic forms without written permission of Idea Group Inc. is prohibited.

You will now EVALUATE the second person who was a participant in the ONLINE group which you led. It's basically the same quiz again ... sooo

Appendix E

GL → Participant IN-CLASS Peer Evaluation

Please answer the following questions by filling in the blanks:

Your name:

Chapter and page of case study:

Name of the person evaluated (i.e., name of the group participant you are evaluating on this form):

What was the strongest addition that this person contributed to the group effort?

What was the weakest point this person brought to the group—what would you have liked to have been able to change about this participant's group work?

Other general comments:

Now, please circle the answer which most closely matches how you saw this person's participation during the PREPARATION of the Case Study (CS):

1. *The quantity of X's participation was* (you may circle multiple answers):*

    A. Beyond the call of duty—excellent

    B. Very good

    C. Average

    D. Poor

    E. Definitely too little

    F. Actually too much—the person "took over"

    G. X did not participate in preparing the CS.

2. *The type of participation by X was**

    A. Creative and helpful

    B. Creative but off the wall

    C. Informative

Copyright © 2006, Idea Group Inc. Copying or distributing in print or electronic forms without written permission of Idea Group Inc. is prohibited.

  D. Rather average

  E. Mundane

  F. Trite

  G. Useless

  H. Off the wall—simply confused issues

3. *The quality of participation was:*

  A. Excellent

  B. Good

  C. Average

  D. Poor

4. *Overall this participant:*

  A. Greatly enhanced the group

  B. Added to the group work appropriately

  C. Could have more actively participated in activities

  D. Was having a really bad time and didn't help at all

5. *If I were to choose a group member to work with in the future, I would:*

  A. Choose this person without a doubt

  B. Choose this person if there were no other available or she or he was being left out

  C. Not choose this person regardless

  D. Leave town rather than work with her or him again

Now, answer the following questions with reference to this participant's work during the presentation for the class and during class discussion:

6. *The quantity of X's participation was* (you may circle multiple answers):*

  A. Beyond the call of duty—excellent

  B. Very good

  C. Average

  D. Poor

  E. Definitely too little

  F. Actually too much—the person "took over"

  G. X did not participate in preparing the CS

Copyright © 2006, Idea Group Inc. Copying or distributing in print or electronic forms without written permission of Idea Group Inc. is prohibited.

7.   *The type of participation by X was*:*
   A. Creative and helpful
   B. Creative but off the wall
   C. Informative
   D. Rather average
   E. Mundane
   F. Trite
   G. Useless
   H. Off the wall—simply confused issues

8.   *The quality of participation was:*
   A. Excellent
   B. Good
   C. Average
   D. Poor

9.   *If I were to describe this person's in class contributions, I'd say:*
   A. Great job overall—useful, flexible, creative, organized, and so on
   B. Flexible and creative
   C. Organized and useful
   D. Unhelpful, just there
   E. A detriment to a good discussion
   F. Does not contribute at all
   G. Was she or he in class with us??

Fill in the blanks now:

This person's strongest addition to our in-class presentation was:

This person's greatest weakness during the in-class presentation was:

Other comments about this person's in-class participation during the whole group discussion:

My grade for _____'s participation for the in-class Case Study is: _____.

Copyright © 2006, Idea Group Inc. Copying or distributing in print or electronic forms without written permission of Idea Group Inc. is prohibited.

Appendix F

Participant → GL ONLINE Quiz

On this "quiz" format, you will EVALUATE your two ONLINE GROUP/ DISCUSSION LEADERS. Do not evaluate your IN-CLASS group/discussion leaders here! You will do BOTH on the same quiz.

Enter your name:

Enter the name of the GROUP LEADER you are evaluating:

Enter the ONLINE GROUP page and date posted:

Enter your group members (include the LEADER and yourself, as well as the others):

1. *The group leader gave a clear introduction to get the group work started.*

    Strongly Agree

    Agree

    Disagree

    Strongly Disagree

2. *The group leader encouraged each member to participate.*

    Strongly Agree

    Agree

    Disagree

    Strongly Disagree

3. *The group leader asked thought-provoking questions/stems when working with the group on this Case Study.*

    Strongly Agree

    Agree

    Disagree

    Strongly Disagree

4. *The group leader added her orhis own critique to discussion.*

    Strongly Agree

    Agree

Copyright © 2006, Idea Group Inc. Copying or distributing in print or electronic forms without written permission of Idea Group Inc. is prohibited.

Disagree

Strongly Disagree

5. *The group leader kept the Case Study group work on task—to creatively modify or improve the comments of members and achieve a strong final product.*

Strongly Agree

Agree

Disagree

Strongly Disagree

6. *During the group work, inappropriate remarks or criticism rather than critique were handled in a professional manner.*

Strongly Agree

Agree

Disagree

Strongly Disagree

7. *During group work, particularly insightful or creative comments and suggestions were appropriately and effectively brought out and summarized.*

Strongly Agree

Agree

Disagree

Strongly Disagree

8. *Additional comments on this group leader's performance while working together on the Case Study online:*

9. *The group leader asked thought-provoking questions/stems when starting the online discussion for the whole class.*

Strongly Agree

Agree

Disagree

Strongly Disagree

10. *The group leader either personally or asked a group member to summarize periodically before moving on when in the online discussion with the whole class.*

Strongly Agree

Agree

Copyright © 2006, Idea Group Inc. Copying or distributing in print or electronic forms without written permission of Idea Group Inc. is prohibited.

Disagree

Strongly Disagree

11. *The group leader kept the discussion with the whole class (during the two weeks online) on task—to creatively modify or improve the Case Study prompts.*

Strongly Agree

Agree

Disagree

Strongly Disagree

12. *With the whole class discussion, inappropriate remarks or criticism rather than critique were handled in a professional manner.*

Strongly Agree

Agree

Disagree

Strongly Disagree

13. *Particularly insightful or creative comments and suggestions were appropriately and effectively brought out and summarized during the whole class online discussion.*

Strongly Agree

Agree

Disagree

Strongly Disagree

14. *Additional comments on this group leader's performance while leading the whole class discussion of the case study online:*

15. *Numerical grade:*

You will now evaluate your SECOND group leader for the second half of this quiz (the questions then repeat).

Copyright © 2006, Idea Group Inc. Copying or distributing in print or electronic forms without written permission of Idea Group Inc. is prohibited.

Appendix G

Participant → GL IN-CLASS Peer Evaluation

Please answer the following questions by filling in the blanks:

Your name:

Chapter & page of Case Study:

Name of person evaluated (i.e., name of the group leader you are evaluating on this form)

What was the strongest addition that this person contributed to the group effort?

What was the weakest point this person brought to the group—what would you have liked to have been able to change about this leader's style?

Other general comments:

Now, please circle the answer which most closely matches how you saw this person's leadership during the PREPARATION of the Case Study (CS):

1. _____ *as group leader gave a clear introduction to get the group work started during our in-class prep time and whenever we met outside of class.*

    A. Strongly Agree

    B. Agree

    C. Disagree

    D. Strongly Disagree

2. *This group leader encouraged everyone to participate.*

    A. Strongly Agree

    B. Agree

    C. Disagree

    D. Strongly Disagree

3. *This group leader asked thought-provoking questions/stems when working together on the CS preparation.*

    A. Strongly Agree

    B. Agree

Copyright © 2006, Idea Group Inc. Copying or distributing in print or electronic forms without written permission of Idea Group Inc. is prohibited.

C. Disagree

D. Strongly Disagree

4. *The group leader added her or his own critique to discussion.*

A. Strongly Agree

B. Agree

C. Disagree

D. Strongly Disagree

5. *The group leader kept the CS group on task—to creatively modify or improve the comments of members and achieve a strong final product.*

A. Strongly Agree

B. Agree

C. Disagree

D. Strongly Disagree

6. *During the preparation for the CS, inappropriate remarks or criticism rather than critique were handled in a professional manner by this group leader.*

A. Strongly Agree

B. Agree

C. Disagree

D. Strongly Disagree

7. *During our group work, this group leader appropriately and effectively brought out and summarized insightful or creative comments.*

A. Strongly Agree

B. Agree

C. Disagree

D. Strongly Disagree

Now, answer the following questions with reference to the group leader's presentation for the class during the class discussion:

8. _____ *as group leader gave a clear introduction to get the class started during our in-class discussion.*

A. Strongly Agree

B. Agree

Copyright © 2006, Idea Group Inc. Copying or distributing in print or electronic forms without written permission of Idea Group Inc. is prohibited.

C. Disagree

D. Strongly Disagree

9. *This group leader encouraged everyone to participate.*

A. Strongly Agree

B. Agree

C. Disagree

D. Strongly Disagree

10. *This group leader asked or had a group member ask thought-provoking questions/stems when starting the discussion of the case study in class.*

A. Strongly Agree

B. Agree

C. Disagree

D. Strongly Disagree

11. *The group leader added her or his own comments to discussion.*

A. Strongly Agree

B. Agree

C. Disagree

D. Strongly Disagree

12. *The group leader kept the class on task—to creatively modify or improve the comments of one another.*

A. Strongly Agree

B. Agree

C. Disagree

D. Strongly Disagree

13. *During the class discussion, inappropriate remarks or criticism rather than critique were handled in a professional manner by this group leader.*

A. Strongly Agree

B. Agree

C. Disagree

D. Strongly Disagree

Copyright © 2006, Idea Group Inc. Copying or distributing in print or electronic forms without written permission of Idea Group Inc. is prohibited.

14. *During the class discussion, this group leader or an indicated member of the CS group appropriately and effectively brought out and summarized insightful or creative comments.*

   A. Strongly Agree

   B. Agree

   C. Disagree

   D. Strongly Disagree

15. *I would work with this group leader again.*

   A. Gladly

   B. If I had to

   C. Against my better judgment

   D. Not ever, in no way, NO!

Fill in the blanks now:

This leader's strongest addition to our in-class presentation was:

This leader's greatest weakness during the in-class presentation was:

Other comments about this person's leadership during the in-class whole group discussion:

My grade for _____'s leadership for the in-class Case Study is: _____.

Thank you for submitting this in a timely manner (within two weeks of the end of your class discussion) and definitely before April 21.

Copyright © 2006, Idea Group Inc. Copying or distributing in print or electronic forms without written permission of Idea Group Inc. is prohibited.

Chapter III

Peer and Self Assessment in Portuguese Engineering Education

Natascha van Hattum-Janssen
University of Minho, Guimarães, Portugal

Pedro C. C. Pimenta
University of Minho, Guimarães, Portugal

Abstract

This chapter describes the implementation of peer and self assessment in two first-year engineering courses at the University of Minho in the north of Portugal. The results of a case study that was aimed at improving student learning by changing the assessment of learning, aim to illustrate the use of assessment as a powerful instrument to influence learning. The first section pays attention to learning and the influences of peer and self assessment, with special attention to assessment within engineering courses. The second section focuses on the case study previously mentioned and illustrates how students assumed responsibility in their own assessment process. Advantages and disadvantages of peer and self assessment are discussed. The opportunities for e-learning in this case study are discussed in the penultimate section, whereas the last section highlights some of the lessons learned from the case study.

Copyright © 2006, Idea Group Inc. Copying or distributing in print or electronic forms without written permission of Idea Group Inc. is prohibited.

Student Learning and Assessment

The learning process is one of the core processes of a university. Traditionally, learning was regarded as a teacher-centered activity. The teacher takes the initiative, determining what to learn, when to learn and how to learn. The teacher is responsible for the whole process and aims to transfer knowledge to his students. The learner is the passive recipient of knowledge and relies on the teacher.

In recent theories about learning, however, learners are no longer regarded as passive consumers of information (Biggs, 1999; Dochy & Moerkerke, 1997). They are seen as constructors of knowledge. Because students construct knowledge by themselves, they are in charge of their own learning process. Responsibility for the learning no longer resides entirely with the teacher, but also in large part with the learner. Enabling students to be responsible for their own learning process implies a change in the roles of teachers and students in many factors that influence the learning process, such as how teachers teach, curriculum design, materials used, and assessment of students The way students are assessed has an enormous influence on the way they learn. It is a powerful factor in determining the hidden curriculum (Sambell & McDowell, 1998). In the literature, assessment is often mentioned as a way to influence student learning (Baillie & Toohey, 1997; Barnett-Foster & Nagy, 1996; Biggs, 1996, 1999; Hager & Butler, 1996). Assessment of learning is a key to changing learning. Dochy and Moerkerke (1997) pointed out that as assessment changes, learning and teaching will change as well. Although there are many internal and external motivating factors that influence students, a good test result is normally a strong incentive for a student not only to learn, but to learn in a certain way. If the assessment demands memorizing facts in order to pass exams, that activity is adopted by many students (Thomson & Falchikov, 1998). Students adapt their learning strategies to what is required by the assessment.

Scouller (1998) found that not only were students more likely to adopt a surface approach when preparing for a multiple-choice test, students with deep-learning strategies performed poorly on a multiple-choice test. A deep approach, aimed at understanding, was discouraged by this method of assessment. Students perceived a multiple-choice test as solely assessing knowledge and not intellectual skills such as application and comprehension. This finding showed that assessment guides students' learning strategies to a great extent. Apart from the influence of assessment format on learning strategies, Birenbaum and Feldman (1998) identified a personal preference that may strengthen the relationship between assessment format and learning strategies. They stated that students who favor multiple-choice questions have an unfavorable attitude towards open ended questions and are characterized by a low academic self concept and poor

Copyright © 2006, Idea Group Inc. Copying or distributing in print or electronic forms without written permission of Idea Group Inc. is prohibited.

learning skills, whereas students who have a favorable attitude towards the open-ended format and with an unfavorable attitude towards multiple-choice questions are characterized as having a high academic self concept and good learning skills. However, deep learning can involve memorization and a surface approach is likely to be related to a certain level of understanding (Entwistle & Entwistle, 2003). If students are to be autonomous, reflective, and independent learners, their assessment needs to incorporate all these qualities (Stefani, 1998). The strong impact of assessment on learning makes it a powerful instrument for institutions, course directors, individual teachers, and others charged with the responsibility of improving the quality of education. Apart from the short-term effect of assessment on learning within a subject, Thomson and Falchikov (1998) also argued that study patterns that are established early in the university career can persist into subsequent years. Teachers need to realize that the way they shape the learning processes of their first-year students, may have a long-term influence on student learning during their entire course. Boud, Cohen, and Sampson (1999) summarized some effects of assessment on learning, effects that illustrate even more the strong impact of assessment as previously mentioned. In the first place assessment traditionally emphasizes the individual. In most institutions, individual, competitive norm referenced testing is the common practice. Competition is more important than cooperation and criterion referenced assessment is relatively rare. Assessment, secondly, exercises power and control over students. It is the main mechanism used to control students and promotes forms of self surveillance that encourage following a set of strict assessment rules instead of learning. Boud et al. also pointed out the so-called backwash effect on learning that inappropriate forms of assessment appear to encourage a surface approach to learning:"… that is they emphasize rote learning, conforming the narrowest interpretations of assessment tasks and working to 'beat the system' rather than engage in meaningful learning" (p. 418).

A deep approach to learning is discouraged by an overload of assessment tasks. If peer and self assessment are only used as supplements to traditional tests and exams, students' workloads may become too high, and the assessment may encourage only surface learning, in spite of the stated purposes of the peer and self assessment tasks. Concerning the outcomes of the learning process, the authors stated that assessment needs to be matched to the outcomes and needs to encourage self assessment to foster lifelong learning.

The introduction of new forms of learning such as project-based learning, group learning, and problem-based learning is the result of a new way of thinking about learning. The constructivist nature of learning and the need for it in meaningful, real-life situations ask for a reflection on the learning environment. As Birenbaum (1996) stated, with regard to the goals of current higher education:

Copyright © 2006, Idea Group Inc. Copying or distributing in print or electronic forms without written permission of Idea Group Inc. is prohibited.

... successful functioning in this era demands an adaptable, thinking, autonomous person, who is a self regulated learner, capable of communicating and co-operating with others. The specific competencies that are required of such a person include

(a) *cognitive competencies such as problem solving, critical thinking, formulating questions, searching for relevant information, making informed judgements, efficient use of information, conducting observations, investigations, inventing and creating new things, analysing data, presenting data communicatively, oral and written expression;*

(b) *meta-cognitive competencies such as self reflection and self evaluation;*

(c) *social competencies such as leading discussions and conversations, persuading, co-operating, working in groups, etc; and*

(d) *affective dispositions such as for instance perseverance, internal motivation, responsibility, self efficacy, independence, flexibility, or coping with frustrating situations.* (p. 4)

As assessment and instruction need to be in harmony, assessment must also change. Jonassen (1992) described a number of criteria for assessment in a constructivistic learning environment. Firstly, assessment needs to be more goal-free and instead based on outcomes. He recommends the use of needs-assessment methods to determine what the goals of education should be. Another criterion is the process of knowledge construction. Assessment of learning needs to focus on learning outcomes that reflect the process of knowledge construction. The product of the learning process, in a constructivistic view, is no longer the only focus of evaluation. The process of knowledge construction should also be part of the evaluation process. Students need to learn to reflect on their own process of knowledge construction and create a metacognitive awareness that improves their learning and the results of their learning. Higher order thinking skills need to be the object of assessment. Assessment of learning should be more of a self analysis and metacognitive tool rather than a reinforcement or behavior control tool, as argued by Jonassen (1992). Assessment should go beyond measuring the reproduction of information; because this kind of assessment does not assess forms of learning involving the construction of meaning by the student or the development of strategies for approaching new problems and learning tasks (Dierick & Dochy, 2001). In the last decade, assessment practices have been changing. Dochy (2001) referred to assessment as a broad concept, not only measuring knowledge gained, but also student involvement, their application of that knowledge, integration in the

Copyright © 2006, Idea Group Inc. Copying or distributing in print or electronic forms without written permission of Idea Group Inc. is prohibited.

learning environment, knowledge construction instead of knowledge reproduction and real life situations. Because students, in his view, should be regarded as independent, autonomous and exploring individuals who direct their own learning processes, their role in the assessment process is different and depends less on the teacher and more on themselves. Assessment and instruction are becoming more integrated. Assessment is no longer an isolated, summative activity, with little connections to learning activities. Instead, it is integrated in the instructional process and can be regarded as a tool to enhance the learning processes of the students (Dochy, 2001).

New forms of assessment raise three questions:

1.   What is assessed?
2.   How does assessment take place?
3.   Who assesses?

The first question, what is assessed, refers to a shift from knowledge to skills. Instead of evaluating the reproduction of factual knowledge, the application of what is learned in specific skills becomes more important. Brown, Bull, and Pendleburry (1997) too, noticed a change in what was being assessed: from the content of the learning material to the competencies the students are supposed to have at the end of the subject. This change placed more emphasis on the students and the meaning of what was learned for them and their skills. The focus is more on the change in performance of the students, than on the content of the course, as this change in performance is the ultimate goal of the course.

The change in what is assessed is illustrated in detail by Hager and Butler (1996), who distinguished three levels of assessment, as shown in Table 1.

Looking at the changed perspectives on learning, the first level of assessment, that is still dominant, is no longer the most appropriate level of assessment. Nowadays, learning is aimed at critical thinking, problem solving, efficient use of information, metacognitive skills, for example self reflection and affective

Table 1. Three levels of assessment according to Hager and Butler (1996)

Knowledge, skills, and attitudes	Students are usually evaluated by tests, exercises and exams, the dominant level in current education
Performance in simulated or practice domains	The student is placed in a simulated situation and has to perform on a higher level
Personal competence in the practice domain	In a real situation, the student has to show that he has integrated knowledge, skills, and personal qualities into reflective and integrating thinking

Copyright © 2006, Idea Group Inc. Copying or distributing in print or electronic forms without written permission of Idea Group Inc. is prohibited.

dispositions, such as motivation and responsibility. The first level does not assess these competencies, skills, and dispositions at all. Simulations and real-life situations are much more appropriate means of assessment to evaluate student performance.

To answer the second question, how does assessment take place, some general trends can be identified (Brown et al., 1997). Written examinations are replaced by coursework. Students do more assignments and are given fewer formal exams. The chronic pressure of assignments replaces the acute stress of exams. Written examinations measure the capacity to recall factual information, to think structurally and to write quickly under pressure, whereas coursework demands the capacity to retrieve and select information from external sources, deeper understanding and the development of problem-solving strategies. It also means a shift from competition to collaboration among students, because written exams do not require any form of collaboration. The emphasis is on the final mark, which creates a competitive atmosphere among students. Assignments ask for collaboration. Given the fact that most assignments are group work, working together for a good result becomes more important than competing against each other for an extra point.

Biggs (1999) described a similar change in what is assessed. He distinguishes a quantitative and a qualitative way of looking at learning. A quantitative way of looking at learning implies that learning performances are measured in quantifiable units, like words or ideas. These words or ideas are equivalent to points that can be counted; each unit is either correct or incorrect, and units are translated into indices of learning along a single scale. The value of each unit is the same. The value of individual correct answers is not important, as long as there are enough correct answers. This could mean in practice that, for example, a medical student can pass a practical exam because he or she performed well on most of the operation, although the patient died due to an error of the student in part of the operation.

A qualitative perspective on learning has different implications for assessment. In this view, learning depends on previous knowledge and becomes more complex all the time. Hence it appears that assessment should inform about the present state of complexity, instead of comparing students. Biggs argued that learning outcomes should be assessed holistically—in a qualitative way—not analytically—in a quantitative way. Furthermore, each student's assessment should be independent of any other student's. Overall assessment and portfolio assessment are more appropriate methods of assessment than are the traditional tests and exams.

The third question, who assesses, is a central one when discussing student responsibilities in learning. Dochy (2001) gave several answers to the question. He presented a continuum with the teacher on one end and the student on the other end. He explained how, in a traditional situation, the teacher carries out

Copyright © 2006, Idea Group Inc. Copying or distributing in print or electronic forms without written permission of Idea Group Inc. is prohibited.

each assessment task. He determines criteria for assessment, evaluates the performances of students, and gives feedback. He called this teacher-controlled assessment. Dochy also explained student-controlled assessment, where students are involved in stating criteria, evaluating their own performance, and giving feedback. In between these two extremes, there are a number of possibilities. In coassessment, students and teachers cooperate in the assessment process. They discuss assessment criteria, and students can evaluate each other, but in the end, the teacher takes the final decisions. Students have the opportunity to experience the role of the teacher. They learn to see what it is to evaluate and make judgements. Furthermore, students learn to evaluate themselves and reflect on their own performances. In peer assessment, which implies less teacher involvement than coassessment, students evaluate each other. It is used to encourage deeper learning. Self assessment is the opposite of traditional assessment. Students are very much involved in the assessment process and they have a central role in their evaluation. The teacher is no longer solely responsible person for the assessment process. Students take part in both development of criteria and the evaluation of their own and their colleagues' performance (Houston & Lazenbatt, 1996; McIlveen, Greenan, & Humphreys, 1997; Sheppard, Johnson, & Leifer, 1998; Sluijsmans, Moerkerke, van Merriënboer, & Dochy, 2001).

In student-centred assessment, students choose their tasks and experience an increased ownership and commitment to their learning process. Furthermore, assessment criteria are more explicit. It is no longer the unique interpretation of a teacher that determines the mark of a student. The students get a role in the determination of criteria and understand why they have received a certain mark. In some studies, students even choose the method of assessment (Cook, 2001). Participation in the assessment can give students an insight into their learning process and to accomplish this, they look more closely at their own performances. Involvement helps to enhance student motivation because the student is part of his or her own assessment. The student has a responsibility and is no longer a passive "consumer" of education.

Apart from the advantages of student involvement in assessment, there are also some difficulties, especially when introducing peer, self and co-assessment for the first time.

- Students may not be used to criticize themselves and others and may feel inexperienced in judging others.
- They are afraid of getting an unfair judgement of their colleagues.
- Explicit marking procedures and guidance of students is necessary for them to gain confidence in assessing each other and to assure an adequate and fair assessment.

Copyright © 2006, Idea Group Inc. Copying or distributing in print or electronic forms without written permission of Idea Group Inc. is prohibited.

Studies in, for example, civil engineering describe possible peer assessment methods that help students to be fair and accurate to each other (Lejk, Wyvill, & Farrow, 1996, 1997; Rafiq & Fullerton, 1996). A study at the Hong Kong Polytechnic University showed significant differences in the grading of tutors and peer groups (Kwan & Leung, 1996), who assessed a simulation training exercise of third year students. They argued that self assessment is a skill that becomes more reliable with practice. The benefits of self and peer assessment greatly outweigh the possible difficulties they found, like disagreement between tutor marks and peer marks.

Looking at different fields of study, Neuman et al. (2002) distinguished between hard pure knowledge, such as physics and chemistry, soft pure knowledge, such as history and anthropology, hard applied knowledge—typified by engineering—and soft applied knowledge—such as education and management studies. They claim that assessment in engineering shows a clear preference for examination, including multiple-choice, covering a large body of factual knowledge. Part of the assessment involves problem-solving, the rest assessment of practice-related skills.

The kind of assessment chosen by a teacher has a profound impact on the way students learn. Students tend to learn for assessment and in this way assessment provides part of the learners' motivation. In engineering courses, motivation for learning is often difficult in the first years of the course (Baillie & Toohey, 1997). Students have problems understanding the relevance of the subjects they study and are often not motivated intrinsically for the materials they have to learn, especially in engineering courses, where the first year consists mainly of mathematics and physics subjects for which students are not highly motivated.

Ditcher (2001) argues that students are often driven by the external demands of the assessment system, rather than by internal motives such as interest. Assessment now becomes a crucial motive for learning. In the last years of the course, students may be motivated, because of a real interest in their course, but in the first years, their interest in the content of the course is not the most important reason for learning. Changing the motivational impact of assessment in the early years of an engineering course could probably contribute to a higher quality of student learning.

The need for changes in assessment in engineering courses is clearly described by Rompelman (2000). The traditional engineering with a profound body of scientific knowledge that the student can apply to technical problems no longer meets the requirements of today's changing society. Students nowadays need to have the following abilities:

- *an ability to apply knowledge of mathematics*
- *an ability to design and conduct experiments, as well as to analyse and interpret data*

Copyright © 2006, Idea Group Inc. Copying or distributing in print or electronic forms without written permission of Idea Group Inc. is prohibited.

- *an ability to design a system, component, or process to meet desired needs*

- *an ability to function on multidisciplinary teams*

- *an ability to identify, formulate, and solve engineering problems*

- *an understanding of professional and ethical responsibility*

- *an ability to communicate effectively*

- *the broad education necessary to understand the impact of engineering solutions in a global and societal context*

- *a recognition of the need for, and the ability to engage in, lifelong learning*

- *knowledge of contemporary issues*

- *an ability to use the techniques, skills, and modern engineering tools necessary for engineering practice.* (Rompelman, 2000)

The first three abilities are rather general for engineers and were the basis for traditional engineering courses. Although they are still very valid, other competencies became necessary as well (Teixeira, Teixeira, Pile, & Durão, 1998). The remaining competencies, as previously mentioned, illustrate the shift from knowledge-based to competency-based learner-oriented engineering education. In recent engineering education, this shift from teacher-centred to learner-centred thinking about education that took place in many engineering courses, caused a change in educational approaches, characterized by project or problem-based learning. (Creighton, Johnson, Penny, & Ernst, 2001; Powell & Weenk, 2003). The accomplishment of the next set of abilities and understandings, as identified by Rompelman (2000), from functioning in multidisciplinary teams to effective communication, ask for learning methods that stimulate interaction between and incorporate a strong component of reflection on one's own thinking and performance. Assessment, being part of the learning method, needs to show these characteristics as well.

Edward (2003) reports, that engineering students have an ambivalent attitude to assessment. On the one hand they had a strong dislike of having to complete coursework and study for examinations, but on the other, they suggested that if more of the work were assessed they would take it more seriously. Assessment, in their opinion, allowed the better and more conscientious student to be distinguished from less industrious or able peers. They also acknowledged the need to maintain standards if their qualification were to have credence among employers. Students will adopt effort, approach, and strategies both to topics and to the explicit criteria of assessment. If the criteria are not explicit many students will passively or actively look for indication of what is asked from them.

Copyright © 2006, Idea Group Inc. Copying or distributing in print or electronic forms without written permission of Idea Group Inc. is prohibited.

Student-centred assessment methods can provide a framework for the enhancement of student responsibility with regard to the abilities and understanding as previously identified.

In this case study, the assessment process was carried out in the classroom and at certain moments, students had to assess the work of their peers outside the classroom.

Peer and Self Assessment in Portuguese Engineering Education: A Case Study

In Portugal, students are allocated to universities and to courses based on the marks they obtain during their last three years at secondary school and at the national exam. The higher the mark is, the more likely students can be placed in their first choice of course. Courses like medicine, law, and psychology are very popular. Many students nominate these as their first choice, so only students with high entrance marks are accepted into these courses. Engineering courses are not as popular as those previously mentioned, so students do not need such high entrance marks to be allocated to an engineering course. Weaker students know they stand a better chance of qualifying for an engineering course, so they are more likely to opt for these courses. Subsequently, many engineering courses in Portugal have a student population that is not highly motivated, does not have clear expectations of the course, and is not as successful as it could be. In 2001 and 2002, only 64% of the engineering students were allocated to their first-choice course. Of the students involved in the case study, for around 40% of the students, their course was actually their first choice. Many of the students enter a course that is not their most wanted course, and they all start with a first year that mainly consists of mathematics and physics subjects, offering very little learning opportunities that are directly related to materials of their own engineering courses. The high workload of mathematics and physics subjects, combined with a poor mathematics and physics preparation of many of the engineering students at secondary school, also contributes to a low motivation of part of the student population. Given these characteristics, working on methods that influence student motivation becomes more and more important to a university. The University of Minho, and especially the School of Engineering, decided to work on methods to improve the results of the first year engineering students in the long term. The main intention was to deepen the learning process of students by using assessment methods that would enhance student involvement, increase their responsibility, and stimulate their motivation.

Copyright © 2006, Idea Group Inc. Copying or distributing in print or electronic forms without written permission of Idea Group Inc. is prohibited.

This section describes the case study of the School of Engineering where peer and self assessment are implemented as a method to improve student learning. Because of the low motivation of many of the engineering students, the complaints of many teachers about the poor retention of materials that were offered at the beginning of the course, the lack of student responsibility during the course and the poorly developed study skills of first-year students, the Council of Engineering Courses decided to implement student-centered assessment, according to the concepts of Dochy (2001). The following model (see Figure 1) was used as a framework for the implementation of peer and self assessment (van Hattum-Janssen, Pacheco, & Vasconcelos, 2004). In student-centered assessment, responsibilities shift from teacher to students. The have more tasks in the assessment process and need to be more involved with the material. A larger involvement and an increased responsibility can affect the intrinsic motivation of students, especially if the assessment tasks appeal to the personal interest and future professional practice of the students. The higher motivation was supposed to deepen the learning approach of the students and therefore enhance the quality of learning. For this case study, three assessment moments were designed in which increasing student responsibility and student involvement. This assessment method was implemented in two subjects of first-year engineering courses: Industrial Electronics and Textile Engineering with both around 60 students enrolled at the first year. These courses were selected because of the heterogeneity and number of first-choice students. Industrial Electronics in general attracts better-prepared and more motivated students, whereas Textile Engineering tends to have less motivated and weaker students. Teachers of both courses had some freedom to design and make adjustments to the assessment tasks and the exact timing of assessment moments.

Figure 1. A model for the enhancement of quality learning

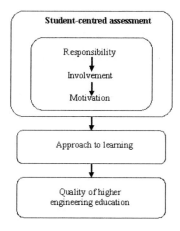

Copyright © 2006, Idea Group Inc. Copying or distributing in print or electronic forms without written permission of Idea Group Inc. is prohibited.

In general, the first assessment moment had to be a peer assessment moment with considerable teacher involvement. The second assessment moment also had to be peer assessment moment, but with less teacher participation. The third assessment moment was supposed to be a self assessment moment with a large component of student responsibility in his or her own assessment process. The Industrial Electronics teacher decided to start off with a group assignment in which students were required to write a detailed report on their futures as an industrial electronics engineer. A peer group assessed the report. The second assessment moment consisted of an individual take-home assignment that was assessed by a peer student. At the third assessment moment, students wrote a test. The textile engineering students started with a test and then wrote a group report as their second assessment task. Their last task was an individual assignment that had to result in a report on the spinning process. Students' responsibilities in the assessment process increased from the first to the last moment. Students were involved in

- **Defining the Assessment Criteria:** In a plenary session with all the students participating in the project, students were asked to propose relevant criteria for the assessment of the work.
- **Correcting Work of Peers or Peer Group:** At the first and the second assessment moment, students reviewed the work of their peers, assessing reports in groups or individually, applying the assessment criteria that were formulated in a plenary session.
- **Correcting Own Work:** At the last assessment moment, students corrected their own work.
- **Grading and Justifying the Grading of Assessments:** At both peer and self assessment moments, students marked assessment results. They were also asked to write an extensive justification of the mark for two reasons: The justification increases on the one hand enhance a more correct and fair mark as students need to show the motive to attribute a certain mark and on the other hand it serves as feedback to the assessed student or group of students.
- **Making Recommendations:** Students were asked to make recommendations for future improvement of the performance of the assessed student.
- **Writing Reflections:** At the end of the project, students wrote a personal reflection of the assessment method.

At the first assessment moment, the teacher input was high, especially with regard to the definition of assessment criteria. Correcting and grading the work of peers and performing self assessment was considered difficult at the

Copyright © 2006, Idea Group Inc. Copying or distributing in print or electronic forms without written permission of Idea Group Inc. is prohibited.

beginning and especially by weaker students, but in general students such assessments were considered to be accurate (van Hattum-Janssen et al., 2004). Because of the experimental nature of the project, the teachers also graded the assignments and tests to enable comparisons between teacher grades and student grades. The involvement of the teacher in the assessment process was important at the first assessment moment to encourage students in their new role as assessors. During the semester, most of the students involved gained confidence in all the new tasks they had to carry out. They started to understand what is involved in assessment and that assessment results are not something that happen to them, but something that are the result of their own performance. A low or a high grade is no the punishment or reward of the teacher, but a direct result of the input of a student in his or her assessment task. Apart from this fundamental understanding, students developed deeper learning approaches as measured with the Inventory of Learning Styles (Vermunt, 1992).

This inventory identifies four components of learning styles.

- **Processing Strategies:** Processing strategies are the mental activities used by students to process information. They process information to obtain certain learning results. The subscales of this scale are deep processing, stepwise processing, and concrete processing.

- **Regulation Strategies:** On a higher level, students use regulation strategies to control, plan, and monitor their learning process and their processing strategies. The subscales of this scale are self regulation, external regulation, and lack of regulation.

- **Learning Orientations:** These are personal ideas, aims, expectations, and so on that students have. They may include reasons for going to university or wanting to obtain a certain degree. Subscales are certificate-oriented, profession-oriented, test-oriented, personally oriented, and ambivalent.

- **Mental Models of Learning:** Mental models of learning refer to the ideas students have concerning knowledge, learning and education, and definitions of learning. The respective subscales are absorption of knowledge, accumulation of knowledge, use of knowledge, and the stimulation of education.

In this project, students' processing and regulation strategies became more profound after the change of assessment methods during the first semester of the first year. Learning orientations and mental models of learning did not show a significant change.

Copyright © 2006, Idea Group Inc. Copying or distributing in print or electronic forms without written permission of Idea Group Inc. is prohibited.

The model that was developed in which student centred assessment served as a tool to improve student learning in engineering education appeared to be useful in the process of remodelling education in such a way that student learning became deeper. The experience showed that education and assessment must complement one another if they are to make any significant change in the way students learn, as pointed out earlier. It also showed that a significant change in the assessment process implies serious changes in the instruction process. Students were supposed to assess their own work and the work of others within lecture hours, so less time was dedicated to traditional lectures, and students spent more time reflecting on their own performance and that of peer students.

E-Learning Opportunities

In this case study, e-learning was not used to enhance the quality of the learning process. There are, however, a number of interesting opportunities for e-learning that can be identified, especially when looking at e-learning experiences in later similar projects. In this case, blended learning is considered a better term, as e-learning is combined with traditional classroom education. Classes will still take place, but where possible the assessment process is facilitated electronically. For a non-experienced teacher, it is a considerable challenge to find the balance between face-to-face and computer-mediated communication. When face-to-face communication in a classroom situation is compared with computer-based communication, two main differences emerge. Firstly, face-to-face communication/discussion normally does not leave any records, as opposed to a discussion supported by a forum, where each contribution is formally recorded and in that way made available for the future. Secondly, face-to-face discussion is oral, compared to computer-based communication that is mainly text-based. Oral communication tends to be more informal; written tends to be more reflected and formal.

In this case study, a number of different activities in peer and self assessment can be distinguished to indicate e-learning opportunities. The first stage of peer and self assessment is the definition of assessment criteria. In a preparatory classroom situation, it is necessary that the teacher explains what is to be assessed and why. The assessment criteria need to be defined by students and teacher together, and negotiation of the relative value of each criterion needs to take place. In the case study, criteria have been defined in a class discussion in a lecture room. In later projects, teachers asked students to propose assessment criteria to them by e-mail or discuss them on a forum. The results of these experiences were not very promising. Students found it difficult to propose criteria without any group interaction or support of the teacher. The number of

Copyright © 2006, Idea Group Inc. Copying or distributing in print or electronic forms without written permission of Idea Group Inc. is prohibited.

reactions was low, whereas in classroom group discussions teachers received useful reactions from students and were able to define a set of assessment criteria.

The following step is the summarization and organization of the criteria by the teacher (or by teacher and students) by electronic means like forums and distribution lists and the distribution of the criteria to all the students. This balance between face-to-face and computer-mediated communication is not trivial; and, although one might be tempted to use a forum for the definition of criteria, experiences in later projects show that this face-to-face interaction moment is crucial for both teacher and students to clarify all aspects of the assessment process and prepare for a well-structured online communication.

After setting criteria, students have to hand in their assignments. In the case study, students handed in paper versions of their assignments and test papers. In later peer and self assessment projects, students sent their reports to a mailing list or to an online repository that was created by the Department of Information Systems to store class projects and reports.

The actual peer and self assessment processes in the case study mainly took place in the classroom. Group reports and individual assignments were redistributed by the teacher and, either in groups or individually, assessed and graded. Because the students involved were first-year students, they did not have any experience with peer and self assessment and it was useful to assist the assessment and grading process and help students with their doubts. In later projects, students assessed and graded work of themselves and their colleagues using Web sites both in groups and individually. The individual assessment and grading processes showed large difficulties of students in attributing fair and balanced grades in comparison with teacher grades. The group marking showed more accurate grades.

On all occasions, both in the case study as well as in later projects, students had to write justification for the grades they gave. This happened on an assessment form that was completed at every assessment moment. On this form, students wrote down the grade and a justification for each grade they gave for each criterion. In later peer and self assessment projects, students send the assessment forms to the online repository or to the mailing list, in order to be accessible for all the students involved. Both students and teacher had access to all the assessment forms and students had to opportunity to read the feedback of their peers on their assignments and test papers.

The opportunities for blended learning as described here are still in an initial stage. More research needs to be done to determine in what way the introduction of blended learning can contribute effectively to the enhancement of learning quality in peer and self assessment. Electronic support of peer and self assessment can facilitate the assessment process to a large extent. Moore's

Copyright © 2006, Idea Group Inc. Copying or distributing in print or electronic forms without written permission of Idea Group Inc. is prohibited.

theory of transactional distance states that distance is a pedagogical more than a geographical phenomenon (Chen, 2001) and distinguishes three types of interaction: learner-instructor, learner–content, and learner–learner. In the different stages of peer and self assessment as described in this chapter, interaction between teacher and students is used to shift responsibilities from the teacher to the students. Students help to define assessment criteria, they assess and grade work, and they give feedback. From the case study and from later experiences in similar projects where part of the classroom activities have been replaced by e-learning activities, it is not clear yet to what extent classroom activities can be replaced by online activities without loosing valuable classroom teacher-learner and learner-learner interaction or what kind of e-learning activities can be used to accomplish the degree of interaction that is necessary to support students in their changing role towards responsible individuals who are in charge of their own assessment process.

The written communication that is a consequence of e-learning has several advantages. The online availability of student work and its assessment record enhances transparency and enables students to easily compare their grades and the consideration of their peer assessors. Another characteristic of this computer-mediated process is that it facilitates the keeping of the records of what happened to show future students and so explain the positive and negative aspects of previous processes. User authentication capabilities, as well as the ability to record the date and time of submission can help teachers to keep track of submission dates and times.

Future Improvements of the Assessment Methods

In general, the implementation of student-centred assessment methods has many advantages for the students, as previously illustrated. There are, however, some points of contention that need to be taken into account. First, students have to learn how they do peer and self assessment. In this case study, it appeared that the weaker students especially had problems with self assessment tasks. They found it difficult to assess their own performance and grade their own work. They had little confidence in their own capacities as assessors. In general, students had to get used to peer and self assessment and gain confidence as the semester progressed. Performing the first assessment task in a group helped them to acquire the skills needed to assess assignments and test results.

Copyright © 2006, Idea Group Inc. Copying or distributing in print or electronic forms without written permission of Idea Group Inc. is prohibited.

Second, peer and self assessment depend to a great extent on a good definition of assessment criteria. In this project, both stronger and weaker students showed capacities to assess their peers and themselves. They depended highly on well-elaborated assessment criteria that guide them through the correction process. The initial stage of discussing and defining these criteria and their relative weights is highly important. It is a first step to make the assessment process transparent and it gives a certain confidence to students who feel insecure about their own capacity to assess their peers or themselves.

For the teachers, the implementation of peer and self assessment implied extra workload for various reasons. They not only had to create more assessment tasks during the semester instead of one traditional exam at the end; but they also had to accompany students during the correction and grading exercise. Apart from these activities, the teachers in this case study, as mentioned before, also corrected each assignment and test paper to be able to compare student marks with the teacher marks and examine the accuracy of student grading. This process was time consuming, although not strictly necessary. In a non-experimental setting, teachers could also draw a random sample of student work to verify the accuracy of their grading or decide not to check the grading process of their students. Because of the multiple assessment moments, more grades are attributed, so the teacher must handle more administration. The higher workload of a teacher was, in this case study, partly compensated by the fact that peer and self assessment completely replaced the final exam.

The implementation of peer and self assessment was limited to one subject per course for this trial. The workload increased for both students and teachers. It is important to fully research the influence of implementing styles of assessment which increase student responsibility to determine:

- How learning styles change,
- If workload demands are fair, and
- How long term study results are affected.

Implementing various assessment moments during a semester requires good coordination between teachers to guarantee a well-balanced workload and a reasonable distribution of assessment tasks.

In the case study as described here, e-learning or blended learning could make a significant difference to the assessment process. Classroom activities can provide important teacher-learner and learner-learner interaction, especially when defining assessment criteria and during individual assessment and the grading process of assignments and test papers. Online activities are useful at

Copyright © 2006, Idea Group Inc. Copying or distributing in print or electronic forms without written permission of Idea Group Inc. is prohibited.

other stages of the peer and self assessment. Continuous access of students to their own work, the work of their peers, assessment and feedback forms, and grades helps students to reflect more on their own work and the work of their peers and in that way enhances the quality of the learning process.

Conclusion

The case study at the Engineering School of the University of Minho in Portugal, where peer and self assessment were implemented in two first-year engineering courses, showed that it was possible to increase student participation in groups of around 60 students by changing from traditional assessment to student-centred assessment. The teachers of both subjects did not make any significant changes to the content of their subjects and the teaching methods. The higher student involvement in the process turned assessment into a learning tool. Students start to understand how and why they are assessed and learn from their own performance as well as the performance of their peers. Because peer and self assessment were, in this case study, incorporated in a frequent assessment scheme, students started working and studying immediately after the start of the semester and had opportunities to reflect on their own behavior shortly after. As they were first-year students with no other assessment experiences, they did not question the assessment method and participated fully in peer and self assessment. Looking at the results of the Learning Style Inventory that was applied at the beginning and at the end of the semester, processing and regulation activities became more aimed at deeper learning during the semester.

Although the changes in the assessment process were mainly positive, there are some important lessons that can be learned from the case study. The process of defining criteria is crucial for a high-quality transparent assessment process. Students need clear and well-discussed criteria to enable a fair and unambiguous interpretation and grading process. Ill-defined criteria can lead to a wide variety of interpretations of test papers and reports and difficulties to attribute a fair grade. It is also important to emphasize the written justification of each given grade. The explicit justification of grades increases the feedback value of peer and self assessment. Students are less likely to attribute undeserved high grades and are forced to explain why they gave a certain grade.

It can be concluded that in many ways peer and self assessment show advantages over traditional assessment, or as phrased by one student in a questionnaire about the assessment method:

Copyright © 2006, Idea Group Inc. Copying or distributing in print or electronic forms without written permission of Idea Group Inc. is prohibited.

This assessment method is innovating and more interactive. It appeals to the critical mind of the students and enables contact with the work of our colleagues, so that we can see what their methods are and where they went wrong. The assessment method has become a way of learning.

References

Baillie, C., & Toohey, S. (1997). The "power test": Its impact on student learning in a material science course for engineering students. *Assessment & Evaluation in Higher Education, 21*, 33-48.

Barnett-Foster, D., & Nagy, P. (1996). Undergraduate student response strategies to test questions of varying format. *Higher Education, 32*, 177-198.

Biggs, J. (1996). Assessing learning quality: Reconciling institutional, staff and educational demands. *Assessment & Evaluation in Higher Education, 21*, 5-15.

Biggs, J. B. (1999). *Teaching for quality learning at university.* Buckingham: SRHE & Open University Press.

Birenbaum, M. (1996). Assessment 2000: Towards a pluralistic approach to assessment. In M. Birenbaum & F. J. R. C. Dochy (Eds.), *Alternatives in assessment of achievements, learning processes and prior knowledge* (pp. 3-30). Boston: Kluwer Academic.

Birenbaum, M., & Feldman, R. (1998). Relationships between learning patterns and attitudes towards two assessment formats. *Educational Research, 40*, 90-98.

Boud, D., Cohen, R., & Sampson, J. (1999). Peer learning assessment. *Assessment & Evaluation in Higher Education, 24*, 413-426.

Brown, G., Bull, J., & Pendleburry, M. (1997). *Assessing student learning in higher education.* London: Routledge.

Chen, Y. J., (2001). Dimemsions of transactional distance in the World Wide Web learning environment: A factor analysis. *British Journal of Educational Technology, 32*(4), 459-470.

Cook, A. (2001). Assessing the use of flexible assessment. *Assessment & Evaluation in Higher Education, 26*, 539-549.

Creighton, S. D., Johnson, R. L., Penny, J. Y. & Ernst, E. (2001). A comprehensive system for student and program assessment: Lessons learned. *International Journal of Engineering Education, 17*(1), 81-88.

Copyright © 2006, Idea Group Inc. Copying or distributing in print or electronic forms without written permission of Idea Group Inc. is prohibited.

Dierick, S., & Dochy, F. (2001). New lines in edumetrics: New forms of assessment lead to new assessment criteria. *Studies in Educational Evaluation, 27,* 307-329.

Ditcher, A. K. (2001). Effective teaching and learning in higher education, with particular reference to the undergraduate education of professional engineers. *International Journal of Engineering Education, 17*(1), 24-29.

Dochy, F. (2001). A new assessment era: Different needs, new challenges. *Research Dialogue in Learning and Instruction, 2,* 11-20.

Dochy, F. J. R. C., & Moerkerke, G. (2001). Assessment as a major influence on learning and instruction. *Educational Testing and Assessment, 27,* 415-432.

Edward, N. S. (2003). Mark my words: Self and peer assessment as an aid to learning. *European Journal of Engineering Education, 28*(1), 103-116.

Entwistle, N., & Entwistle, D. (2003). Preparing for examinations: The interplay of memorising and understanding, and the development of knowledge objects. *Higher Education Research & Development, 22,* 19-41.

Hager, P., & Butler, J. (1996). Two models of educational assessment. *Assessment & Evaluation in Higher Education, 21,* 367-378.

Houston, K., & Lazenbatt, A. (1996). A peer-tutoring scheme to support independent learning and group project work in mathematics. *Assessment & Evaluation in Higher Education, 21,* 251-265.

Jonassen, D. H. (1992). Evaluating constructivistic learning. In T. M. Duffy & D. H. Jonassen (Eds.), *Constructivism and the technology of instruction.* Hillsdale, NJ: Lawrence Erlbaum Associates.

Kwan, K., & Leung, R. (1996). Tutor versus peer group assessment of student performance in a simulation training exercise. *Assessment and Evaluation in Higher Education, 21,* 205-214.

Lejk, M., Wyvill, M., & Farrow, S. (1996). A survey of methods of deriving individual grades from group assessments. *Assessment & Evaluation in Higher Education, 21,* 267-280.

Lejk, M., Wyvill, M., & Farrow, S. (1997). Group learning and group assessment on undergraduate computing courses in higher education in the UK: Results of a survey. *Assessment & Evaluation in Higher Education, 22,* 81-91.

McIlveen, H., Greenan, K., & Humphreys, P. (1997). Involving students in teaching and learning: A necessary evil? *Quality Assurance in Education, 5,* 231-238.

Neumann, R., Parry, S., & Becher, T. (2002). Teaching and learning in their disciplinary contexts: A conceptual analysis. *Studies in Higher Education, 27,* 407-417.

Copyright © 2006, Idea Group Inc. Copying or distributing in print or electronic forms without written permission of Idea Group Inc. is prohibited.

Powell, P. & Weenk, W. (2003). *Project-led engineering education.* Utrecht: Lemma.

Rafiq, Y., & Fullerton, H. (1996). Peer assessment of group projects in civil engineering. *Assessment & Evaluation in Higher Education, 21,* 69-81.

Rompelman, O. (2000). Assessment of student learning: Evolution of objectives in engineering education and the consequences for assessment. *European Journal of Engineering Education, 25*(4), 339-350.

Sambell, K., & McDowell, L. (1998). The construction of the hidden curriculum: Messages and meanings in the assessment of student learning. *Assessment & Evaluation in Higher Education, 23,* 391-402.

Scouller, K. (1998). The influence of assessment method on students' learning approaches: Multiple choice question examination versus assignment essay. *Higher Education, 35,* 453-472.

Sheppard, S., Johnson, M., & Leifer, L. (1998). A model for peer assessment and student involvement in formative course assessment. *Journal of Engineering Education, 87,* 349-354.

Sluijsmans, D. M. A., Moerkerke, G., van Merriënboer, J. J. G., & Dochy, F. J. R. C. (2001). Peer assessment in problem based learning. *Studies in Educational Evaluation, 27,* 153-173.

Stefani, L. A. J. (1998). Assessment in partnership with learners. *Assessment & Evaluation in Higher Education, 23,* 339-350.

Teixeira, I. C., Teixeira, J. P., Pile, M. & Durão, D. (1998, May). *From continuing education to continuing learning using self assessment and process monitoring.* Paper presented at the 7th World Congress on Continuing Engineering Education—The knowledge revolution, the impact of technology on learning, Torino, Italy.

Thomson, K., & Falchikov, N. (1998). Full on until the sun comes out: The effects of assessment on student approaches to studying. *Assessment & Evaluation in Higher Education, 23,* 379-390.

van Hattum-Janssen, N., Pacheco, J. A., & Vasconcelos, R. M. (2004). The accuracy of student grading in first-year engineering courses. *European Journal of Engineering Education, 29,* 291-298.

Vermunt, J. D. H. M. (1992). *Leerstijlen en sturen van leerprocessen in het hoger onderwijs. Naar procesgerichte instructie in zelfstandig denken.* Lisse: Swets & Zeitlinger Publishers.

Copyright © 2006, Idea Group Inc. Copying or distributing in print or electronic forms without written permission of Idea Group Inc. is prohibited.

Chapter IV

Learning and Assessment:
A Case Study – Going the Full Monty

Mary Panko
Unitec New Zealand, New Zealand

Abstract

This chapter reflects on the lessons learned by the developers of a course about self, peer, and group assessment for adult educators, large elements of which were carried out via online discussion forums. In particular, this chapter will look in detail at the ways in which the learners used online discussion forums and also examine particular exchanges to show how the group projects were developed in an online environment. From these reflections come a number of pointers that may enable facilitators to either make changes to the way in which their courses are organised or highlight aspects to their students to enrich and simplify their learning experience. This case study represents the first iteration of an action research cycle where future investigations will lead to increasingly effective integration of e-learning in the form of online discussions and the development of more straightforward self, peer and group assessment.

Copyright © 2006, Idea Group Inc. Copying or distributing in print or electronic forms without written permission of Idea Group Inc. is prohibited.

Introduction

When my colleagues and I began to design a new course within our programme for adult educators, we started with a fundamental belief: that to truly achieve independent learning a wholehearted experiential approach must be taken. Therefore, responsibility had to lie in the hands of the student and this had to apply to both the content of the course and the assessment of the learning process. This turned out to be less straightforward then we had imagined.

This chapter is intended to reflect on the lessons learned by the course developers about self, peer, and group assessment for adult educators, large elements of which were carried out via online discussion forums.

In particular, this chapter will look in detail at the ways in which the learners used online discussion forums and will also examine particular exchanges to show how the group projects were developed in an online environment. Out of these reflections have come a number of pointers that will either allow us to make changes to the way in which the course is organised or enable us to highlight aspects of it to the participants, to possibly enrich and/or simplify the learning experience. We hope that our sometimes-cautionary tale may also help other teachers and developers who are intending to apply peer and self assessment techniques.

Background

The course we designed, Learning and Assessment, was delivered in a blended mode, partly through face-to-face sessions, and partly at a distance using whatever mechanisms the students felt they needed, whether that was e-mail, phone, or online discussions through the Blackboard learning-management system. In the case of the latter, all of the participants had some prior experience of online discussions in previous courses in which the teacher had contributed to the discussion as an e-moderator and where their postings had been summatively assessed. In these earlier situations, the discussion element had therefore been a compulsory part of the course requirements.

The course at the centre of this case study, Learning and Assessment comprised two main threads: First, it focussed on independent learning theories and stratagems; and, second, it was designed around collaboratively assessed group projects.

Copyright © 2006, Idea Group Inc. Copying or distributing in print or electronic forms without written permission of Idea Group Inc. is prohibited.

Rationale

The reason for the significance of independent and experiential learning (Jarvis, 1998) would not surprise anyone involved in adult and tertiary education and was part of our drive to encourage constructivist and interactive forms of teaching and learning.

The need for practice and reflection on group project work by students grew out of the increasing reliance placed upon this form of endeavour in many courses in tertiary educational institutions, combined with a frequent lack of assessment expertise in this area. Anecdotal evidence indicates that a number of lecturers who have introduced self, peer, or group assessment procedures have discovered too late, the complexities associated with the assessments and the lack of emphasis that had been directed to support up-skilling students in the techniques of peer assessment. The effects of this realisation have tended to discourage extending this form of project work and its associated assessment strategies—being frequently relegated to the "too-hard basket."

Nevertheless, the overarching strategy of group project work has long been advocated as a way of promoting deep learning approaches to learning (Karabenick & Collins-Eaglin, 1997). Established writers on this topic have recognised the values of collaborative interactivity for the enhancement of the learning experience, ranging across the decades from the initially preonline writings of Johnson and Johnson (1986), and later to that of researchers in online interactivity such as Bonk (1998) and Garrison and Anderson (2003). And yet, few of these authors would dispute that assessment of group work can be fraught with difficulties and inequities.

The Assessment of Tasks

In the course Learning and Assessment groups of five or six students were self selected and then each group chose an independent learning stratagem to research and deliver as a one-hour presentation to their colleagues. They were particularly asked to include assessment techniques applicable to the particular theory they had chosen. The exact description of the assessment can be seen in Figure 1.

Students were provided with basic "starter packs" of resources for each area of independent learning, these included seminal readings, case studies of practical examples and reference lists. However, it was made clear to the participants that if they had some alternative independent strategy their group wished to pursue,

Copyright © 2006, Idea Group Inc. Copying or distributing in print or electronic forms without written permission of Idea Group Inc. is prohibited.

Figure 1. First assessment for the course learning and assessment

This assessment event incorporates Learning Outcomes 1[a] and 3[b] and involves working as a project group:

- researching an independent learning strategy and its associated assessment issues (Possibilities: problem-based learning, contract learning, collaborative learning, experiential learning, resource-based learning, discovery learning).
- presenting the results to the course participants and lecturers.
- peer assessing the presentations of other groups.
- peer assessing the contribution of your own group members.
- self assessing your contribution to the group project..

The Assessment Task

Part One: Project Group Presentation
Your task as a group is to work collaboratively to select an independent learning strategy and then develop and deliver a group presentation that clearly demonstrates the following learning outcomes:

- Review current theories of the specific independent and student centred learning strategy.
- Describe the application of the independent learning strategy by outlining how the selected strategy encourages independent and student centred learning, especially with regard to assessment.

Part Two: Undertake Self- and Peer assessment
Assessment Method
1. **Assessment of Presentation**. Your peers will use a criteria schedule to assess the presentation of your group. The criteria sheet will be developed in class.

2. **Assessment of contribution to group project.** Your group will develop and use a schedule of criteria to assess individual contributions to the group project.

[a]*Learning Outcome 1: Develop advanced learning strategies that are student centred and encourage independent learning.*
[b]*Learning Outcome 3: Work collaboratively to develop and deliver a group presentation on a specific topic.*

this would be equally acceptable. Having selected their topic, the learners then had to determine grading criteria and how they were going to collaboratively allocate their grades to themselves and to their colleagues.

In total, the members of each group were required to perform three assessments (see Figure 2). The first was to self assess their own contributions to the group task, and the second required them to grade all the other members of their group. Thirdly, they were asked to also assess the other groups who were presenting. In the case of the latter assessment, both groups decided to jointly develop and then share their intergroup criteria but separately develop their own forms of intragroup assessment.

Although it was obvious that three separate assessments were needed, the breakdown of decisions that had to be made in order to arrive at workable outcomes were not so apparent. The major issues that the students gradually discovered they needed to address are indicated in Figure 2 and the questions that

Copyright © 2006, Idea Group Inc. Copying or distributing in print or electronic forms without written permission of Idea Group Inc. is prohibited.

Figure 2. The context of participants' assessment decisions

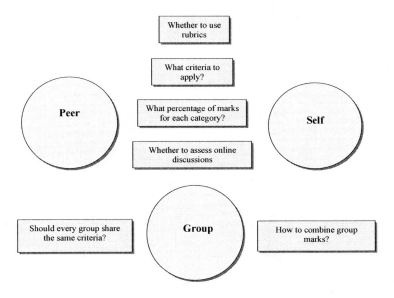

they raised, as previously shown, applied to some or all of the assessment tasks. The wide extent of this student-determined assessment was described by one of the lecturers on the course as "going for the full-Monty" and it was made clear to participants that in their own teaching they might well decide to limit the extent to which their students carried out the individual steps of this process. In other words, they might feel that as an initial step, they might prefer to supply solutions for some of these issues, such as, how group marks were to be calculated or whether their students should be directed to assess online discussions.

The design that we instigated was developed to parallel Biggs' (1999) constructivist alignment, in which he recommends that small group assignments, based on real-life situations, should involve learners at all three stages of the assessment process, that is: setting the assessment criteria; selecting the evidence; and making a judgement about performance. Biggs argues that this approach is designed to increase student realisation of the depth of learning offered by the dialogue, and develop a sense of ownership in the process. Our application of these guidelines did appear to enhance the students' depth of learning even though there were times when we might have wished we were to be able to "pull rank" on the students.

Although substantial face-to-face time was allocated to these steps, by the end of the course the participants discovered that the finer points of their assessment

Copyright © 2006, Idea Group Inc. Copying or distributing in print or electronic forms without written permission of Idea Group Inc. is prohibited.

strategies needed to be reconsidered in light of the presentations from each group. In addition, the participants realised that they had not established the way in which they were going to combine their individual marks into a group assessment of the other teams. The course facilitators saw these realisations as a mark of success of the process, a valuable reflective experience, but perhaps the participants saw them as one more layer of frustration. Falchikov (2002) reported a similar conflict of views when she compared her own perceptions of the success of a peer assessment exercise with the evaluations provided by her students. She countered this by increasing the nature and quality of feedback provided by students to their peers, particularly during the preparation phase, and by reducing the proportion of peer graded assessments to only 20% of the final coursework mark. Nevertheless, we decided that we preferred the students to experience the full impact of self and peer assessment, and left that at a 60% contribution.

Working Online

Within the first few days of the course starting, group members demanded access to Blackboard online discussion forums and proceeded to make ever-increasing use of them to share their findings and work out their preparations for their final presentation. They primarily utilised the private group forums and, to a lesser extent, the discussions which were open to the whole class. By adopting the online approach the record of online postings had the potential to be used as an element of their intragroup assessment but it is interesting to note that the participants did not use the online discussions as part of their own assessment strategies. The reason for this could be because considerations to include this method did not arise at the outset when the students were determining their grading criteria.

When statistics of discussion usage were examined at the end of the course, it was found that almost all the participants took part in both reading all the postings of their colleagues and also contributing postings themselves.

This high participation rate in a non-assessed and non-teacher-moderated discussion confounds current accepted wisdom about the use of discussions in teaching and learning. For example, Klemm and Snell (1996) and Roblyer and Wiencke (2003) have provided evidence that shows assessment is normally the major positive motivational factor in encouraging online postings and that non-assessed discussions are little used by students. On the other hand, Bullen (1998) has been more cautious about the relationship between online discussion and compulsory assessment. He revealed that mandatory participation in discussions, as determined by proportion of the marks awarded, could have a detrimental effect on the nature and frequency of the contributions. His research

Copyright © 2006, Idea Group Inc. Copying or distributing in print or electronic forms without written permission of Idea Group Inc. is prohibited.

indicated that for some students the marks became part of an ongoing type of cost benefit analysis that they engaged in to determine how to apportion their time. This finding is similarly reported by Cartwright (2000) who investigated 82 undergraduate nursing students' satisfaction with asynchronous discussion and found that many thought they had spent more time online than the allocation of their marks reflected. Rainsbury and Malcolm (2003) identified that for a total mark of 5%, the number of students participating in the five discussions gradually dropped as the course continued. This unsurprising finding supports Cartwright's assertion that the level of effort required for a discussion-forum activity normally has to equate fairly to the grade allocated, regardless of the students' satisfaction with the knowledge gained.

In addition, in relation to the expectation of having a teacher acting as an e-moderator, Collison, Elbaum, Haavind, and Tinker (2000) consider that this element is also a necessary procedure and recommend a variety of strategies to either "sharpen the focus of the dialogue . . . or help participants dig deeper into the dialogue," (Collison et al., p. 127). These included processes through which the teacher identifies direction, sorts ideas for relevance, focuses on key points, uses full-spectrum questioning, makes connections, and honours multiple learning perspectives. While some of these mechanisms are required to be incorporated into the preliminary design of the discussions, the majority are recommended for use by the e-moderator during the dialogue itself.

In light of internationally accepted discussion guidelines (Collison et al., 2000; Salmon, 2000), it is all the more interesting to recall that the discussions in this case study were non-assessed and non-moderated. It is possible that the reason for their success was that the students developed a significant level of ownership of the course; and, although they received no online grading, they made a major commitment to the self and peer assessment process that they expressed though their interactions.

The Nature of Online Teamwork

McCarthey and McMahon (1992) indicated that student teamwork might be seen to exist across a continuum of student-centred strategies, ranging from co-operative techniques, often closely controlled by the teacher, to collaborative learning, where the student has more control over the process. Indeed, Althauser and Matuga (1998) warn that in the co-operative model, learning can become compartmentalised and the extent of learning can be limited.

Using these terms designated by these authors, the behaviours adopted by the students on this course initially demonstrated a tendency toward co-operative learning, as they used the discussion board as a method of facilitating a division

Copyright © 2006, Idea Group Inc. Copying or distributing in print or electronic forms without written permission of Idea Group Inc. is prohibited.

of labour between members of the group. On the other hand, as the process progressed and the outlines of their presentations were posted online, a more collaborative approach became apparent. Students commented on the content of the postings, suggested modifications, and added additional ideas. This combination of individual and group activity enabled the discussion to reinforce student development by reducing the extent of isolated and independent work.

As well as collaborating online, the students also worked face-to-face on their projects within class hours as well as at weekend sessions in cafes. Such a combination of face-to-face and computer-supported collaborative learning is supported by Cavanaugh (2001) who showed in a metaanalysis of 19 empirical studies integrating interactive technology with traditional classroom studies, that this combination tended to result in positive learning achievements.

The Nature of the Discussion

The pattern of student use of the discussion forum took a similar path in both groups. To begin with, there was a degree of experimentation with the communication systems, as individuals familiarised themselves with the opportunities provided through the Blackboard communication system. This stage rapidly merged into a sharing of resources where initial references were made to the materials provided as part of the starter pack. Rapidly, these resources were left behind as students pursued other possibilities such as sites on the Web, additional texts, and their own colleagues who contributed practical examples of independent teaching and learning strategies. However, this acquisition of others' skills was not restricted to a process of inert material capture but led to the development of their own capabilities as exemplified in the following posting:

In case we decide to run with using Blackboard as our Group Project I have located a contact in Learning Technologies, [N] who is happy to facilitate a small workshop on the use of Blackboard. This may help us in formulating a coherent learning strategy. What do you think? [A]

Although this step was not taken further, following the sharing of resources and techniques, co-operative learning became transformed into a collaborative approach as groups began planning ways to integrate the resources into a complete presentation. One group recognised that the process they were undertaking was an example of discovery learning and discussed the advantages they might gain as learners if they recorded the events of the experience as a journal:

Copyright © 2006, Idea Group Inc. Copying or distributing in print or electronic forms without written permission of Idea Group Inc. is prohibited.

I like the idea of using our blackboard experience as an example of discovery learning—perhaps we should each have a diary of our hopes, expectations, joys and frustrations to help depict what is happening for the student. [R]

This suggestion was supported by a reply that read, "Great idea [R]. Having kept one for another Graduate Diploma in Higher Education (GDipHE) course it has become an invaluable tool for reflection and learning" [A]. This posting demonstrates that the students were sharing their concepts of the values of reflection and that they had moved into the higher or metacognitive levels of learning, as described by researchers such as Biggs (1999). This finding shows that through the use of an online discussion forum, students can increase their active engagement with learning tasks.

Both groups decided to structure their delivery around a PowerPoint® presentation, and it was at this stage that the maximum flow of postings occurred. Individuals put their own ideas and amendments into the discussion and responded to one another on a daily basis, but some found they needed a more rapid exchange of views than is normal with asynchronous discussions. To overcome any delay, one group turned the process into a semisynchronous one, by text messaging one another when they were about to go online, and then working synchronously for several hours into the late evening, only signing off when they were exhausted. This adaptation of an established technology into a more vibrant communication system is noteworthy and highlights the way in which online discussions can support the establishment of e-learning communities (Palloff & Pratt, 1999).

Towards the end of the course, each group presented their reports during an interactive face-to-face session and immediately following, each group graded the work of the other groups. These three grades were then combined to produce 60% of their final course grade, the remaining 40% being achieved on the basis of their performance on a more standard, individually written assignment, graded by the teacher.

The course ended with a debriefing session designed to reinforce the experiential learning that had occurred, and participants were encouraged to reflect on the advantages and disadvantages of self, peer and group assessment. They were also asked to examine the principles and issues associated with group project assessment tools, as applied to their own teaching contexts. Towards the end this debriefing session the students took total charge of the feedback role and worked with one another to extend their reflections on the process that had taken place.

Copyright © 2006, Idea Group Inc. Copying or distributing in print or electronic forms without written permission of Idea Group Inc. is prohibited.

Solutions and Recommendations

The question is: Did the techniques of self, peer, and group assessment that we applied in the course Learning and Assessment work effectively? The answer to that is yes—and no. In the first instance, by observing and questioning the students during their presentations, it was obvious that they had developed a thorough and deep understanding of the principles of independent learning as well as the particular theory they had investigated. Secondly, the participants' awareness of the benefits and pitfalls of self, peer, and group assessment had also greatly expanded. It was also clear that the students had seized the opportunities offered by the online discussion process in order to drive their projects to a well-balanced conclusion.

Furthermore, at the end of the presentation session, one participant commented online to her own group, "To everyone, thanks for this morning—it was fun and I enjoyed the journey as much as the destination." The group then shared their debriefing and feedback, within their online discussion, with one of their members who had been unable to attend the day's presentation session.

What was interesting was that during their presentations the issue of any form of assessment was given only perfunctory treatment. As developers, we found it curious that this latter step, which we had considered fundamental to a course of this nature, was given the least attention by the participants. On one hand, this could point to a requirement on our part to highlight the significance of this section. On the other, it might be seen as another aspect of the success of the course: that the participants were focussed on the learning experience and the credentialing of that learning took a back seat.

The remaining, and less surprising outcome of their peer assessment was that they tended to allocate maximum grades to their peers on an almost universal basis. Nevertheless, while they may have seen this unlikely result as a valid reflection of their peers' work, at the very least it has allowed the participants to recognise the issues they face when using self, peer, and group assessment in their own teaching. In other words, in a truly experiential manner, they had not only done it but felt it as well.

Issues for Reflection within the Case Study

Once the course was completed, the teaching team reflected on their perceptions of its delivery and on the feedback provided by the participants in their end-of-course evaluations. We identified a number of issues that needed further consideration before the next delivery cycle.

Copyright © 2006, Idea Group Inc. Copying or distributing in print or electronic forms without written permission of Idea Group Inc. is prohibited.

- **Course timing.** It became clear that as this course required a significant process of independent learning and reflection by the participants, it was not a process that should be rushed. The initial timetable had allowed for this by having sessions spread out over a number of weeks. This enabled students to focus on both the content of their material and also allowed them to develop measured grading criteria.

- **Teacher direction vs. student autonomy.** From the perspective of the teachers, the students gained immensely from their own struggles with the development of assessment criteria. Nevertheless, the participants reported that they would have appreciated an increased degree of teacher direction and assessment structure. Although a variety of examples were shown to them at the early stage of the course, it is possible in future that we encourage them to make their decisions during the classroom sessions so that gaps or inconsistencies in their criteria are identified at an earlier stage in the course so that the context and complexities of self and peer assessment become more obvious.

- **Proportion of student-allocated grading.** This issue has both psychological and practical considerations. For both participants and teachers, student grading of their own work removes an emotional security blanket as well as raises issues of quality assurance. However, although international experience has opened up different findings in relation this issue, several researchers (Elwood & Klenowski, 2002; Falchikov, 2002) have demonstrated that peer and teacher assessments do not generally differ significantly from one another. In light of this, and despite problems that we encountered in this area, we have decided that our emphasis on student responsibility for their grades should continue, but that we would attempt to increase their skill base in developing assessment criteria.

- **Overmarking and undermarking.** To enable students to become more discriminating with the grades they allocated to one another, these aspects should be highlighted at an early stage. Possibly an assessment rubric might help to overcome these problems.

- **Role of course facilitators.** Once assessment responsibility is placed into the hands of the students, what role should the course facilitators take when the student presentations were being made? If it is felt that providing feedback into the project reports is an essential contribution, this needs to be overtly discussed in advance with the participants so that at the end of the course there are no unpleasant surprises.

- **Whose job is it anyway?** One common issue that we did not encounter in this case study—probably as a result of the participants all being tutors of adults themselves—was the view that marking is the teacher's job and we should be doing what we are paid for. Falchikov (2002) has countered this

Copyright © 2006, Idea Group Inc. Copying or distributing in print or electronic forms without written permission of Idea Group Inc. is prohibited.

by explaining "why I was requiring them to take part in assessment (they would benefit from the experience) and what I saw as my job (to aid student development and independent lifelong learning)" (p. 71). This aspect is discussed more fully in other sections of this book.

Future Trends: To Assess or Not to Assess Online Discussions?

In this case study we were provided with a rare opportunity to observe the practical application of an online discussion that required no input from the course teachers.

As discussions play a more and more significant role in online course design, the question of assessment in this domain becomes increasingly pivotal. The way in which these assessments are undertaken—whether self, peer, or teacher-assessed—seems most closely tied to the teaching beliefs of the individual e-moderator. In some situations, the criteria a teacher applies are likely to be centred on the coverage of course content, and the e-moderator will tend to allocate marks in relation to a list of anticipated key responses (Samuelowicz & Bain, 2002). These teachers appear to be less likely to provide *bonus* marks when students provide commentary of material not directly required by the provided criteria. The use of rubrics as primarily information-based scoring guides can also be observed in the writings of Huba and Freed (2000). Huba and Freed list five issues:

- levels of mastery indicating the students' level of overall achievement,
- dimensions of quality demonstrated through intellectual or knowledge competencies,
- organisational groupings using multidimensional skills such as collaboration,
- commentaries that are the defining feature of the task, and
- descriptions of consequences in which metacognition and relevance to practice is highlighted.

However, it seems to be unlikely that students, at the outset of a course, would have the content knowledge to devise assessment criteria of this nature and so this form of assessment is unlikely to become assimilated into self, peer or group assessment in e-learning. It is therefore worth considering the option of gradually extending or adding to the criteria as the course progressed and the content

Copyright © 2006, Idea Group Inc. Copying or distributing in print or electronic forms without written permission of Idea Group Inc. is prohibited.

knowledge of the participants expanded. On the other hand, this integrative option would also serve to increase the already complex range of decisions that is required and in a short course this would not seem to provide a successful strategy.

While recognising that a rubric may clarify student expectations about online assessment performance, I would argue that not only do they tend to normalise the postings, but if used as the basis of scoring guides, they can become a "box-ticking exercise" which can destroy many of the opportunities offered by potentially constructivist and engaging online discussions. Samuelowicz and Bain (2002) referred to this when they conclude their paper on academics' orientations to assessment practice by saying, "It is not difficult to understand why, faced with seemingly irreconcilable assessment objectives, some students opt for a cynical 'give them what they want' approach to their learning" (p. 198). This is particularly evident when teachers or e-moderators inform their learners that open, wide-ranging and reflective responses are required and yet supply the student with assessment criteria that focus heavily on factual content.

Nevertheless, as described earlier, the tasks and assignments set by e-moderators are usually as intimately involved in the process of online teaching as they are in the face-to-face context. Proponents of detailed assessment methods (Garrison & Anderson, 2003) emphasise that not only does this process provide extrinsic motivation for the learners, it also determines the level of learning that is likely to be attained by learners.

On the other hand, teachers from a more constructivist background will tend to focus on the learning process, emphasising the type of interactive and participatory qualities suggested by Roblyer and Wiencke (2003) in their recent assessment rubric. Students can be guided to consider these criteria as part of their initial assessment design where issues such as, practical contribution to end product or research, analysing and evaluating material get allocated a distinct score out of 5 or 10.

In this case study, the participants encountered assessment methods demanding a deep learning approach, and an opportunity to exercise responsible choice in the method and content of study. The success of this experiential method was supported by the participants' development and application of the online discussion forums.

Conclusion

Group projects tend to set up tensions within teams; the summative assessment of each individual becomes bound up with the performance and cooperation of

Copyright © 2006, Idea Group Inc. Copying or distributing in print or electronic forms without written permission of Idea Group Inc. is prohibited.

all other members. When this complexity becomes overlaid with the additional tensions associated with peer and group-assessment practices, relationships have the potential to become destructive and learning opportunities can be lost within a welter of emotions. On the other hand, group projects in association with online discussion forums can lead to the establishment of communities of inquiry (Garrison & Anderson, 2003; Palloff & Pratt, 1999) that are often impossible to achieve in most educational circumstances, let alone those whose main form of contact is the e-learning environment. The groups that formed in this case study, in the main, became very supportive of one another, encouraging each other's work and becoming very protective when they considered outsiders (such as the course lecturers) were providing advice with which they did not agree.

This endorses the findings of Palloff and Pratt (1999) who emphasised that such online discussions can encourage critical and demanding interactive communication between learners and lead to the foundation of successful learning communities. They used Shaffer and Anundsen's (1993) definition of a learning community as an interactive, dynamic whole that emerges when people:

- share common practices,
- are interdependent,
- make decisions jointly,
- identify themselves with something larger than the sum of their individual relationships, and
- make long-term commitments to the well-being of the group.

Although these characteristics were originally drawn up in the context of face-to-face teaching, Palloff and Pratt (1999) contended that similar characteristics could also be found in online communities of learners, and I have found that these features are central when facilitators are attempting to establish collaborative assessment environments. In this case study in particular, all of these points could be identified within the collaborating groups, and to a major extent, this was due to the combination of self and peer assessment techniques being applied in an interactive online environment. For these reasons I would encourage other professionals working in the area of online teaching and learning to explore the ways in which discussion forums can contribute to the wider assessment experience for their students.

This case study is most definitely a work in progress. It represents only the first iteration of an action research cycle where future investigations will possibly lead to increasingly effective integration of e-learning in the form of online discussions and the development of more straightforward self, peer and group assessment.

Copyright © 2006, Idea Group Inc. Copying or distributing in print or electronic forms without written permission of Idea Group Inc. is prohibited.

KINGSTEC LIBRARY

References

Althauser, R., & Matuga, J. A. (1998). On the pedagogy of electronic instruction. In C. J. Bonk & K. S. King (Eds.), *Electronic collaborators: Learner-centred technologies for literacy, apprenticeship, and discourse* (pp. 183-208). Mahwah, NJ: Lawrence Erlbaum Associates, Inc.

Biggs, J. B. (1999). *Teaching for quality learning at university: What the student does.* Philadelphia: Open University Press.

Bonk, C. J. (1998). *Pedagogical activities on the "Smartweb": Electronically mentoring undergraduate educational psychology students.* Paper presented at the American Educational Research Annual Meeting, San Diego, CA.

Bullen, M. (1998). Participation and critical thinking in online university distance education. *Journal of Distance Education, 13*(2), 1-32.

Cartwright, J. (2000). Lessons learned: Using asynchronous computer-mediated conferencing to facilitate group discussion. *Journal of Nursing Education, 39*(2), 87-90.

Cavanaugh, C. S. (2001). The effectiveness of interactive distance education technologies in K-12 learning: A meta-analysis. *International Journal of Educational Telecommunications, 7*(1), 73-88.

Collison, G., Elbaum, B., Haavind, S., & Tinker, R. (2000). *Facilitating online learning: Effective strategies for moderators.* Madison, WI: Atwood Publishing.

Elwood, J. & Klenowski, V. (2002). Creating communities of shared practice: The challenges of assessment use in learning and teaching. *Assessment & Evaluation in Higher Education, 27*(3), 243-256.

Falchikov, N. (2002). Unpacking peer assessment. In P. Schwartz & G. Webb (Eds.), *Assessment: Case studies, experience and practice from higher education* (pp. 70-77). London: Kogan Page.

Garrison, D. R., & Anderson, T. (2003). *E-learning in the 21st century: A framework for research and practice.* London: Routledge Falmer.

Huba, M. E., & Freed, J. E. (2000). *Learner-centered assessment on college campuses: Shifting the focus from teaching to learning.* Boston: Allyn & Bacon.

Jarvis, P. (1998). *The theory and practice of learning.* London: Kogan Page.

Johnson, D. W., & Johnson, R. T. (1986, January). Computer-assisted cooperative learning. *Educational Technology,* 12-18.

Copyright © 2006, Idea Group Inc. Copying or distributing in print or electronic forms without written permission of Idea Group Inc. is prohibited.

Karabenick, S. A., & Collins-Eaglin, J. (1997). Relation of perceived instructional goals and incentives to college students' use of learning strategies. *The Journal of Experimental Education, 65*(4), 331-338.

Klemm, W. R., & Snell, J. R. (1996). Enriching computer-mediated group learning by coupling constructivism with collaborative learning. *Journal of Instructional Science and Technology, 1*(2).

Lehtinen, E. (2003). Computer-supported collaborative learning: An approach to powerful learning environments. In E. De Corte, L., Vetschaffel, N. Entwistle, & J. Van Merrieboer (Eds.), *Unravelling basic components and dimensions of powerful learning environments*. Oxford, UK: Elsevier.

McCarthey, S. J., & McMahon, S. (1992). From convention to invention: Three approaches to peer interaction during writing. In N. M. R. Hertz-Lazarovits (Ed.), *Interaction in cooperative groups* (pp. 17-35). Cambridge, UK: Cambridge University Press.

Palloff, R. M., & Pratt, K. (1999). *Building learning communities in cyberspace: Effective strategies for the online classroom*. San Francisco: Jossey-Bass.

Rainsbury, L., & Malcolm, P. (2003). Extending the classroom boundaries: An evaluation of an asynchronous discussion board. *Accounting Education, 12*(1), 49-61.

Roblyer, M. D., & Wiencke, W. (2003). Design and use of a rubric to assess and encourage interactive qualities in distance courses. *The American Journal of Distance Education, 17*(2), 77-98.

Salmon, G. (2000). *E-moderating: The key to teaching and learning online*. London: Kogan Page.

Samuelowicz, K., & Bain, J. D. (2002). Identifying academics' orientations to assessment practice. *Higher Education, 43*, 173-201.

Shaffer, C., & Anundsen, K. (1993). *Creating community anywhere*. New York: Perigee Books.

Copyright © 2006, Idea Group Inc. Copying or distributing in print or electronic forms without written permission of Idea Group Inc. is prohibited.

Chapter V

A Case Study of the Integration of Self, Peer, and Group Assessment in a Core First-Year Educational Psychology Unit through Flexible Delivery Implementation

Rozz Albon
Curtin University of Technology, Western Australia

Abstract

This chapter provides a case study of one lecturer's approach to innovative assessment in a first year unit of university study of 188 students. Many insights are provided into the training, preparation, and assessment experiences of self, peer, group, and lecturer assessments bound together by technology for flexible delivery. The dynamic and complex forms of assessment support the coproduction of knowledge sharing to harness the

Copyright © 2006, Idea Group Inc. Copying or distributing in print or electronic forms without written permission of Idea Group Inc. is prohibited.

synergy of collective knowledge. Specifically, this chapter presents the author's use of theory used to inform selected assessment strategies. General issues surrounding group assessments, and the impact of graduate attributes and technology on assessment, introduce the case study and reinforce the fact that assessment drives the learning. The author hopes that by sharing her insights, higher-education practices can better meet the need for students to learn collaborative and team skills required for the future world of work.

Introduction

Achieving the benefits of self, peer and group assessments within the context of e-learning, requires the implementation of many processes. It is the processes themselves that move the mindsets of students from one of passivity towards assessment to one that values high interactive engagement in the assessment process. Textbooks document the role of assessment in the learning cycle but rarely explain how assessment relates to learning outcomes, specific university contexts, or e-learning. Nor do textbooks show lecturers how to support students during the peer and group assessment process.

This chapter is a case study of how one lecturer moved students towards an interactive engagement in their own assessment and describes the contribution this move made to students' learning. This chapter also illustrates how case studies can be used in e-learning as an instructional approach. The insights provided by the author into the training and preparation necessary to enable students to function and learn from their engagement in the assessment have been carefully woven into the role and function of assessment in learning. Further, this chapter also demonstrates how a complex, flexible, and dynamic learning environment that includes a variety of assessment approaches has been prudently designed to ensure deep and meaningful learning while maintaining control over assessment. The inclusion of self, peer, and group assessment within a single unit of study has supported a coproduction of knowledge and typified a knowledge-sharing approach to harness the synergy of collective knowledge. The future world of work provided an impetus to reconsider andragogical approaches to learning and better align them with flexible delivery. The present case study will demonstrate the integrated role of e-learning with face-to-face learning by describing many strategies and processes. The case study involved 188 first year Educational Psychology students drawn from both on- and off-campus contexts who had to complete major assessment tasks in groups.

Copyright © 2006, Idea Group Inc. Copying or distributing in print or electronic forms without written permission of Idea Group Inc. is prohibited.

It is the author's belief that many educators want to change their practice but are unable to do so because of the lack of tools or theories about how learning occurs for adults in higher education context, one often without walls or classrooms. This chapter presents:

- The author's use of theory and the role of assessment in learning
- Presentation of the assessment debate
- A case for creating opportunities for students to achieve graduate attributes, and how these then impact on assessment, particularly peer and group assessment
- The role of technology in assisting students to achieve the learning outcomes
- The case study of assessments
- A brief outline of how students were prepared developmentally for a complex and dynamic group assessment
- Summary and conclusion
- The future

Background: The Role of Assessment in Learning

The Framework to Authentic Assessment

Understanding how learning occurs is the key to designing authentic assessments that drive deep and meaningful learning (Biggs, 1999). That is, assessments require students to demonstrate that they can use their understanding to respond to open-ended tasks and ill-defined problems. Designing and integrating authentic assessment early in students' learning experiences can foster deep and intellectually superior higher education (Newmann, 1997). However, the success of authentic assessment depends upon a number of factors, not least of which is carefully integrating and balancing several forms of self, peer, group, and lecturer assessment (traditional assessment by the lecturer), facilitated by flexible delivery through technology, mainly computers. The andragogical approaches to learning of choice, autonomy, and negotiation are integral to the assessment tasks presented in this chapter. They are reflected in the philosophical and teaching approaches underpinning the authentic task described throughout this chapter as represented in Figure 1.

Copyright © 2006, Idea Group Inc. Copying or distributing in print or electronic forms without written permission of Idea Group Inc. is prohibited.

Figure 1. The principles and features of authentic assessments that drive deep and intellectual quality learning in higher education

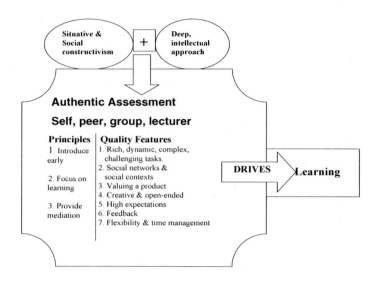

In sum, it is the theoretical conceptualization of how learning occurs which frames the holistic approach to teaching presented in this chapter, in which assessment is integral. Figure 1 states what drives learning for students and the tasks presented in the case study can be tracked back to these theories as explained in the following.

The Role of Situated Tasks in Learning (*Situative*)

The learning design described here is situative because it focuses the attention of all students on a common, relevant learning environment (education in Western Australian schools) mediated by WebCT—a learner management system which unifies students' interactions with each other, with the material, and with the informational and social resources provided. It is further supplemented with personal interactions occurring daily at the university and within similar courses presented by the university's Department of Education.

Copyright © 2006, Idea Group Inc. Copying or distributing in print or electronic forms without written permission of Idea Group Inc. is prohibited.

The Role of Social Interactions in Learning (*Social Constructivism*)

Having direct experiences and actions involving knowledgeable others lie at the heart of social constructivism. The socially constructivist nature of the assessment framework reported here required students to communicate with each other and the wider community as part of their learning. Students' learning was facilitated by a variety of mediated processes both online and face-to-face during the completion of the assessment. The choice, flexibility, and open-ended tasks provided the impetus for groups to engage socially, seek clarification, and apply theories in a classroom context. In fact, the task depended on this. Students could not achieve the task by themselves, in isolation, or by sole engagement with a textbook. A later discussion about mediated learning further explains its function in social learning. Identifying the differences between and the role of social learning and learning alone is fundamental to educators wishing to adopt authentic approaches such as those suggested in this case study.

The Role of Deep Intellectual Approaches in Learning (*Deep Intellectual Approach*)

A deep intellectual approach also drove the learning. The assessment tasks were designed to engage students in critical thinking, synthesis of knowledge, and problem identification and problem solution. Discussions, reading materials, and interviews focussed on theoretical concepts that are widely applicable in teaching or that transfer to other contexts. Concrete data and information were provided as support materials only. The tasks were complex, requesting students to find links between research-based theories and classroom behavior, as were the processes of learning which were open-ended and enabled students to establish the group momentum and synergy. Students were expected to demonstrate high levels of thinking, evidence of reasoning, freedom of choice, and group interaction. The tasks required students to work with real problems and real audiences and emphasized the intent of the assessment task to transform information rather than summarize other people's research and conclusions. Such deep and intellectual learning engaged students in evaluating the work of their peers as the marks they allocated actually contributed to each student's final mark and therefore their final grade. So, as represented in Figure 1, theories of situative and social constructivism and deep intellectual approaches to learning were used as the framework to plan authentic assessment.

Copyright © 2006, Idea Group Inc. Copying or distributing in print or electronic forms without written permission of Idea Group Inc. is prohibited.

The Role of Technology in Learning (*Facilitating E-Learning*)

The previous features and principles did not exist in isolation. They comprised the thinking framework used to design assessment tasks. Newer tools of technology were used to enhance the learning processes and the ability of students to assess themselves, their peers, and the group. Technology was therefore an important consideration in designing the learning opportunities. Technology itself may not improve learning, but when used as a cognitive tool (Jonassen & Carr, 2000) it enabled different learning environments and processes to be created, which in turn fostered further or other learning. The uses of technology in the case study are presented later in the chapter.

Authentic Assessment: Principles and Features

If authentic assessment is to make a real impact on learning, then several principles are recommended. Firstly, the assessment tasks should be introduced as early as possible within a unit of instruction as doing so provides the students with the necessary time to consider the complexity of the task and sets them up as the driver of their learning. Students need time to pull the task apart before they can begin to put it back together again. Secondly, the task should focus on learning and not on assessment. The focus on teaching in universities is about student learning and whereby they all have to be assessed, sometimes the assessment has become the focus to the detriment of "real" learning. Students need to obtain a variety of knowledge and skills to be able to competently deal with new and unseen problems in the future, and providing the means to understand knowledge is key to their success. Therefore learning, and not assessment, is the focus presented in the case study. The third principle states that the educator should provide mediation. That is, not only does the educator act as facilitator, but also walks the journey of learning with the students. A mediator can offer advice, critique students' suggestions, and ask provocative questions as well as "what if" questions in order to increase students' awareness of the complexities of problems and possible future situations. Mediation is about assisting students to produce their best work before it is submitted for grading, in contrast to offering it after the submission. A mediator is similar to a coach whose role is to get the athlete to be at their peak performance in order to compete for the prize

This list of features is offered as a checklist to ensure that assessment drives the learning. All group-authentic tasks should be rich, dynamic, and complex, making them incredibly challenging for the group and certainly for individuals, for it is

Copyright © 2006, Idea Group Inc. Copying or distributing in print or electronic forms without written permission of Idea Group Inc. is prohibited.

only when these features are included is the group motivated to begin and work out what needs to be done and how it will be done. Self, peer, group, and lecturer assessment can be built into creating this complexity as demonstrated in the case study presented in a later section. Situating the task beyond learning in the four walls of a classroom or within the confines of textbook embraces the strengths and differences individual students bring to the task, and expands their interpersonal and intrapersonal knowledge and skills. Each student has a rich and diverse knowledge base and setting tasks that draw on this resource enables each student to contribute to the task, thus building perspectives and knowledge in socially constructivist ways.

Instead of writing an assessment task merely as a hoop that students must jump through, positioning the task as a valued product creates a sense of pride, interest and raises the quality of the group submission. It counters the lack of motivation often seen in students who have to complete routine, mundane and meaningless tasks. Proposals such as models, Web sites, reports, films, law-court backgrounds, and journal articles are just some examples of valuable products.

An authentic task should not stifle creativity but value it. Innovative solutions to future ill-defined problems are dependent on students being able to think both divergently and convergently. Ensuring that tasks encourage creativity poses issues for assessment, but these are not insurmountable, as illustrated in the case study. Designing open-ended tasks, ill-defined problems, and case studies, incidents, or scenarios are examples of how this feature of creativity is addressed in the case study.

It is assumed by the author that university students are highly intelligent, capable, knowledgeable in different disciplines and work experiences, and easily motivated if the task is engaging and meaningful, and provides them with some autonomy over their learning. Conveying these expectations is essential to raising the quality of assessment submissions. Students need to believe in themselves and the lecturer can empower students by assuring them they have what it takes to achieve the task and by suggesting time management strategies. Opportunities for conveying these expectations arise in mediation with the students.

Feedback is immediate when the principle of mediation is employed. When the educator sat with groups of students discussing emergent issues in their work and development of the valued product, she listened, evaluated, and responded. She did not provide solutions or answers but raised issues and alternative views or promoted further thought on ways to improve the students' product.

An educator who understands the developmental phase of young adults, earnest in making their own decisions but still needing that reassuring adult as support, is aware that sport, work, family commitment, and health, to name a few, impinge on their lives. Building flexibility into tasks assists students not only to become

Copyright © 2006, Idea Group Inc. Copying or distributing in print or electronic forms without written permission of Idea Group Inc. is prohibited.

autonomous learners, but exemplifies your respect to them. It additionally acts as a motivator because their self esteem is maintained or enhanced. Building time management strategies into the task assists students to navigate the semester of study as well as the flexible, open-ended authentic tasks of the case study unit. It is difficult for students to manage complexity and group tasks; but, as illustrated in this case study, assisting them with time management strategies assures the task is manageable and completed to a high standard. Many students reported that if all group work tasks at university were managed like that presented in this case study, they would willingly engage in group work than shy away, because the outcomes they achieved in terms of content knowledge and life skills were valued and exceeded their expectations.

In sum, it is the implementation of these three principles and seven features which really drive the learning, and, as illustrated in Figure 1, emerge from two main theoretical perspectives of situative and social constructivism and a deep intellectual approach. There is no one way to teach in higher-education contexts, but these principles and features are offered as a guide for educators across disciplines to focus on learning through self, peer, and group assessment. Each is embedded in the case study that follows and perhaps the reader can be challenged to identify them.

The Role of University Graduate Attributes in Learning (Role of Assessments in Achieving Desired Graduate Attributes)

University graduate attributes have also impinged on the learning design presented in this case study and therefore assessment. The introduction of graduate attributes and outcomes in a university context, such as Curtin University of Technology, has challenged teachers to reconceptualize assessment and move away from the existing testing paradigm to one that is consistent with an outcomes-based approach to learning and assessment. The need for students to achieve the graduate attributes appears to have legitimized self, peer, and group approaches to assessment. Acceptance of graduate attributes also affirms the value of critical, creative thinking and communication skills in the learning opportunities for students, all of which reflect how deep intellectual learning can be achieved. Therefore, it was incumbent on the author to provide opportunities for students to acquire these attributes and this was achieved by adopting the "assessment drives the learning" approach. These opportunities were embedded in the authentic assessment tasks in the case study.

Copyright © 2006, Idea Group Inc. Copying or distributing in print or electronic forms without written permission of Idea Group Inc. is prohibited.

Integrating Assessment in Learning: The Assessment Debate

The issue of who is responsible for assessing student's learning has been subject to ongoing debate for many reasons. Assessment by lecturers is the most common approach used to judge student achievement, but is less debated and critiqued than self, peer, and group approaches. This lack of debate and critique of assessment by lecturers is a paradox because the literature reports that students appear to engage in deeper learning experiences when they are involved in the assessment procedures (Biggs, 1999), than when lecturers assess. If this

Table 1. Debate between self, peer, group, and lecturer assessment: summary of issues

Issues	Positive Outcomes	Negative Outcomes
When should group assessments occur?	Group assessment contributes to learning	Time consuming to organize and manage peer and group marking
How do individuals receive a fair and equitable mark?	Group assessment contributes more to the process of assessment	Time consuming negotiating the logistics of collating self-, peer, and group marks
Do the benefits of peer and group assessments outweigh lecture assessments?	Another teaching strategy for staff; better and more strategic use of time spent assessing student work	Need to be creative to develop application to eliminate plagiarism; not all are creative
Are particular tasks more effective in learning than others? Do some have greater impact on learning than other methods of learning?	Bigger and more realistic tasks can be set	Need creative design to eliminate freeloaders
Students need to be taught the skills of group work and assessment prior to becoming involved; this consumes learning time.	Increase student responsibility to own learning	Creative design to award effort and learning in group-assessment tasks
Reliability of assessment	Students benefit from peers, process and knowledge, feedback, view work of others, restate own learning standards or goals	Students need time allocated within timetable for common meeting times; impinges on space-utilization management
	Assessment and learning are more likely to be meaningful because of connection or integration	Too difficult to develop integration of content, assessment, and university attributes
	Increased understanding of individual processing styles and work ethics by students and lecturer	Unreliability of computers to record and assess when it is relevant
	Generation of new learning strategies—for example, mediation.	Students' inability to use computers for assessment purposes
	Students increased knowledge of group dynamics, negotiation, and interpersonal skills	
	Student development of conflict-resolution skills	

Copyright © 2006, Idea Group Inc. Copying or distributing in print or electronic forms without written permission of Idea Group Inc. is prohibited.

is so, then why do lecturer assessments remain the most popular form? The debate, as understood by the author, is summarized and presented in Table 1. The key issues and concerns of academics about peer and group assessments gleaned from debates at meetings, conferences, and around the photo copier are listed as well as the positive and negative outcomes that may arise from the implementation of self, peer, and group approaches.

It seems from Table 1 that opposition to self, peer, and group assessment focuses on issues of (a) reliability of the assessment, and (b) time, effort, and resources required to implement such assessment. On the other hand, support for self, peer, and group assessment focuses on improved learning outcomes. These learning-outcome advantages of group-based learning and assessment validate its place in the social and situative learning design articulated in this chapter. Although group work and group assessment dominate the learning design reported in this case study, a strong role for self and peer assessment also exists. In sum, the author believes the value of, and impact on, learning should be the primary consideration to using particular assessment approaches. The problems that might emerge as a result of instantiating a particular assessment approach are secondary, and although they should be seriously considered in a lecturer's workload, they should not solely direct assessment practices.

This section was included to raise awareness of issues and to encourage the reader to consider the various positions alongside the authentic assessment presented in this chapter. Sometimes the debate is fuelled by limited views and outmoded practices. In the remaining discussion, deliberate reference has been made to lecturer or tutor in contrast to academic, as it is the lecturer who usually designs and delivers units of study and the tutor who delivers them and not necessarily the academic.

Creating Opportunities for Learning through Self, Peer, and Group Assessment

Students' ability to acquire graduate attributes and achieve university, faculty, and unit outcomes has placed a responsibility on lecturers to create opportunities in which these can be achieved. While it may be argued that students are given the opportunity to apply professional skills during laboratory sessions, tutorials, or workshops, others would argue that these contexts militate against their acquisition. For example, essays are rarely required in the professional world, but reports are, and therefore students should become more proficient in writing reports than essays.

Copyright © 2006, Idea Group Inc. Copying or distributing in print or electronic forms without written permission of Idea Group Inc. is prohibited.

Curtin University of Technology, like many others, articulated a list of attributes that graduating students expected to achieve after many years of study. Table 2 lists the desired Curtin University graduate attributes, a possible assessment approach, and the kind of opportunity that must be created to achieve that attribute. Readers may like to add to this list, as it is not claimed to be a complete list.

Each study unit must therefore contain opportunities to achieve those desired graduate attributes. Creating learning opportunities that are focussed on desired outcomes and attributes and addressed through assessment avoids the need to separately track student achievements in desired learning outcomes and attributes, as well as their marks/grade. It is important to the achievement of

Table 2. Curtin University graduate attributes, suggested assessment approaches, and opportunities for students to achieve them

CURTIN UNIVERSITY OUTCOMES	ASSESSMENT APPROACH	OPPORTUNITIES
1. Applying discipline knowledge, principles and concepts	Self, peer, group, lecturer	• To construct, adapt, design, perform • To compare/contrast • Investigate/research • Produce a product
2. Thinking critically, creatively and reflectively	Self, peer	• To analyse the components of an issue • To identify problems, issues within a bigger complex task/issue • To generate/produce innovative solutions • To review and compare • To investigate
3. Accessing, evaluating and synthesising information	Peer, group	• Identifying the most appropriate information to solve a problem • Synthesising information in order to evaluate an approach, the technology • Evaluate different sources • Gathering information from variety of sources
4. Communicating effectively	Peer	• Accounts for the audience in the development of a tangible product • Writing to authors/companies for specific information /clarification • Clarifying complex tasks
5. Using technologies appropriately	Group	• Design a program of work using appropriate technologies, which identify and utilise the potential of each. • Using technology for intra-group communication • Use technologies to provide alternate approaches to understanding or presenting a context.
6. Utilising lifelong learning skills	Group	• Employ a problem- based case approach • Ensure research is embedded in students' tasks • Work in teams as well as groups
7. Recognising and applying international perspectives	Peer, Group	• Design xxxx to suit specific contexts or cultures. Analyse the differences • Detail adaptations which would make xxxx more suitable to a temperate climate • Prepare a presentation to suit international audiences
8. Demonstrating cultural awareness and understanding	Peer, Group	• Influence the formation of multicultural groups • Groups participate in the assessment of multicultural group work
9. Applying professional skills.	Self, Group	• Prepare a case for ..... • Collect data information from authentic sources • Interview xxxx and synthesise information • Review data/reports, write own report • Communicate with – patients/parents, clientele as a data gathering process
10. Create knowledge through research	Self, Peer, Group	• Use historical search to find...... • Present a literature review and several research questions • Identify the limitations ....propose an alternative which wilL account/address these limitations

Copyright © 2006, Idea Group Inc. Copying or distributing in print or electronic forms without written permission of Idea Group Inc. is prohibited.

specific learning outcomes and attributes that peer and group *work* as well as self, peer and group *assessment* are implemented in various combinations. This in turn enables fairness to be transparent.

Understanding the fundamental processes of learning allows powerful learning opportunities to be created within the course and study unit. Alexander and Boud (2001) affirm that "students still need to actively engage with what is to be learnt; they still have to have ways of expressing their understanding if they are to be confident that they have learnt and they need to feel that what they are doing is worthwhile" (p. 4). A rich, dynamic assessment and a complex environment drove the learning process and assessment in the case study. Students built their knowledge by providing information and pointing things out to one another, asking questions, arguing, elaborating on each other's ideas (Resnick, 1991), and critiquing each other's work. Technology enabled this interaction and integration of social constructivism through the creation of group-developed and group-assessed Web sites to create an e-learning environment in every sense of the word, as was the task in the case study. The suggested opportunities emphasized active engagement and deep meaningful learning.

There should also be a transparent alignment between university attributes, course goals, unit goals, and assessment (Biggs, 1999). Too often, assessment bears little relation to the intended or desired learning outcomes from any one unit. For example, if participation in classes is deemed essential and therefore assessable, then this criterion should be reflected in the University attributes or course/unit goals. Likewise, if the quantity of a discussion board is to be assessed, then the frequency of postings should be the only factor to be monitored. However, if the purpose of the discussion board is to facilitate debate, exchange ideas, and promote deep intellectual learning then the quality of discussion must become the assessable task. Checking only that the performance of a skill has been demonstrated is a waste of precious workload time. Checking the application of the skill in context (authentic assessment) is more productive and this translates into lecturers or learning designers creating the opportunity to learn using assessment. The student can apply the knowledge and skills to pass the authentic assessment or they cannot.

Technology can ease the difficulties that emerge when designing assessments that drive learning in directions aligned with university and course objectives. This is demonstrated in the case study in various ways, but is described explicitly in the assessment of the quality of discussion in an online environment. The author argues that greater critical, creative, and reflective thinking is achieved when students not only work in pairs or groups, but are also involved in the assessment of that work. As the ultimate responsibility of academics is to ensure students learn, then designing in opportunities should operate as a priori and the problems that may be created in marking should follow and be addressed, not the reverse.

Copyright © 2006, Idea Group Inc. Copying or distributing in print or electronic forms without written permission of Idea Group Inc. is prohibited.

The case study in this chapter was designed to achieve one clear outcome: Students enrolled in a Bachelor of Education degree were to be fully cognisant and familiar with learning theories in education. A case study/scenario was presented to students who then had to identify the problem/s and collect information and data in the hope of positing a solution. This problem-based approach to learning initiated the transfer of learning, as it not only introduced a process, but a goal or reason for students to learn. Students were empowered to create their own meaning and purpose. Quality solutions were best obtained from group work and their discussions in which issues could be thrashed out. Solutions were reflected in the group-assessment task. Inherent in the design were the opportunities to achieve, or work towards achieving, many of the graduate attributes.

Three Roles of Technology in the Case Study Learning Environment

Technology played three roles in the academic unit in which the case study was embedded. The first role was administration and information dissemination (which is now common with online units).

The second role of technology was as a tool to facilitate communication. Its flexibility and capability opened doors for authentic group tasks and group assessment and offered greater opportunity to develop effective group processes of collaborating, organizing, creating, monitoring, evaluating, publishing knowledge, and communicating. Technology and learning theories were integrated as equal partners in the design process; technology enabled access to video lectures and online communications, and theories provided a framework for designing an e-learning environment able to prepare future teachers for their role as change agents in schools (Sherry & Gibson, 2002) and in the information computer technology education of a future generation of learners. The final design offered future teachers opportunities to be critical builders as well as consumers of technology based learning and resources. Traditional institutional boundaries to expertise and knowledge were diminished, allowing students to acquire knowledge from a variety of sources, experts, and chats on the Internet (Rudestam & Schoenholtz-Read, 2002).

The third role of technology was as a tool for constructing knowledge. Jonassen and Carr (2000) argue that "representing what learners know in a single way engages a limited set of cognitive skills. ...constrains their understanding of whatever they are studying" (p. 165). They not only advocate using multiple forms of knowledge representations in assessment, but also recommend request-

Copyright © 2006, Idea Group Inc. Copying or distributing in print or electronic forms without written permission of Idea Group Inc. is prohibited.

ing this from students. Students "function as interpreters, organizers and designers of their personal knowledge" (p. 167) when they use computers as knowledge-construction tools (mindtools). Knowledge-construction tools provide "structural, logical, causal, systemic, or visuospatial formalisms that scaffold different kinds of thinking and knowledge representation" (p. 167) and possibly enable learners to think in ways not previously possible. The case study used a Web site as the ultimate space in which all learning was synthesized for each group.

These three roles of technology within the case-study unit are summarized as follows:

1. Information dissemination
    - Unit outline, i-lectures (video lectures integrated with PowerPoints®)
    - Administration issues
    - Assessment issues
    - Weekly tuteshop tasks (a combination of a tutorial and a workshop)
    - Microsoft® PowerPoint® of weekly lectures
    - Database/register of all groups
2. Communication tools
    - Inform peers of new information
    - Advertise and disseminate each group's constructed quiz
    - Completion and mailing of quiz
    - Requesting group members, if necessary
    - Synchronous chats online
    - Asynchronous café chats
    - Exchange of subcomponents for proofing by group members
    - E-mailing meeting times, venues, agendas
    - Weekly asynchronous discussion of content from lecture (PoCR = **Po**st, **C**hallenge, **R**eflect)
    - Occasional synchronous tuteshop
    - Facilitate mentoring role of particular members (coenrolled in a technology unit)
3. Information Building tool to create a valuable product
    - Create a quiz
    - Create PowerPoints®
    - Create mind-maps/semantic/concept maps

Copyright © 2006, Idea Group Inc. Copying or distributing in print or electronic forms without written permission of Idea Group Inc. is prohibited.

- Create Web site
- Internet searches
- Word processing
- Integration of multimedia

The focus of the remaining chapter is on the case study and the use of technology as a mindtool to enable desired student learning outcomes to be achieved.

The Case Study Description

First-year, second-semester students studying for a bachelor's degree of early childhood, primary, or secondary, as well as several students completing double degrees were enrolled in this core educational psychology unit. Students were considered adult learners with work and family commitments. This cohort of students was well suited to an online environment that enabled them to control their own learning. Rudestam and Schoenholtz-Read (2002) note that "adult students seek to be effective collaborative partners in the learning process and seem to thrive in academic settings that offer a facilitative and supportive milieu" (p. 7).

The unit was focused on teaching, learning, and assessment. The theories presented in the unit formed the basis of the unit design so that students had first-hand experience of their application. The unit was delivered via WebCT to multiple campuses with a total enrolment of 188 students. Seven tutorial groups were based on the main campus while another seven tutorial groups, representing diverse geographical areas of Western Australia, were administered from a Regional Centre as depicted in Figure 2.

Figure 2 illustrates the way that the learning materials were delivered. At Curtin University, the units were delivered through seven tuteshops (each tuteshop is a prepared set of tasks beginning with a problem specific to the topic which directs students' attention to the link between theory and practice). The same materials supplied to the Centre for Regional Education were delivered to groups of students at seven separate campuses spread throughout Western Australia.

Copyright © 2006, Idea Group Inc. Copying or distributing in print or electronic forms without written permission of Idea Group Inc. is prohibited.

Figure 2. The administrative structure and delivery of the single core educational psychology unit of study

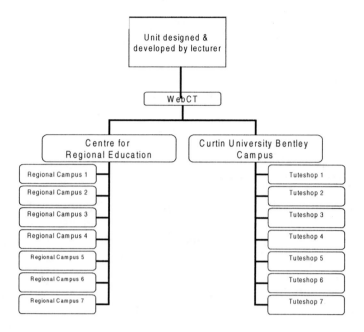

Key Terms in the Case Study

Self assessment is an approach used in both learning and formal assessment in which students award themselves a mark or grade. The contribution of self assessment to a student's final grade is determined by the lecturer, the unit design, and the graduate attributes the unit seeks to achieve. Students assess their personal learning by reflecting on a combination of effort, achievement of unit outcomes, and achievement in relation to the academic unit of study. Students can develop their own criteria for the awarding of marks, be guided by the lecturer, or use criteria provided by fellow students. In the case study, individual tutorial groups decided on the criteria as well as the marks allocated to each criterion. This meant assessment criteria differed between the numerous tutorial groups.

Peer assessment occurs when an individual student marks or grades the work of another student who is a participant in the same unit of study. In the case study, the selection of criteria by peers was extrapolated from the objectives and intended outcome(s) of the assessment task. Like self assessment, this differed between tutorial groups.

Copyright © 2006, Idea Group Inc. Copying or distributing in print or electronic forms without written permission of Idea Group Inc. is prohibited.

Group assessment has similarities to peer assessment except that a group of students instead of individuals are responsible for assigning the final grade/mark. In the case study, students arrived at the criteria through discussion, which they then applied to the completed work of another group. However, in the case study, the criteria were refined through discussion in each of the multiple tutorial groups until consensus was reached. Each group then applied the same criteria to judge the assessment task completed by other groups.

Lecturer assessment is based on the application of a set of criteria to individual or group tasks and made explicit to students, usually before engaging in the task so that it also serves an educative purpose. In this case study, criteria were presented one third of the way through the unit and were consistent with the group-assessment criteria developed through consensus. Both the lecturer- and group-assessment criteria were made public through WebCT concurrently.

Combining Approaches. Any single task can be assessed by a combination of any of the previous approaches as illustrated in the case study. Assessment validity improves when several persons mark or judge the same completed task.

Figure 3. Excerpt of assessment from the unit outline

> **Assessment is self, peer, group and lecturer based.**
> **Criteria are decided weekly by each tuteshop group for tutesheets and challenges.**
> **Criteria for the Web site is not available ahead of time but will be developed by the cohort during the semester.**

Assessment item

1	All tuteshops have an online and tutesheet component. ❖ Each week one challenge must be posted (in a similar manner as the questions were post in Semester 1). However, your response to any challenge must be made in a particular role which is allocated to you each week (See Table 1–Challenge Roles). *PEER ASSESSED* A challenge should emanate from the lecture. The idea is to challenge others. Therefore it should take on the following: ❖ Something you are confused about ❖ Something you are uncertain or unclear about ❖ You require an example of how xxx will work in a classroom *PEER ASSESSED* ❖ Each tutesheet must be completed individually in class to be eligible for a grade *SELF ASSESSED*	18%
2	Contract and analysis of own learning. *LECTURER/TUTOR ASSESSED*	10%
3	Quizzes: Each person must complete three. *PEER /GROUP ASSESSED*	12%
4	Web site **Part a** Journal of Andragogy (Marks to be decided by cohort consensus, awarded by lecturer/tutor) **Part b** Design a quiz. **Part c**– Teacher & student interview & critique (Marks to be decided by cohort consensus, & lecturer/tutor) **Part d**– Remaining tasks – journals, video review, Web links, concept map chapter summary (Marks to be decided by cohort consensus, & lecturer/tutor) *PEER /GROUP ASSESSED and LECTURER/TUTOR ASSESSED*	60%

Copyright © 2006, Idea Group Inc. Copying or distributing in print or electronic forms without written permission of Idea Group Inc. is prohibited.

One approach offered in this case study is the combination of both group and lecturer assessment.

Explanation of the Processes in Designing Complex and Challenging Quality Learning

An excerpt taken from the unit outline is provided in Figure 3 to orient the reader as to how self, peer, and group assessment was implemented in the case study, the focus of this chapter. As noted from Figure 1, challenge was inherent in all assessment tasks. However, assessment item 1, Figure 3, uses challenge in a slightly different way. In item 1, students had to identify a concept or issue from the lecture that appeared worthwhile exploring. They then had to phrase this into an open-ended question in such a way that this would challenge their peers' thinking sufficiently as to incite debate or encourage the sharing of different perspectives. This was an extension from semester one where all students were required to post two questions online derived from their readings and bring these and the prepared answers to the face-to-face tuteshop.

Assessments in the Case Study

As documented in the previous extract from the unit outline (Figure 3) four assessment tasks were set for the unit of study. Each is presented in the following sections like a description of a recipe rather than the recipe itself, to enable adaptations by the reader to other discipline areas.

Assessment 1

Background to this assessment: The unit has a regular two-hour tuteshop schedule. A one-hour tuteshop was set aside for the whole of class, face-to-face activities, which elaborated theories presented in the weekly lecture. The second hour was dedicated to creating the Web site and was a common time for all members to meet as a group and with the lecturer/tutor. It was set within a computer lab so that students can access the resources required to complete the assessment. The provision of this common hour contributed to the flexible delivery of the unit. Students could work totally online and/or away from the campus according to their needs. The one-hour weekly tuteshop also had two components: online and face-to-face.

Copyright © 2006, Idea Group Inc. Copying or distributing in print or electronic forms without written permission of Idea Group Inc. is prohibited.

Figure 4. Example of a weekly tuteshop designed using problem-based learning

TUTESHEET5
Individual Differences

PROBLEM: Assuming that teaching students is about accomodating individual differences, what guiding principles should be used to enfure that each student will learn?

1   PoCR – resolve any outstanding issues

2   (I)You are given the IQ scores of a number of students in your class. You notice they range from 82 to 148. What does this mean to you?

3   (P) Using two columns list the reasons why you would and would not use ability grouping in the classroom.

4.   (Grp) Complete the man/woman exercise (provided by lecturer). Identify your own learning style. Discuss with a partner. What could a teacher do to accommodate you in the classroom?

5.   (Gps 4) List the kind of behaviours you would expect from students who are highly creative. Discuss. Prepare two role plays one to demonstrate how you could accommodate their creativity, the other to demonstrate how you could discourage it.

6.   (Gps 4) Mime activities/behaviours to show the differences between cognitive styles & learning styles, and between the different cognitive styles. Present the mime to the tute group who will identify the styles.

KEY: (I) = individual; (P) = pair; (Grp)=group

   RESOLUTION/SOLUTION

Face-to-face class activities were set within a problem-solution framework. An example is presented in Figure 4. In this framework, the lecturer introduced the tuteshop by posing a problem and left it open until the end of the class, at which time students responded with a solution, usually individually and in writing. The problem was related to the topic focus for the week and bridged theory with practical applications to a classroom. Sometimes the single tuteshop was generic across early-child, primary, and secondary degree programs, and at other times a specific tuteshop was written for the specific program groups.

During the tuteshop, students completed the activities as listed in the weekly tutesheet (a guide to weekly individual, pair, or group activities). The activities were specified to be completed either individually, in pairs, or as a small group. At the conclusion of the tuteshop, students used the new information gathered during the activities to write a response to the problem. During the tuteshop, the

Copyright © 2006, Idea Group Inc. Copying or distributing in print or electronic forms without written permission of Idea Group Inc. is prohibited.

lecturer moved from group to group, listening to the debates or discussion, or was asked by groups to join a discussion. Generally she facilitated the progression from one activity to the next. Often, the activities required a table to be constructed and students were encouraged to facilitate the building of the table. Each activity was often concluded by a whole-group summary, albeit briefly. As this was an education unit, many strategies of learning were implemented and no two weeks were identical. Charts, tables, drawings, sketches, and evidence of WebCT questions and responses were to be recorded as students worked through the activities. No expectation was made that it be retyped, organized, tidied, or "prettied" up. These collations of tuteshop work were not collected for lecture/tutor marking but acted as a record of work and were self and peer assessed. Students in each tuteshop group allocated themselves a mark based on criteria determined by group consensus at each tuteshop. The implementation of this self assessment had been developed in the previous semester and is described in detail in the following (see "Preparing Students: A Scaffolded Approach to Self, Peer, and Group Assessment"). Although this chapter is not about an evaluation of the case study presented here, it can be reported that students found weekly tuteshops a most valuable part of their learning; so much so, they claimed they would do everything in their power to attend each tuteshop. They were also heard advising the following cohort of students the same information.

Students were advised to use a scrapbook to collate the tutesheets, preparatory notes, and all hands-on class work. It was considered a working document in which content and thinking was documented for later reflection.

All tuteshops had an online component. Each week, students were encouraged to post to the WebCT discussion board to enable them to socially construct their knowledge by participating in meaningful and rewarding dialogues (rather than posting because it is a requirement). Derry, Gance, Gance, and Schlager (2000) used an index of apprenticeship to query the effectiveness of the online medium for social construction of knowledge, noting it may not be functioning or, if it is, it may not necessarily be effective. They noted lack of effectiveness was attributed to overdominance by leaders, ineffective mentorships, or overly difficult tasks for the group. An organizational structure was imposed on the discussion in the case study to counter these factors. The structure was designed to allow discussion to take its own path, reflect the needs of students, and provide opportunities to socially construct knowledge.

The author expected students to be motivated by participation and knowledge construction through discussion and that this motivation would therefore promote further discussion. Thus, discussion postings were designed with both an intrinsic and an extrinsic aspect. There was a strong element of freedom and flow within the structure of the design so that students were not engaged in meaningless postings. In line with elements suggested by Hudson (2002), story telling and

Copyright © 2006, Idea Group Inc. Copying or distributing in print or electronic forms without written permission of Idea Group Inc. is prohibited.

personal anecdotes were encouraged, both for constructing learning and for making the communication experience enjoyable. Hudson argues that the virtual or e-learning environment fosters alternative forms of interaction. However, to implement the ideas suggested in this case study and other similarly alternate ideas, the mindset of a classroom, classroom lesson plans, and learning dominated by memorization must be removed or eliminated from thinking to enable the freedom and flow to emerge and carry the interaction. This aspect of freedom and flow is integral in the design of online discussions. And, as expected, anecdotes, sayings, jokes, and stories all emerged as students wrestled with identifying examples of life experiences to demonstrate their understanding of theory. Frequent exclamations were heard from students along the line that they did not feel like they were learning but on reflection they were astonished at how much they actually had learnt.

In the words of one student: "I thought that it was great, the discussion was good and ideas thought provoking and I learnt a lot. Once again I enjoyed today" (1st year student, 2003).

The peer assessment of the discussions was based on the relative amount and quality of discussions contributed each week. No length was stipulated and no penalties were imposed for brief discussions. The aim of the assessment was to encourage students to socially construct their knowledge online and take responsibility for the content and nature of that knowledge. These points are elaborated in the following sections.

How was Such Freedom and Choice Structured and Implemented?

Firstly, students were given a role to play or thinking lens to use each week according to a timetable as illustrated in Figure 5. Roles were allocated for three

Figure 5. The PoCR timetable for the semester

WEEK	Last initial A-F	Last initial G-L	Last initial M-R	Last initial S-Z
1	PoCR	Green	white	red
2	red	PoCR	Green	white
3	white	red	PoCR	
4	Green	white	red	PoCR
5	PoCR	Green	white	red
6	red	PoCR	Green	white
7	white	red	PoCR	Green
8	Green	white	red	PoCR
9	PoCR	Green	white	red
10	red	PoCR	Green	white
11	white	red	PoCR	Green
12	Green	white	red	PoCR

Copyright © 2006, Idea Group Inc. Copying or distributing in print or electronic forms without written permission of Idea Group Inc. is prohibited.

of DeBono's six thinking hats (red, white and green) and a PoCR. They were allocated by surname initial and, because they were rotated each week, each student performed each role three or four times during the semester. This eliminated dominance by some members, shared the mediation of discussions, and transferred the decision-making from the lecturer to the students.

PoCR represented the role of "Post, Challenge, and Reflect." Students in this role were required to select content from the lecture and reframe it so it would challenge their peers, or cause them to reflect on some experience in addition to resolving a personal query. Several students could be in the PoCR role simultaneously and each would create a new thread. Each thread could take on a unique dimension. If students did not find the thread challenging, it would die from lack of interest; however, if it were of great interest to students, it would consume much of the tutegroup's postings. Students acted as mediators of online

Sample 1.

Example PoCR:
There are many different cultures of the world each with their own individual perspective on the world. Appropriate behaviour is not a universal concept. There are many diffrent [*sic*] forms of behaviour which is socially acceptable in one country but looked upon as inappropraite in others.
If you have a child in your lower primary class that continuously portrays what you consider to be inappropriate behaviour but was acceptable in their home culture how do you control or explain why they should no longer behave in that manner?

GREEN HAT THINKER
I think an extremely useful idea would be to do role-plays in class. For example, you may think of the action that is deemed inappropriate in the culture where the school is, such as spitting. In your own time, you could list how it may affect others; students, elderly people, other people outside the school context. You can then get the children to act out role plays, getting them to visualise and imagine how other people feel when somebody spits (elderly person may not see that there is spit on the ground and could slip, infections, germs, etc). Make sure that the children
discuss amongst themselves what reactions different people would have—this is so they may challenge one anothers [*sic*] beliefs. If the teacher tells them the reactions people would have, the children will act the situations outmeaninglessly [*sic*]. That is, theyll [*sic*] think ,"this is what the teacher wants me to do so im [*sic*]going to do it like that."
The children could act out the scenarios, swapping roles to make sure they get a chance to see different sides of the story and how the inappropriate behaviour may affect others.

Maybe a person from the school community or from outside school—a health worker, etc could come in and do activities with the class. This may be an indirect way to correct inappropriate behaviours.

Or you could read them a story—the children could discuss the reactions of the characters, which may influence the way the children act.

Non-disclosed hat:
I agree with Amanda. We cant [sic] treat students and children as if they are stupid. I think sometimes we just need to tell them how it is. Explain that different behaviours are considered acceptable in different cultures, and that they may do this behaviour at home but not at school. Children have to learn what behaviours are acceptable in different
places as well. Many children will get away with a lot more at home than they would at school. It is all part of social development and learning what is socially acceptable. I think the idea of a parent-teacher interview if this doesnt [*sic*]work is a great idea.

Copyright © 2006, Idea Group Inc. Copying or distributing in print or electronic forms without written permission of Idea Group Inc. is prohibited.

discussion, reading, responding, and being provocative if necessary. The lecturer reviewed all discussion postings prior to the scheduled face-to-face tuteshop. Inconclusive issues and main debates were summarized and presented to the group. Where the inconclusive issues were thought to be beneficial to students' learning they were debated further until closure was achieved. If, as happened on several occasions, the discussions got off course or too much anecdotal information was presented, then the lecturer made a group posting to redirect the discussion, and/or privately emailed the PoCR students for that week to assist them in redirecting the discussion. The following sample shows three original postings from an initial PoCR. They illustrate the depth and commitment students had to this activity, as well as a window into how students were involved in the process of constructing their knowledge.

Figure 6. Discussion page of WebCT, listing the groups and the number of postings as at week 4 of semester

Discussions

Compose message ■ Search Topic settings
Click on a topic name to see its messages.

Topic	Unread	Total	Private	Anonymous	Locked
Admin issues	2	27			
Assessment	0	5			
Quizzes to do	69	101			
Cafe chat	6	37			
ECE 1	65	115			
Hi 8	123	359			
10-12	80	141			
2-4	0	71			
Early birds sec	6	21			
Sec 2	6	117			
Esperance	3	3			
Gero	116	123			
Kalgoorlie Rollers	58	60			
Northam	20	22			
Kal quizzes	7	7			
KalMMM	31	31			
All	592	1240	Update		

Copyright © 2006, Idea Group Inc. Copying or distributing in print or electronic forms without written permission of Idea Group Inc. is prohibited.

Figure 6 records the lecturer's view within WebCT of the discussion postings up to and including week 4 of second semester by students from the main campus and the Centre for Regional Education. As can be noted, the first four topics are of a general nature to which all students can respond. Questions about enrolment, assessment dates, and invitations to social gatherings were posted along with soapbox topics such as teachers' right to breast-feeding in school. The next six topics relate to the main-campus students and the remaining six topics relate to the Center for Regional Education (note: student groups gave themselves their discussion name for the purpose of easy group identification). Given that during the first week students were still navigating their way into the discussions, it was rewarding to see the number of postings during the early part of the semester. It can be noted that the Hi 8 group had posted 359 times in four weeks. At the time of printing 123 messages had yet to be read by the lecturer, indicating the possible postings in one week alone. This group concluded the semester with 520 postings.

As stated previously, other roles available to tuteshop group members were based on DeBono's red, green, and white thinking hats to represent the emotional, creative, and factual lens for thinking. These roles also prevented them from writing the first (often uncritical) response that came to mind. This was a problem experienced in past discussion boards. The thinking hat roles also encouraged students to probe more deeply and persist with a particular topic. Students expressed how difficult this was and at times wanted others to know that this was not their very personal opinion and stated the color of their hat prior to their views, as illustrated in the previous posting by the green hat thinker. Dividing messages into threads enabled all members to read those preceding theirs and later those which followed relating to a particular challenge.

A strong feature of this flexible but structured approach to discussion, apart from posting in role, was the rotation of roles. The role of PoCR is quite demanding, as it requires students to regularly check all postings, respond, mediate the discussion, and summarize or conclude. For this reason, students played this role only three to four times during the semester. In the following weeks, students participated in each of the thinking-hat roles. Not only did they respond and reflect but they also experienced for themselves the difference between the three nominated ways of thinking. Sharing knowledge is fundamental to social constructivism. Although expert knowledge was not always available in the discussion sessions, opportunity was provided at the beginning of every face-to-face tuteshop for unresolved issues to be further discussed with the lecturer present.

Quality of discussion was obviously a significant goal for promoting deep learning and understanding. Not all PoCRs were equal in their ability to achieve this goal. Some postings died, others engendered little discussion, while others created

Copyright © 2006, Idea Group Inc. Copying or distributing in print or electronic forms without written permission of Idea Group Inc. is prohibited.

monumental postings in length, number, and quality. As there were several PoCRs for each tutoral it was not essential that every discussion was taken up or debated at length. For some individuals it was a relief not to have to manage excessive postings, as most required the PoCR to know the area intensively to be able to mediate the discussion. Where it was felt some less assertive or quiet, shy students needed help, an e-mail was sent with suggestions and encouragement. On some occasions, some students did not post. This did not become an issue because of its rarity. Students were involved in this activity and appeared motivated to post whenever possible, some weeks more often than others. However, students who did not post missed the allocation of marks for that particular week.

Participating in all four roles gave each student the experiences of being both facilitator and responder. Many students commented that this assisted them in understanding how important it was to respond, even if were to ask questions themselves to increase the discussion or move the discussion to deeper or more relevant aspects of teaching. Increases in weekly postings over the duration of the semester suggest that students learned the format and participated extensively, many responding to several PoCRs during any one week. The lecturer did not berate students who did not post. Following the principles listed in Figure 1, encouragement was provided through a mediated approach, and students also knew it was their responsibility in their own learning journey to participate. It appeared that there was no need for the lecturer to take this action further as students did this themselves.

The assessment for PoCR had a generic format. Students in PoCR allocated marks or "smiley faces" to the students in thinking-hat roles. During the weekly tuteshop class, students in PoCR roles gathered together as a group to assess their peers so that a mutually agreed mark/smiley was recorded against each student's name. Nonparticipants received a sad face or zero marks. Although it was intended that students in the role of PoCR did not receive marks, but only awarded marks to others, the quality and commitment of students in this role indicated that the lecturer should reward them for their contribution. While assessing the discussions was the responsibility of students and not intended to be marked by the lecturer, it was in the lecturer's interests to read students' concerns and note the discussion and comment privately where appropriate. Behavioral learning theory suggests that an "intermittent" response or contribution to the discussion informs students that the lecturer is listening and values their commentary. This in turn motivates students to participate further. This indeed was found to be the case. Students proudly told their peers that they had a personal comment from the lecturer about their posting and this in turn created aspirations in others that they too would get a positive response. For example, one student routinely asked deep questions to which few and sometimes no one responded. A response was mailed to him commenting not only on the quality and

Copyright © 2006, Idea Group Inc. Copying or distributing in print or electronic forms without written permission of Idea Group Inc. is prohibited.

insight apparent, but an informed and provocative response was made. Others tried to emulate this kind of posting and it became an enjoyable and humorous feature of this particular tutegroup. And, as noted previously, not every student believed the view they posted and some wanted others to know they were in role.

The words of students offer insight into the value of this approach.

It was good to see the questions in a different perspective. I often got new information out of the weekly questions....It (the questions) challenges you to think and apply what you have learnt in the text....Posting questions was interactive and good practice for years to come.

Using an e-learning, asynchronous approach to the task provided students with a time frame that enabled them to be reflective, refer to the text or other readings, and be more critical in their response. This is not possible in face-to-face spontaneous discussions. Face-to-face meetings were used for grade allocation, as this is most difficult and time consuming when done online. Face-to-face meetings were an economical way for students to reflect on postings in both qualitative and quantitative ways. This division of online and face-to-face activities put the emphasis on learning and not on the allocation of marks. Some students did not care to follow through about the marks they received as they believed they had made sufficient contribution and were more informed as a result of having been engaged.

Assessment 2

The main assessment task for the unit was complex and involved several activities. To enable students to complete the task and therefore manage their time, a contract system was imposed. A model of a contract was provided which students could present in a format of their choice. Key information such as a group name, group members, rules, goals, outcomes, and a 10-week plan followed by signatures of all members, were required. This was allocated minimum marks by the assessor/lecturer. Contracts could be altered or modified as students became more informed of the nature of each task and the length of time each would take to complete, but all changes were to be documented.

The strategy for promoting continued reflection and understanding of how learning occurs required each student to analyse his or her own learning at the conclusion of 10 weeks. This analysis was lecturer/tutor assessed. A minimum of 10 entries was required to indicate a clear understanding of the learning theories encountered in the unit. No maximum limits were imposed and students were encouraged to add more than the minimum 10, which represented one theory and one posting for each week. The context and application of the theory was open and did not have to reflect learning at a university.

Copyright © 2006, Idea Group Inc. Copying or distributing in print or electronic forms without written permission of Idea Group Inc. is prohibited.

Assessment 3

This assessment required participation in the development of a quiz as well as completing quizzes as illustrated in Figure 7. Students in self selected groups of four were required to construct one quiz. All students enrolled in the study unit were to complete three separate quizzes to ensure that quizzes were of a high quality and were a valued approach to learning. The range of topics selected by the students for these quizzes was advertised on WebCT. All students corresponded with the quiz developers, who forwarded them the quiz, and marked it on its completion. Each group was responsible for marking and recording all marks, as these counted toward a final assessment result. Thus, peer marking contributed to a valid component of the overall assessment grade. Some students sought out mindtools (knowledge construction computer software application tools that learners learn with, not from; Jonassen & Carr, 2000) to develop, disseminate, and mark a quiz; others used a combination of hard copy and mindtools. The recording format of quiz takers and their marks was also left open to choice. Some students selected a word-processing and table format and others selected a spreadsheet format (Excel®).

Figure 7. Completed process of quiz design, from construction to completion and to the final grade

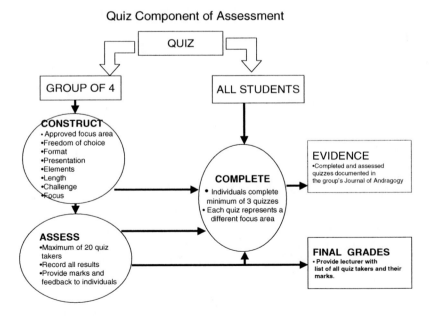

Copyright © 2006, Idea Group Inc. Copying or distributing in print or electronic forms without written permission of Idea Group Inc. is prohibited.

Assessment 4

Students working in self selected groups of four were required to construct a Web site and maintain a journal of andragogy to document the complete process of learning. Figure 9 documents the subtasks of the Web site. This diagram of the bigger and holistic assessment illustrates its complexity. The whole task of producing a valuable product, in this case a Web site, incorporated a group contract, a problem-based approach, several subtasks, documentation of the group process, and peer marking. The process of assessing this process is detailed in the following discussion.

The process of assessment had the underlying motives to enable students to experience first hand various approaches to assessment as well as empathize with the emotional aspects of self, peer, and group assessments. As future teachers, these students will forever be involved in the processes of evaluation and assessment and it was important they experience group dynamics, empathy, workload ethics, validity and reliability, rather than just read about it. So, how was such a complex task assessed?

Figure 8. Mark allocation between students and lecture

Marking of the Web site was divided into two parts: peer assessment and lecturer assessment.

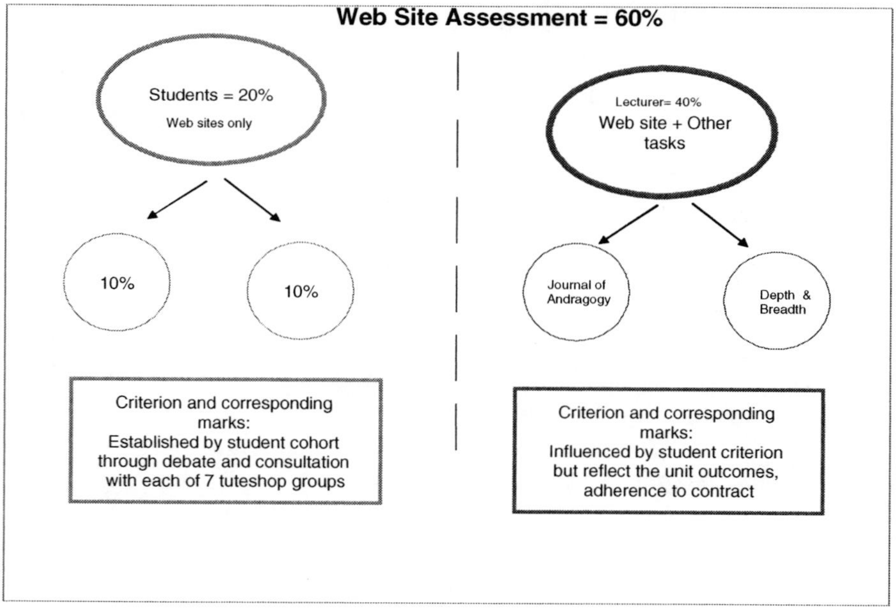

Web Site Assessment = 60%

Students = 20%
Web sites only

10%

10%

Criterion and corresponding marks:
Established by student cohort through debate and consultation with each of 7 tuteshop groups

Lecturer= 40%
Web site + Other tasks

Journal of Andragogy

Depth & Breadth

Criterion and corresponding marks:
Influenced by student criterion but reflect the unit outcomes, adherence to contract

Copyright © 2006, Idea Group Inc. Copying or distributing in print or electronic forms without written permission of Idea Group Inc. is prohibited.

Marking of the Web site was divided into two parts: peer assessment and lecturer assessment. The Web site assessment contributed 60% to the final marks of the students. Student assessment of the Web sites contributed to 20% of their final marks, and lecturer assessment contributed to 40% of the final marks. Student assessment was based on criteria established by the entire student cohort through consultation with each of the student tuteshop groups. The lecturer assessment was based a balance between the criteria decided by the student cohort, and the desired learning outcomes specified for the course. The division of all assessments and the allocation of 60% to the Web site have been determined to be the effective and less stressful than other combinations of marks in previous years, some of which were substantially higher.

The development of the criteria was invigilated as a process and was therefore undertaken during the weekly lecture topic of assessment. The process began with the first tuteshop who proposed a structure, some criteria, and some idea of marks. This was typed during the class and distributed to the next tuteshop group, who then continued to refine the structure, criteria, and allocated marks. This process continued for the seven Bentley Campus Tuteshop groups. The final edition was then posted to WebCT, along with the lecturer's criteria. Ultimately, the timing of this student-developed assessment was critical in the learning process. Had the criteria been developed earlier than its placement in week 5, it would not have addressed the intensity and complexity of the tasks as students would not have had the required experience in this stage of the development of the Web site. Had the process occurred later, it would have denied students the opportunity to work towards the criteria which of itself should be fair, educative, comprehensive, valid, and explicit (Curriculum Framework, WA). The process empowered students and strengthened their goals. They not only knew what was expected of their group but knew how to judge the work of their peers.

Validating Assessment

Validity was addressed in one specific way. In most group tasks, it is usual or common practice for the lecturer to do the assessment. In this case study, the assessment was structured so that peers not only assessed but contributed to another student's mark. This translated into nine pairs of eyes (eight students and the lecturer) marking the Web site instead of the usual set of one providing increased validity to the assessment. Peer marking which contributes to a final grade is usually raised as a contentious issue when students first discuss this process and their responsibility. They are concerned about fairness, and particularly the bias of the groups who will mark their site. When the issue of anonymity and the high correlation of all three sets of marks is presented from previous

Copyright © 2006, Idea Group Inc. Copying or distributing in print or electronic forms without written permission of Idea Group Inc. is prohibited.

cohorts of student data, uncertainty and trepidation are replaced by confidence in, and fairness of, the process.

The process was as follows. The two Web sites to be assessed by groups were emailed only to each marking group who then submitted the completed criteria to the lecturer. Most groups were unaware who marked their sites; however some groups were comfortable in disclosing this, as they wanted to verbally congratulate the group on the interest and learning value of the site.

The allocation of markers to sites was made at the conclusion of the semester. Student groups were e-mailed the names of two group Web sites they were to assess. Each group of four then allocated a mark to two other Web sites using the criteria developed by the entire cohort of students. Students will have accessed and viewed the Web sites online and used a hard copy of the criteria for marking. The assessment criteria sheets were submitted to the lecturer and the marks were transferred to the larger mark sheet (*Excel*® document of all students and marks).

The quality of learning from this type of group assessment was captured in the feedback of students. They reported having peers mark their work increased their motivation for competence and arrive at sound theoretical conclusions to the many subtasks and solutions to the main problem. This motivation was apparent in the finer debates and discussions about what eventually was placed on line for marking. Students also claimed the impact of being marked solely by the lecturer is less stressful than that of group assessment. They viewed group marking as highly critical because it is the group who would "talk" about their site. Their reputation as individuals was at stake and so they strove to be seen as competent and intelligent students rather than "stupid" or loose face in front of friends and peers.

Using Mediation

To alleviate the acknowledged stress and drive the quality of learning, the lecturer used mediation extensively as a guiding principle of learning. However, to use mediation effectively the lecturer had to firstly acknowledge the complexity and challenging nature of the task and make this quite explicit to students. Such recognition was critical if the lecturer intends to interact positively and help students move from an uncomfortable state of disequilibrium (a state of extreme discomfort) to a comfortable state of equilibrium. It was also assumed that this discomfort motivates students to learn, and drives them into understanding content in order to reduce the level of discomfort. In sum, the stress must be approached from both the lecturers and the student's perspective, as leaving it to the students may prove too overwhelming. The demanding nature of the task

Copyright © 2006, Idea Group Inc. Copying or distributing in print or electronic forms without written permission of Idea Group Inc. is prohibited.

also meant that the possible stress could be carried for the duration of a semester, a significantly longer time than traditional assessment completed in 3 to 5 weeks.

To counter these factors, mediation was implemented in a deliberate way. The lecturer became the "fellow explorer" (Feurerstein, 2001) in a student's learning journey. As noted, students attend a 1-hour tuteshop with the lecturer and then have a second hour to construct their Web sites. In this second hour students were encouraged to invite the lecturer to any, or all of their group meetings, of which two were compulsory. At these meetings (which can take place outside the computer labs) students and lecturer sat together and discussed emerging concerns about the process, tasks, content, solutions, interview questions, or concept-map interpretation, or indeed anything they wished to reflect on which contributed to the development of their Web site, thus employing a constructivist and sociocultural approach to learning. During these chat sessions with students, emphasis was placed on what they had accomplished and what was yet to be accomplished. The journey and process of learning was made apparent to students and their potential to learn and achieve, in line with Vygotsky's zone of proximal development (Woolfolk, 2003), was recognized and supported. The meeting schedule incorporated two compulsory meetings, not for the benefit of the students who managed time well, but for the students who were not skilled in time management or indeed were recalcitrant. It enabled the lecturer to monitor those who needed assistance in this area and provided additional mediation. Failure to follow up on these students may have resulted in unnecessary stress in the final weeks leading up to the submission of the assessment or worse, failure.

In addition to the group assessment, other processes—contracts, problem-based learning, and mediation—were implemented which impacted on the ability of each group to function more as a team, thereby providing peer support during this stressful time. Each group was encouraged to allocate a "driver" to each of the subtasks who then became responsible for the data gathering, synthesis, and final production and high quality of one particular subtask. They requested assistance from their peers to achieve their personal goals of the subtask. For example, the teacher interview is dependent on asking relevant questions. The driver of this subtask is to ask each member to compose four to five questions they would like to ask the teacher or student and then reflect on all contributions to arrive at a sensible and feasible list. The final list is then presented to the group for approval and which can then be presented to the mediator (lecturer) for further comment and critical reflection. In this way the group, which is both cooperative and collaborative, functions as a team as the responsibility of driving one subtask is significant in the final outcome of the group to produce the Web site and address the case-study problem.

So, the implemented structure of "driver" achieved two functions: one to alleviate student's stress and the other to facilitate further mediation. That these

Copyright © 2006, Idea Group Inc. Copying or distributing in print or electronic forms without written permission of Idea Group Inc. is prohibited.

first year students arrived at the end of this learning journey having been through a state of disequilibrium is evident from the sense of pride, accomplishment, competency, and joy expressed in their journal reflections as in the following:

This rich assessment task has allowed us to further understand our learning styles, how the other members in the group and how we work and how we needed to appreciate and make use of these differences in order to complete the assignments to the standard to which we were pleased. Working together has enabled everyone's talents to be utilized and we were able to gain new knowledge from one another by scaffolding each other's progress. We now feel confident in participating in a school environment where we will be required to work and contribute to planning and classroom management with other staff. (1st-year student, 2003)

And, "High expectations for preparation and persistence of independent learning throughout the unit. A high bar was set which has helped me to develop a university mindset over the course" (1st-year student, 2002).

Figure 9. The overview of the authentic task and the related subtasks

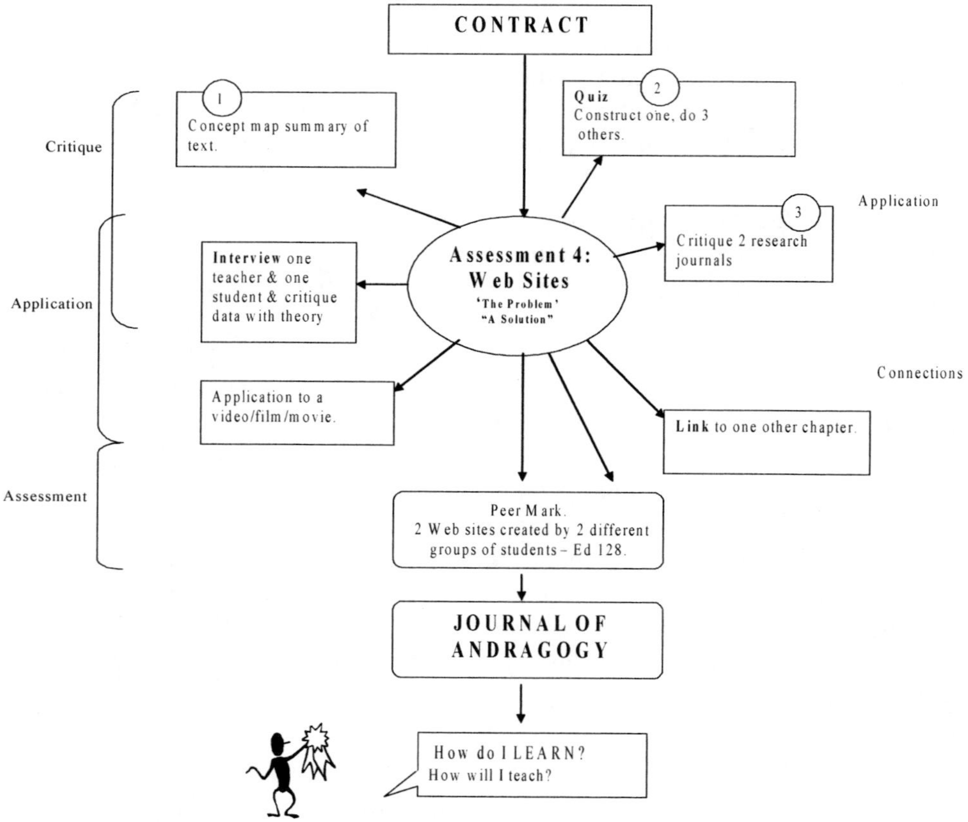

Copyright © 2006, Idea Group Inc. Copying or distributing in print or electronic forms without written permission of Idea Group Inc. is prohibited.

Using Roles, Structured Meetings, and a Journal of Andragogy

Another functional and successful process was the use of structured meetings. Students rotated the role of scribe at the meetings and documented the time, duration, members present, venue, agenda, actions required for the next meeting, actions achieved and often questions for the lecturer. This process assisted in the equitable and fair allocation of marks, a common criticism of group work, as each member could review the records for information if disagreement arose. Documentation of the process made individual's contributions public, furthering the motivation to participate fairly. The meetings notes were compiled and presented in the group's *Journal of Andragogy*, another process approach explained in the following. Structured meetings provided self feedback to the group as they compare their planned agenda to the actions achieved. From this students evaluated their progress as documented in the initial contract. However the main objective of the documented meetings was for all group members to confidently agree they all received the same group mark or different marks in extreme cases.

The *Journal of Andragogy* contained all authentic documents such as field notes, drafts, story boarding diagrams, logos, and photos. Students chose to divide this journal into the requested subtasks and often added other sections such as communication, and research into a theorist (who had to be presented in the group title in some way). It provided a comprehensive picture of the group's industriousness, as well as the learning of the group and as such was only to be assessed by the lecturer.

Using Groups

As discussed in the introduction to this chapter the current assessment task was developed partly from the need to create opportunities for students to achieve the unit outcomes and university graduate attributes, and partly from the nature of assessment, which suggests that the kind of assessment planned for students will determine what and how they learn. Group work was perceived to be an experience that students should have, given the information age the world of work is confronting and therefore this need for group work, collaboration, and cooperation dictated the assessment procedure. Other issues were addressed such as: how to stucture assessment, how many members should be in each group, what the group responsibilities would be and how students' time management strategies would be enhanced.

Copyright © 2006, Idea Group Inc. Copying or distributing in print or electronic forms without written permission of Idea Group Inc. is prohibited.

From yearly unit evaluations students nominated a group size of 4 as being the most effective for group work. After experiencing a number of groups' poor time management or lack of time-management strategies, several processes were devised to assist the groups to better achieve the outcomes. These were making meeting notes compulsory, making two meetings compulsory, creating a data-base in which all students were to submit their group name, focus area, and focus question/problem and appointing drivers to each of the subtasks. A meeting timetable was provided outside the lecturer's door so that students could see not only all the appointments, but offered an opportunity for an informal chance meeting with me, their lecturer.

Preparing Students: A Scaffolded Approach to Self, Peer, and Group Assessment

Students were prepared for their assessment roles through a scaffolding process prior to the implementation of the case study. In this scaffolding process, the author delivered a first-semester, first-year unit via a 1-hour lecture (both audio and face-to-face) as well as a 2-hour tuteshop, which was synchronous in some weeks or a combination of asynchronous and face-to-face in other weeks. Scaffolding was introduced within the tuteshop in two main ways. The first of these involved training students to be able to self assess. The second form of scaffolding involved training students to develop criterion for assessment. Both of these scaffolds were removed in second semester, as the same students undertook both units.

The training of students to be able to self assess occurred at the conclusion to each tuteshop, and involved a variety of learning experiences with which students were to self assess.

Students were trained to respond to the question: "What do you want a mark for?" following some joking and good humor based on why no marks were to be allocated for participation. This prompted students to think more critically about how they wished to be assessed. Preparation was required for each tuteshop. This took the form of a chapter summary (in any form, length, colour, design, as long as it was perceived to be effective by the student); the posting of two questions to WebCT, (with the responses recorded); and the selection of one question to which they individually chose to respond. The questions were all posted and therefore selected from WebCT. Responses were made prior to attending the tuteshop as it was the social context that was imperative to the ensuing tuteshop discussion, debate, and therefore learning.

Over the duration of the semester, students began to understand that no work or participation resulted in no knowledge and therefore no marks for tuteshops.

Copyright © 2006, Idea Group Inc. Copying or distributing in print or electronic forms without written permission of Idea Group Inc. is prohibited.

Collectively, students nominated several criteria in response to the question they composed and allocated marks to each. They then used the criteria to self mark and entered this mark themselves into a weekly mark sheet. So, in sum, they learnt over a period of one semester how to be critical of the work they were doing, in terms of effort and especially of learning outcomes. Many students became defensive, arguing that criteria such as the response to their posted question should be considered as well as their originality.

In the second form of scaffolding, students worked in groups of 3 writing six case-study scenarios and a theoretical interpretation for each. They passed three of these scenarios to another group who made their own theoretical interpretation and returned it for marking. Each group of students set up criteria and mark allocation for each of these three scenarios.

These two scaffolds proved critical in preparing students for the task ahead in the following semester. Students were learning while they were assessing. Although the time the lecturer spent marking was reduced, additional time was spent talking with students about their interpretation of the assessment, and thus contributed positively to the quality of their interpreted scenarios. They were looking for something that was black and white and could be replicated by everyone. The investment of time to assess in this way set the stage for authentic assessment in semester 2. Students went about the task in semester 2 uncon-

Diagram 1. Two approaches to scaffolding students' ability to self, peer, and group assess employed in semester 1

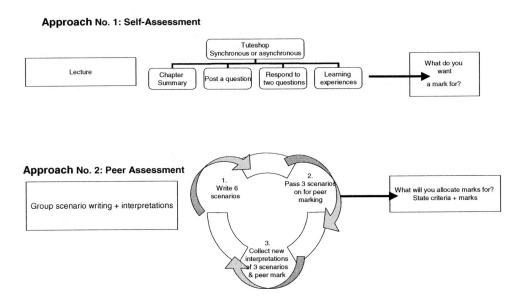

Copyright © 2006, Idea Group Inc. Copying or distributing in print or electronic forms without written permission of Idea Group Inc. is prohibited.

cerned about the issue of cloned assessments. They relished the opportunity to be creative and were excited about employing their ideas. In turn, their products were inspirational to mark and the diversity among the product, a Web site, was astounding. The marking task had been transformed from one of endurance to one of excitement and anticipation.

Summary of Case Study

It is critical that university educators get the mix of online learning and face-to-face design correct, since educators cannot escape the need to incorporate this in their curriculum of the world's future citizens and workers. The educational sector (in contrast to other courses and units which do not use computers), has a responsibility to ensure that the online learning design is correct, and would be deemed negligent if it failed to do so. The online learning design impacts on the quality and effectiveness of learning, as well as personal satisfaction and motivation. The unit was delivered in a flexible mode and therefore did not draw the criticism leveled at solely online units. Students engaged in critical and higher level thinking, managed their time well and cooperated and collaborated effectively to create a team product. They communicated extensively in writing via WebCT facilities, and gave and received feedback sensitively and effectively. They initiated and built some interpersonal contact online between campuses. In the words of two students:

I liked the way the assignments were set. You had to investigate in depth, to answer set objectives. This encouraged deeper learning in turn gaining a wider knowledge base. It left no room for "skimming" through, so to speak (1st year student, 2002).

And, "The course is by no means easy but due to its design and implementation I never feel as though it is going over my head" (1st year student, 2004).

As a visual means of summarizing, Table 9 has been included. The philosophy and pedagogy that underpinned the design of the authentic task, presented in Figure 1, has been translated into the specific principles and features. Further, the quality features for each task presented in the case study is listed to assist the reader to see the major group-assessment task in its entirety.

Task: Develop a Web site using a focus area to address the shortcomings or problems evident in a case-study school. Eleven subtasks, the compilation of a journal and a contract are required.

Advice was provided on how to work productively in a group, with drivers to be nominated for each subtask and each member contributed to each of the same subtasks. The sequence of the first three tasks and meeting format were suggested. Two compulsory meetings were scheduled with the lecturer.

Copyright © 2006, Idea Group Inc. Copying or distributing in print or electronic forms without written permission of Idea Group Inc. is prohibited.

Table 9. Overview, subtasks, and quality features of the assessment task

PRODUCT: Website	
Group Sub-Tasks	**Summary of Strategies and Quality Features**
1. Choose a focus area (e.g., discovery learning, motivation, metacognition)	Grp review topics in text. Discuss the implications of the topic to the subtasks & case study & its problems. Decide focus area, restate into a question/problem. ***Comment: Quality Features 3, 4, 5 were dominant. Mediation was provided by discussing focus areas, approving each to prevent duplication, & encouraging groups to restate the focus in terms of a question which would assist the case study school/problem.***
2. Complete the contract	Grp to complete the group goals, outcomes, rules for grp timetable, state focus area, question, group name and group members. ***Comment: Quality features 3, 5, 6, 7. Mediation was provided as groups embarked on the completion of the contract. The contract completed and submitted in week 2. Changes were to be expected. A proforma was produced as a model only.***
3. Summarize chapter in text	Grp decide the format – diagrammatic, mind map, headings & text. ***Comments: Quality features 1, 2, 4, 5, 7. Creativity encouraged to transform the text material into a stronger visual & meaningful presentation. Mediation available as students trialled various approaches. Some groups divided the task & then the 'driver' collated contributions, & all proofed final product.***
4. Choose teacher to interview, write questions, synthesize data, provide critique of teacher's application of theory	Story telling of personal experiences leading into questions, the selection of a teacher, and finally synthezing data and critiquing it against the text. ***Comment: Quality features 1, 2, 3, 4, 6, 7. Mediation was provided usually after questions were constructed and after the data was synthesized. Many groups elected to interview more than the one mandatory teacher. Transferred theory by liaison with professionals.***
5. Choose a video/film to analyze and apply focus area/theory (related to learning)	Narrating personal views of several videos/films. Discussing the potential of each film to demonstrate the theory/focus area. Selecting & then writing how the video demonstrates the theory. ***Comment: Quality features 1, 2, 3, 4, 5, 6, 7. Students watched several films before settling on the most applicable. During this selection they were constantly applying theory to interpret and explain the actions in the film. This usually occurred on weekends at each other's residences. Students considered this to be extremely challenging.***
6. Choose a Web site to support the focus area	Matching websites to theoretical position. Explaining how the site uses the theory. ***Comment: Quality features 2, 7. An abundance of Web sites to select. This task opened the possible variety and number of resources available with appropriate and relevant classroom applications. This moved students aware from theory and to finding good ideas based on the theory.***
7. Select research journals, appraise several (7) before selecting three to critique	Individuals tell group members the content/issues/ theoretical constructs in each journal. They write a critique in which all members proof read. ***Comment: Quality features 1, 2, 3, 5, 7. Mediation was used extensively as students grappled with research in education as a new concept. Application of theory to a variety of contexts was encouraged.***

Conclusion

In support of comments made by Rudestam and Schoenholtz-Read (2002), a shift in thinking is required by educators wishing to utilize the learning opportunities afforded by technology. It is not appropriate to use old and practiced pedagogies in a new technological e-learning environment. Viewing technology as a management system only limits its potential to enhance learning, but when viewed as a system to support cooperation, collaboration, development of relationships, and socially constructed learning, then technology can be seen as a medium for creating productive environments (Schrage, cited in Rudestam &

Copyright © 2006, Idea Group Inc. Copying or distributing in print or electronic forms without written permission of Idea Group Inc. is prohibited.

Table 9. cont.

PRODUCT: Website	
Group Sub-Tasks	**Summary of Strategies and Quality Features**
8. Construct a quiz as a group and individually complete three group quizzes; Advertise quiz on discussion board	Group reviewed knowledge of quizzes, then decided on format. Produced numerous items and allocated a marking criteria. Groups were responsible for sending out their quiz and collecting quizzes for marking. A summary of all quizzes and results was to be maintained. *Comment: Quality features 1, 2, 3, 4, 5, 6, 7. This strategy enhanced learning as something scholarly and fun. It provided a simulated teaching experience. Mediation was provided as students sought validation on the type of questions asked, the length and the challenge within.*
9. Link focus area to two other areas of learning in the text	Develop meaningful connections between three theoretical approaches. *Comment: Quality features 1, 2, 3, 5, 6, 7. Students linked using mind maps, or identifying overlaps in the theoretical approaches.*
10. Peer marking of 2 Web sites	Application of knowledge, valuing creativity, providing critical audience for the final product. *Comment: Quality features 1, 2, 3, 4, 5, 6, 7. Students identified individuality of knowledge & presentation. Transferred criteria developed in tuteshops to each site. The marks allocated were 'real' and contributed to final mark.*
11. Respond to the initial problem	Data from the focus area used to resolve the identified problems or issues in the problem case study. *Comment: Quality features 1, 2, 3, 4, 5, 6, 7. This provided the real focus and purpose for collecting data from a variety of sources including theoretical and practical. The nature of each focus area of study meant each group had the freedom of using their particular 'lens' to see the problem. Students felt comfortable and proud in the resolutions they provided. A most challenging task requiring mediation.*

Schoenholtz-Read) as clearly illustrated in the previous case study. One student had the following to say: "I have not encountered any other units that have the same innovative style as you present, and that give the feeling of achievement to me personally" (2nd year student, on reflection).

The success of e-learning is premised on the ability of designers of learning to focus on making learning available by using course content, readings, and listed assessment tasks, rather than focusing on delivering instruction. What is required is a fluid and interactive environment to spawn learning. Conversations, as an example of engendering this fluidity, expedite learning in a virtual space. It is clear the power of messages, their psychological interpretation, the intended and unintended nuances, the boundaries created by these communications, the sense of presence, all need to be factored into types of assessment suitable for e-learning and their related contexts. Shaw (2001), in his alert to educators about the mistakes made in designing online learning, identifies two: an underestimation of the time and resources required, and the ill-considered simplicity of transferring face-to-face delivery to online. The case study is but one example of how face-to-face delivery has not been transferred but reconceptualized to exploit the opportunities of technology to enhance learning. Within this reconceptualization, individuals were empowered in their learning through an integrated assessment approach based on knowledge sharing, likened to a team approach. The depth of learning through the assessment approach may not have been possible if it were not for the integration of technology. The words of one

Copyright © 2006, Idea Group Inc. Copying or distributing in print or electronic forms without written permission of Idea Group Inc. is prohibited.

student used to sum her experience seemed to say it all: "It was exciting, at times frustrating… but darn it, I learnt so much!" (Nicole, 2003)

The theories of situative and social constructivism and deep intellectual approaches to learning along with the principles and features which were represented in Figure 1, and used as the framework to plan authentic assessment, have been operationalized throughout the discussion of the assessments offered within the case study and their integration with technology. It is hoped the reader has been able to follow these through and is informed sufficiently so as to create their own for their learning context.

The Future

The move away from a testing paradigm may be apparent by the use of peer and group assessment and while they are still being perpetuated as a means of learning the author has proposed future learning designs be reconceptualized within a team-centered approach. This is significantly different from group learning, embracing such features as noted by the New Zealand America's Cup syndicate in 1995 as:

- *Works in an environment which encourages every member to make meaningful contribution*
- *Has a high degree of personal integrity and honesty*
- *Recognises personal goals but not hidden agendas*
- *Continuously monitors and improves its [team] performance*
- *Is fun to be in.* (Gilson, Pratt, Roberts, & Weynes, 2000)

The future, fast-paced world and its emphasis on knowledge management and sharing of knowledge resources must transcend the way educators design and deliver courses and units of study. The case study is an example of strong alignment with teams. The inclusion of self, peer and group assessment within a single unit of study has supported a coproduction of knowledge and typified a knowledge sharing approach to harness the synergy of collective knowledge. Although this case study was positioned in education its design has application to a variety of teaching contexts in which team and knowledge sharing through e-leaning is valued.

Copyright © 2006, Idea Group Inc. Copying or distributing in print or electronic forms without written permission of Idea Group Inc. is prohibited.

References

Alexander, S., & Boud, D. (2001). Learners still learn from experience when online. In J. Stephenson (Ed.), *Teaching and learning online: Pedagogies for new technologies*. London: Kogan Page.

Biggs, J. (1999). *Teaching for quality learning at university*. Buckingham: Open University Press.

DeBono, E. (1999). *Six thinking hats*. MICA Resources.

Derry, S. J., Gance, S., Gance, L. L., & Schlager, M. (2000). Toward assessment of knowledge-building practices in technology-mediated work group interactions. In S. P. Lajoie (Ed.), *Computers as mindtools: No more walls* (pp. 165-196). NJ: Lawrence Erlbaum Associates.

Feurerstein, R. (2001). *What is mediated learning experience?* Retrieved January 17, 2002, from http://www.icelp.org

Gilson, C., Pratt, M., Roberts, K., & Weynes, E. (2000). *Peak performance: Business lessons from the world's top sports organisations*. Netley, SA: Harper Collins Business.

Hudson, B. (2002). Critical dialogue online: Personas, covenants, and candle-power. In K. E. Rudestam & J. Schoenholtz-Read (Eds.), *Handbook of online learning*. Thousand Oaks, CA: Sage Publications.

Jonassen, D. H., & Carr, C. S. (2000). Mindtools: Affording multiple knowledge representations for learning. In S. P. Lajoie (Ed.), *Computers as mindtools: No more walls* (pp. 165-196). NJ: Lawrence Erlbaum Associates.

Newmann, F. (1997). *Let's focus on intellectual quality*. Retrieved July 20, 2004, from http://www.wcer.wisc.edu/publications/WCER_Highlights/Vol.9_No.1_Spring_1997/Focus_intellectual_quality.html

Resnick, L. B. (1991). Shared cognition: Thinking as social practice. In L. B. Resnick, J. M. Levine, & S. D. Teasley (Eds.), *Perspectives on socially shared cognition* (pp. 1-20). Washington, DC: American Psychological Association.

Rudestam, K. E., & Schoenholtz-Read, J. (Eds.). (2002). *Handbook of online learning*. Thousand Oaks, CA: Sage Publications.

Shaw, K. (2001). Designing online learning opportunities, orchestrating experiences and managing learning. In J. Stephenson (Ed.), *Teaching and learning online: Pedagogies for new technologies* (pp. 175-181). London: Kogan Page.

Copyright © 2006, Idea Group Inc. Copying or distributing in print or electronic forms without written permission of Idea Group Inc. is prohibited.

Sherry, L., & Gibson, D. (2002). The path to teacher leadership in educational technology. *Contemporary Issues in Technology and Teacher Education, 2*(2). Retrieved from http://www.citejournal.org/vol2/iss2/general/article2.cfm.

Woolfolk, A. (2003). *Educational psychology* (8th ed.). Boston: Allyn & Bacon.

Copyright © 2006, Idea Group Inc. Copying or distributing in print or electronic forms without written permission of Idea Group Inc. is prohibited.

Chapter VI

Culture of Critique:
Online Learning Circles and Peer Reviews in Graduate Education

Margaret Riel
Pepperdine University, USA

James Rhoads
Citrus College, USA

Eric Ellis
Treasure Valley Community College, USA

Abstract

In this chapter, we explore a strategy, "online learning circles," for helping students develop their own authority and trust in evaluating research and a respect for the authority of their peers. Our goal is to examine this online collaborative structure and its ability to foster a culture of constructive critique in graduate-school education. The data we analyze includes peer-review messages and survey responses. Student message data are coded for type and quality of peer review. The survey data is used to understand the students' perspective about their experience in learning circles and their judgment of the quality of feedback they offered and

Copyright © 2006, Idea Group Inc. Copying or distributing in print or electronic forms without written permission of Idea Group Inc. is prohibited.

received from their peers. This research addresses two important issues. First, it evaluates a structure, learning circles for group work in graduate online education; and second, it explores the type and form of peer feedback from within this collaborative structure. Learning circles did provide a structure for peer review but there are reservations and issues involved in helping students to develop the trust needed to work together effectively. The second issue revolves around authority in the process of peer review. Under what conditions are students willing to be critical and to accept criticism from their peers as legitimate? To do this involves a process of reacculturation that is difficult to create in courses of limited duration but may be one argument for the advantages of creating a cohort model of education in either on-campus or online programs of study.

Introduction

Much of early schooling requires students to acquire knowledge alone with limited opportunities for inquiry, interpretation, design, and critique. In contrast, graduate education, either online or on-campus, requires students to engage in a creative process of analytic interpretation, question-driven inquiry, and crucial reflection with the eventual goal of creating new knowledge. Group projects or peer feedback on projects engage students in deeper learning because these activities often involve a discussion of alternative interpretations and some accommodation to different strategies for accomplishing a task. This requires a trust in thinking and a willingness to experiment with ideas and approaches, some of which may need to be discarded.

Moving from knowledge acquisition to knowledge construction can be very difficult for students, who often vary in their ability to work collaboratively or offer constructive criticism. Peer review requires students to make evaluative judgments on the progress of their peers. This process requires a shift in many of the cultural assumptions students hold about school in general and graduate education in particular.

One reason a "culture of critique" is difficult to develop stems, in part, from graduate students' expectations of their relationship to their instructors. Many students come to the university with the expectation that they will learn from the experts, their instructors. These same expectations are greater in online courses where students frequently ask for more feedback from their instructors. While online instructors might appear to be available more frequently, they face the same time constraints of on-campus university teaching, limiting their ability to engage in extensive one-on-one interaction.

Copyright © 2006, Idea Group Inc. Copying or distributing in print or electronic forms without written permission of Idea Group Inc. is prohibited.

Students have been conditioned to think of evaluative feedback as personal and private. However, the comments made by instructors to students are often very repetitive. If students were willing to receive their feedback in a public online forum accessible to all students in the class, the instructor could use examples to highlight problems that are likely to be encountered by a number of students in the class. Since graduate students often return from years of work experience, they bring valuable additional perspectives to the discussion. This valuable knowledge can only be exploited, however, if students can develop the trust and authority to offer and accept constructive criticism.

Building this trust is not easy. Many of the graduate students are in workplace positions where it was the role of a supervisor, for example a principal, to provide constructive feedback. Peer critique necessitates a reacculturation of students to help them develop a sense of trust in their own authority to evaluate the work of others and respect the authority of peer evaluation (Bruffee, 1999). This seems to be especially true when the graduate students are themselves involved in K-12 education. The traditional approach to education has fostered a school culture that displays a strong avoidance of wrong answers, constructive critique, or intellectual conflict.

Classroom habits carry over into professional dialogue; and, though teachers often have extensive critiques of their peers, they rarely develop the interpersonal trust to convey information in a way that constructively improves practice. Critique is viewed as the function of the administration. The consequence is a weakened professional community that loses the value of learning from one another.

A final factor challenging the creation of a culture of constructive critique in online programs has to do with the self selection of students into educational programs. Compared to students enrolled in on-campus programs, students in some online classes have been found to score higher on independent learning-style scales and score lower on collaborative- and dependent-learning-style scales (Diaz & Cartnal, 1999). If this finding is valid, then placing students in highly cooperative learning contexts is contrary to the way they approach learning and could lead to some dissonance. It should, it would follow, be even more difficult for them to work in a collaborative, interdependent framework than students who attend university classes on campus.

Peer Review

This book represents the burgeoning research interest in collaborative student learning and methods to evaluate group work in online education. The online

Copyright © 2006, Idea Group Inc. Copying or distributing in print or electronic forms without written permission of Idea Group Inc. is prohibited.

practices are in many ways similar to those that are described in research for peer evaluation in on campus education (Bruffee, 1999; Roberts, 2003; Topping, 1998). Peer review is often used for either summative or formative assessment of student effort, technical skills, and social attitudes (Brook & Ammons, 2003; Conway & Kember, 1993; Lejk & Wyvill, 2001; Li, 2001). Less often, peer review involves a process—shared learning through discussion of the ideas and negotiation of plans and goals for action or project work (Bruffee).

Studies of peer review divide into two groups. The first group of studies assumes peer review is an assessment process related to grading and fair assignment of credit for different parts of an assigned task. The second set of studies focuses on peer review as either a peer tutoring or peer group collaborative learning process. After considering these studies, we explore the use of "learning circles" as a structure for online peer review.

1. Peer Review as Assessment: Advising on Grade Assignment

Group tasks in university courses tend to be practice activities, games, or written tasks assigned by the instructor rather than selected by the students. Student learning is regulated by grades serving as a system of incentives or pressures. Any collaborative work is often completed outside of university class time and therefore not visible to the instructor. The final work or project is turned in to the instructor or sometimes presented to the class. University instructors, not always comfortable giving all of the students in the group the same grade, look to peer review as a strategy to help extract individual grades from group products. In this use, peer review is a monitoring of student effort and time on task (Brooks & Ammons, 2003; Conway & Kember, 1993).

Li (2001) reviews a number of strategies and formulas that have been created to determine individual grades by using students' "peer review" or evaluations of the relative effort of their partners on a set of component tasks. These formulas weight the aggregate scores from peers and the relative importance of the task with the project grade to calculate individual student grades. Students bring different conceptual and social skills and level of commitment to a group task, as well as different relationships with one another. The precision of the numerical scores masks the much more difficult issues of fairness of the assessment.

Peer review of the relative effort of one's partners evaluated early enough can increase the effect of external rewards on behavior. Students who are not working—"free-riders" or "social loafers"—can lower the morale of the group when the other students feel the work load is unfairly distributed (Brook &

Copyright © 2006, Idea Group Inc. Copying or distributing in print or electronic forms without written permission of Idea Group Inc. is prohibited.

Ammons, 2003). To address this problem, Brook and Ammons experimented with having students give (and withhold) rewards throughout the process of group work, rather than solely at the end. Since these experiments were conducted with students in business courses, they gave each student a finite amount of "pay" to distribute to the group members based on contribution to the group, attendance at group meetings, and social attitudes as they worked within their simulated company. As a result, peer review took place at multiple times through the course using specific evaluative criteria. This process of early identification of "lagging students" gave them a chance to improve, and also clarified the evaluative criteria of the project.

However, simply "telling" who did the work and identifying free-riders, either at the middle or end of a project, does not exploit students' ability to help one another. From the students' perspective, this form of evaluation of their friends is likely to be viewed as a form of treason, and group criticism of the less-popular students may lead to scapegoating. In either case, it is different than seeing students as social resources for one another's learning.

2. Peer Review as Negotiated Learning and Identity Transformation

Other characterizations of learning focus less on external factors and more on the social dimension of cognition (Bransford, Brown, & Cocking, 1999). Learning in this tradition is described as a process of enculturation into a community of practice (Bruffee, 1999; Vygotsky, 1978; Wenger, McDermott, et. al, 2002). Learning how to think, value, and work with the physical, technical, or mental tools of a community contributes to the transformation of the identity of the learner (Gee, 2003; Wenger et al., 2002). Identity as a member of a community is further shaped when a person creates new forms of knowledge that are valued by the community. The community then provides the feedback for reflecting on the change created by the creative work.

In order for students to gain mastery in an area that involves moving beyond a reception of information, they need to be invested in their work. This involves not only acquiring knowledge but also adopting the practices, using the rules of evidence and sharing the values of the people who do the work. In effect, students are trying on the identity of the people in the field they are studying. This level of investment is hard to create without a design which gives students choice in their learning projects. Graduate students are encouraged to select an area in which to develop their expertise so that they can become a member of that knowledge-building community. Learning in this area is tied with acquiring a new identity as a member of the intellectual community. Once students have a strong

Copyright © 2006, Idea Group Inc. Copying or distributing in print or electronic forms without written permission of Idea Group Inc. is prohibited.

interest in learning how to take on new roles, the grade becomes feedback on the process of change, rather than the motivation for their actions. But trying to create such a context where the work of learning is driving the student effort, rather than a preoccupation with grades, requires a transformation of the way that students approach schooling and the way instructors teach.

Rather than have students work together, and then try to divide up the work after it is done, it is possible to structure the work so that both the individual and group efforts are part of the learning landscapes.

3. Learning Circles as a Structure for Peer Review

Online learning circles are teams of learners situated in diverse locations who share a common goal of acquiring a deeper understanding of topics arranged around themes (Riel, 2004). Learning circles (also called study circles) have a history as an informal method for adult learning and social change. The Chautauqua Assembly in New York used this method in 1870 as a vehicle for providing higher education to people who were unable to attend college. Instead of formal classes, people sent for discussion materials, and then assembled in small groups to discuss them. They learned from one another in a democratic fashion, without the formal direction of a leader (Campbell, 1998). Over time and across countries, civic organizations, neighborhood communities, trade unions, churches, and social-justice groups have used learning circles to empower their members to make choices and take action.

Learning circles have also been used as a tool in the process of constructing a community of practice in schools (Collay, Dunlap, Enloe, & Gagnon, 1998; Funk, 2002). As a professional development strategy for teachers, learning circles are defined as small groups of professional educators who are committed to improving their practice and that of their larger community by mutual support of each other in teaching and learning a specified task. A synthesis of the essential characteristics of these learning circles includes democratic leadership, relational trust, constructivist learning, shared culture, assessment of group process, and documentation of circle work. Learning circles are viewed as nested in a larger community of practice and serve as the working units of the larger community (Funk).

Learning circles have been used online for student learning (Riel & Polin, 2004) and more recently in online graduate education (Riel, 2005). Electronic learning circles have supported the learning of elementary and high-school education for several decades (Levin, Riel, Miyake, & Cohen, 1987; Riel, 1985, 1990). At the present time, more than 5,000 elementary and secondary students around the world participate in learning circles on the International Education and Resource

Copyright © 2006, Idea Group Inc. Copying or distributing in print or electronic forms without written permission of Idea Group Inc. is prohibited.

Network (iEARN). This structure was designed in response to observations that the teachers and students who created an online project were much more invested in the learning than those who passively participated. In learning circles, each group sponsors a project and everyone participates in the projects of others. This local ownership makes it easier to align global project-based learning with local curriculum. The distinguishing characteristics of online learning circles are diversity of participants, development of relational trust, project-based learning with both individual and group ownership of projects, reciprocity of work on multiple projects, distributive leadership, phase-structured interactivity, collaborative publishing (Riel, 2004).

Using online learning circle structure to help graduate students support their action research projects required some minor modifications; however, the structure remains very similar (Riel, 2005; Riel & Polin, 2004). Distributed leadership, diversity, and constructed learning are essential elements. Fostering trust (Bryk & Schneider, 2002) is essential for success. The task is similar to that of professional development learning circles with continual dialogue around assessment and documentation an essential part of their action research. The small group exchanges are used to support the development of action research in areas that were important to the students. The network of ties can be a valuable resource for the people in the learning circles, but these ties are only valuable if the participants are willing to go past the perfunctory comments about each other's work and really engage in serious review of one another's work. It requires the work to build a culture in which critique is a resource, not a negative sanction.

Peer Review, Identity and Learning Circles: A Culture of Critique?

In this chapter, we explore how small group exchanges in the structure of learning circles make use of the educational resources represented by the collective knowledge of the group. In these learning circles, the task is the improvement of the quality of action research projects. Learning circles were used in this context to balance independent ownership of part of the process with reciprocal interdependence. The technology for collaboration visually displays the group work throughout its progress, taking away the need for students to report on who is, and is not, participating because the instructor can see for him or herself.

A second difference between this approach and peer review in university courses on campus is that without the physical ties to a single working location—the university—it is often easier to have students design projects situated in authentic workplace settings. When student learning is connected to their work,

Copyright © 2006, Idea Group Inc. Copying or distributing in print or electronic forms without written permission of Idea Group Inc. is prohibited.

it is likely to have more consequences for their professional development and identity (Wenger, 1998). This can make grades less salient as the form of reward for learning.

The circles were reformed each semester to give students the opportunity to work with most of the students in the cadre as this increases the exposure to different ideas. The goal in the setting is to extend the role of peer review to one of intellectual consultant rather then task manager. While students may be familiar with peer review, which involves rating the work habits of their peers, it is uncommon for them to offer evaluative feedback on the quality of peer thinking or problem solving. This form of review takes preparation and explicit instruction; it involves the work of creating a "culture of critique."

Research Questions

The questions we explore are:

- Can online learning be structured so that students are comfortable with giving and receiving public, rather than private, evaluations of their progress?
- Can students, over time, develop sufficient trust and authority to give and receive constructive critique from their peers?
- What type of critique do students provide for one another, and does it change over time working together?
- How do students evaluate the quality of their work in learning circles in comparison to working independently?

The Research Context

This research focuses on students enrolled in a 13-month Master of Arts in educational technology program taught primarily online with three face-to-face meetings. The students meet face-to-face at the beginning and middle of the program for 4 days each of intensive learning. At the end of the program, 4 days are used for reflections and final presentations of research projects. The rest of the educational experiences take place online in a range of contexts, employing both synchronous and asynchronous communication. The program uses a cohort model in which the same group of students moves through a set of courses together. This study examines one group of 20 students from their first course

Copyright © 2006, Idea Group Inc. Copying or distributing in print or electronic forms without written permission of Idea Group Inc. is prohibited.

in a summer—Introduction to Distributed Learning—and follows them through a three-semester course of action research with a culminating project presentation at the end of the program. This introductory course and the yearlong action research seminar were taught by the same person (one author of this chapter) who served as research advisor for the action-research projects. The yearlong sequence provided a context for examining how students developed their peer review skills.

The explicit goal of the graduate program is to help students develop a program of action research situated in their workplace. An equally important goal is to develop "service" leadership skills in the area of educational technology. This form of leadership places high value on the authority of one's peers and respects each person's authority to contribute to the community. The graduate program is structured to help students develop their action research while experimenting with different strategies of team leadership. The open structure of leadership in learning circles lends itself to this process and students are encouraged to take responsibility for the quality of all of the action-research projects in their circle. This might involve challenges to the approach that a student is considering. For many, this is not a simple process. It involves a serious reacculturation process (Bruffee, 1999) to create a learning culture that values open, constructive feedback from peers.

The role of the instructor as single "expert" was de-emphasized and students were encouraged to see the expertise was distributed. The instructor consciously modeled peer feedback. This distributed approach to expertise requires students to examine their experiences and draw connections between theoretical constructs and their life stories. To facilitate this type of work, the 20 students in this cohort were arranged in a series of smaller learning circles. The students were directed to meet with their learning circle each week to review their progress. This meeting was held synchronously in Tapped In®, a professional arena for group chats. The instructor joined one of the circles each week to discuss progress. The students in the learning circles also had asynchronous "threaded" discussions where their comments on each other's work were publicly available to all students in the course. The major work of supporting their action-research plans and projects were facilitated by these learning circle interactions.

The 20 graduate students were placed in a series of four learning circles over each of the four terms, with different circle partners each term and with evolving goals and tasks for each circle. This created a total of 16 learning circles (four circles each semester with five students in each circle). These online learning circles were similar to those used in primary and secondary education and those used in professional-development contexts in a number of important ways. They assumed a process of distributed learning with no person identified as the leader. Diversity was increased by having an opportunity to work with each of the members of the class in these small units. The students saw each other face-to-

Copyright © 2006, Idea Group Inc. Copying or distributing in print or electronic forms without written permission of Idea Group Inc. is prohibited.

face at the beginning, middle, and end of the program for 4 days at each time, and community circles were also used as a tool during these times to further build group trust.

Each of the graduate students pursued their own action research subject. The role of the others on their project was not as clear as with school-based learning circles. The students were each asked to serve as an advisory board or as "critical friends" in the design, implementation, reflection, and final presentations of action research. While each student designed action research in their own setting, the students were evaluated for their role as researcher and advisor on the research of others. In this way, each student had an advisory board independent of the instructor.

Research Methods and Data Analysis

To examine our research questions around peer review, we examined the work of a cohort of 20 students in Pepperdine University's Master's in Educational Technology Graduate program. The student work comes from three sequential one-unit courses on action research taught in the fall (September-December), spring (January-April), and summer (April-July).

In each session, students were asked to serve as consultants giving their learning-circle partners feedback on their work. While positive comments serve to reinforce students, the goal was to help students learn how to give and receive more extensive feedback in a context that improved actions, reflections, and writing. When the constructive criticism that the instructor supplied was made in public, it helped all students see how work could be improved. Therefore, the student reviews and instructor reviews were delivered in the public forum. If or when a student was unwilling to accept public comments, they could ask for and receive a private review through e-mail. Several students asked for private reviews, but in most cases the students were willing to have their work reviewed in the public setting. The instructor used student work as an opportunity to talk about how to improve research skills or work on some aspect of writing.

We drew on two sources of data for this analysis. First, we used the student messages that provided peer feedback exchanged in online learning-circle interaction. Before using this data, the students were informed by e-mail of the purpose of this analysis and given the option of having their materials removed. No student took this option. The second data source was student surveys evaluating learning-circle interaction. These surveys were completed after their second learning-circle session and again at the end of the year, with students

Copyright © 2006, Idea Group Inc. Copying or distributing in print or electronic forms without written permission of Idea Group Inc. is prohibited.

providing their perceptions of the value of peer review in this structured format. The surveys were voluntary and anonymous.

Student Messages Evaluating Peer Work

The students made use of many forms of technology (synchronous chats, e-mail, instant messaging, interactive Web journals, etc.) to facilitate learning-circle interactions, however the messages exchanged in online discussion forums were the most public part of their work. These forums are open to all students and faculty in the Pepperdine community and the students were aware of this open access. While we recognize that the messages we use do not represent the whole of their interactions, we think it represents a reasonable sample of the forms of help they provided one another.

In each of the courses, the students and the instructor exchanged between 600 and 800 messages in threaded discussion forums. Some messages were posted in the whole-class discussion forums and others were posted in threads only for learning-circle participants (groupings of five students). In the fall, the writing centered mostly around creating a literature review with messages coming from the second half of the 14-week course. For the spring session, learning-circle discussions centered on helping students refine, conduct, and write about their action research. In the first two courses, the discussion took place as learning circles—threads of dialogue in the larger course discussion forums. In the final spring course, each learning circle used the discussion boards of Tapped In®, a collaborative messaging and chat tool for learning circle interactions making it easier to separate the learning-circle messages from the class discussion forums.

The instructor read and responded to the action-research projects in the learning circles to provide explicit models of different ways of giving constructive feedback. Her goal was to move students past positive comments (affirmations) towards thinking collaboratively about the process of action research and to develop the ability to give thoughtful feedback to one another. Since the instructor's messages serve as models, we include them in the analysis, but keep them separated from the student's messages.

Coding Student Forum Messages

A modified method of discourse analysis was used to look at the forms of evaluation that students provided to one another in the threaded discussion of the online (asynchronous) environment. It involved coding messages that students

Copyright © 2006, Idea Group Inc. Copying or distributing in print or electronic forms without written permission of Idea Group Inc. is prohibited.

posted in the threaded discussion across 10 months (September to July), while engaged in action research.

Student messages were extracted from newsgroup or forum discussions and numbered by time and thread. Messages were read and coded in order of their thread—that is, all messages were ordered first by topic, and then by date and time. Messages sometimes referred to comments in previous messages or continued an online dialogue. Each message was coded in three main categories; either as a solicitation, evaluation, or reaction (cf. Mehan, 1979) or was determined to not be a part of the review process following the guideline in Table 1. These distinctions were easy to make with very high intercoder reliability.

Procedural messages and sociability comments were excluded from the analysis. Table 2 shows the total set of messages that were coded for this analysis.

The evaluation messages were then coded based on their content as containing one or more of the following affirmations: editorial/technical comments, extension of ideas, or constructive critique. Each evaluation message could receive up to four codes based on the presence or absence of these different forms of feedback.

Table 1. Messages coded as part of the review cycle

SOLICITATIONS—Help-seeking
　　Learning-circle messages that asked for specific help or offered materials for students to review. This might include listing a Web site or attaching files for review.
EVALUATIONS—Help-giving
　　Learning-circle messages that offered some form of response to the work of a peer. These messages contained different forms of feedback such as comments, editorial or technical help, suggestions of resources, strategies, or alternative approaches.
REACTIONS—Help-taking
　　Learning-circle messages that acknowledged help, responded to questions, or described changes made in a student's approach or writing.
NOT PART OF THE REVIEW PROCESS
　　Learning-circle messages that were not part of the peer-review cycle and were not include in the analysis. These included messages that focused on course logistics, assignments, or social issues.

Table 2. Total number of learning-circle messages related to review of student's work

	PEER REVIEW	INSTRUCTOR REVIEW	REVIEWED MESSAGES
FALL	59	14	74
SPRING	219	57	276
SUMMER	162	55	217
TOTALS	440	126	566

Copyright © 2006, Idea Group Inc. Copying or distributing in print or electronic forms without written permission of Idea Group Inc. is prohibited.

Table 3. Coding categories for content of evaluation messages

EVALUATIONS—Help-giving
- **AFFIRMATION**: Supportive, appreciative statements about the work, but without information that would lead the work to be revised. Comments about the student's work, use of colors, quality of writing, or general appreciation all fell into this category. Indirect compliments or encouragement (e.g., "You're on the way to having a publication.") also were coded as affirmations.
- **EDITORIAL/TECHNICAL:** Encompassed anything that could be construed as mechanical advice, but did not suggest major conceptual changes to the student's work. Misspellings, grammatical corrections, typographic errors, broken or missing Web site links, and font or color changes all represented situations where this code was appropriate.
- **EXTENSION**: Represented feedback from peer to student that was intended to give more to consider or new directions to explore. Personal stories that might be helpful, links or suggestions for new information locations, or other discussions of theory all represented extension. Importantly, extension contained no implied critique or attempts to question, reorient, or challenge ideas of the author.
- **CRITIQUE**: Constructive critique was used for feedback that challenged any aspect of what the student had written or presented and offered a different direction for the student to consider. Comments suggesting a different method, questioning an outcome, or suggesting a different approach were coded as critiques. Sometimes the critique also represented a "kickstart" for a lagging student; if the message suggested that the student was not fully exploring the subject or taking advantage of the peer-review process, this was coded as Critique.

Initially, each message was coded independently by two coders and then checked for concurrence. In situations where the coders scored the message differently, the coders recoded the messages to resolve inconsistencies. Once intercoder reliability was consistently higher then 85%, one coder coded the remaining data. The test of reliability at the conclusion of coding was 94%.

Student Surveys Evaluating Learning Circles

The same 20 students were also asked to complete a survey to evaluate their learning-circle experience across three semesters in terms of their trust, commitment, investment in the work of others, rate of participation, quality of the feedback and leadership. These voluntary, anonymous surveys were collected twice, once at the end of the second spring session (reporting on fall and spring) and again at the end of the summer session. Sixteen students completed the first survey; nine completed the final survey.

The surveys were completed via e-mail, and students used a code to link them. They were transmitted to a person who removed all identification except the code so that they could be analyzed anonymously. There was no way to identify nonrespondents so we do not know their reasons for not responding. While recognizing that the number of student surveys at the end of the year is low, the surveys do provide a student perspective on some of the issues of trust and quality that are not evident from coding messages. The survey responses are examined in the next section to provide students' perceptions of the collaborative process of peer support in learning circles.

Copyright © 2006, Idea Group Inc. Copying or distributing in print or electronic forms without written permission of Idea Group Inc. is prohibited.

Findings

Data Set 1: Peer Review Messages

As noted in Table 2, there were 566 messages that were part of the learning-circle review cycle across the year. Of these 566 messages, students posted 440, and the instructor posted 126. When the 440 student messages were coded into the three review categories, 148 (34%) messages were solicitations, 198 (44%) were evaluations, and 98 (22%) were reactions. The total number of messages from the first session, 59, increased to 219 in the spring session, then decreased in the fall session to 162. The evaluations became the set of messages used for looking at how students provided feedback to each other.

Instructor Critique of Student Work

The 129 messages posted by the instructor in the review cycle were all evaluations, since the instructor was not sharing work for students to review. In these 129 messages, there was an average of 2.2 different forms of evaluation per message across the year (Table 5).

For the fall session, the instructor's messages averaged 2.1 forms of feedback per message with almost all of the messages (14 out of 15) containing positive

Table 4. The number (and percent) of messages by code and session

	SOLICITATIONS	EVALUATIONS	REACTIONS	TOTALS
FALL	29 (49%)	17 (29%)	13 (22%)	59 (100%)
SPRING	77 (35%)	93 (43%)	49 (22%)	219 (100%)
SUMMER	42 (26%)	84 (52%)	36 (22%)	162 (100%)
TOTALS	138 (44%)	194 (44%)	98 (22%)	440 (100%)

Table 5. Forms of evaluation (affirmation, editorial, extensions, and critique) contained in messages posted by the instructor

	AFFIRMATIONS	EDITORIAL	EXTENSIONS	CRITIQUE	TOTAL EVAL.	TOTAL MSG.	TOTAL EVALS. PER MSG.
FALL	13 (41%)	2 (6%)	9 (28%)	8 (25%)	13 (22%)	14	229
SPRING	42 (40%)	20 (19%)	27 (26%)	15 (14%)	49 (22%)	60	1.73
SUMMER	33 (27%)	27 (22%)	38 (31%)	26 (21%)	36 (22%)	55	2.25
TOTAL	88 (34%)	49 (19%)	74 (28%)	49 (19%)	98 (22%)	129	2.02

Copyright © 2006, Idea Group Inc. Copying or distributing in print or electronic forms without written permission of Idea Group Inc. is prohibited.

feedback (Affirmations). The second form of feedback was almost equally likely to be an extension or a critique and less likely to be editorial.

In the spring session, the number of evaluation messages increased substantially from 14 to 60 messages. The number of codes per message dropped slightly (1.7). While 70% of the messages contained positive comments, this contrasted with 97% in the fall. There were 8 messages with single codes and these were equally distributed across the four types of types of evaluation. The decrease in positive comments was accompanied by an increase in editorial comments with about the same rate for extensions and a slight decrease in critical critique relative to the other forms of feedback.

In the summer, the instructor's messages averaged 2.3 different forms of feedback, with 33 of the 55 messages (60%) containing positive feedback. While the relative frequency of positive comments decreased, the use of extensions increased with almost 70% of the messages containing an extension of the student's ideas. Overall, 49 of the 129 instructor's messages (38%) contained critical or constructive criticism.

Students' Peer Critique

The students posted 194 evaluation messages with an average of 1.5 forms of feedback per message. They posted substantially more reviews during the middle session with a slight drop during the final session.

Of the 17 evaluation messages posted during the fall session, 11 of them (65%) provided positive feedback and more than a third (35%) contained some help in extending the ideas. Less then one-fifth of the messages (18%) contained constructive critique.

In the spring session, the number of forms of feedback per message was only slightly higher (1.3 forms of feedback per message) however the number of messages increased dramatically. The relative number of affirmations increased from fall session to spring with 68 out of the 93 messages (73%) containing positive feedback.

By the spring session, students' positive comments were slightly less frequent; 52 (62%) of the messages exchanged during that session included positive comments. There was an increase in the number of codes per message (1.82), which signals longer messages. Constructive or critical criticism appears to be the hardest form of feedback for students to give each other. It only accounts for 7% of all of the students' evaluations and was found in only 11% of the students' messages compared to 38% of the instructor's messages.

Copyright © 2006, Idea Group Inc. Copying or distributing in print or electronic forms without written permission of Idea Group Inc. is prohibited.

Data Set 2: Student Surveys on Learning Circles for Critique

In the first set of data, we looked at the forms of evaluation that students provided to one another in their learning-circle groups. The survey explored the students' opinions about the learning-circle collaboration. Questions explored the perceptions of individual student performance within the group, how the group reciprocated with invested time and communication, and the quality and usefulness of the communication. Structural questions about leadership, and whether the learning-circle membership should be periodically reorganized, were also included. While 75% of the students completed the survey for the first two sessions, the less than 50% return at the end of the year suggests caution in any assumption about trends over the whole year.

The Quality of Peer Review

Students were asked to evaluate the quality of the feedback they gave to their peers and the quality of the work they received from their circle partners (Table 7). In the fall, the students' rating of their skill took the shape of a normal distribution with 60% in the middle, 20% at the high end, and 20% at the low end. Over the course of the year, by self report, students gained skill in their ability

Table 6. Forms of evaluation (affirmation, editorial, extensions, and critique) contained in messages exchanged by students

	AFFIRMATIONS	EDITORIAL	EXTENSIONS	CRITIQUE	TOTAL EVAL.	TOTAL MSG.	TOTAL EVALS. PER MSG.
FALL	11 (52%)	1 (5%)	6 (29%)	6 (29%)	21 (100%)	17	1.24
SPRING	68 (58%)	16 (14%)	30 (26%)	30 (26%)	117 (100%)	93	1.26
SUMMER	52 (34%)	44 (29%)	42 (27%)	42 (27%)	153(100%)	84	1.82
TOTALS	131 (45%)	61 (21%)	78 (27%)	78 (27%)	291 (100%)	194	1.5

Table 7. Perceived quality of peer review

	THE QUALITY OF FEEDBACK PROVIDED			THE QUALITY OF FEEDBACK RECEIVED		
	LOW	MEDIUM	HIGH	LOW	MEDIUM	HIGH
FALL (n=15)	20% (3)	60% (9)	20% (3)	13% (2)	40% (6)	47% (7)
SPRING (n=16)	19% (3)	37% (6)	44% (7)	25% (4)	44% (7)	31% (5)
SUMMER (n=16)	0% (0)	44% (4)	55% (5)	11% (1)	44% (4)	44% (4)

Copyright © 2006, Idea Group Inc. Copying or distributing in print or electronic forms without written permission of Idea Group Inc. is prohibited.

to engage in the process of peer review. At the end, 55% of the students rated their feedback as high in quality and no one rated him or herself as low. While this change might signal a change in quality, it might also represent an increase in the development of confidence in students' ability to help their peers. There was almost no change in their perceptions of quality of the feedback that they received from their peers.

Student Investment in Group Success

The goal of action research is for students to select a critical problem or issue in their workplace. While some succeeded at selecting a problem they were passionate about, most of the students were working in areas in which they were invested. Students were less concerned about grades because the goal was to affect their career trajectory directly through their actions in their communities, and not indirectly with report cards. Learning circles involve a process of shared responsibility for work. It was not clear if students would be invested in the work of their peers. Students were asked to rate the sense of responsibility they felt for the quality of the action research of their circle peers (Table 8). They were also asked about the inverse: that is, did students feel the others in their circle invested in their work?

Students reported their investment in the work of their peers was moderate (81%) to high (21%) in the fall. There was a decrease in the spring with a high rate in the summer. Students' perception of the investments of others was consistent with the collective report of the students. In the spring, the students' perceptions of the investment and reported investment mirrored each other exactly. One fourth of the students were not invested in the work of their peers and did not believe that others were invested in their work. The rest of the students split equally between those that invested and perceived investment to be high and medium. In the summer, a mismatch can be seen. Over three fourths of the students (78%) report high investment but did not find this investment from their peers. It is possible that the respondents are the ones who were highly invested in the learning-circle process and the nonrespondents were those who

Table 8. Perceived reciprocal investment in student work

	STUDENT'S INVESTMENT IN THE SUCCESS OF THE ACTION RESEARCH OF OTHERS			STUDENT'S PERCEPTION OF THE INVESTMENT OF OTHER IN HIS OR HER WORK		
	LOW	MEDIUM	HIGH	LOW	MEDIUM	HIGH
FALL (n=16)	0% (0)	81% (13)	19% (3)	6% (1)	63% (10)	31% (5)
SPRING (n=16)	25% (4)	38% (6)	38% (6)	25% (4)	38% (6)	38% (6)
SUMMER (n=9)	0% (0)	22% (2)	78% (7)	22% (2)	33% (3)	44% (4)

Copyright © 2006, Idea Group Inc. Copying or distributing in print or electronic forms without written permission of Idea Group Inc. is prohibited.

were perceived as less engaged. The percentages reported on Table 8 are very similar for the nine students who responded to all three sessions.

Student Ability to Communicate Their Ideas and Solicit Help

Throughout the yearlong program, students needed to be able to communicate their action research in writing in a way that made it clear what help they needed from their peers. The circle work changed over time, but each semester students needed to review their work and ask their new partners for help. Generally, the tasks facing the circles each semester were:

- **Fall:** Generate action research questions, develop a literature review
- **Spring:** Conduct their action research cycles (1 & 2), and write reports
- **Summer:** Cycle 3—Report and write final action research report.

Students were asked how well they felt they communicated the nature of their work to the group and how clearly they understood the projects of others (Table 9). After the fall session, fewer than half the students (44%) felt that they communicated their project to others clearly and 56% felt that they understood the projects of others. By the end of the year, 89% of the students claimed that their communications were well specified while only 44% thought that their partners had clearly specified their projects. It appears from this data that students were not as effective in communicating their ideas as they thought they were.

Trust and Commitment

Willingness to share substantial comments on one another's work requires a sense of trust and responsibility to the group (Bruffee, 1999). The students were

Table 9. Perceived quality of communication with peers

	STUDENT COMMUNICATION OF PROJECT TO OTHERS			STUDENT UNDERSTANDING OF PROJECTS OF OTHERS		
	VAGUE	SOMEWHAT CLEAR	WELL SPECIFIED	VAGUE	SOMEWHAT CLEAR	WELL SPECIFIED
FALL (n=16)	6% (1)	50% (8)	44% (7)	0% (0)	44% (7)	56% (9)
SPRING (n=15)	7% (1)	17% (4)	67% (6)	7% (1)	47% (7)	53% (8)
SUMMER (n=9)	0% (0)	11% (1)	89% (8)	11% (1)	44% (4)	44% (4)

Copyright © 2006, Idea Group Inc. Copying or distributing in print or electronic forms without written permission of Idea Group Inc. is prohibited.

Table 10. Reported trust and commitment to the learning circle

	SENSE OF TRUST IN THE CIRCLE			STUDENT UNDERSTANDING OF PROJECTS OF OTHERS		
	WEAK	MODERATE	HIGH	WEAK	MODERATE	HIGH
FALL (n=16)	6% (1)	31% (5)	62% (10)	6% (1)	19% (3)	75% (12)
SPRING (n=16)	6% (1)	44% (7)	50% (8)	6% (1)	56% (9)	38% (6)
SUMMER (n=9)	0% (0)	44% (4)	56% (5)	11% (1)	11% (1)	78% (7)

asked to rate their sense of trust in the circle (weak, moderate, strong) and their level of commitment to their circle partners (Table 10).

The sense of trust that students felt in their learning circles seemed to hold relatively steady throughout the program. Students reporting a high level of trust in the circle started at 62%, this declined slightly to 50% and then increased to 56%.

The commitment of students to the circle increased slightly over the year, with 75% listing a high commitment in the first session and 78% at the end. Four students reported a weak commitment to their circle during one of the sessions, and only one student reported this for two sessions. The commitment to the circle may have more to do with the specific people in the circle than change over time.

Circle Leadership

No one was assigned to lead the groups. Students were directed to work as a team of leaders. Therefore, we asked students "Did this work or would it have been better to assign one person the role of facilitator or leader?"

After the first session, 88% of the students were confident that leadership was not a problem, and 94% indicated there was no need for an assigned leader (Table 11). This confidence remained high until the last session. A few more students at the end felt that some assigned leadership or structure would have helped the circle progress.

Table 11. Perceived need for leadership in learning circles

	LEADERSHIP WAS A PROBLEM IN THE LEARNING CIRCLE (n=13)			IT WOULD BE BETTER TO HAVE AN ASSIGNED FACILITATOR (n=13)		
	AGREE	NOT SURE	DISAGREE	AGREE	NOT SURE	AGREE
FALL (n=16)	0% (0)	12% (2)	88% (14)	94% (15)	0% (0)	6% (1)
SPRING (n=16)	19% (3)	6% (1)	75% (12)	88% (14)	6% (1)	6% (1)
SUMMER (n=9)	11% (1)	11% (1)	78% (7)	56% (5)	22% (2)	22% (2)

Copyright © 2006, Idea Group Inc. Copying or distributing in print or electronic forms without written permission of Idea Group Inc. is prohibited.

Table 12. Perceived usefulness of learning circle on individual research

	STUDENT WOULD HAVE LEARNED MORE WORKING ON HIS OR HER OWN			STUDENT'S WORK WITH OTHERS WAS CRUCIAL IN DEFINING MY ACTION RESEARCH PROJECT		
	AGREE	NOT SURE	DISAGREE	AGREE	NOT SURE	AGREE
FALL (n=16)	6% (1)	31% (5)	63% (10)	6% (1)	31% (5)	63% (10)
SPRING (n=16)	25% (4)	25% (4)	50% (8)	25% (4)	38% (6)	38% (6)
SUMMER (n=9)	11% (1)	11% (1)	78% (7)	11% (1)	22% (2)	67% (6)

Learning Outcomes

Interactions in learning circles take time and effort. We asked the graduate students if they thought that working with peers in the learning-circle structure helped or interfered with their progress on their action-research projects (Table 12).

Across the three sessions, more than half of the students rejected the premise that they would have learned more if they worked on their own research without helping their peers or being helped by their peers. About two thirds of the students in the fall (63%) and summer (67%) reported that their work with others had been crucial in defining their action research. In the spring, there is a drop to these reports. This pattern is essentially the same for the 9 students that responded for all sessions, suggesting that missing data is not responsible for the differences between fall, spring, and summer.

Analysis

Giving and Receiving Feedback in the Public Forum

Our first research question addressed the issue of student comfort in receiving and giving public, rather than private, feedback on action-research projects. With the exception of final grading and special requests, all of the instructor's feedback on student work was shared in the public forum. This allowed for a much higher rate of feedback from the instructor, and also strengthened the modeling of providing constructive criticism, helping students understand how such feedback increases the quality of performance, while minimizing the personal reaction. One source of evidence of increased comfort with public evaluation was the fact that there were few requests for private evaluation during the year and none during the final summer quarter.

Copyright © 2006, Idea Group Inc. Copying or distributing in print or electronic forms without written permission of Idea Group Inc. is prohibited.

A look at the content of student messages written as reactions to peer evaluations suggested that they accepted the concept of giving and receiving public critique. There were no messages that expressed any concern or challenged a review. Instead the messages expressed gratitude, responded to questions, and described how the feedback helped them change their focus or led to a new document.

Identifying the degree to which students become more comfortable with this process of public critique is more challenging. The results of the survey suggest that the students became more convinced of the value of others' input on their own research as the program progressed. This response, however, does not speak directly to how they preferred to receive their peers', or instructor's advice or criticism.

Providing Peer Feedback: Developing Trust and Authority

Our second question addressed students' ability to give and receive constructive critique. While difficult to create with one semester, it was unclear if a yearlong course would provide enough time to develop trust and authority that underlies the student-review process. Looking at students' feedback to their peers (Table 6), there is evidence that students did, in fact, learn to give and receive extensive feedback. More difficult to quantify is the students' comfort in offering criticism. There was undoubtedly significant private interchange between students that was likely underreported in their public postings; several messages referenced critiques that had been sent between students via e-mail. Significant feedback was exchanged in the public forums, but how authoritative students felt in offering this advice is unclear. Perhaps most telling is the increase from 20% to 55% in students who reported their belief that they were giving high-quality feedback. It seems likely that a student who feels they have something significant to offer will be more likely to do so than a student with doubts about the quality of their input.

Another possible marker of increased comfort can be drawn from the average number of codes per message. Message length was not coded as messages often contained embedded repetition of previous messages, quoted text from prior messages, or copied parts of student's work. Our analysis did not attempt to code the number of repetitions of an evaluative move since it would be very difficult to determine when one move ended and a new one started. However, generally messages that received multiple codes were longer and provided more in-depth feedback. With the rise from 1.3 to 1.8 codes per message over the course of the program, it seems fair to say that the student feedback became more complex as the year progressed.

Copyright © 2006, Idea Group Inc. Copying or distributing in print or electronic forms without written permission of Idea Group Inc. is prohibited.

Changes in Forms of Feedback

Our third question was concerned with forms of feedback that students would provide for each other. The largest increase was in the extensions, which are easier to provide then constructive critique. While constructive critiques increased over the year, students signaled their difficulty in providing this form of feedback by expressing their concern, "Please don't take this wrong"; discounting their expertise, "I don't pretend to know a lot about your work, but …"; or appealing to authority "I am only saying this because [name] said it to me."

Whether offering that feedback was more difficult is hard to say. It is important not to place too high a value on evaluative acts of criticism, since not every situation calls for the student to be redirected or corrected. With that in mind, however, it does seem that while students increased in their willingness to offer critique over the course of the program, they continued to be more likely to offer more technical, editorial comments. If we compare the instructor's evaluations with those of the students, the difference is that the students were more likely to give positive feedback (45% of the students' evaluations compared to 35% of the instructor's were affirmations) and the instructor was more likely to offer constructive critique (19% of the students' evaluations compared to 7% of the instructor's were critiques). Other than that, the relative percentages for editorial and extensions were very similar.

Student Assessment of Learning-Circle Collaboration vs. Independent Work

Finally, and now relying on the responses to the learning-circle survey, we wanted to understand the value the students placed on collaborative work in learning circles.

The survey responses suggested a contradiction: Students generally felt that over the year they were communicating better, offering better advice, and generally being more invested in the works of others; yet, they did not appear to see this progress in the work of others. It seems possible to envision a situation where students' reluctance to say hard things about each other's work would lead them to offer extension from their personal experience in hopes of making a difference, while at the same time hoping for very concrete constructive critique to make their own work better.

As a result of social concerns of students, the combination of the hope for the serendipitous discovery, and the desire for concrete assistance, seem to coexist. The trends shown in the coding of the messages suggests that possibly the students were breaking through this paradox as they completed the program, or

Copyright © 2006, Idea Group Inc. Copying or distributing in print or electronic forms without written permission of Idea Group Inc. is prohibited.

perhaps not. It is interesting to consider what a second year of interaction among these students would have been like, especially if they had been asked to start a new cycle of research after having completed their first cycle of research and presentation. Would they have returned to a more affirmative tendency, or would their baseline have been shifted to a more critical (or more extension-inclined) interaction? The results of this study do not give a clear picture, but seem to hint at the latter alternative.

Conclusion

The purpose of this analysis is to explore the creation of a culture of critique in an online education program. Difficult to create in a 14-week class, doing so in a 13-month program may have higher odds of success, but still requires significant effort and a conducive environment in order to establish the trust needed for effective public critique.

That students need trust is crucial to appreciate. Students are far less experienced with giving and receiving critique publicly; their educational history and professional career experiences are generally marked by private reviews between themselves and the instructor. An important part of convincing students to participate in a culture of critique is to show how others frequently make similar errors, or face similar challenges. Addressing these similarities publicly allows the collective group to develop deeper understandings and explore more ways to change the individual's work.

Constructive critique then rests heavily on dispelling the fear of getting wrong answers. Making critique public, or exposing to public comment the continual rethinking that is a part of learning, encourages distancing the student from the work so that they can consider alternative perspectives and develop a theoretical approach to problem-solving.

This research addressed two important issues: First, it evaluated a structure, learning circles for group work in graduate online education; and second, it explores the type and form of peer feedback from within this collaborative structure.

Learning Circle Structure

Students are often drawn to online learning for the perceived flexibility it offers. They expect this to mean they will work alone and at their own pace. Working as part of a cadre, and specifically within learning circles, represents a significant

Copyright © 2006, Idea Group Inc. Copying or distributing in print or electronic forms without written permission of Idea Group Inc. is prohibited.

shift from their expectations. This team-based approach to exploring and solving real problems in a community of practice provided a strategy to situate knowledge and skills in their own community.

Students rated the level of trust achieved in the group from moderate to high by the end of their experiences in learning circles. Another measure of trust was the willingness for the students to accept feedback in the open setting. In the first two sessions, some of the students' evaluations were sent through e-mail to individuals, but by the summer trimester all student feedback was shared in the group forum. This developed trust allowed written comments on students' action research to be addressed to the student and the class simultaneously, providing additional feedback for students and reducing the number of times the instructor needed to address a similar issue in student papers. The instructor often referred students to comments on similar papers, or used the research reports of other students as a possible model to consider in making revisions. This gave students many examples to guide their work and encouraged them to use peer resources. The amount of feedback that the instructor was able to provide on student work in learning circles was significantly increased by the open nature of the critiques while the energy spent repeating similar comments was diminished.

Each semester, learning circles were reformed with a different combination of students. This was done to increase the diversity of the people who offered help and to develop the ties to the larger cadre. However, it also required students to periodically stand back from their action research and summarize what they had accomplished for their new circle members. These retellings of the plan and process were practice for their final presentation where they would describe their research to a community audience. Asked about this process of regrouping, a third of the students found the process of changing circles disruptive and recommended fewer changes, but the rest of the students who responded found it valuable to shift to new partners. However, a structure that encouraged peer responses is subject to evaluations of uneven quality. While many students demonstrated skill, talent, and creativity in the review of the action-research projects of others, not all students were as comfortable making substantial suggestions. Each learning circle was a unique set of people who created a specific learning context. It may be that the difference in group makeup, and not increased experience in this form of learning, was responsible for the differences in perceptions about the success of learning circles. Student feedback provides one way of understanding how students experience this effort to have them work not independently but rather as members of a circle with communal responsibility for the work of others.

It is worth noting that most of the survey items show a definite dip in the students' assessment of the quality and value of the learning-circle experience during the middle of the program. This might be an artifact of the overall stress of the action

Copyright © 2006, Idea Group Inc. Copying or distributing in print or electronic forms without written permission of Idea Group Inc. is prohibited.

research cycle, or of the push to engage in peer evaluation. It is worth marking this pattern for comparisons in the future. It may represent initial concerns about distancing oneself from one's ideas and participation in a culture of critique.

Not surprisingly, students wanted to remain in circles that they saw as effective and switch out of circles that were less successful. While there was not a steady upward trend, this student's comment suggests that the intensity of preparing for final exhibition inhibited group work during the final semester: "the sense of responsibility to the group helped keep the work moving forward until the end when the work got so intense that participation fell off." One student reported difficulty in a circle that was less successful, "when a group isn't working hard but there is a high level of friendship—you don't want to report to the teacher that things are not going well." Another student reported using the learning-circle structure in her teaching, saying "the experience was very helpful and has changed the way I teach larger groups. I now use the small groups and make students accountable to each other."

Process of Peer Review

The second issue revolves around authority in the process of peer review. Under what conditions are students willing to be critical and to accept criticism from their peers as legitimate? Through all phases of their action research, students provided feedback to one another. This acceptance and participation in a community that provides regular, public, constructive criticism represents a significant shift from the practice of competitive grading. This shift involves a move away from student competition for the best grades to a commitment to help each member of the group to do well, and engages students in interpretive dialogue that crosses community lines.

Over the course of the year, the instructor's comments shifted from always including positive comments to including either praise or an extension. Extensions of ideas, a form of thinking with the student, may have served as an indirect form of positive feedback. Students also wrote fewer messages that contained only positive comments over the year, however they were more likely to make suggestions that extended the work of a peer in the same direction, rather than take the risk of suggesting a redirection.

The results of analysis show a definite increase in the willingness of students to engage in a public evaluation of peers' work. While the students generally felt the value of other students' input stayed the same throughout the program, they increased their rating of their own ability to provide quality feedback higher over the duration of the program. Squaring this reported disparity—improved outgoing critique without improved reciprocal critique—presents some challenges, but the

Copyright © 2006, Idea Group Inc. Copying or distributing in print or electronic forms without written permission of Idea Group Inc. is prohibited.

students' increased willingness to participate in a culture of public critique is clearly evident.

References

Bransford, J. D., Brown, A. L., & Cocking, R. R. (Eds.). (1999). *How people learn: Brain, mind, experience and school.* Washington, DC: National Academy of Sciences—National Research Council.

Brooks, C., & Ammons, J. (2003). Free riding in group projects and the effects of timing, frequency, and specificity of criteria in peer assessments [electronic version]. *Journal of Education for Business, 78*(5), 268-272.

Bruffee, K. A. (1999). *Collaborative learning: Higher education, interdependence, and the authority of knowledge* (2nd ed.). Baltimore: The Johns Hopkins University Press.

Bryk, A. S., & Schneider, B. (2002). *Trust in schools: A core resource for improvement.* New York: Russell Sage Foundation.

Campbell, S. L. (1998). *Guide for training study circle facilitators.* Study Circles Resource Center. Retrieved July 23, 2004 from http://www.studycircles.org/pdf/training.pdf

Collay, M., Dunlap, D., Enloe, W., & Gagnon, G. (1998). *Learning circles: Creating conditions for professional development.* Thousand Oaks, CA: Corwin Press.

Conway, R., & Kember, D. (1993). Peer assessment of an individual's contribution to a group project [electronic version]. *Assessment & Evaluation in Higher Education, 18*(1), 45-57.

Diaz, D. P., & Cartnal, R. B. (1999). Students' learning styles in two classes: Online distance learning and equivalent on-campus. *College Teaching, 47*(4), 130-135. Retrieved March, 15, 2005, from http://www.LTSeries.com/LTS/html_docs/grslss.htm

Funk, C. (2002). *Creating learning communities through circles of learning.* TX: Sam Houston State University.

Gee, J. P. (2003). *What video games have to teach us about learning and literacy.* New York: Palgrave/St. Martin's.

Lejk, M., & Wyvill, M. (2001). Peer assessment of contributions to a group project: A comparison of holistic and category-based approaches [electronic version]. *Assessment & Evaluation in Higher Education, 26*(1), 61-72.

Copyright © 2006, Idea Group Inc. Copying or distributing in print or electronic forms without written permission of Idea Group Inc. is prohibited.

Levin, J., Riel, M., Miyake, N., & Cohen, M. (1987). Education on the electronic frontier: Tele-apprentices in globally distributed educational contexts. *Contemporary Educational Psychology, 12*, 254-260.

Li, L. (2001). Some refinements on peer assessment of group projects [electronic version]. *Assessment & Evaluation in Higher Education, 26*(1), 5-18.

Mehan, H. (1979). *Learning lessons: Social organization for the classroom.* Cambridge, MA: Harvard University Press.

Riel, M. (1985). The Computer Chronicles Newswire: A functional learning environment for acquiring literacy skills. *Journal of Educational Computing Research, 1*, 317-337.

Riel, M. (1990). Telecommunications: A tool for reconnecting kids with society. *Interactive Learning Environments, 1*, 255-263.

Riel, M. (2004). Electronic learning circles. In A. Kovalchick & K. Dawson (Eds.), *An Encyclopedia of Educational Technology: Vol. 2.* (pp. 407-414).

Riel, M., (2005). Building communities of learners online. In G. Kearsley (Ed.), *Online learning.* NJ: Educational Technology Publications.

Riel, M., & Polin, L. (2004). Learning communities: Common ground and critical differences in designing technical support. In S. A. Barab, R. Kling, & J. Gray (Eds.), *Designing for virtual communities in the service of learning.* Cambridge, MA: Cambridge University Press.

Roberts, T. S. (Ed.). (2003). *Online collaborative learning: Theory and practice.* Hershey, PA: Idea Group Inc.

Topping, K. (1998). Peer assessment between students in colleges and universities. *Review of Education, 68*(3), 249-277.

Vygotsky, L. S. (1978). *Mind in society: The development of higher psychological processes.* Cambridge, MA: Harvard University Press.

Wenger, E. (1998). *Communities of practice: Learning, meaning and identity.* New York: Cambridge University Press.

Wenger, E., McDermott, R., & Snyder, W. (2002). *Cultivating communities of practice.* Boston: Harvard Business School Press.

Copyright © 2006, Idea Group Inc. Copying or distributing in print or electronic forms without written permission of Idea Group Inc. is prohibited.

Chapter VII

Learning English for Technical Purposes: The LENTEC Project

Anne Dragemark
Göteborg University, Sweden

Abstract

This chapter presents some research findings in the area of self assessment, obtained from the European Leonardo Project: Learning English for Technical Purposes (LENTEC), carried out 2001–2003. In this project, upper-secondary vocational students solved problem-based learning cases in a virtual environment. The project aimed at stimulating upper-secondary vocational school students from six different European countries to improve their English-language skills. It also aimed at helping foreign-language teachers to develop their skills in online tutoring. A validation study was undertaken and the results underscored that students need time and practice to assess their own results. According to students and teachers, a majority of the students became more aware of their own language-learning development. The teachers in the project developed a new teacher role where some of the responsibility for assessment moved from them to the students themselves. This not only motivated the students but also gave them added time for actual language learning.

Copyright © 2006, Idea Group Inc. Copying or distributing in print or electronic forms without written permission of Idea Group Inc. is prohibited.

Introduction

The aim of the chapter is to describe the use of self assessment in the LENTEC project, the materials used, and how the involved partners tried to validate the results obtained when using this approach to assessing language learning in an online environment.

The LENTEC project, which was carried out between 2001-2003, involved upper secondary vocational students from six different European countries. The students solved problem-based learning cases in a virtual environment to improve their English language while giving their foreign language teachers an opportunity to develop their online tutoring skills.

Questions investigated in relation to assessment were: Did students feel that their language skills improved? What opinions did their teachers express? In what ways could progress of learning be recorded or measured? To what extent did students make reliable self assessments?

Theoretical Background

Autonomous learning and the ability to evaluate one's own learning has become an educational aim in many European school systems. This is reflected in a range of national modern-language syllabi and curricula and in European language policy in general (Delors et al., 1996). It is one way to prepare young people for lifelong learning and thus prepare young people for increased work mobility in Europe. Especially, the smaller countries have realized that a basic knowledge of languages other than their own is essential to promote their own products and make use of technology from abroad (Perkins, 2004b). A central aspect of the lifelong learning concept is to be able to assess one's progress and attained results and, on the basis of this, make judgements on learning goals. When learners become more independent, it is neither possible nor desirable for teachers to be the ones to assess the students' learning in all areas. In fact, formal or traditional language testing is seldom used as the sole instrument for placement, diagnosis, and measurement of achievement outside educational bodies. Instead, language assessment has become increasingly more authentic and direct as it involves students in tasks in which they would normally be involved in their daily lives. The assessment in such situations is primarily formative and process-focused rather than summative and product-focused. As maintained by Gipps (1994), assessment is becoming part of and a way to support the learning and teaching process. Educational theory supports this development, especially modern constructivist theories of how knowledge is constructed. The importance of autonomy is often stressed (Holec, 1988).

Copyright © 2006, Idea Group Inc. Copying or distributing in print or electronic forms without written permission of Idea Group Inc. is prohibited.

According to many researchers, the metacognative function plays an important role in the construction of new knowledge, as it has to do with planning, understanding, and the control of learning (Allwood & Jonsson, 2001; Purpura, 1997). "Access to metacognitive processes for pupils can come from a process of guided or negotiated self assessment, in which the pupil gains awareness of his or her own learning strategies and efficiency" (Gipps, 1994, p. 28).

Research has shown that learners often have a comparatively accurate picture of their actual ability levels and results. Oscarson (1980, 1984) found that adult language learners' self assessment showed strong relations to other more objective criteria such as test results and teacher assessments. In an overview, Blanche and Merino (1989) concluded that there is a "consistent overall agreement between self assessments and ratings based on a variety of external criteria" (p. 315). Bachman and Palmer (1989) investigated validity in self ratings with the help of confirmatory factor analyses and found that "self assessments can be reliable and valid measures of communicative language abilities" (p. 22). On the basis of a metaanalysis of 10 correlation studies, Ross (1998) established that "self assessment tends to provide robust concurrent validity with criterion variables" (p. 16). This also seems to hold true in other areas. Falchikov and Boud (1989) compared "self assessed marks and teacher marks" in different subjects and came to a similar conclusion.

Some less successful studies have also been reported. In a Canadian study with English-speaking pupils in French immersion classes, Peirce, Swain, and Hart (1993) could only find weak correlations between self assessments and test results of listening, reading, speaking, and writing skills. Similar results were found by Janssen-van Dieten (1992), who investigated immigrants' assessments of their skills in Dutch as a second language.

Other aspects which may influence students' ability to evaluate their own language learning are their interpretation of what is to be evaluated, their language learning background and experience, as well as their self esteem (Oscarson, 1998). Varying degrees of self esteem and self confidence can also influence the assessment of one's own knowledge in different ways. Students from cultures where it is not the norm to assess one's own achievements may score lower on a self assessment rating than when ranked by peers or teachers. Research on gender differences in this area seems to be inconclusive.

Research conducted by Falchikov and Boud (1989) and Prohaska and Maraj (1995) also suggests that beginners and students with rudimentary skills have a tendency to overestimate their abilities, while students who are more proficient are inclined to underestimate their abilities.

According to the theory of transactional distance (Moore, 1997), distance learning is not only about learners being separated from others in their learning environment, that is teachers or other students with whom they are collaborating,

Copyright © 2006, Idea Group Inc. Copying or distributing in print or electronic forms without written permission of Idea Group Inc. is prohibited.

it is a pedagogical concept that includes aspects of the nature and degree of the learner's autonomy and self directedness. The greater the transactional distance, that is the space or time between this interaction, the more autonomy the learner will need to exercise and in this way share responsibility for his or her learning process (even in the case of not fulfilling the set goals). Moore found that distance programs that were "more structured than dialogued" encouraged students to be teacher-independent. When students have not reached the stage where they are able to practise productive self directed learning, it is the teacher's responsibility to help them attain these skills. Dialogues between learners, for example on a Web site in virtual groups or in pairs, are one way to help students learn through interaction. This way, distance learners are able to share in their own construction of knowledge.

Problem-based learning (PBL)—in a distance, online environment where the students are forced to express themselves in writing and comment on each other's work in the form of so-called metacomments—is believed to develop the students' ability to self reflect on their own progress and learning (Björk, 2004).

The TENTEC and LENTEC Projects

In 1999, a European Union project (Leonardo da Vinci programme), *Teaching English for Technical Purposes* (TENTEC, 1999–2000), was undertaken by Sweden, Austria, France, the Netherlands, and Slovenia. One of its aims was to improve teaching practice through cooperation between English-language teachers, vocational teachers, and industry by using a PBL model, where English was used as the medium of communication when the students jointly solved technical problems. In a PBL situation, students have to brainstorm around the given problem and identify what new knowledge they need. After this, the group members carry out the "research" and report their findings or solution. A Web site was created where new learning approaches and different "cases" were presented. Teachers were able to use the site, test methods and problems, and also had the opportunity to exchange and evaluate experiences with teachers in other European countries. The concept of self assessment was introduced to the teachers. The project focused on teachers and the use of PBL.

The logical continuation of this work was another project, *Learning English for Technical Purposes* (LENTEC, 2001-2003), coordinated by Polly Perkins, educational adviser modern foreign languages, Centrum voor Innovatie van Opleidingen (CINOP), the Netherlands. In LENTEC, the focus of project activities shifted from teachers to learners. LENTEC aimed at stimulating upper-secondary vocational students to improve their English-language skills and at helping foreign language teachers to develop their skills in online tutoring. Students from the six participating countries—Sweden, Denmark, France, the

Copyright © 2006, Idea Group Inc. Copying or distributing in print or electronic forms without written permission of Idea Group Inc. is prohibited.

Netherlands, Estonia, and Slovenia—were to discuss problem-based cases with each other in a PBL setting using an electronic learning environment called Blackboard (www.blackboard.com). The students were to "cross borders virtually" and cooperate on their tasks (cases) using English as their common working language. Curriculum models were to be developed and a guide published.

Arguments for the Use of Self Assessment

Self assessment is the practice when the student or learner evaluates or assesses his or her own learning in relation to set criteria. This can be anything from when a school child tries to jump a certain height in gymnastics to deciding that one has to learn a new language well enough to negotiate a business contract. There is a strong traditional belief that only teachers can assess students' knowledge, but most people have a fair idea of what they know or do not know within a particular skill area. Self assessment thus becomes important in all learning situations as it is only when one is aware of what one already knows that the areas that need to be focused on for further learning are apparent.

The use of self assessment was new to the majority of the partners in the project, with the exception of the teachers who had also participated in the previous enterprise, that is TENTEC. Four strong arguments for self assessment practices as formulated by Oscarson (1998, 1999) were adopted as the theoretical underpinnings of activities in the LENTEC project.

In the *pedagogical-educational* argument, one may assume that students who practice self assessment become more aware of their learning needs. This awareness helps them see what they need to concentrate on in their language studies, and in this way motivate and enhance the students' sense of responsibility and in consequence, their learning results. In an online, digital environment it is just as important that students are aware of the communicative language skills needed to effectively participate in a virtual environment as they may not get immediate feedback on their communication. Written language used in e-mail communication and chat rooms is more spontaneous and open to interpretation than language used in, for example, essays and letters. The latter type of language would normally be revised before being read by others and would be closer to spoken language.

The *practical-pragmatic* argument suggests that there is more time left for learning and teaching when the responsibility for language assessment does not rest solely on the teacher. Time in the classroom may be spent on actual learning activities instead of being spent on extensive "testing." In the project, it was felt that time should be spent working on the cases at hand, and that it would be difficult to use traditional language tests to measure language improvement.

Copyright © 2006, Idea Group Inc. Copying or distributing in print or electronic forms without written permission of Idea Group Inc. is prohibited.

The *logical-philosophical* argument implies that it can be difficult for someone else to know better than the learners themselves how well they can understand and communicate in another language and in what areas they feel the need to improve most. There are many situations that are not possible to simulate in the language classroom. Hence, there are many skills that the students will not be able to show the language teacher. In LENTEC, the teachers could set up topics for discussion and follow the students' interchanges on the net to a certain extent, but the students continued their communication outside of Blackboard on different levels.

Finally, there was the *empirical* argument, based on research findings, which suggests that learners are, if trained, able to assess their abilities and results fairly realistically.

Neither the students nor the teachers in the project had previously used self assessment, and the teachers were quite sceptical about it at the beginning. Talking about self assessment during a seminar one teacher described how her colleagues first looked at her and said: "Are you crazy? Have students assess themselves? Impossible!" and many students may feel the same way. The validity of self assessments may of course be different in "high-stakes" assessment situations, but here this would not be the case.

Other factors which may influence self assessment ability—but where research has not shown any conclusive evidence as to their impact, for example culture and gender—were further interesting aspects of the work, but they were not specifically studied.

Research Questions and Participants

The issues investigated in the LENTEC project mainly focused the question of whether the teachers and students felt that the students' language skills improved through self assessment practices and to what extent the students made reliable self assessments of their progress and results.

The students from Sweden, Denmark, France, the Netherlands, Estonia and Slovenia, worked on common problems or cases virtually. The students cooperated on the common technical problems that were designed by their teams of teachers. The teachers and their students worked in groups of two or three schools and countries, and used English as their common working language when solving cases of the type "The Motorcycle Helmet—how protective can it be?," with reference to design, properties, and materials used, and "A nasty shock," concerned with electrical installations.

All the partner schools were upper-secondary schools or vocational colleges and all the students were following a technical course. Their ages ranged from 16 to

Copyright © 2006, Idea Group Inc. Copying or distributing in print or electronic forms without written permission of Idea Group Inc. is prohibited.

early 20s. The students' levels of English-language skills varied considerably, as the students had studied English between 2 and 12 years, with the average being 8 years. The teachers assessed the students to be at level A2–B2, on the 6-level (A1 – C2)[1] Common European Framework of Reference scale,[2] a description of language ability commonly referred to as the CEF (Council of Europe, 2001a). The CEF is a document produced by the Council of Europe, which among other things describes standards and competences to be attained at different stages of language learning from *Breakthrough* through *Mastery*, in a comparable manner. None of the students had had any previous training in self assessment.

Six teachers of English participated (1 male and 5 female). They were all experienced language teachers and had taught English between 13 and 34 years at upper-secondary to college and university level. None of them had English as their native language.

Instruments and Method

It is especially important that assessment criteria are transparent and easy to understand when students and teachers from different countries work together on a common project (Perkins, 2004a). In order to define the students' strong and weak language skills, both a language portfolio and self assessment instruments were used. The language portfolio enabled the students to assess their own language levels and register them at the beginning of a course. It also enabled them to become aware of the skills they needed to acquire in order to attain a certain level.

Due to the students' wide range of language proficiency in English, it was considered appropriate to make assessments using the Dutch and Swedish versions of the European Language Portfolio (ELP) (http://culture2.coe.int/portfolio/inc). The ELP consists of three parts: a *Language Passport*, a *Language Biography* and a *Language Dossier*. It exists in a large number of versions in different European languages (Council of Europe, 2001b).

Through these portfolios, students had access to common assessment criteria in the form of the six CEF levels as well as self assessment grids in the form of "can-do" statements. The students were, for example, asked to assess their own mastery of the situation. An example: "You can send a personal letter or e-mail to a foreign acquaintance." It could be answered by either: "I can do this: (a) not yet; (b) with difficulty; (c) with ease; or by (d) I want to learn this."

Another important instrument employed was *The Swedish Self Assessment Material*, designed for the Swedish educational system, in particular the Swedish Upper Secondary School, English Course A (http://www2.educ.umu.se/~provb/engelska/prov/index.html). This course is estimated to correspond to

Copyright © 2006, Idea Group Inc. Copying or distributing in print or electronic forms without written permission of Idea Group Inc. is prohibited.

level B1 of the CEF scale according to the results of a study reported by Oscarson (2002). The *Student Material* includes a *Student Background Questionnaire*[3] that aims to give teachers and students information on which to base the planning of the course of study, an *English Usage Checklist*[4] to help the students become aware of how much English they already use in everyday life, and a *Self Assessment Questionnaire*[5] to help the students reflect on their linguistic skills in relation to set criteria. Each part can be used separately and adapted to teacher and student needs. In conjunction with the *Student Material*, there is also a brief manual for the teacher and student, which includes a description of the purpose behind the material, theoretical background, and additional things to consider when using the material (National Agency for Education, 2001).

Together with in-depth interviews with three of the participating teachers and six of the Estonian students, the other instruments used in the small-scale validation study were:

- The *Students' Self Assessment Questionnaire I* and *II* where the students answered questions on their language background and assessed their general level of English on a five-point scale from "unsatisfactory/poor" to "excellent" as well as how they would manage to speak and understand English if they were alone with a group of peers. They were also asked if and how often they discussed their English skills with their teachers and classmates and how often they thought about this themselves.

- The *Teachers' Self Assessment Validation Questionnaire* which asked the teachers to assess the individual students' general level of English as well as their listening comprehension skills and some questions pertaining to how they perceived the students' self confidence.

- A *Teacher Questionnaire—for teachers of English* and a *Teacher Questionnaire—for vocational teachers,* both of which posed questions on previous and current use of self assessment and what their experiences of the self assessment materials used in the project were.

Data Collection

Assessments were made at the following stages of the project:

- At the beginning (the exact time differed in each group due to each participating country's school calendar), the participating students filled in *Self Assessment Questionnaire I.* This was done with the purpose of

Copyright © 2006, Idea Group Inc. Copying or distributing in print or electronic forms without written permission of Idea Group Inc. is prohibited.

helping the students to become aware of the skills needed to carry out the problem-solving aspects of the PBL cases and communicate with their foreign partners. The students sent this to the researchers involved by e-mail (as well as other spontaneous communication from time to time).

- During the project to assess students' progress of learning and attitudes to project materials and activities. The students used the ELP and/or the *Swedish Self Assessment Material* at some time during the project but this material was not collected. The *Validity Study* was also undertaken during the project to see to what extent the teachers' assessments and the students' self assessments corresponded to the results of a listening-comprehension test administered.

- At the end, to assess whether students and their teachers were able to perceive improved language skills and results due to their involvement in LENTEC activities. A modified *Self Assessment Questionnaire II* was administered but due to unexpected administrative complications at the end of the term, only two groups were able to complete it. The *Teacher Questionnaire—for teachers of English* and a *Teacher Question-naire—for vocational teachers* were answered and sent by e-mail to the researchers after the student phase of the project was completed. All of the participating teachers of English (but only two of the vocational teachers) completed the questionnaire. Towards the end of the project, the teacher and student interviews were recorded.

The Validity Study

A small-scale study was undertaken within the LENTEC project in order to investigate the validity of the students' own assessments of their general level of English and, in particular, their level of listening comprehension. In order not to tire the group with too many questionnaires, the questions used were part of the *Student Self Assessment Questionnaire I.* The self assessments that were used are therefore the students' initial assessments of their language skills before any training in self assessment had been given.

For the sake of comparison between the groups, a standardized semiauthentic listening-comprehension test was administered (by permission of Citogroep,[6] Arnhem, the Netherlands) to the participating students towards the end of the project. A listening-comprehension test was chosen to make test administration and general conditions around the test for the students as similar as possible. In conjunction with this, the students' teachers were asked to make personal independent assessments of the students' listening comprehension skills as well as of their general level of English.

Copyright © 2006, Idea Group Inc. Copying or distributing in print or electronic forms without written permission of Idea Group Inc. is prohibited.

Of the 111 students that participated (and for whom a complete set of data is available) 81% were male and 18% female. Forty percent were from Sweden, 12% from Holland, 14% from Estonia, 23% from Slovenia, and 11% from France. (The Danish students did not participate in the *Validity Study*). Twenty-eight percent of the students had a different mother tongue than that of the country where they lived. Eighty-three percent of the females and 69% of the males had studied English for 8 years or more.

General Results of Student Questionnaires and Interviews

According to the questionnaire, only 1% of the students assessed their own general level of English as "poor" and 21% as "fair." Seventy-four percent assessed it as "good" or "very good," and only 4% as "excellent." Their teachers, on the other hand, considered as many as 12% of the students as having a "poor" and 26% as having a "fair" general level of English. Fifty-six percent were assessed as "good" or "very good," and 6% as "excellent."

There is a tendency among the weaker students to overestimate their general language level while the better students are often more realistic in their assessments and they show a slight tendency to underestimate their ability.

The students were also asked to estimate the degree to which they discussed their language skills with their teacher and peers and thought about their own language learning. There was comparatively little communication between the parties in both cases (student-teacher and student-peers). Only 1 student in 6 had frequent talks with the teacher in this matter. That is, the vast majority of students

Figure 1. Assessment of students' general level of English

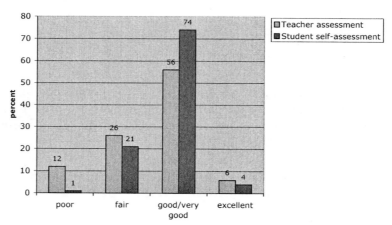

Copyright © 2006, Idea Group Inc. Copying or distributing in print or electronic forms without written permission of Idea Group Inc. is prohibited.

(83%) only seldom ("sometimes" or "never") discussed their English-language skills with their teacher. The picture is much the same when it comes to student-peer contacts. In slight contrast to this, there is a tendency for learners to more often think about their English individually, rather than discuss it with somebody else, including the teacher. More than a third of the students (36%) thought about his or her English more or less all the time ("always" or "often"). Only 7% never reflected on the question at all. It thus appears that the students' individual reflections on their ability in English is in fact a more common activity than either student-teacher "conversational" assessment or peer assessment, that is student-peer assessment.

Overall, the large majority of students (89%) answered that they knew fairly well or very well how good they were in English and even more (95%) believed that they could speak and understand English fairly or very well if they were alone in a group of English-speaking people their own age. Their teachers also assessed them at this level or even higher.

Many of the students (74%) answered that they themselves knew best what they had learned in English while working on a PBL case while the rest of the students thought that the teacher (21%) or the group members (5%) knew best.

Over half the students (61%) reported that the self assessment grids in the ELP had helped them see what they needed to work on more in English.

The student interviews also took place towards the end of the project, in Estonia. The Estonian students knew of the researchers through the Web site and some had been in touch when they sent in their questionnaires. They were all willing to talk about the project. All of them were also aware of the reason why they needed to learn English and they had a definite opinion of how well they knew English:

I know Russian quite good and Estonian almost like Russian and the English is, as I think, I don't know it very well but I, I can speak. I can tell people my thoughts and in this country now it's. I don't need more at the moment but I think if I'm gonna find a work or other things abroad I can I need more skills in English. (Estonian Student 2)

They also expressed that they felt that they could assess some of their language skills themselves:

In some way I can, but I'm not sure. ... I know that I don't know grammar for example at all. Almost all the things I write, I think for example: Do you have to put the word in [the] right form the verb? I think about how it should [be]. I think about ... how it sounds best. (Estonian Student 2)

Copyright © 2006, Idea Group Inc. Copying or distributing in print or electronic forms without written permission of Idea Group Inc. is prohibited.

... well the teacher can't actually say or tell you how well you can listen ... you have to find it out yourself. (Estonian Student 5)

Furthermore, some students thought that there were some skills that the teacher may miss in the classroom assessment situation or that are not focused as much as other skills:

But listening is more something which I do outside the class. ... An examination in English includes the same, the listening part but in [the] classroom I don't remember that we practised this way. (Estonian Student 2)

I'm [the] kind of a person that talks very much and I think my teacher (I've been studying here for three years) I think that now *she knows pretty much what I do know.* (Estonian Student 4)

The students also expressed that taking responsibility for their own learning and assessment was something worthwhile.

[The] positive side is of course you learn more...because you have to work yourself...more time...you have to think what you want to do in class. ... But during this you learn the language, the words and everything. ... I think the negative side, it's more negative than positive though, is lots of selfwork. ... and you have to do your homeworks everytime and think. (Estonian Student 3)

School isn't the one that should teach you, [you] have to learn yourself. School just shows the way to that, to the way of learning or the learning itself. The process itself, but you have to learn by yourself. Always. (Estonian Student 6)

The way that the students worked in the project gave them the opportunity to practice self assessment in a way they had not done before. A majority of students discussed and thought about their own language skills. To a lesser degree they also discussed their language skills with their teachers and peers. According to the teachers, the students also became better at assessing their own language learning and more aware of their own language-learning needs during the project. As has been noted in previous research, the more advanced students were those who tended to underestimate their language ability in

Copyright © 2006, Idea Group Inc. Copying or distributing in print or electronic forms without written permission of Idea Group Inc. is prohibited.

English, while those with lesser language skills tended to overestimate their abilities somewhat.

Teacher Questionnaires and Interviews

Five out of six of the participating teachers of English used student assessment in their classes during the project. The students were sometimes assessed by their classmates, and often by self assessment. All of the teachers felt that their students could assess their own language skills in English fairly or very well. The teachers' explanations often coincided: "For the first-year students it is sometimes difficult to assess themselves fairly, but next [year] they already know how to do that;" "Most students are actually quite aware of their weaknesses;" and "They know rather well what their skills are." Two of the involved teachers had had previous experience working with self assessment in other European projects, and three of the teachers had asked the students to assess themselves at some time before they took part in the project.

Four of the teachers had used the *Swedish Self Assessment Material* with their students and found that this helped to give them a better picture of their English. "The self assessment questionnaires have quite exact and clear questions about different skills and this helps them to understand what they know and what they do not know."

Four of the teachers had used the self assessment grid in the ELP and believed that it gave the students a realistic picture of their English skills.

The six teachers had different opinions as to who best assessed what the students had learned while working on their PBL cases, and several of them marked more than one alternative, because "they constitute a team" and "there are different roles for everyone involved."

The teachers who were not familiar with self assessment practices in previous projects were sceptical of the approach at the beginning of the project and also reported the same general attitude from their colleagues. As the project progressed, there was a marked overall change. The teachers experienced a change of attitude from the students towards assessment. They also found their own role as a teacher changed as a consequence of the participation in the project.

The first questionnaire [of three] was horrible, ... Now they assess themselves more fairly. They seem to be more honest, more realistic. They become more realistic and they find out what do they really know and what do they really want/need to know. ... Now they know what they have to work on. (Estonian teacher)

Copyright © 2006, Idea Group Inc. Copying or distributing in print or electronic forms without written permission of Idea Group Inc. is prohibited.

I have actually gone from teaching to coaching and from teaching to learning. I find it's such an eye opener. When I heard this for the first time, "It's not about teaching, it's about learning." I tell the students I am responsible for the quality of the learning that can take place, you are responsible for your own learning. (Dutch teacher)

The teachers also experienced the material used as valuable:

Even outside this project I use the Swedish Self Assessment material. ... I have students from all over the school, even those who I haven't taught before and I don't know them or what they know and I use the Student Background Questionnaire to find out what they know or at least to get the first picture to start from and it's good. (Estonian teacher)

I think that the European Language Portfolio is a gift from heaven. They have a description of skills...very concrete 'can-do statements'—any level you want—the only drawback is it's a lot of text for my not very language minded students. I can just tell my students what criteria I expect them to reach and they know beforehand. I think they have a right to know what they are going to be judged on. (Dutch teacher)

The reasons the teachers found for using self assessment was that it was conducive to independent learning and that traditional assessment does not always give enough to give a fair picture of the students' skills.

We are not objective sometimes and don't assess them [the students] fairly. People are different and some are afraid of speaking in the classroom. It depends on the student of course. It's quite difficult, as I said, to assess the student who is afraid of speaking even if he can do it quite well. They are afraid, they have had quite little practice and few possibilities to talk. (Estonian teacher)

The teachers found that their teaching role changed and became less demanding as the students themselves could take more responsibility for their own learning. According to the teachers, a majority of the students became more aware of their own language-learning development and more motivated for their language studies. The teachers in the project developed a new teacher role where some of the responsibility for assessment moved from them to the students themselves. This motivated and gave the students added time for actual language learning.

Copyright © 2006, Idea Group Inc. Copying or distributing in print or electronic forms without written permission of Idea Group Inc. is prohibited.

Results of the Validity Study

The minimum score attained by the students on the listening comprehension test was 2 points and the maximum was 17 out of 17. The mean score was 9.32 with a standard deviation of 3.21.

There was, not surprisingly, clear agreement between the teachers' assessment of the students' listening-comprehension ability and the listening-comprehension score even if the correlation was only moderate (r=.57).

The unexpected findings were that, in the whole group, there was a surprisingly low correlation (r=.24) between the teachers' and the students' opinion of how well the student would manage to speak and understand English in a group of English-speaking peers. The correlation between the teachers' and the students' assessment of the individual student's general level of English was also very low (r=.34) as a whole (N= 111). However, in the largest of the participating sub-groups, Sweden (n=45) (Figure 2) there was a moderate correlation (r=.47) between the teachers' and students' assessments of the general language level,

Figure 2. The correlation between Swedish students' and teachers' assessment of individual student's level of English (r=.47). Scale: 1=poor, 2=fair, 3=good, 4=very good, 5=excellent.

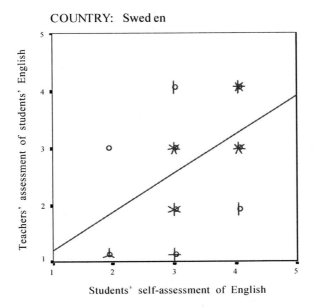

Copyright © 2006, Idea Group Inc. Copying or distributing in print or electronic forms without written permission of Idea Group Inc. is prohibited.

in comparison with the next largest group from Slovenia (n=25) (Figure 3) where there was no significant correlation at all.

There are also unexpectedly low correlations in the large group between the number of years that the students had studied English and their listening comprehension scores (r=.28). Only the Dutch group, which was very small (n=12), showed a strong correlation (.76). The correlation between the listening comprehension scores was also low (r=.29).

Another unforeseen finding was that there was no significant correlation between the teachers' and students' perception of how well the student knows how good he or she is in English. There was also no correlation between the teacher's opinion of the student's general level of self confidence and the students' assessments. On the other hand, there was a sizeable correlation between the teachers' estimates of the students' self confidence and their estimates of students' general level of English (r=.61). There was also correspondence between the teachers' assessment of the students' self confidence and their assessment of how well the students would be able to communicate with a group of English-speaking peers (r=.56).

Figure 3. The correlation between Swedish students' and teachers' assessment of individual student's level of English (r=.17). Scale: 1=poor, 2=fair, 3=good, 4=very good, 5=excellent.

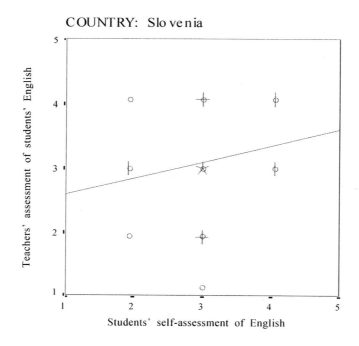

Copyright © 2006, Idea Group Inc. Copying or distributing in print or electronic forms without written permission of Idea Group Inc. is prohibited.

Figure 4. The correlation between teachers' assessment of students' self-confidence and conversational skills (r=.56). Scale: 1=poor, 2=fair, 3=good, 4=very good, 5=excellent.

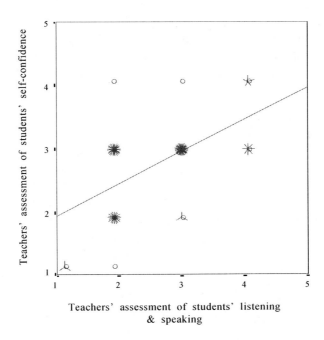

Teachers' assessment of students' listening & speaking

At the beginning of the project, the students' general self assessment of their ability to *speak and understand* English in a group of peers correlated only moderately (r=.42) with their results on the test. The association between the two measures was thus quite weak. However, the students estimated their *conversational* skill (i.e., speaking and understanding), not just their listening skill, so a much higher correlation coefficient should probably not be expected.

Discussion and Conclusion

The development of language awareness does not come by itself. Training is needed for the students to be able to reflect and become independent when it comes to the assessment of learning results. Talking to them about their results and own assessment is one way to increase awareness and become autonomous learners. Letting them talk to each other about learning experiences is another way. Towards the end of the project, all the teachers of English felt that their students could self assess their English skills fairly or very well.

Copyright © 2006, Idea Group Inc. Copying or distributing in print or electronic forms without written permission of Idea Group Inc. is prohibited.

As has been noted in previous research, results obtained showed that the more advanced students were the ones who tended to underestimate their language ability somewhat. Furthermore, the more familiar the students were with self assessment practices, the more realistically they assessed themselves. Teachers need to be more aware of the students' own beliefs about their abilities as this is something which may influence the learning situation.

These results accentuate the fact that students need to be given the opportunity to practice self reflective evaluation of their own results. The students in the study had not had any training in self assessment when they filled in the student questionnaire for the first time.

The *Validity Study* showed some unexpected results. The fact that the students represented no less than 15 different mother tongues and five different countries, all with their different academic traditions, may be one possible explanation. There are different traditions in language teaching in the participating European countries; and listening-comprehension, for example, may not be one of the skills traditionally focused on in all of them.

In countries such as Sweden and The Netherlands, we know that the students are surrounded by much more English in everyday life and are more exposed to English from an earlier age compared to the Eastern European countries and France where students traditionally have not been exposed to the same amount of, for example, English music and films. This may have had an effect on the results. One of the larger groups of students in the study was from Sweden. It was also the only group where there was any correlation between the teachers' and the students' assessments of the individual student's general level of English. Sweden has clearly formulated curricula and syllabi goals that emphasize reflective student behavior. They also express an explicit communicative approach to language learning. One major underlying aim in Swedish language education in general is that the student "should want to" and "have the courage to" speak the language in question. It is possible that this has had a certain impact and makes students better at assessing their own skills in English.

The fact that the teachers' and students' perceptions differ so much with regard to students' confidence and general ability should have implications for language education. Clearly, teachers need to become more aware of their students' own perceptions of their ability to be able to help them to become proficient at assessing their own language skills and develop their language learning skills in general.

As access to "virtual mobility projects" (such as the one reported on here) and working in a virtual environment increases and becomes the norm, students must and will, of necessity, take more control of their own learning. By finding independent ways of working and learning, new assessment models will logically become more student-determined. Teachers can no longer be there to test every

Copyright © 2006, Idea Group Inc. Copying or distributing in print or electronic forms without written permission of Idea Group Inc. is prohibited.

new area taught or every skill practiced. Students need to learn and practice the art of self assessment and reflection. The more independent their learning is, the more essential this is. In e-based learning environments, it seems imperative for everyone within the realm of education to help both learners and teachers to reflect on their learning and teaching practices.

Summary

Working online in the LENTEC project gave the students involved the opportunity to train the use of self assessment practices in a way they had not done before. A majority of students discussed and thought about their own language skills. To a lesser degree, they also discussed their language skills with their teachers and peers. According to the teachers, the students also became better at assessing their own language learning and more aware of their own language-learning needs during the project.

As has been noted in previous research, the more advanced students tended to underestimate their language ability in English, while those with lesser language skills tended to overestimate their abilities somewhat.

The results of the *Validity Study* show some unexpected results, which may be due to the different language teaching and learning traditions and conditions in the participating European countries. The results also underscore the fact that students need time and practice to become proficient at assessing their own language skills.

A full description of the project is to be found in the guide published, *The LENTEC Guide to Learning English: Problem-Based Learning in Virtual Mobility Projects* (Perkins, 2004a).

Language learning is changing, as are also, by necessity, assessment practices. Students cross borders virtually to work and study. They need the tools to assess their own results to be able to continue learning in a rapidly changing world.

You have to learn yourself. School just shows the way to that, to the learning process itself. But, you have to learn by yourself, always. (Estonian student)

[The students can assess their own language learning] but it has not been common until now. I hope it will come. (Estonian teacher)

Copyright © 2006, Idea Group Inc. Copying or distributing in print or electronic forms without written permission of Idea Group Inc. is prohibited.

Further information about LENTEC can be accessed at http://www.pedc.se/lentec/

Acknowledgments

Grateful thanks are extended to all the participating LENTEC teachers and students as well as Polly Perkins, project coordinator, educational adviser modern foreign languages, Centrum voor Innovatie van Opleidingen (CINOP), the Netherlands, and fellow research student Sylvi Vigmo who transcribed the student and teacher interviews. The author is greatly indebted for the support of Professor Mats Oscarson at the Language and Literature Unit of Göteborg University, Sweden.

References

Allwood, C. M., & Jonsson, A. C. (2001). Om betydelsen av elevers metakognitiva förmåga [On the significance of students' metacognitive ability]. In G. Svingby & S. Svingby (Eds.), *Bedömning av kunskap och kompetens [Assessment of knowledge and competence]* PRIM-gruppen (pp. 79-97). Stockholm: Lärarhögskolan i Stockholm, Institutionen för undervisningsprocesser, kommunikation och lärande.

Bachman, L., & Palmer, A. S. (1989). The construct validation of self ratings of communicative language ability. *Language Testing, 6,* 14-25.

Björk, U. (2004). *Distributed problem-based learning: Studies of a pedagogical model in practice.* Doctoral dissertation, Göteborg Studies in Educational Sciences 221, Göteborg University.

Blanche, P., & Merino, B. J. (1989). Self assessment of foreign language skills: Implications for teachers and researchers. *Language Learning, 39,* 313-340.

Council of Europe (2001a). *Common European framework of reference for languages: Learning, teaching, assessment.* Cambridge, UK: Cambridge University Press and author.

Council of Europe, (2001b). *European language portfolio.* Cambridge, UK: Cambridge University Press.

Delors, J., Mufti, I. A., Amagi, I., Carneiro, R., Chung, F., Geremak, B., et al. (1996). *Learning: The treasure within.* Paris: UNESCO Publishing.

Copyright © 2006, Idea Group Inc. Copying or distributing in print or electronic forms without written permission of Idea Group Inc. is prohibited.

Falchikov, N., & Boud, D. J. (1989). Student self assessment in higher education: A meta-analysis. *Review of Educational Research, 59*(4), 395-430.

Gipps, C. (1994). *Beyond testing: Towards a theory of educational assessment.* London: The Falmer Press.

Holec, H. (Ed.). (1988). *Autonomy and self directed learning: Present fields of application.* Strasbourg: Council of Europe, Council for Cultural Co-operation.

Janssen-van Dieten, A. M. (1992). *Zelfbeoordeling en tweede-taalleren [Self assessment in second language learning].* Unpublished doctoral dissertation, Katholieke Universiteit, Nijmegen, The Netherlands.

Moore, G. M. (1997). Theory of transactional distance. In D. Keegan (Ed.), *Theoretical principles of distance education.* New York: Routledge.

National Agency for Education (2001). *The Swedish self assessment material: English course, A.* Retrieved from http://www2.educ.umu.se/~provb/engelska/prov/index.html

Oscarson, M. (1978). *Approaches to self assessment in foreign language learning.* Strasbourg: Council of Europe, Council for Cultural Co-operation. Also published in 1980 by Pergamon Press, Oxford.

Oscarson, M. (Ed.). (1980). *Behovsanpassad undervisning och självbedömning av färdigheter i moderna språk: Några försök. Språkpedagogiskt centrum, Göteborgs universitet.* [Needs-oriented teaching and self assessment of modern language skills: Some case Studies. Work papers from the Language Teaching Research Center, No. 28. Göteborg University, Department of Education.]

Oscarson, M. (1984). *Self assessment of foreign language skills: A survey of research and development work.* Strasbourg: Council of Europe, Council for Cultural Co-operation.

Oscarson, M. (1998). Om självbedömning av språkfärdighet—empiri och reflektioner [On self assessment of language skills—Empirical data and reflections]. In B. Ljung & A. Pettersson (Eds.), *Perspektiv på bedömning av kunskap [Perspectives on the assessment of knowledge].* Lärarhögskolan i Stockholm, Institutionen för pedagogik.

Oscarson, M. (1999). Estimating language ability by self assessment: A review of some of the issues. In *Papers on Language Learning Teaching Assessment.* Festskrift till Torsten Lindblad, Göteborgs universitet, Institutionen för pedagogik och didaktik.

Oscarson, M. (2002). *En steg/framework-jämförelse.* [A comparison of Swedish grading levels ('Steg') and the Council of Europe framework levels]. Skolverket, Stockholm, och Institutionen för pedagogik och didaktik, Göteborgs universitet. [Unpublished report.]

Copyright © 2006, Idea Group Inc. Copying or distributing in print or electronic forms without written permission of Idea Group Inc. is prohibited.

Peirce, B. N., Swain, M., & Hart, D. (1993). Self assessment, French immersion, and locus of control. *Applied Linguistics, 14*, 25-42.

Perkins, P. (Ed.). (2004a). *The LENTEC guide to learning English: Problem based learning in virtual mobility projects.* Malmö: The Board of Education and The European Commission: Leonardo da Vinci Programme.

Perkins, P. (2004b). *LENTEC: Problem based learning in virtual mobility projects.* Paper presented at EfVET (European federation of Technical and Vocational Education and Training). Maastricht.

Prohaska, V., & Maraj, F. (1995). *Low and medium ability students confidently overestimate all their grades.* Paper presented at the Seventh Annual Convention of the American Psychological Society. New York.

Purpura, J. E. (1997). An analysis of the relationships between test takers' cognitive and metacognitive strategy use and second language test performance. *Language Learning, 47*(2), 289-325.

Ross, S. (1998). Self assessment in second language testing: A meta-analysis and analysis of experiential factors. *Language Testing, 15*(1), 1-20.

Endnotes

[1]   A1: Breakthrough, A2: Waystage, B1: Threshold, B2: Vantage, C1: Effective Operational Proficiency, C2: Mastery

[2]   http://www.culture2.coe.int/portfolio/documents_intro/common_ framework.html

[3]   http://www.skolverket.se/nat/provbanken/engelska/public_html/prov/ student_background.pdf

[4]   http://www.skolverket.se/nat/provbanken/engelska/public_html/prov/ english_usage.pdf

[5]   http://www.skolverket.se/nat/provbanken/engelska/public_html/prov/ self_assessment

[6]   Centraal Instituut voor Toetsontwikkeling/Dutch National Institute for Educational Measurement

Copyright © 2006, Idea Group Inc. Copying or distributing in print or electronic forms without written permission of Idea Group Inc. is prohibited.

Chapter VIII

Self and Peer Assessment in Problem-Based Learning:
Learning English by Solving a Technical Problem – A Case Study

Bernarda Kosel
University of Ljubljana, Slovenia

Abstract

The purpose of this case study is to offer some suggestions on assessing student-centered groups, and show how self and peer assessment can complement a teacher's assessment. The case study reports on which assessment tools have been developed to measure students' work in two European Leonardo da Vinci projects. The project used problem-based learning to teach English by combining this with a technical subject. A brief report about the experiences on using an e-learning environment

Copyright © 2006, Idea Group Inc. Copying or distributing in print or electronic forms without written permission of Idea Group Inc. is prohibited.

(Blackboard) in which the second project was carried out is also given. Assessment is divided into the process and product strands. The assessment tools for each strand are proposed. These include rating scales for assessing the presentation and report, as well as self and peer assessment questionnaires for assessing the learning process.

Introduction

As a teacher of English for Specific Purposes at the tertiary level, I took part in two European Leonardo da Vinci projects: Teaching ENglish for TEChnical Purposes (TENTEC 1999-2000) and a logical continuation of it, Learning ENglish for TEChnical Purposes (LENTEC 2001-2003). Both projects made use of the problem-based learning (PBL) model, which is becoming a widespread educational innovation strategy in which learning is centered on a problem given to a group of students to solve. One of the best-known examples of computer-based PBL is the Jasper Woodbury series (Cognition and Technology Group at Vanderbilt, 1992) designed to enhance problem solving in mathematics for grades four and up. Over the last decade, the use of PBL has also been growing rapidly in European schools. It has become a buzzword in the field of educational innovation and has been practiced a great deal especially at the upper secondary and tertiary level.

Centering around a problem emphasizes "learning by doing" as proposed by Papert (1980) who has provided one of the greatest influences on educational philosophy by underlining that teaching (instructionism) is important but learning by doing (constructionism) is much more important. The proposed problem should be relevant to the group and realistic enough to arouse and maintain their interest. Solving the problem is done by teamwork in the group. Social learning or cooperative learning is an important component of PBL. It produces better quality learning outcomes than any individual student could manage, which is consistent with Vugotsky's proposal (1978) that social interaction profoundly influences cognitive development.

In the TENTEC and LENTEC projects we have basically followed the PBL model as described by Woods (1994). What was new or specific to the projects was that students were solving a discipline-related problem in combination with learning English as a foreign language. (To learn more about this approach, see the section on problem-based learning on the project Web site www.pedc.se/lentec; Kosel, 2002.) The first project was carried out under normal classroom circumstances, whereas the second was an e-learning project, which also included an element of virtual mobility. For example, a group of students from

Copyright © 2006, Idea Group Inc. Copying or distributing in print or electronic forms without written permission of Idea Group Inc. is prohibited.

Slovenia worked on the same problem together with a group of students from Sweden by virtually crossing borders. The results of both projects are presented on the project Web site and also published in a project publication (Perkins et al., 2004).

The projects were innovative in many aspects, one of them being assessment. Teachers working on the projects realized right away that, in a PBL situation, a traditional assessment such as a written test paper could no longer be used simply because it would not measure the skills students are required to develop in PBL. For any serious assessment, assessment tools must be valid for the situation, content validity being one of the important properties of any testing or evaluation (Wharton, 1998). In a PBL environment, the development of an assessment model is not an easy task and there is probably no ideal way of doing it. In the two projects, a team led by Anne Dragemark, Department of Education, Göteborg University, was set up to deal with the problem of assessment. The team came to the conclusion that self and peer assessment should be an important component of the model.

In this case study, assessment from the teacher/student experience perspective will be discussed. For students, all aspects of the project were new. They had never before learned English following a cross-curricular, problem-based learning concept, nor had they learned English or any subject entirely using an e-learning environment. And they had no previous experience in self or peer assessment.

Related Tasks

Most tasks that the students were asked to complete were generated from the given PBL cases. In our PBL situation students had to:

- brainstorm on the problem given;
- identify their current knowledge about it and the new knowledge they need;
- search for new knowledge/information and do out-of-class research;
- select appropriate knowledge and find a solution;
- write a report in English;
- give a group oral presentation in English; and
- function well within a group.

Copyright © 2006, Idea Group Inc. Copying or distributing in print or electronic forms without written permission of Idea Group Inc. is prohibited.

Practical Experiences with an E-Learning Environment

In addition to the previously mentioned tasks, students also needed to develop info-search skills, select relevant information, plan their work as a group, and become familiar with the possibilities offered by an e-learning environment. The e-learning environment that was chosen by the project team was Blackboard. The initial problems were successfully overcome by preparing a simplified version of the Blackboard Guide for both teachers and students and by having a hands-on experience with the program before starting with the PBL cases. In order to make optimal use of a Web-based environment, the project teachers used WebQuest (Dodge & March, 1995), which is a framework structure designed to use the learner's time well and focus on using information rather than looking for it. Each PBL case was carefully structured in a WebQuest framework under several headings, see www.pedc.se/lentec. This contributed a great deal to a smooth flow of the learning process, and the fact that assessment was planned from the very start as an aid to the learning process. Because most of the appropriate source information students found on the Internet was in English, an important requirement was also that they paraphrase the source information and not just "copy and paste" it into their reports. Among the functions offered by Blackboard, all groups found the use of the discussion board particularly useful, more than the virtual classroom. The only problem that occurred while using e-learning was that sometimes the Internet was slow and that not all of the students had an Internet connection at home.

Assessment Dilemmas

In any kind of assessment, the main goal, the tasks student will have to do to achieve this goal, and the skills and abilities they will have to develop, need to be defined.

The main goal of PBL in the e-learning environment was to: "Use a target language as a tool for solving real problems using the e-learning environment to full advantage by communicating with partner-country students, peers, the technical teacher and the language teacher."

Students were divided into groups and worked on the same problem as their partner-country group. For example, Slovene students from the first year of the applied sciences program in Ljubljana, worked together with Swedish students from Malmö Pualiskolan Upper Secondary. Both groups of students were the same age and were interested in science and technology. They were given two

Copyright © 2006, Idea Group Inc. Copying or distributing in print or electronic forms without written permission of Idea Group Inc. is prohibited.

problems to solve. In the first, they were asked to design a motorcycle helmet and discuss the materials to be used. The second problem was an investigation into the use of smart materials, which are a relatively new type of materials that have the capability to respond to stimuli and environmental changes. See www.pedc.se/lentec, Examples of student work.

As an English teacher, I did not know how to assess all of the PBL-related skills and abilities to give each student a final mark, which my school requires.

Dilemmas identified were:

- How to assess the subject-specific content;
- How to assess so many skills/what to assess;
- How to assess an individual within the group; and
- How to arrive at the final grade based on so many components.

Assessment Model

The LENTEC project tried to involve vocational subject teachers to help the language teacher in designing the problems or cases to be solved, and to assess the subject-specific content of students' work. This was one of the good innovative ideas of the project that helped me solve my first dilemma of how to assess the subject-specific content. However, because this kind of cross-curricular teaching had never been practiced at our school, there was some initial difficulty in finding a technical teacher who would be willing to cooperate, although I did find one in the second phase. A colleague who was knowledgeable about technology of materials helped me write the introduction to the problem of smart materials, acted as mentor to the students, and assessed the technical content of students' reports. This was ideal. The fact that this was a European project may have helped to overcome the frequent complications when technical and nontechnical faculty work together on a technology-based problem. Usually, technical and language teachers do not consider working together, which is regrettable, because the cross-curricular approach is a very good idea and worth striving for.

Turning to the assessment of language skills, one of the main problems was the wide range of skills and abilities students needed to develop to complete the PBL work. Which of these skills should be assessed? There was also a need for transparency of language criteria as teachers and students in different partner countries had their own, sometimes official, language criteria. The project team

Copyright © 2006, Idea Group Inc. Copying or distributing in print or electronic forms without written permission of Idea Group Inc. is prohibited.

decided to rely on the Common European Framework of Reference (CEFR), which gives a range of descriptors for the quality of language skills at certain levels of foreign language knowledge, and is a great help in standardizing these levels across Europe. In our project it served as a firm basis for all participating countries, making the criteria more transparent to both teachers and students. Thus language teachers could each be more confident in their own assessment. The very concrete "can do statements" from the European Language Portfolio are a very helpful reference for teachers as well as students. In the partner pair Sweden-Slovenia, we used the Swedish self assessment materials for the Swedish Upper Secondary School, which is deemed to be at the CEFR level B1 (Oscarson, 2001), and is organized in a similar way to the CEFR self assessment as grids. The Swedish self assessment materials consisted of a Student Background Questionnaire, an English Usage Checklist and a Self assessment Questionnaire. The Swedish materials used can be found on the LENTEC Web site.

Having to decide what skills and abilities to assess, it became evident that assessing the products of a PBL case only, that is the report and the group oral presentation, would not suffice. PBL is an educational model in which students and teachers need to know what is going on during the learning process itself. Thus, it was decided that we would not only assess the report and presentation but also the learning process and in this, we would focus on the quality of a student's personal improvement and his or her contribution to group work. These aspects would be gauged through self and peer assessment.

The decision to divide assessment in PBL into product and process strands is also supported by the latest trends in assessment theory. Today, teachers need to develop a new way of thinking about assessment. It should no longer be regarded just as a means of measuring the results (products) but should also act as an aid to the learning process. Assessment is undergoing a paradigm shift from standardized testing and the written examination to a broader model of educational assessment (Gipps, 1994) from which the teacher and the learner should receive formative feedback. Traditional summative assessment at the end of the learning process is simply not enough.

The tools of assessment of the product strand (presentation and report) are well known to the language teacher. A number of rating scales for assessing the presentation and report are available in literature (Brown, 1998; Gibbs, 1995;

Figure 1. Assessment in PBL

Process Strand (Discussions + Team Work)	Product Strand (Presentation + Report)
Peer assessment Self-assessment	Language teacher Subject specialist Formative peer assessment

Copyright © 2006, Idea Group Inc. Copying or distributing in print or electronic forms without written permission of Idea Group Inc. is prohibited.

Lynch & Anderson, 1991), needing only to be adapted to particular needs. To improve the reliability of rating scales it is essential that students are made familiar with the criteria at the very start, and that appropriate guidance is given so they know what is expected of them.

Since students were not prepared to share the same mark for their presentation and the report, there was also a requirement that the report be written so that each individual student's contribution was identifiable, to enable individual marking. The same approach was taken in assessing the group oral presentation. Each student was required to speak for 7 to 10 minutes and was again individually assessed on their own part of the presentation.

Possibilities for Involving Peers in the Product Strand of Assessment

Teachers normally assess products of PBL. However, this does not mean that it is not a good idea to involve peers in assessing products. Several authors have reported on successful involvement of peers in the assessment of products and how useful it has proved (Conway et al., 1993; Dudley-Evans, 1995; Gibbs, 1995). Most of the cases they describe refer to groups of students who were either graduate students or have reached a certain level of maturity. If this is not the case or if students have not had any previous experience as assessors, peer assessment for a mark may become problematic.

Our student population was a mixture of the last year of the upper secondary (Sweden) and first year undergraduate (Slovenia), all aged nineteen. Most of them were not made familiar with any peer assessment in their previous school years. For this reason, we believed that peer assessment should not be included in the final mark. However, after some discussion with the students it was decided to introduce peer assessment in report writing and group oral presentations, for formative purposes. When students were writing reports, they were asked to exchange the first draft with their peers in the group. They were also encouraged to exchange reports with Swedish students, but not many Swedish students were able to respond because at the time they were preparing for an external examination in English. This was unfortunate because it would have provided a true international platform for peer assessment. Nevertheless, reading one another's reports within their own Slovene groups proved quite useful for improving both English and technical content. This was also an opportunity for the better students to demonstrate their knowledge.

Peer assessment for formative purposes was also used in parts of the oral presentation. Peer audiences proved they could be good judges of elements such as: clarity, structure, use of visual aids, delivery, and body language. Our experience showed that suggestions for possible improvements made by peers

Copyright © 2006, Idea Group Inc. Copying or distributing in print or electronic forms without written permission of Idea Group Inc. is prohibited.

were accepted more readily than if they had been made by the teacher. The following rating scales for the report and presentation indicate who we considered would be the best assessor for each element in the scale. A rationale explaining the criteria in each section follows each rating scale.

Rating Scale for Group Report

Refer to Figure 2.

Please assess the report by giving a mark 1–5 (1 = not at all, 5 = very much so) in each of the following categories.

Rationale

In both the presentation and report models, the first element concerns the relevance of the topic. It was desirable that this be judged by the subject

Figure 2. Rating scale for group reports

Please assess the report by giving a mark 1 – 5 (1 = not at all, 5 = very much so) in each of the following categories

Write in the student's name	Student A	Student B	Student C	Student D
Contains relevant information showing insight in the problem. The solution offered is based on factual data. *(preferably assessed by subject specialist)*	4	4	5	3
Demonstrates awareness of structure (Problem / Solution pattern) *(peers)*	5	4	5	3
Shows ability to plan and complete own elements of written team report that fit into the whole *(peers)*	5	4	5	4
Standard of English acceptable appropriate word order appropriate vocabulary spelling *(language teacher)*	4	4	5	4
Meets the standards of technical writing, uses referencing, citation conventions broadly observed *(language teacher)*	3	3	4	3

Kosel, Faculty of Mechanical Eng. Ljubljana

Copyright © 2006, Idea Group Inc. Copying or distributing in print or electronic forms without written permission of Idea Group Inc. is prohibited.

specialist, who could best say whether the topic was well-researched, and whether the solutions offered were based on factual data. Points earned in this part can represent one of the marks in the technical subject. In this way, the technical and language content of the PBL case are marked separately.

The second element was: demonstrates awareness of problem/solution structure pattern. This judged whether the student showed awareness of the required text organization pattern. The pattern that I found especially suitable for writing a report on PBL activities is the problem/solution pattern as proposed by Edge (1998), since many reports on problem solving are likely to be organized in that way. The structure of this pattern has the following parts:

- situation;
- focus;
- response; and
- evaluation.

At the beginning of the report, students first set the problem in the context of the current situation (situation). Then they explained the aspects on which they wanted to focus (focus), described their response and suggested solutions on the basis of factual data (response), and evaluated their response (evaluation). The assessor determines whether this structure is present and how well particular parts are written. Again, it is very important that the problem/solution pattern is explained to students before they start writing.

The third item in the report rating scale was: shows ability to plan and complete own elements of written team report. Since we had decided that individual student's work should be identifiable, we also needed some criteria on how each part fit into the whole. These criteria, which are the same as suggested by Gibbs (1995) for assessing group reports and individual contributions to the group as a whole, should be included in the rating scale, because they show how well individual team members integrate their contribution, and how well they know the work of other team members. This of course requires knowledge of the whole topic and a higher level of cooperation.

The fourth element, Standard of English acceptable, referred to the use of the foreign language: My students were required to reach level B1, Independent User, as defined by the CEFR. This meant that they should be able to write a report about accumulated factual information on matters within their field. The report, or individual parts of it, is judged in terms of: appropriate vocabulary, grammar and spelling, and other writing skills such as use of linking words, paragraph building, paraphrasing, and summarizing. Compared to the presenta-

Copyright © 2006, Idea Group Inc. Copying or distributing in print or electronic forms without written permission of Idea Group Inc. is prohibited.

tion where the emphasis should be on fluency, in the report greater emphasis is to be placed on grammatical accuracy.

The last item in the rating scale was: meets the standards of technical writing (dealing with numbers, graphs, tables, etc.). This criterion focuses on how well the report meets the requirements of the genre and the standards of technical writing, including citation conventions, referencing and bibliography standards, and observation of copyright restrictions.

Rating Scale for Oral Presentation

Refer to Figure 3.

Please assess the student (your colleague) by giving a mark 1–5 (1 = not at all, 5 = very much so) where indicated.

The second and the third elements were: clear and well-structured organization, supported by visuals and delivery style. These refer to assessing presenters in

Figure 3. Rating scale for oral presentation (italics)

Please assess the student (your colleague) by giving a mark 1 – 5 (1 = not at all, 5 = very much so) where indicated.

Write in the student's name	Student A	Student B	Student C	Student D
The topic is relevant, well researched and content appropriate *(subject specialist)*	5	5	4	3
Clear and well-structured organization, supported by visuals *(peers)*	4	5	3	4
Excellent delivery, appropriate body language, can invite questions and answer them successfully *(peers)*	4	5	4	4
Good clear pronunciation, fluent with little hesitation, appropriate vocabulary, use of discourse markers (B1) *(language teacher)*	4	5	4	4

Kosel, Faculty of Mechanical Eng. Ljubljana

Copyright © 2006, Idea Group Inc. Copying or distributing in print or electronic forms without written permission of Idea Group Inc. is prohibited.

terms of clarity and organization, use of visual aids, appropriate body language, and whether questions were invited and answered successfully. In our case, peers judged these elements, since they were actually the audience. Students gave each presenter a mark, but as previously stated, that mark was not included in the final grade because of students' lack of maturity and experience as assessors. The marks were given for formative purposes only, and proved very worthwhile as an awareness-building tool for detecting possible weaknesses in presentations still to be delivered.

The last element in the rating scale was: performance in the foreign language. Presenters were judged in terms of pronunciation of words and sounds, appropriate vocabulary, use of discourse markers, and grammatical accuracy. However, rather than grammatical accuracy, priority was here given to fluency, since this is more important in oral production. With reasonable fluency, the presenter should sustain a straightforward description of a subject within his or her field of interest, see CEFR, B1. The assessor of this element in the rating scale is, of course, the language teacher.

Self and Peer Assessment

Regarding the process strand of PBL in an e-learning environment, it is clear that teachers have little insight into what is going on during the learning process. Only the students know how they themselves have progressed, who was a hindrance to the group, and who came late or did not attend the meetings.

Because of this, the LENTEC project team decided the best way to assess the quality of the learning process would be to introduce self and peer assessment. This required teachers to change their way of thinking about assessment in general, moving away from the idea that marking is solely the job of teachers. Students reacted in a similar way, asking why they should assess themselves, as this is the teacher's job. Teachers also needed to recognize that self assessment especially can be an important complement to traditional assessment. It is an additional tool, reaching beyond the more traditional methods. The main advantage of self assessment is that it widens the perspectives of both teachers and learners, Oscarson (1989, 1999). Learners become more aware of aspects of the learning process, and teachers get feedback for possible modifications or adjustments to the learning process.

Assessment should be an ongoing process and should not be product-focused, or as Brindley (1991) puts it, assessment should not be something that is merely "tacked on" to the end of the learning process (p.153).

Copyright © 2006, Idea Group Inc. Copying or distributing in print or electronic forms without written permission of Idea Group Inc. is prohibited.

Self Assessment: Teacher/Student Perspective

In the project team, Dragemark (2004: 35) pointed out that the aim of using self assessment was to increase the students' reflective capacity about their own learning, and in this way, increase motivation. If students have the opportunity to use self assessment practices, they will also have the opportunity to reflect continuously on their own learning.

In the project, self assessment was a complementary tool to teacher assessment. My group used the Swedish self assessment materials, consisting of a Student Background Questionnaire, an English Usage Questionnaire and an additional Self assessment Questionnaire for PBL and the LENTEC project. All teachers working on the project were sent a Teacher's Guide to Student Questionnaire plus a Teacher Questionnaire for Teachers of English, in which they were asked questions concerning the self assessment materials they used with students, whether they had used self assessment previously, and their opinion of the students' ability to self assess. For details see www.pedc.se/lentec.

Students were given the same questionnaire twice: first, after they had worked on the project for a few months, and again, as close to the end of the course as possible. All answered questionnaires were sent online to the teachers and project-assessment researchers and the use of Blackboard here proved a real advantage.

Within the LENTEC project, a study was also carried out to gauge the accuracy of students' self assessment of their language level of English. Students in all partner countries took a standardized listening/comprehension test that was administered towards the end of the project. All teachers received detailed instructions on how to administer the test to make conditions as similar as possible for all students. Students heard an interview with a young Jewish woman who talked about her family history and her present job. The interview was to be played only once and students had to answer 17 multiple-choice comprehension checks. An independent teacher's opinion was also sought. For each participating student, the language teacher made a personal, independent assessment of the student's listening comprehension skills and general level of English. For details about the validity study, see Chapter VII.

Although this type of assessment was not completely new to me, having used some self assessment materials with previous English for Specific Purposes students, this project reinforced my belief that self assessment is not worth much if it is not done systematically. It is not enough for the teacher to bring the materials into the classroom or put them on the e-learning course Web site and just ask students to respond to them. If self assessment is a new experience for students, they need to know why they should self assess, why assessment is not only the teacher's job, and how self assessment complements other assessment.

Copyright © 2006, Idea Group Inc. Copying or distributing in print or electronic forms without written permission of Idea Group Inc. is prohibited.

Therefore, it is very important to explain that self assessment means self involvement in the learning process and that it raises the students' innermost awareness in a way no teacher can emulate.

The benefits of self assessment became apparent to me after the first questionnaire about student language abilities. To solve their problems, students had to use the Internet as their main source. Because information on the Internet is written in perfect English, they were of course tempted to "copy and paste" it into their reports. Only through the process of self assessment did they realize they were actually in the process of learning English, and that they should try to use their own words and paraphrasing. When the questionnaire asked them to respond to a statement such as "After some preparation I can inform others about something, or describe something that I'm interested in" (Self Assessment Questionnaire), with acceptable answers being "not at all," "a little," "fairly well," "very well," or "perfectly," they understood they were not expected to have a perfect command of English and therefore it was not necessary to pretend they did. Through self assessment, they became aware that they were in the process of becoming an Independent User (B1 on the CEFR scale), and that making mistakes is all part of this process. They also became more careful about the way they described their language competence and performance to peers. In short, they started reflecting on their own learning.

On the other hand, through the language criteria required for self assessment some good students realized that they did not need to learn as much as they had thought. Another positive aspect of self assessment is that by using the English Usage Checklist asking them to answer questions like "Have you read a book in English?" or respond to statements such as "I can understand a typical English entertainment program on TV without subtitles," they became aware that they were learning outside school as well. This is something the teacher cannot know or assess. Students in the project also liked the transparency of criteria for language abilities. When they could see that other European countries, schools, and consequently, employers would use the same criteria, this motivated them to make use of self assessment for learning.

Peer Assessment: Teacher/Student Perspective

One of the assessment dilemmas mentioned at the beginning of this paper was how to assess an individual within the group. Gibbs (1995) points out that the main problem with group work is that it is individuals who gain qualifications not groups, and for this reason assessment of groups is normally considered thoroughly unsatisfactory if no special differentiation is made within the group.

Cooperation in the group is an important element of the PBL process. Contribution to the group, regular, active collaboration, commitment to the common goal,

Copyright © 2006, Idea Group Inc. Copying or distributing in print or electronic forms without written permission of Idea Group Inc. is prohibited.

and readiness to share knowledge are all very important qualities, since PBL cannot function properly without them. If these are present, the learning process will unfold by itself. In our PBL situation, observation of the groups in action was very difficult. It was practically impossible for the teacher to define individual levels of contribution. Members of the group were the only ones who really knew how much individual students had contributed to the process. When a group was asked to look for relevant information and find a solution to a problem, only members of the group knew how much each student had contributed to the common goal and how reliable they had been in carrying out the assignment.

To assess individual contributions within the group, a peer assessment checklist was developed, see Figure 4. The scaling method is based on a comparable scaling method used by Boud (1995) and Sluijsmans et al. (2001). After some discussion within the groups, it was also decided that the checklist should be confidential. If peer assessment is performed in open agreement within the group there is a tendency of over-rating for all members of the group. A study carried out by Lejk and Wyvill (2001) indicates that secret peer assessment would lead to a higher spread of individual marks and perhaps fairer assessment than when assessment is done in open agreement. To be as honest as they could, students decided to keep the checklist confidential.

A very positive aspect of this checklist was that it acted as a catalyst to the learning process. In group work, poor or lazy students may unfairly profit from the efforts of good students, or conversely, good students may suffer from the poor efforts of the others. At the first, or at the latest, the second meeting, the checklist was distributed to each member of the group and students were told that at the end of the course they would have to hand in the completed checklist, in which they would assess one another on how much each group member contributed to the whole, and who was no help at all or even a hindrance to the group. Once the groups learned that their peers would assess their contributions, even the lazy students started working.

Completed peer assessment checklists were handed to the teacher who did the summative assessment. They were written evidence for assessment of the learning process, and for distribution of points by group members. The student with the most points on the checklist also got the highest number of points for his or her relative contribution to group work. Checklist points were then added to the points earned in the report and presentation.

Arriving at the Final Mark

Schools require teachers to give students marks. This is, and will remain, the teacher's professional responsibility. In a PBL environment, assessment be-

Copyright © 2006, Idea Group Inc. Copying or distributing in print or electronic forms without written permission of Idea Group Inc. is prohibited.

Figure 4. Peer assessment checklist

Confidential

Please assess the other members of your group by giving a mark:

3 –	*Better than most of the group*
2 -	*About average for this group*
1 –	*Not as good as most of the group*
0 –	*No help at all*
- 1 –	*Hindrance to the group*

Write in your Colleague's Name	Student A	Student B	Student C	Student D
Attended meetings regularly, accepted fair share of work, and completed by the required time	3	0	2	1
Contributed to the group discussions, helped to identify the key issues of the case problem, made meaningful contributions to the group discussions	3	0	2	1
Positive attitude to the group, encourager, supporter of team decisions	3	-1	3	1
Has researched the topic well, the quality of his or her contribution was	3	1	2	2

Kosel, Faculty of Mechanical Eng. Ljubljana

comes a complex thing. It can be made a bit easier for the teacher if members of each group agree to share the same mark for their report and presentation. However, this is rarely the case. Usually good students will resent being dragged down by poor students, while poor students may unfairly profit from the work of good students. Any perception that the assessment is unfair could undermine cooperative group learning.

However, as stated previously, we felt that assessing only the products did not seem to be sufficient and that some evidence about the quality of the learning process should be considered as well. In the literature, there are a number of suggestions on how to include evidence based on peer assessment into the final mark. One is that students themselves judge the relative contributions to the group. The group is given a certain number of points that have to be distributed between group members, depending on how much each contributed to the whole (Gibbs, 1995; Conway et al., 1993). This method proved quite suitable for our student-centered groups. As evidence for the distribution of these points, the confidential peer assessment checklist was used. The points the student received

Copyright © 2006, Idea Group Inc. Copying or distributing in print or electronic forms without written permission of Idea Group Inc. is prohibited.

from their peers for group work were then added to the points given by the teacher for the report and presentation. Finally, the mark obtained was then compared with the student's self rating level. It is important to point out that assessment of this nature caused no hard feelings and no significant discrepancies.

Conclusion

What teachers dislike most in their work is marking students. It is an odious job, burdened with responsibility. My experience from the project and the way the assessment was done is that self and peer assessment take a lot of time in the classroom or in an e-learning environment, but:

- They are worth doing because they reduce the burden of marking for the teacher. The final mark is a kind of a mutual agreement between the teacher and the student. It is a relief when for example the teacher's mark is only "a pass" to see that the student's answer in the self assessment is " I cannot really do this" or "a little".

- A shift has been made from teaching to coaching and caring for the quality of student learning. Self and peer assessment change both the teacher's and the students' perspective of the learning process. They act as eye openers to what is really going on in the learning process. Teachers become more aware of their responsibility, not for the quality of teaching, but for the quality of students' learning, and students become more aware that personal involvement and their own reflection about learning are irreplaceable and an absolute precondition for progress.

- The e-learning environment proved to be an advantage in many respects. It created a feeling that students were members of an online community with a shared interest. The fact that in this environment each heading, including the heading on assessment, is carefully structured and planned prevents the possibility that assessment would be just attached to the learning process at the end. In addition, the availability of self and peer assessment questionnaires and rating scales provided through Blackboard right from the start gave students the opportunity to continuously reflect about their learning, sometimes also in their spare time.

Copyright © 2006, Idea Group Inc. Copying or distributing in print or electronic forms without written permission of Idea Group Inc. is prohibited.

Tips for the Teacher

During the project, many ideas evolved that could be used by others who are undertaking assessment activities like those described in this chapter. In the following, you will find some useful hints:

• Students need training in self assessment. Only through repeated experience will they develop the ability to reflect on their own learning.

• Make the whole assessment framework clear to students at the beginning. Explain the CEFR or other set of criteria.

• Self assessment increases the amount of organizational work for the teacher. It is a process that takes time. At the beginning, students need to be guided.

• Keep the self and peer assessment questionnaires short, otherwise students will consider it to be too much paperwork.

• Self assessment should be done at least twice: first, at the beginning; and second, in the middle or at the end of the course, for students to be able to judge their progress.

• Peer assessment will act as a motivational tool but only if students are informed about it at the beginning, or at the latest, at the second meeting.

• Make self assessment and peer assessment a natural part of your classroom or your e-learning environment. By doing so, you will gradually change the attitude of your students to their own learning.

Acknowledgments

I wish to thank Polly Perkins, CINOP, the coordinator of both European projects, for many helpful ideas and for editing this chapter. I also wish to thank Dr. Sue Wharton, University of Aston, UK, for her help in designing a valid framework of assessment for a problem-based learning situation.

References

Boud, D. (1995). *Enhancing learning through self assessment*. London: Kogan Page.

Copyright © 2006, Idea Group Inc. Copying or distributing in print or electronic forms without written permission of Idea Group Inc. is prohibited.

Brindley, G. (1991). Assessing achievement in a learner-centred curriculum. In J. C. Alderson & B. North (Eds.), *Language testing in the 1990s*. Modern English Publications in association with the British Council.

Brown, J. D. (Ed.). (1998). *New ways of classroom assessment*. TESOL.

Cognition and Technology Group at Vanderbilt (1992). The Jasper Series as an example of anchored institution: Theory, program, description and assessment data. *Educational Psychologist, 27*(3), 291-315.

Conway, R., Kember, D., Sivan, A., & Wu, M. (1993). Peer assessment of an individual's contribution to a group project. *Assessment and Evaluation in Higher Education, 18*(1), 45-56.

Dodge, B., & March, T. (1995). *Some thoughts about Webquests*. Educational Technology Department, San Diego University. Retrieved from http://webquest.sdsu.edu/webquest.html

Dragemark, A. (2004). *The use of self assessment in the LENTEC project*. Retrieved from www.pedc.se/lentec/self assessment

Dudley-Evans, T. (1995). Common core and specific approaches to academic writing. In D. Belcher & G. Braine (Eds.), *Academic writing in a second language: Essays on research and pedagogy*. Norwood, NJ: Ablex.

Edge, J. (1998). *The foundation module, unit 2*. Aston University MSc in TESOL, Teaching English for Specific Purposes. Gibbs, G. (1995). *Assessing student centred courses*. Oxford Centre for Staff Development.

Gipps, C. (1994). *Beyond testing*. The Falmer Press.

Lejk, M., & Wyvill, M. (2001). The effect of the inclusion of self assessment with peer assessment of contributions to a group project: A quantitative study of secret and agreed assessment. *Assessment & Evaluation in Higher Education, 26*(6).

Lynch, T., & Anderson, K. (1991). *Study speaking*. CUP.

Kosel, B. (2002, March). Problem-based learning in teaching English across the curriculum. *IAFETL ESP SIG Newsletter, 21*.

Oscarson, M. (1989). Self assessment of language proficiency: Rationale and applications. *Language Testing, 6*(1), 1-13.

Oscarson, M. (1999). *Estimating language ability by self assessment: A review of some of the issues* (IPD-rapporter Nr 1999:02). Göteborgs Universitet.

Oscarson, M. (2002). *En steg/framework-jamforelse* (A comparison of Swedish grading levels ["Steg"] and the Council of Europe framework levels). Stockholm: Skolverket och Institutionen for pedagogik och didaktik, Göteborgs universitet.

Copyright © 2006, Idea Group Inc. Copying or distributing in print or electronic forms without written permission of Idea Group Inc. is prohibited.

Papert, S. (1980). *Constructionism vs. instructionism*. [Speech delivered by video to a conference of educators in Japan.] www.papert.org/articles/const_inst/const_inst1.html

Perkins, P., et al. (2004). The LENTEC guide to learning English. In *Problem based learning in virtual mobility projects*. International Programme Office for Education and Training, Leonardo da Vinci Language Project, S/01/B/F/LA- 127024.

Sluijsmans, D., Moerkerke, G., Merrienboer, J., & Dochy, F. (2001). Peer assessment in problem based learning. *Studies in Educational Evaluation, 27*(1), 153-173.

Wharton, S. (1998). *Language testing module, unit 5 validation*. Aston University MSc in TESOL, Teaching English for Specific Purposes.

Woods, R. D. (1994). *Problem-based learning: How to gain the most from PBL*. Hamilton, Ontario: The Bookstore, McMaster University.

Vygotsky, L. S. (1978). *Mind and society: The development of higher mental processes*. Cambridge, MA: Harvard University Press.

Copyright © 2006, Idea Group Inc. Copying or distributing in print or electronic forms without written permission of Idea Group Inc. is prohibited.

Chapter IX

Evaluating Designs for Web-Assisted Peer and Group Assessment

Paul Lam
The Chinese University of Hong Kong, Hong Kong

Carmel McNaught
The Chinese University of Hong Kong, Hong Kong

Abstract

Activities, such as peer-group discussion and peer review, where students assist each other by commenting on and assessing each other's course work, are thought to be beneficial and effective in many aspects. Web-based technology has opened up new possibilities for peer- and group-assessment activities. Three main Web functions—e-resources, e-display, and e-communication—are discussed in this chapter in the context of six cases of teachers using peer and group assessment in a Hong Kong university. These cases use different levels of Web enhancement. Evaluation of the six cases involved student surveys, focus-group interviews, teacher surveys, analysis of forum postings, and counter site logs. The chapter provides an analysis of this evaluation data within the various designs of

Copyright © 2006, Idea Group Inc. Copying or distributing in print or electronic forms without written permission of Idea Group Inc. is prohibited.

*these courses. The data collected generally confirm that Web-enabled peer-
and group-assessment activities can produce positive results. The need for
careful planning for these types of assessment activities is also clearly
illustrated.*

Peer and Group
Assessments in Teaching

Traditionally, learning has been regarded as an individual process, especially
under the influence of individualism in western countries (Webb & Palincsar,
1996). The model was that students would learn on their own in order to compete
with their peers, and their achievements in tests or projects were also assessed
on an individual basis. However, beginning in the 1950s, there have been an
increasing number of studies demonstrating that group learning can be superior
to individual-to-individual transfer of learning (Johnson & Johnson, 1989).
Cooperative interactions were identified as bringing about good learning outcomes. A variety of peer-learning approaches appeared, and students were also
assessed either on a group basis or an individual basis (Sharan & Hertz-
Lazarowitz, 1980; Slavin, 1980, 1995).

Peer assessment involves using peers' comments in assessing the quality of
assignments. Johnson and Johnson (2004) defined group assessment as "collecting information about the quality or quantity of a change in a group as a whole,"
while peer assessment "occurs when peers collect information about the quality
or quantity of a change in a student" (p. 2). Thus, group-assessment activities
involve students working in groups. Very often, group assessments look only at
the group's performance as a whole and ignore the differential performance of
the individuals in the group. A more complete model involves the performance
of the group and its members being assessed not only by the teacher, but also by
their peers in the same or in other groups. These activities involve both peer and
group assessments.

Activities that involve peer assessment take many different forms, such as peer
tutoring (Wagner, 1982), cooperative learning (Kagan, 1985, 1994), peer-group
discussion (Hatano & Inagaki, 1991), and peer review in writing (Gere, 1987) in
which students assist each other by commenting on and assessing each other's
course work. Brown, Race, and Smith (1996) suggested that peer assessment
helps students develop an awareness of the importance of structure, coherence,
and layout in their work; peers can help one another by brainstorming the content
and structure of essays. They can check for correct answers and may be able
to identify exactly where errors have occurred.

Copyright © 2006, Idea Group Inc. Copying or distributing in print or electronic forms without written
permission of Idea Group Inc. is prohibited.

Group-assessment activities also take many different forms. Group-based discussions (Webb & Farivar, 1999), assignments, projects, and debates are common enactments of group learning in classrooms. Group assessment is considered to be highly conducive to learning in a number of ways. Baumeister and Leary (1995) commented that the need to belong to and maintain human relationships is a fundamental benefit. Johnson, Johnson, and Smith (1998) remarked that "the research results consistently indicate that cooperative learning will promote higher achievement, more positive interpersonal relationships, and greater psychological health than will competitive or individualistic efforts" (p. A:32). There are also reports that group projects promote essential learning skills, including organization, negotiation, team work, cooperation, leadership, and problem-solving (Smith, Armstrong, & Tait, 2003).

As Table 1 suggests, peer assessment, group assessment, and peer-and-group assessment of activities can be considered as involving three major steps. There is a *preparing* stage in which students collect information and understand the activity to be done. Group assessment activities may have the preparation done in groups. The *working* stage is where students actually work out a solution, a report, or a piece of writing (alone or in groups). The *sharing* stage is when the worked solutions and writings are circulated for feedback. Additional sharing may occur when the first drafts are revised based on feedback and then resubmitted for further comments. Peer assessment sharing involves peer review at this stage. Group-assessment activities may receive feedback from the teacher. Group activities may also involve peer assessment when their fellow student groups or their fellow classmates are reviewing the group work individually.

Table 1. Stages of peer and group assessment activities

Stage	Assessment activity		
	Peer	Group	Peer and group
Preparing	Preparation and information gathering alone	Preparation and information gathering in groups	Preparation and information gathering in groups
Working	Working alone	Working in groups	Working in groups
Sharing	Presentation of work	Presentation of work	Presentation of work
	Feedback from peers	Teachers' feedback	Feedback from peers
	Refinement of work/enrichment of ideas	Refinement of work/enrichment of ideas	Refinement of work/enrichment of ideas

Copyright © 2006, Idea Group Inc. Copying or distributing in print or electronic forms without written permission of Idea Group Inc. is prohibited.

The Web in Teaching

University teachers are now more willing and able to use e-learning to assist their teaching because the advance of technology has made the development of educational Web sites more convenient. There are now online functions that are widely deemed to have a potential to enhance learning. The present study focuses on the following three functions: e-resources, e-display, and e-communication.

E-resources provide reading and learning materials to students. These materials are potentially more media-rich than traditional text-based materials (Hills, 2003). For example, common online materials in the sciences include animations and well-drawn graphics that can better explain difficult concepts because they assist students to visualize movements of molecules and genes in three dimensions. Online materials can also help students to extend their learning beyond the main requirements of the subject; examples are virtual laboratory video clips or a glossary of terms. Obviously also, the provision of well-organized links to other resources on the Web has a potential to support self-directed and exploratory learning.

The e-display function enables the Web to be a place for showing and exchanging students' work. File accessibility and revision is greatly improved compared with ordinary face-to-face exchange.

Lastly, the e-communication facility promotes student-student and teacher-student dialogues. Communication is considered by many to be essential to learning (e.g., Laurillard's, 2002, conversational model of learning). Using the Web for communication may have certain advantages over face-to-face discussion because it enables the keeping of better track records of the discussion and allows more time for reflective remarks. Communication between students and students, or between students and teachers, is achieved through the use of online discussion forums, chat rooms, and/or other online communication technologies (Kearsley, 2000).

One of the strengths of using the e-mode of handing out resources, displaying files and work, and engaging in communication is that students can access materials and messages an unlimited number of times, and at various times and places; this can increase the opportunities for learning.

When Pedagogy Meets Technology

The three Web functions can be used to facilitate peer and group assessment activities (Figure 1). E-resources can be used to provide materials for prepara-

Copyright © 2006, Idea Group Inc. Copying or distributing in print or electronic forms without written permission of Idea Group Inc. is prohibited.

Figure 1. Possible uses of the e-functions during activities

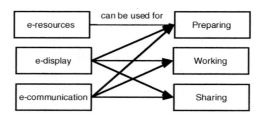

tion. The e-display functions may be used to exhibit students' assignments and ideas, or for critique and review. These drafts and ideas may also help other students' preparation or working process as well. Lastly, the e-communication function has the potential to help all the three stages: Students may use online discussion to search for ideas and information when getting ready for the task; they can discuss online when working on the task; and, as its most frequent use, students use e-communication when they share what they have already written in order to get suggestions for improvements. No one single e-learning design can employ all these possibilities and in Figure 1 we shall look at six different designs.

The Study

This chapter looks at how current Web technology can assist peer and group assessment in higher education by reporting the evaluation of six recent cases of Web-assisted peer or group assessment activities at a university in Hong Kong. These six cases have been chosen to be presented here not because they are all extremely successful. On the contrary, there is a range of effectiveness in these Web-enhanced peer and group assessment attempts. They are reported here because, taken together, they reveal useful patterns.

The Web development and evaluation of the six cases have been supported by the e³Learning (e³L) (i.e., enrich, extend, evaluate learning) project which has been designed to assist teachers to better exploit the possibilities of Web-assisted teaching. Full details of the design of this project are in James, McNaught, Csete, Hodgson, and Vogel (2003) and the project Web site http://e3learning.edc.polyu.edu.hk/. The e³L project operates across three universities: the Hong Kong Polytechnic University, the City University of Hong Kong, and The Chinese University of Hong Kong.

Copyright © 2006, Idea Group Inc. Copying or distributing in print or electronic forms without written permission of Idea Group Inc. is prohibited.

Figure 2. Web-assisted cases of peer and group assessment

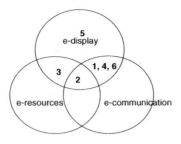

Table 2. Matching of e-functions and activities in the six cases

Web function	Assessment activity		
	Peer	**Group**	**Peer and Group**
	1. online journal 2. clinical cases	3. group case-based activity 4. online debate	5. group role-play 6. group multimedia project
e-resources	2	3	-
e-display	1, 2	3, 4	5, 6
e-communication	1, 2	(3), 4	6

Overview of the Six Cases

As shown in Figure 2, the cases incorporated different designs of using the three functions of the Web. Table 2 shows in more detail the peer assessment, group assessment, and peer-and-group-assessment activities in the six cases and the respective e-functions involved in each case.

The first two cases used the Web mainly to assist peer assessment. Activities carried out were reflective journal writing and discussion of clinical cases. Cases 3 and 4 used the Web for group-assessment activities: group case-based activity and online group debate. The last two cases used the Web to assist activities that have both the peer and group assessment components. The activities involved were group role-plays with peer criticism and Web-assisted group projects.

Five of the courses in these six cases were in the field of nursing. Case 5 involved a course on English-language teaching. All the courses were held in the Hong Kong Polytechnic University either in the 2002-2003 or 2003-2004 academic years.

Copyright © 2006, Idea Group Inc. Copying or distributing in print or electronic forms without written permission of Idea Group Inc. is prohibited.

Figure 3. Evaluation data types

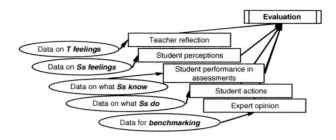

Table 3. Sources of evaluation data for the six cases

Data sources	Case 1	Case 2	Case 3	Case 4	Case 5	Case 6
Teacher reflection on the experience of the course (data on how the teacher *feels*)	Course-end teacher survey	Postings teacher made on the website	Course-end teacher survey	Course-end teacher survey	Course-end teacher survey	Course-end teacher survey
Students' perceptions of their experience (data on how students *feel*)	2 student surveys, (mid-term and course-end); 2 focus-group meetings	Course-end student survey	Course-end student survey	Course-end student survey & focus-group interview	8 task-end student surveys, and 1 course-end student survey	Course-end student survey & focus-group interview
Student performance in assessments (data on what students *know*)	X	Forum posting content analysis	X	Forum posting content analysis	X	Forum postings content analysis
Student actions (data on what students *do*)	Site and forum logs	Site and forum logs	Site logs	Site and forum logs	X	Site and forum logs
Expert opinion e.g. evaluator, peer evaluator, external examiner, employers (data which has *'benchmarking'* validity)	X	X	X	X	X	X

Outline of the Evaluation Model Used

The overall approach of the evaluation is aligned with a constructivist approach rather than with an absolute measurement perspective (Reeves & Hedberg, 2003; Scriven, 1993). Thus, the data collected are not meant to be precise measurements of the learning enhancement. Instead, they are rich descriptions that aim at giving indications of the advantages and disadvantages of the learning intervention. Multiple sources of evaluation data were collected. As shown in Figure 3 and Table 3, five sources of data are used in e³L evaluations: teacher reflection, student perceptions, student performance, student actions, and expert opinions (Lam & McNaught, 2004).

Copyright © 2006, Idea Group Inc. Copying or distributing in print or electronic forms without written permission of Idea Group Inc. is prohibited.

Kennedy (2004) argues that we need to put an increasing emphasis on the cognitive processes of learners. While his work is with learner-content interactions in stand-alone computer environments, his "cognitive interaction model" is of interest in evaluating the possible benefits of online environments. He defines *cognitive interactivity* as being "a continuous, dynamic relationship between instructional events and students' cognitive processes that is mediated by their behavioural processes" (p. 58). In the evaluation studies, we have tried to distinguish between what students *do* and what students *know* in order to tease out some understanding of this relationship.

Table 3 shows that the evaluation strategies of the six cases are varied, depending on the pragmatics of the situation, such as the availability of the teacher and the class. Note that, in these six cases, no expert peer review was used, though it has been valuable in other e³L evaluations.

Case 1: Peer-Review of Reflective Journals (E-Display and E-Communication)

Introduction

The teacher of a nursing course put up a site using the WebCT platform. It was the first time that the teacher had tried to bring e-learning into her teaching. Some parts of the site contained resources including video clips, pictures, readings of various subject themes, and crossword puzzles. More interestingly, the teacher also planned a Web-assisted peer-review activity in which the students were asked to share and comment on each other's reflective journals posted online; this part of the site is the focus of this case. Although the experience was not very successful, the teacher was pleased with this as a first attempt.

Students were asked to submit to the site forum short commentaries (not more than 100 words each) after they had begun their clinical placement. The teacher required that the reflective journals include the following three aspects: (1) students' evaluation of the strengths and weaknesses in their conducting nursing assessment, planning nursing management, and communicating with clients; (2) what the students have gained from the experience; and (3) how the experience has affected their future learning. The teacher also required that students should constantly view their peers' commentaries and give feedback through the forum. Students were also encouraged to refine or provide more information to enrich their journal entries based on the feedback they received. Both the commentaries and the peer feedback on the commentaries were counted in the course grade.

Copyright © 2006, Idea Group Inc. Copying or distributing in print or electronic forms without written permission of Idea Group Inc. is prohibited.

Figure 4. Design of Case 1

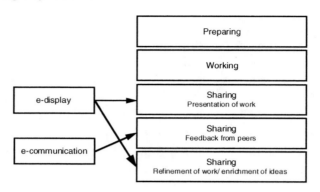

As Figure 4 shows, the peer assessment was assisted by the e-display and e-communication functions of the WebCT forum.

The teacher believed in the benefits of peer learning. She designed this activity of peer-reviewed reflective journals in order for the students to be more engaged in, and give more thought to, their clinical placement experiences. She also hoped that the availability of their peers' stories of clinical experiences online would give students a higher motivation in the course and deepen their understanding of clinical nursing practice.

Evaluation Methodology

Two student online surveys (one at mid-term and one at course-end), and two focus-group meetings (one at mid-term and one at course-end) were conducted. A teacher survey was also conducted after the course was finished to collect opinions from the teacher's point of view. The response rates of the mid-term and course-end student online surveys were 88% (97 students out of the 110 completed the survey) and 51% (56 students out of 110 completed the survey) respectively.

Observed Activity on the Web

E-Display

The e-display function did not work as well as expected. Although the teacher encouraged the students to do the activity and a small amount of the course mark

Copyright © 2006, Idea Group Inc. Copying or distributing in print or electronic forms without written permission of Idea Group Inc. is prohibited.

was attributed to this online activity, only a total of 59 journal entries were recorded. This means that nearly half the students did not write and post their 100-word commentaries.

E-Communication

The online communication function was not very well utilized either. A total of 45 pieces of feedback were recorded on the forum, commenting on the journal entries posted there, but 25 of them were written by the teacher herself.

Results from Surveys and the Focus Group

A moderately positive feeling towards the online commentary was recorded in the two student surveys. For example, a mean of 3.54 (in a scale from 1 to 5, with 5 being strongly agree) was collected when the students were asked whether they liked this activity of writing about clinical practice on the Web site. The mean score was 3.29 when the students were asked whether they thought the activity had helped them learn. The mean was 3.46 when asked whether they agreed that they had learned from reading other students' commentaries. A major problem in the student survey data was that there was a high percentage of students who picked the "cannot decide" option (around 40% in each case), suggesting that many of the students either did not have strong interest in this activity or they might have not done the activity in the first place.

This lack of participation was further confirmed in the focus-group meetings. Students admitted that they found it difficult to find time to look at others' files of clinical experience since there had already been many things to deal with and there were too many postings on the site.

Some of the students blamed the unfriendliness of the WebCT forum for its unpopularity. The messages were arranged in chronological order rather than according to the topics. Students suggested that relevant messages with their replies should be arranged together like a message board. There was also a complaint about the forum's incompatibility with Chinese characters.

Students suggested breaking the class into smaller groups so that each student would need to read the journals within one group only. Students did not feel they knew their classmates well enough to engage in active, even heated, discussion online; they lacked the feeling of an online community. Some others said that the forum would be more interesting if the teacher posted answers to common problems onto the forum.

The teacher observed no significant learning improvement; she noted in the course-end teacher survey: "I see no obvious learning improvement; however,

Copyright © 2006, Idea Group Inc. Copying or distributing in print or electronic forms without written permission of Idea Group Inc. is prohibited.

I noticed that they are more eager to talk about their learning difficulties and share with me on their clinical experience related to subject material learning."

Case 2: Peer Discussion of Cases (E-Resources, E-Display, and E-Communication)

Introduction

The second case is a Web-enhanced peer assessment activity (online case-based discussion) implemented by a teacher of a one-semester course on nursing. The teacher has used the Web in teaching for four years, but it was his first attempt at this kind of activity. The results, however, have turned out to be quite promising.

The teacher provided two multimedia-enriched cases (with photos, simple animations, and sound effects) about a car and a fire accident respectively and asked the students to post their thoughts and remarks on these cases on the site forum. The car-accident case was further split into three stages: the first on the accident scene, the second in the hospital after a preliminary check-up, and the third in the hospital after radiographic scans had been taken. The second case was split into two stages: the accident scene and the hospital. The photos, sound effects, and real hospital reports and scans made the case contextually rich and realistic. There were questions to consider and decisions to be made in each of

Figure 5. Design of Case 2

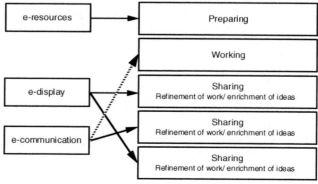

Copyright © 2006, Idea Group Inc. Copying or distributing in print or electronic forms without written permission of Idea Group Inc. is prohibited.

the stages of the cases. There were also links to other Web resources related to the cases. The students posted their suggested decisions and their justifications of their decisions onto the forum, while the peers commented on each other's solutions. The cases were also used as materials for face-to-face discussion in the tutorials.

The teacher motivated the students to participate in the online discussion by constantly monitoring the progress on the site and regularly added his timely comments to help build the atmosphere and the sense of community. Participation in the online discussion was counted as part of the course assessment. As Figure 5 shows, facilitation of this case-based activity was achieved by all the three Web functions we have identified.

The teacher believed that it is important for students to go through real cases in his course in order for students to practice decision-making, which is a key skill in the students' future nursing profession. The reason for the teacher's decision to introduce a peer-discussion component to his cases was that he believed the feedback and comments from the peers would enable students to better consider the different aspects of a case and be more engaged in the case.

Evaluation Methodology

The response rate of the course-end student online survey was 85% (76 students out of 89 completed the survey). In addition, five students gave their opinions in the focus-group meeting, and the teacher gave feedback on the Web site. Site log data and forum postings were also analyzed.

Observed Activity on the Web

E-Resources

Students mentioned in the focus-group meeting that the multimedia representation of the cases were "high-tech" and interesting to look at, and thus had attracted their attention. They regarded the cases as being realistic. They also remarked that cases with the possibility of showing animation and videos are most useful to show sequences of events and procedures.

The links to other Web resources were highly appreciated as well. Students noted that they quoted information from textbooks, journals, or Web sites more readily and that they considered searching for information on the Web convenient.

Copyright © 2006, Idea Group Inc. Copying or distributing in print or electronic forms without written permission of Idea Group Inc. is prohibited.

Figure 6. Distribution of students' frequency of posting

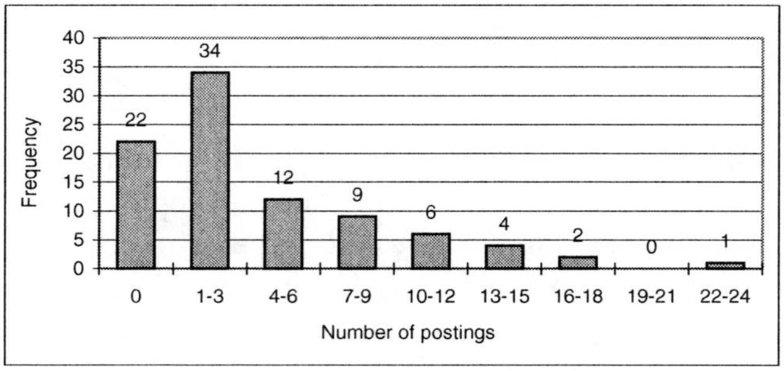

E-Display and E-Communication

The site forum (in which both the e-display and e-communication took place) attracted good participation. The forum logs revealed a satisfactory to high degree of use of the forum for discussion. The total number of postings recorded in the forum was 449. Of the postings, 79 were written by the teachers. On average, each student (in a class of 89) posted about 4.2 messages. Over 75% (67 out of 89) of the class participated in the online discussion. While most of them had posted one to three times throughout the course, five students participated actively in the forum, with postings ranging from 15 to 23 each (Figure 6).

Students reported that there were keen discussions on the site. Many of them would look at the postings more than once a week during the most active period of the forum. They admitted that they posted messages onto the forum because marks were allocated to the online participation. However, they thought that once they were accustomed to visiting the forum, they found accessing it and using it very useful. They also appreciated that the teacher often read their postings on the forum and wrote replies in the forum as well.

Students in general preferred to have online discussions before working on the papers, so they could pinpoint the most relevant information. Through the online discussion, they clarified misunderstandings and thus avoided interpretation errors when writing their essays. This was not expected and is shown as a dashed line in Figure 5.

Copyright © 2006, Idea Group Inc. Copying or distributing in print or electronic forms without written permission of Idea Group Inc. is prohibited.

Results from Surveys and the Focus Group

Generally speaking, the online case discussion activities were valued highly by the students. Most students (~70%) found completing the cases helpful and felt that they had learned from doing so.

With respect to the comparison between face-to-face discussions and the online forum, many students thought it was effective and efficient to use the Web for the discussion (~60% agree or strongly agree). With respect to the quality of criticism, over half of the students thought their peers could give a high-quality critique (~55% agree or strongly agree) and most of them thought the Web had enabled them to receive feedback (80% agree or strongly agree).

The majority of students agreed that they received good ideas or comments from their peers (~70% agree or strongly agree) and that the feedback was informative (~75% agree or strongly agree). Suggestions for improvement included providing more background information in the cases, lengthening the time of working on the cases, and removing the assessment scheme.

All students agreed that they had few opportunities to express their ideas in tutorial classes due to the limited class time (two hours) and the relatively large class size. The online discussion thus provided more opportunities for students

Table 4. Forum postings classification categories related to the SOLO taxonomy

SOLO Taxonomy (Biggs, 1999) categories	Explanation of SOLO categories	Postings classification categories	Type of posting
Prestructural	Misses the point	Non-substantive	• Social
Unistructural	Single point	Substantive	• Adding new points
Multistructural	Multiple unrelated points		• Enhancement and clarification of points
Relational	Logically related answer	Elaborated substantive	• Making clear contrary statements
Extended abstract	Unanticipated extension		• Developing complex arguments • Referring to material with a new perspective • Using fresh and different reference material

Copyright © 2006, Idea Group Inc. Copying or distributing in print or electronic forms without written permission of Idea Group Inc. is prohibited.

to discuss. All in all, the students affirmed the appropriateness of conducting the discussion in e-format.

Although the teacher did not notice any significant improvement in student-student and student-teacher interactions throughout the course, he believed that the Web activities improved students' understanding of the subject matter. In the Web site, he thought the discussion forum was the most effective component.

Analysis of Forum Postings

The students were able to give good comments to each other. On the forum, 23 randomly sampled threads with 102 postings were selected for further analysis. The 102 randomly selected postings (23% of the overall postings) were analyzed with reference to their nature and quality of content. Postings were classified as nonsubstantive (usually social; Although we do recognize the value of social interaction in community-building online, in this case another public forum was the social arena), substantive (i.e., related to the topic), and elaborated substantive. These classifications are related to the Structured Observation of Learning Outcomes (SOLO) classification (Biggs, 1999), as shown in Table 4. A summary of the data is shown in Table 5. The data indicate a good level of engagement in the forum; the percentage of elaborated substantive postings is high.

Case 3: Group Case-Based Activity (E-Resources and E-Display)

Introduction

The third case is a Web-enhanced group activity in nursing. The teacher provided audio case clips, mainly to be listened to by the students online in their free time and then used as materials for discussions in tutorials.

Table 5. Summary of the analysis of the forum postings in Case 2

No. of postings analysed	102
% of postings analysed	23
% of non-substantive postings in sample	9
% of substantive postings in sample	30
% of elaborated substantive postings in sample	61

Copyright © 2006, Idea Group Inc. Copying or distributing in print or electronic forms without written permission of Idea Group Inc. is prohibited.

Figure 7. Design of Case 3

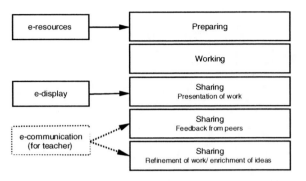

There was also a more elaborated case called the SARS (Severe Atypical Respiratory Syndrome) case (enriched with photos and audio). The students in groups handled this case. Each of the groups wrote a report describing how they would handle the SARS case. The teacher and peer students submitted these reports on the site for viewing. The teacher also posted in the same presentation area her feedback and grades on each of the group reports.

The main roles the Web played in this design of the case-based activity related to the e-resources and e-display functions (Figure 7). The e-resources function provided the students with realistic audio-recorded cases. The e-display function (using the presentation feature in WebCT) allowed the students to post their group reports onto the site for reviews. Discussion of the cases, and commenting on the group reports were not explicitly required to be done online. In fact, the teacher had allocated ample time for case discussions and feedback on reports in classes. Nevertheless, a forum was also set up on the course site to facilitate students who opted for additional e-communication online.

As in Case 2, the teacher in this case also believed in the benefits of using real cases in her course in order to train students' decision-making skills in applying theories and concepts to clinical situations. The teacher decided to use group work in this case-based teaching design because she believed students would "learn to learn" in groups through actively considering the feedback and comments from peers.

Evaluation Methodology

The evaluation data came from a course-end student online survey, a teacher survey, and the site-log information. The response rate of the course-end student

Copyright © 2006, Idea Group Inc. Copying or distributing in print or electronic forms without written permission of Idea Group Inc. is prohibited.

online survey was high—95% (145 students out of the 153 completing the survey).

Observed Activity on the Web

E-Resources

The students welcomed the resources of the cases. The site recorded heavy traffic during the course. Over 50% of the students who responded the survey said they visited the Web site a few times each week. The site logs recorded a high number of visits. Among the different pages of the Web site, the course schedule page was visited most (2,753 accesses) and audio cases page, including the SARS case, came second (919 accesses).

E-Display and E-Communication

The e-display function also seemed to function as expected. All 19 student groups posted their assignments on the forum, displaying their work to their peers for comments. The e-communication did not work well for student-student interactions. There was feedback from the teacher to each of the assignments, but no feedback from the students was recorded despite the fact that the teacher had encouraged the students to give peer feedback to each other.

Results from Surveys and the Focus Group

The students really enjoyed the Web-based cases. About 60% of the students found audio-enhanced cases helpful to their learning. Moreover, ~80% of the students had accessed and listened to the audio clips on the site, and over 50% of the students said the cases increased their interest in the course. Indeed, the main suggestion for improvement of the site was requesting more cases in video or audio formats.

The students also found the e-display function to be useful. Over 65% of the students responded with either "strongly agree" or "agree" to the survey statement "reading the work of the other groups was helpful to my learning" (mean score 3.69 out of 5). This suggests that, although the students did not make much use of the e-communication function, they took advantage of the e-display and benefited from reading their peers' work.

Copyright © 2006, Idea Group Inc. Copying or distributing in print or electronic forms without written permission of Idea Group Inc. is prohibited.

At the end of the evaluation, the teacher was so impressed by the students' positive reactions towards the e-resources that she indicated in the course-end teacher survey that her next plan was: "more learning resources can be uploaded to the website e.g. case studies and useful references & links."

Case 4. Group Online Debate (E-Display and E-Communication)

Introduction

The course in this fourth case was a nursing course for part-time students taking place over two months in the summer. It was the teacher's first attempt to use an online forum for a debate about controversial issues concerning nursing home care in Hong Kong. Each student group selected one discussion topic from four alternatives and could debate from either the proposing (i.e., affirmative) or the opposing side. The four debate topics were about home care and hospitalization and were as follows:

1. There is a need for change to meet the home-care needs of people in Hong Kong.
2. Increased home-care services can save health-care costs.
3. Home care is an alternative to hospitalization.
4. Home is always the best place for patients.

Figure 8. Design of Case 4

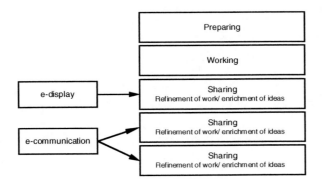

Copyright © 2006, Idea Group Inc. Copying or distributing in print or electronic forms without written permission of Idea Group Inc. is prohibited.

The proposing side was given one week to post their arguments to support the statement while the opposing side used the week following to post their arguments (as a group or on an individual basis). Then, the third week would go back to the first group again. At the end of the debate, each student had to submit his or her personal views on the topic in the form of a short essay. Marks were allocated according to the students' performance in the online debate and their individual course-end essays.

As Figure 8 shows, facilitation of this case-based activity was achieved by mainly employing the e-display and e-communication functions. The e-display functions used the site forum to host the student groups' arguments for or against the motion. The e-communication part (also using the forum) allowed the opponent groups to post their counterviews.

The teacher chose the format of an online debate to motivate the students to be more engaged in the subject, to be able to appreciate the complexity of the issues surrounding home care, and to be able to acquire some important learning skills such as analytic and argumentative skills. The teacher expected the assistance of the Web would lead to a smoother exchange of dialogue for her students who were mostly part-time students who had full-time work in the daytime.

Evaluation Methodology

Altogether five instruments were used to collect both the qualitative and quantitative data for this online debate attempt. An online course-end survey intending to elicit students' feelings about the online debate was conducted with a response rate of 50% (58 out of the 114 students). In the course-end focus-group meeting, 10 students enthusiastically expressed their ideas about various aspects of the online debate. A site log was installed to track students' use of the debate forum. A content analysis was also done on the debate postings. Lastly, the teacher's feedback was collected with a course-end survey.

Observed Activity on the Web

E-Display and E-Communication

The forum logs showed that the attention paid to the forum was intense. There were 212 postings on the forum: an average of 1.88 postings for each of the 114 students in the class. The total number of visits paid to the debate section of the forum over the period amounted to 11,663. On average, each student visited the forum 114 times, either browsing through the messages or posting their own

Copyright © 2006, Idea Group Inc. Copying or distributing in print or electronic forms without written permission of Idea Group Inc. is prohibited.

messages. On average, each student read 58 articles posted on the forum. For each topic, there was sufficient discussion—an average of 31 postings per topic—and the arguments were quite balanced with both sides of the debate well represented.

Results from Surveys and the Focus Group

Quantitative figures from the online survey showed students' liking of the online debate. Over 70% of students indicated their liking for online debate activity in the survey, and nearly 80% of students agreed that online debate added fun to the routine learning processes. This was echoed in the focus-group meeting with students appreciating the time flexibility and commenting that their critical and logical thinking had been strengthened. However, in the focus-group meeting, a strong minority of students condemned the online debate because it lacked immediate feedback, was time-consuming, and was more difficult being the opposing side of the debate.

In the survey, students agreed that they spent more time reading and finding additional information from other sources in order to complete the online debate task. Over 80% of students thought that they had engaged in real and meaningful arguments when they did the online debate. The positive appraisal might possibly be due to the self-recognized improvement in the argumentative skills but might also be due to the better preparatory work students had done.

Students supported the use of online debates over traditional ones, since (1) they could have a longer time to prepare, think more thoroughly, and thus absorb and assimilate the materials acquired more effectively; and (2) the greater credibility of debate sources enhanced academic soundness.

Students, by and large, agreed that they could analyze both pros and cons of an issue in a more systematic manner. Students stressed thinking beforehand as a learning benefit of the course. New angles of thinking were allowed in the discussion, with more new ideas being thrown out.

Improvements suggested by the students concerned streamlining the logistics, such as ways to improve grouping of students, more guidelines on debating and argumentative writing skills, introduction to the flow of the debate before it

Table 6. Summary of the analysis of the forum postings in Case 4

No. of postings analysed	123
% of postings analysed	100
% of non-substantive postings	2
% of substantive postings	44
% of elaborated substantive postings	54

Copyright © 2006, Idea Group Inc. Copying or distributing in print or electronic forms without written permission of Idea Group Inc. is prohibited.

begins, allowing the students to write longer pieces, and having longer time frames for the writing.

Analysis of Forum Postings

Using the SOLO taxonomy-based classification system described in Case 2, we found over 98% of the postings were substantive comments (presenting new points and clearly explaining positions), and many of the students were able to explain their comments in an elaborated way (e.g., able to quote external fresh information to support their points and linking arguments clearly). The first speakers usually posted the overview of the stance of the group, all of which were new points, and the second speakers of both sides adopted high quality replies in terms of essay articulation, content, and number of proper citations. The online discussions were shown in this sense to be quite genuine and meaningful. In addition, students demonstrated above-average analytical skills in this course assignment.

Case 5: Group Role-Play with Peer Criticism (E-Display)

Introduction

The fifth case involved role-play activities that had both peer- and group-assessment elements. The course was an English language for marketing course for a group of 12 business students. The teacher had been using role-plays to

Figure 9. Design of Case 5

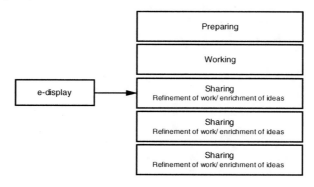

Copyright © 2006, Idea Group Inc. Copying or distributing in print or electronic forms without written permission of Idea Group Inc. is prohibited.

assist teaching for many years already but it was the first time that she had used the Web extensively for a series of role-play activities. Students were asked to roleplay two roles: (1) company with a new product or service, and (2) an Internet marketing company. They needed to complete eight tasks on the Web, including putting up home pages, writing e-mails, writing a press release, designing marketing research questionnaires, and finding Web resources. These activities were all done in groups.

The peer assessment part came from the constant peer feedback in the work the students created because, although each of the groups played two roles, they did not market their own product. Each group had to find another group of students whose product they would sell, and so they constantly monitored the other group's work to check whether their promotional materials were up to standard and suited their needs.

E-display was employed to facilitate the eight role-play activities. The function was mainly achieved by the forum of the site, in which the groups posted up their work as attachments for the teacher and their peers to see. The following diagram shows how the e-display functions helped the presentation of work and the housing of the final versions of the work. Peer comments on the e-tasks, however, were not collected on an online format but were mostly done in class or face-to-face outside class hours.

The teacher believed that the role-play activities would give students realistic practice in how to use the English language appropriately in marketing products. Also, by asking students to monitor each other's work, they would learn more about how to judge the quality of promotional materials and in turn would also produce materials that were of high quality as well. It was further hoped that the Web would facilitate the document exchange mechanism that was deemed critical in view of the complexity of the activity design and the relatively large number of e-tasks involved.

Evaluation Methodology

The evaluation strategies employed included eight end-of-task online student surveys, one course-end online student survey, one end-of-course focus-group meeting with the students, and one course-end teacher survey.

Copyright © 2006, Idea Group Inc. Copying or distributing in print or electronic forms without written permission of Idea Group Inc. is prohibited.

Observed Activity on the Web

E-Display

The students visited the course Web site very often; most of them did this a few times a week or more often. Of the 12 students, 8 claimed that they put up e-tasks onto the site quite often or very often, and 7 of the students reported that viewed the e-tasks of the other groups quite often or very often.

Results from Surveys and the Focus Group

Overall, the students' comments on the whole e-learning experience were positive. They generally thought the e-tasks as a whole helped them learn a great deal about using English for marketing (mean score 3.92 out of 5).

Nearly all of the e-tasks were considered to be quite difficult to do by the students. Some commented that they encountered difficulties in setting up home pages; some said they could not distinguish a press release from a promotional letter; some mentioned the difficulty in writing long questionnaires; some talked about the challenge of writing findings in a report; some had problems drawing graphics and making attractive poster designs. The e-tasks that required them to write e-mails and business letters seemed to be comparatively easier than the other e-tasks.

More uniform opinions were collected about the meaningfulness of the various e-tasks. All e-tasks were regarded as meaningful by most of the students surveyed. One interesting remark concerned with the setting up of a home page in E-task 1. The student remarked that at first he or she thought it was meaningless setting up a home page in an English course but later found that he or she had learned a lot by so doing.

Although the design of the e-tasks emphasized roleplay and peer help, the data collected did not show that students appreciated the feedback they got from their peers; rather, they preferred the feedback they obtained from the teacher. It was thought that more time might be explicitly allocated for student groups to critique each other either in class or online.

Copyright © 2006, Idea Group Inc. Copying or distributing in print or electronic forms without written permission of Idea Group Inc. is prohibited.

Figure 10. Design of Case 6

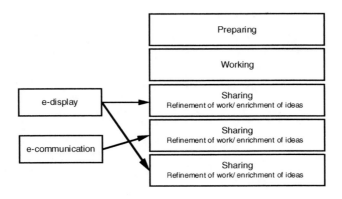

Case 6: Group Multimedia Projects with Peer Assessment (E-Display and E-Communication)

Introduction

The final case was also a combination of both group work and peer assessment. The teacher in this case asked her students to prepare multimedia projects in groups, which she called "Cybernet Shows," for a public health course. The finished projects were supposed to be deliverables that could be viewed online to promote any one of the issues covered in the course. The projects could take the form of a PowerPoint® show, a Web site, or a video strip. The site contained an assignment submission system through which the students posted their multimedia projects for teacher and peer revision. Furthermore, there was a discussion forum for the exchange of comments. Interaction mainly came from the teacher and the students' peer comments on each other's work in the forum.

The project activity took three stages: (1) Students were required to form groups of around 10 students and each group needed to produce and upload a draft Cybernet Show on the course site; (2) these shows were subjected to criticisms and comments from students of a preassigned group in the forum; and (3) students revised the drafts according to both the teacher's and their classmates' comments.

Copyright © 2006, Idea Group Inc. Copying or distributing in print or electronic forms without written permission of Idea Group Inc. is prohibited.

The Web facilitation of this case-based activity was achieved by the e-display and the e-communication functions. The e-display (putting the links to the materials onto the site forum) enabled the students to exhibit their multimedia projects for peer review. The e-communication function (i.e., forum) then enabled exchanges of opinions. Lastly, the e-display function played a role again as the teacher took the time to design an online exhibition page to repost the revised versions of the projects for the class to see at the end of the course (Figure 10).

The teacher aimed to improve creativity and the students' engagement with the subject through the group multimedia project. She expected that the assistance of the Web would facilitate the whole file exchange and idea exchange process, so necessary in this kind of activity design that involved cross-group interactions.

Evaluation Methodology

Data from both the teacher and the students were collected. A course-end student survey with a response rate of 38% (87 out of the 229 students responded) was conducted. Also, a focus-group meeting with eight students occurred. The postings on the forum were also collected and a forum-postings analysis was conducted to gauge how involved the students were in the forum. Average thread length, average postings per students, and the postings' content type (whether the messages contained substantive or nonsubstantive information) were analyzed. On the teacher side, a seven-item teacher survey was conducted. The teacher also made qualitative comparisons with students' work in previous years.

Observed Activity on the Web

E-Display and E-Communication

The site forum was active (the Cybernet-Show-related component was the largest share of the forum). The forum logs recorded 20,170 visits and 10,174

Table 7. Summary of the analysis of the forum postings in Case 6

No. of postings analysed	78
% of postings analysed	100
% of non-substantive postings	13
% of substantive postings	81
% of elaborated substantive postings	6

Copyright © 2006, Idea Group Inc. Copying or distributing in print or electronic forms without written permission of Idea Group Inc. is prohibited.

instances of an article being read. On average then, each of the 229 students paid 88 visits to the various places on the forum and each of them read 44 postings. The e-display function seemed to have operated very well.

The e-communication part, however, was not outstanding. The total number of postings in the Cybernet-Show section of the forum was 133. From this number, several postings need to be deducted—13 posts that were the links of the Cybernet Shows, 3 posts that were self-corrections of errors, and 39 posts that were teachers' comments—leaving 78 peer-review postings contributed by the 229 students in the class. The average thread length on the forum was 2.8, which meant that, on average, one or two replies were given to each leading post. Overall, online peer review was not actively carried out.

Results from Surveys and the Focus Group

Despite the fact that e-communication was not very active, the students still largely confirmed in both the survey and the focus-group meeting that the Cybernet Show on the whole was a good learning exercise. More than 80% of the respondents of the student survey showed positive responses to the statement: "Revising other group's presentation was a meaningful activity that helped my learning." However, participants in the focus-group meeting noted that the instructions for, and the layout of, the forum were quite confusing. Students were confused whether they should give feedback to individuals or to a group as a whole.

The forum-posting analysis generally shows that students were able to give constructive and useful comments to each other. There is still room for improvement, though, on the quality of the comments students give at this peer-revision stage. Although 81% of the postings were substantive comments (presenting new points and clearly explaining positions), few (6%) students were able to explain their comments in an elaborated way (e.g., able to quote fresh external information to support their points).

Students also generally found it helpful to learn to go through the second stage that required them to criticize each other's work. Sixty percent of the respondents agreed with the statement "After the cyber-show activity, I found that I was more willing to and am more able to give critical comments on the work of others." Nearly 80% of the respondents felt that they were now more willing to listen to and accept others' criticism, and they also felt they were able to learn from others' ideas.

As for the third stage of the activity (the modification of the Cybernet Shows based on the comments received), more than 80% of the respondents of the student survey agreed that it was useful to make amendments based on other

Copyright © 2006, Idea Group Inc. Copying or distributing in print or electronic forms without written permission of Idea Group Inc. is prohibited.

students' comments and criticisms. However, the focus-group meeting revealed that not many students did actually modify their shows. Students in the meeting said that they were not motivated to modify their project because the amendments were not marked. Also, there were practical problems in amending their projects. This discrepancy between student-survey data and focus-group opinions shows how important it is to triangulate evaluation data. The reality is that students will not do extra work (even if they acknowledge it could be beneficial), and so it is important for the course teacher to provide sufficient incentive to students.

In general, in both the focus group and the survey, students agreed that the multimedia-project work enhanced their creativity, trained them in a number of important skills (e.g., team-collaboration skills, computer skills, video-filming skills, and analytic skills), and helped them understand more about, and have more confidence in, really promoting public health care. The project also gave students a sense of satisfaction, especially when the deliverable product was finished. The project helped the students to integrate and articulate the course concepts and theories through the process of producing Cybernet Shows. The activity also helped them to associate personal values to the different public health issues. In this sense, the project has enabled students to move beyond application of course material in an academic way into a personalized expression of the material.

The teacher also reported that she saw more involvement from the students when the task was conducted online compared with the in-class presentations in the past. She also remarked that she saw great improvement on students' work too, perhaps as a result of the fact that the students got more feedback on their tasks when the tasks were online for their classmates' viewing. The teacher remarked that she enjoyed the addition of the Web component to her course and she observed that students got learning satisfaction, too. Apart from the student-student communication required by the Cybernet Show activity, the teacher also remarked that the forum had provided a better channel for teacher-student communication, an aspect she also valued very highly, although measures should be taken to foster a more active use the next time the activity is to run.

Discussion

Accommodating Complexity

The six cases reveal that peer- and group-assessment activities are relatively complex in design. Figure 11 shows that in these six cases more consideration

Copyright © 2006, Idea Group Inc. Copying or distributing in print or electronic forms without written permission of Idea Group Inc. is prohibited.

Figure 11. Complexity of peer and group assessment designs

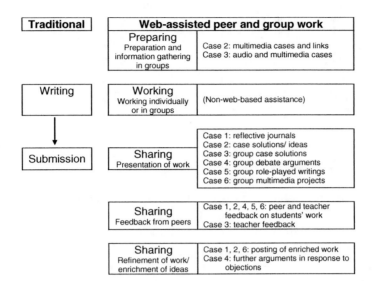

has been put into guiding students through the preparing, working, and sharing stages in peer- and group-assessment activities than occurs with the simple write-and-submit type of traditional assignments.

Figure 11 also shows how the six cases had different focuses in the various stages of the activities. For example, Cases 2 and 3 took care to assist students with the preparation stage of the activity by providing case materials and/or other readings on the Web. All the cases designed some form of work-sharing and work-reviewing mechanism. Cases 1, 2, 4 and 6 were even designed in such a way so that the students further reflected on their work and made revisions or enrichments based on the feedback received.

From these six cases, it becomes clear that the Web's strength lies in providing multimedia online materials (e-resources), providing a storage place for student-generated work and ideas, awaiting comments (e-display), and providing an archivable platform for ideas to flow between students in a time- and place-independent fashion (e-communication). This flexibility aids in solving the logistical problem of a complex activity design.

Students mentioned many times the flexibility and convenience of the assistance provided by the Web, and that they enjoyed the peer and group assessment: "I like the process of doing the cyber-show activity. It let us to discuss and co-operate with classmates. Since everyone has [their] own idea and opinions, I can learn and know different views they have on the issues;" "[I like] the interactive

Copyright © 2006, Idea Group Inc. Copying or distributing in print or electronic forms without written permission of Idea Group Inc. is prohibited.

way of learning from comments from classmates;" and "more videos like the scenario of SARS, can make the teaching more interesting."

However, not all is plain sailing. For example, in Case 1, students did not participate in online peer review actively as expected; and, in Case 6, nearly half of the students did not give online remarks to their peers' Cybernet Shows. The use of e-functions do not automatically lead to success. We will take a closer look at each of the three functions and try to identify some factors to success based on the experience of the six cases.

E-Resources

Students' and teachers' feedback towards the e-resources function tends to be, in general, very positive. Its use in the facilitation of peer and group assessment seems to be confirmed. In Table 8 is a summary of the strengths and weaknesses (if any) collected from the Cases 2 and 3 using e-resources. The wide acceptance of the e-resources function is not difficult to understand. Students usually do not object to teachers doing more work!

E-Display

The e-display function is not as popular as the e-resources. As can be seen from Table 9, both strengths and weaknesses were observed from the six cases concerning this function.

The strengths of this function are that in many cases the students actively view the displays and they agreed that viewing their peers' work is helpful to their learning. One main problem concerns the convenience of use. If uploading the

Table 8. Strengths and weaknesses of e-resources

	Strengths	Weaknesses
Case 2	• multimedia cases attract students' attention • animation and videos can show sequences of events and procedures clearly • searching information on the Web convenient – more frequent citations can be seen in students' work	• preparing cases is very time-consuming for teachers
Case 3	• students find audio-enhanced cases helpful • students want more • materials are viewed frequently	• preparing cases is very time-consuming for teachers

Copyright © 2006, Idea Group Inc. Copying or distributing in print or electronic forms without written permission of Idea Group Inc. is prohibited.

Table 9. Strengths and weaknesses of e-display

	Strengths	Weaknesses
Case 1		• participation not good • not easy to post and check messages in WebCT • can add too much to students' workload
Case 2	• achieved a good participation • students posted original ideas	
Case 3	• all students displayed assignments • students considered that reading the work of the other groups is helpful	
Case 4	• students posted their first statements as scheduled • intense attention given to reading postings	
Case 5	• all students posted their work for sharing successfully • students visited the work often	• encountered technical problems making web materials • encountered technical problems in posting materials online • did not generate much peer review
Case 6	• all students' posted work for peer review • revised students' work exhibited online • students viewed their peers' work	• encountered technical problems making web materials • encountered technical problems in posting materials online

materials for display can be made easier, more students will be willing to do this and do this more frequently.

Another major problem concerns workload. This e-component normally adds more work to students' course work rather than simplifying work for them. It is a key issue that teachers should foresee the additional workload brought about by the introduction of any extra online activities. In the case of e-display, there is a danger that students find more materials on display than they can handle. The more successful cases in our study used grouping to help students shortlist the materials and focus their attention.

Copyright © 2006, Idea Group Inc. Copying or distributing in print or electronic forms without written permission of Idea Group Inc. is prohibited.

Table 10. Strengths and weaknesses of e-communication

	Strengths	Weaknesses
Case 1	• teacher found students more eager to talk about their learning difficulties	• few critiques recorded • not easy to post and check messages in WebCT • too many journals to read • lack of teacher's attention
Case 2	1. keen discussion 2. teacher responded and monitored the discussion 3. helped clarification of concepts and ideas 4. improved exam and assignment performance 5. students able to give quality feedback to their peers 6. students considered system effective 7. students considered system convenient	
Case 3		• no feedback from students, only from teacher
Case 4	o most students preferred web-based debates to face-to-face ones o added fun to the routine class teaching o ideas on the forum well substantiated with evidence	(a) lacking immediate feedback (b) time-consuming for frequent checking of updates
Case 6	• students generally appreciated peer review	1. not a high quantity of online discussion on their peers' work 2. quality of feedback was not high. 3. instructions and layout of forum confusing

E-Communication

The e-communication function is found to be yet more difficult to use. As can be seen in Table 10, there are cases (2 and 4) where online discussions really worked and brought along benefits, while on the contrary, there are cases (1 and 3) where meaningful and active online discussion just did not happen and students did not enjoy the experience.

The main weaknesses relate to difficulty of use, scarce replies, and lack of immediate responses. The strategies used in the more successful cases to bring

Copyright © 2006, Idea Group Inc. Copying or distributing in print or electronic forms without written permission of Idea Group Inc. is prohibited.

about successful communications included the provision of clear guidelines specifying how, how often, what and when to interact online. Also, when teachers make it clear that e-communication is a required part of the course, then the forum is more likely to be populated. Populating the discussion forum is of utmost importance even if students are forced to do so, in order to get a sequence of discussions rolling. To a certain extent, this suggestion is in opposition to the belief that e-learning should be self-directed and e-communication should be self-motivated. However, judging from the experience reported here, this kind of genuine and active virtual learning space is not fostered easily, especially in places like Hong Kong where there is a limited tradition of e-learning.

The quality of the discussion will improve gradually, when (1) the students are more used to seeking help online; (2) an online learning community is built (Wenger, 1998); or (3) teachers demonstrate the usefulness of online discussion by leading one or a few meaningful discussions on the Web.

Progressive Development

Of course, the need to induct students into any new activity is well-known. Our experiences echo and reinforce those of other practitioners and researchers. Salmon's (2000) five-stage model of (1) access and motivation, (2) online socialization, (3) information exchange, (4) knowledge construction, and (5) ongoing development can be seen quite clearly in our cases. Case 1 had limited success because students did not feel comfortable with this online group; Stage 2 had not been reached. In several of the cases there was clear information exchange (Stage 3) but limited knowledge construction (Stage 4). In none of our cases is there evidence of students taking on independent ongoing development through their own initiatives (Stage 5).

The discussion of the e-communication function, in particular, highlights the importance of group dynamics and participation. This resembles the concept of group processing (Johnson & Johnson, 1989, 2004) which establishes that group members need assistance and guidance on collaborative skills before group work. In the same vein, it is observed here that online peer and group work needs support for the development of online group processing skills.

Both teachers and students are relative novices in the world of online learning. Even students who have spent considerable time online are not necessarily experienced in formal online learning situations. In our six cases, only the teacher in Case 2 was an experienced online teacher and even he was new to online peer review. Staff working in e-learning support need to constantly remember this and refrain from suggesting learning designs that are too ambitious for the teachers and students involved.

Copyright © 2006, Idea Group Inc. Copying or distributing in print or electronic forms without written permission of Idea Group Inc. is prohibited.

The experience of these six cases can now be fed back into future development work with teachers here in Hong Kong. There is no doubt that guidelines developed locally are more persuasive than totally foreign cases. The synergy we see here between our Hong Kong contexts and the reported experience of others elsewhere strengthens our guidelines and affirms our endeavors.

Acknowledgments

Funding support from the University Grants Committee in Hong Kong is gratefully acknowledged, as is the collaborative support of colleagues in the e³L project. We would like to pay an especial tribute to the teachers with whom we worked: Wong Wai Lin, Marian; Sarah Kong; Cynthia Wu; Tong, Tak Fai; Loretta Chung—all from the School of Nursing—and the Hong Kong Polytechnic University and Sima Sengupta, formerly of the Hong Kong Polytechnic University. Their commitment to their students and their enthusiasm to seek new ways to enhance their teaching are the keystones of the e³L project.

References

Baumeister, R. F., & Leary, M. R. (1995). The need to belong: Desire for interpersonal attachments as a fundamental human motivation. *Psychological Bulletin, 117*(3), 497-529.

Biggs, J. (1999). *Teaching for quality learning at university.* Buckingham: SRHE and Open University Press.

Brown, S., Race, P., & Smith, B. (1996). *500 tips on assessment.* London: Kogan Page.

Gere, A. R. (1987). *Writing groups: History, theory, and implications.* Carbondale: Southern Illinois University Press.

Hatano, G., & Inagaki, K. (1991). Sharing cognition through collective comprehension activity. In L. Resnik, J. Levine, & S. Teasley (Eds.), *Perspectives on socially shared cognition* (pp. 331-348). Washington, DC: American Psychological Association.

Hills, H. (2003). *Individual preferences in e-learning.* Hants: Gower.

James, J., McNaught, C., Csete, J., Hodgson, P., & Vogel, D. (2003). From MegaWeb to e³Learning: A model of support for university academics to effectively use the Web for teaching and learning. In D. Lassner & C.

Copyright © 2006, Idea Group Inc. Copying or distributing in print or electronic forms without written permission of Idea Group Inc. is prohibited.

McNaught (Eds.), *Proceedings of the 15th Annual World Conference on Educational Multimedia, Hypermedia & Telecommunications, ED-MEDIA 2003,* Honolulu, Hawaii (pp. 3303-3310). Norfolk, VA: Association for the Advancement of Computers in Education.

Johnson, D. W., & Johnson, R. T. (1989). *Cooperation and competition: Theory and research.* Edina, MN: Interaction.

Johnson, D. W., & Johnson, R. T. (2004). *Assessing students in groups: Promoting group responsibility and individual accountability.* CA: Corwin Press.

Johnson, D. W., Johnson, R. T., & Smith, K. (1998). *Active learning: Cooperation in the college classroom* (2nd ed.). Edina, MN: Interaction.

Kagan, S. (1985). Dimensions of cooperative classroom structures. In R. Slavin, S. Sharan, S. Kagan, R. Hertz-Lazarowitz, C. Webb, & R. Schmuck (Eds.), *Learning to cooperate, cooperating to learn* (pp. 67-96). New York: Plenum Press.

Kagan, S. (1994). *Cooperative learning.* CA: San Juan Capistrano.

Kearsley, G. (2000). *Online education: Learning and teaching in cyberspace.* Belmont, CA: Wadsworth/Thomson Learning.

Kennedy, G. E. (2004). Promoting cognition in multimedia interactivity research. *Journal of Interactive Learning Research, 15*(1), 43-61.

Lam, P., & McNaught, C. (2004). Evaluating educational websites: A system for multiple websites at multiple universities. In L. Cantoni & C. McLoughlin (Eds.), *Proceedings of the 16th Annual World Conference on Educational Multimedia, Hypermedia & Telecommunications, ED-MEDIA 2004,* Lugano, Switzerland (pp. 1066-1073). Norfolk, VA: Association for the Advancement of Computers in Education.

Laurillard, D. (2002). *Rethinking university teaching: A framework for the effective use of educational technology* (2nd ed.). London: Routledge Falmer.

Reeves, T. C., & Hedberg, J. G. (2003). *Interactive learning systems evaluation.* NJ: Educational Technology Publications.

Salmon, G. (2000). *E-moderating: The key to teaching and learning online.* London: Kogan Page.

Scriven, M. (1993). *Hard-won lessons in program evaluation.* San Francisco: Jossey-Bass.

Sharan, S., & Hertz-Lazarowitz, R. (1980). A group-investigation method of cooperative learning in the classroom. In S. Sharan, P. Hare, C. D. Webb, & R. Hertz-Lazarowitz (Eds.), *Cooperation in education* (pp. 14-46). Provo, UT: Brigham Young University Press.

Copyright © 2006, Idea Group Inc. Copying or distributing in print or electronic forms without written permission of Idea Group Inc. is prohibited.

Slavin, R. E. (1980). Effects of student teams and peer tutoring on academic achievement and time-on-task. *Journal of Experimental Education, 48,* 252-257.

Slavin, R. E. (1995). *Cooperative learning* (2nd ed.). Boston: Allyn & Bacon.

Smith, C. C., Armstrong, S. E., & Tait, S. J. (2003). Enhancing transferable skills development in group projects. *LTSN Engineering.* Retrieved March 9, 2005, from http://www.ltsneng.ac.uk/downloads/miniproject/transferable _skills.pdf

Wagner, L. (1982). *Peer teaching: Historical perspectives.* New York: Greenwood Press.

Webb, N. M., & Farivar, S. (1999). Developing productive group interaction in middle school mathematics. In A. M. O'Donnell & A. King (Eds.), *Cognitive perspectives on peer learning* (pp. 117-149). Mahwah, NJ: Erlbaum.

Webb, N. M., & Palincsar, A. S. (1996). Group processes in the classroom. In D. Berliner & R. Calfee (Eds.), *Handbook of educational psychology.* New York: Macmillan.

Wenger, E. (1998). *Communities of practice: Learning, meaning and identity.* Cambridge, UK: Cambridge University Press.

Copyright © 2006, Idea Group Inc. Copying or distributing in print or electronic forms without written permission of Idea Group Inc. is prohibited.

Chapter X

How's My Writing?
Using Online Peer Feedback to Improve Performance in the Composition Classroom

Vanessa Paz Dennen
Florida State University, USA

Gabriel Jones
San Diego State University, USA

Abstract

This chapter presents a case study of how online peer feedback was used as a formative learning and assessment activity in a required, university-level composition course. The authors argue that such activities, if designed effectively, contribute significantly toward a student's sense of audience, authority, and empowerment as a productive member of a larger discourse community. In the study, students were divided into small workgroups and shared their work by posting it on the class discussion board. They were asked to provide feedback on specific parts of their classmates' work. Issues such as preparing students to provide peer feedback, quality and usefulness of the peer assessment, and student attitudes toward the peer assessment process are addressed.

Copyright © 2006, Idea Group Inc. Copying or distributing in print or electronic forms without written permission of Idea Group Inc. is prohibited.

Introduction

Composition courses are intended to teach students critical thinking and writing skills. No matter what the subject matter or focus used as a means of exploring writing-related concepts, the intent is always to help students be better able to write clearly, effectively, and persuasively. Peer assessment in the composition classroom can be an effective activity toward accomplishing these goals for a variety of reasons. From a learning standpoint, students have the opportunity to improve their writing skills through seeing each other's work, practicing their critique skills, and receiving feedback from classmates. Additionally, from an administrative standpoint, peer assessment can help an overloaded instructor increase the amount of feedback that students receive without increasing the instructor's workload and ideally increase the speed with which every student in the class can receive feedback.

Perhaps most importantly, however, peer assessment impresses upon students a sense of audience, of a community where ideas are created and shaped within a specific context and affected by the writer's understanding of her or his readers' knowledge, concerns, and response strategies. One of the most pressing tasks in a composition class is to give students a sense of responsibility for their ideas and of empowerment within a discourse community and the ways that power, authority, and responsibility play out within the classroom environment—both in terms of how students respond to their audience, both instructor and fellow students, and of how students are able eventually to assert their own authority with confidence—are deeply influenced by the ways that peer-assessment activities are structured and by the roles that instructors and students play within those activities.

This sense of community—of ideas shaped within a particular context that is developed by its members and influenced by the particular ways writers and readers respond to each other—is, we suggest, among the most important lessons that students can learn in the composition classroom, both for under-standing how writing and communication are created in the first place but also to instill a sense of ownership and investment in one's own ideas and of responsibility and interest in others' ideas. Peer feedback is also important in removing the typical, and to some degree debilitating, belief among some students that feedback is the sole responsibility of the instructor and instead can show that effective student critique can be helpful toward reading actively and, thus, productive collaboration in building writing communities in the classroom and beyond.

In a traditional classroom-based course, writing instructors may encourage peer critique by having students exchange physical copies of their writing, read them, and discuss them in small groups. These activities are generally considered good

Copyright © 2006, Idea Group Inc. Copying or distributing in print or electronic forms without written permission of Idea Group Inc. is prohibited.

ways to teach and reinforce writing concepts. However, there remain some challenges: Teachers can have difficulty monitoring critique discussions effectively, students often have to provide on-the-spot and thus generally nonreflective feedback, and responses are spoken (and temporary), not written. These activities can easily be moved online using commonly available courseware tools such as Blackboard or WebCT. Web-based asynchronous discussion can overcome the drawbacks of face-to-face feedback, allowing easy exchange of work, reflection, and teacher monitoring of the feedback process, as well as producing written artifacts of student work as it progresses.

This textual environment that students collectively create online with their instructors through peer critique activities can effectively create a strong sense of empowerment in writers and of active readership, thus replicating in small form the sorts of discursive communities where ideas get shaped and communicated both in academic and popular discourse. Online peer feedback can be one of the most powerful means toward giving students a sense of investment in the collaborative construction of such communities and of both their own and others' ideas within those communities.

Composition courses, we argue, should above all aim to help students develop their own voices as writers and as readers by giving them a sense of productive membership within a discourse community and by stressing the actual value of their contributions as editors. Through this, students develop a sense of responsibility and investment in both their own and their fellow students' ideas, which is doubly important because it gives them a feeling not only of ownership over their own writing—all too often attenuated, unfortunately, when feedback is solely in the instructor's hands—but also of empowerment within a discourse community because they feel partially responsible for shaping the quality and substance of that community. In this chapter, then, we examine the effects of an online peer feedback activity in a blended, college-level composition course in order to understand how best to help students productively understand their roles as both writers and readers within such communities.

Brief Review of Literature

Sharing student work online, upon completion or in-progress, is not a new concept. Student assignments presented in online portfolios can be used as a launching point for student-student interactions. Peers may provide each other with feedback on their assignments or enter a dialogue about a particular concept or technique represented within the body of work being critiqued (Bonk, Kirkley, Hara, & Dennen, 2001; Flanagan & Egert, 2000). The value of peer critique is multifaceted: It can allow students to see each other's work and share ideas, more advanced students can benefit from having to articulate to others what they

Copyright © 2006, Idea Group Inc. Copying or distributing in print or electronic forms without written permission of Idea Group Inc. is prohibited.

may have only intuitively understood, and learners who are uncertain about how to approach an assignment can gain a better grasp of it through seeing how other students responded to it (Bonk et al., 2001).

Peer feedback also can raise the quality of student work and emulate a professional work environment. Computer conferencing works well in a writing curriculum because the collaborative nature of a Web-based conference emulates many real-life writing situations. Although academics, lawyers, journalists, and business people may write on their own, activities such as peer critique are regular parts of their composition experiences, and their written products are always written with a clear sense of audience in mind (Bateman & Benson, 1999). Schools traditionally do not encourage students to write for an external audience, however, and in such circumstances students at best simply develop an ersatz sense of audience by tailoring their papers to what they perceive to be their instructors' interests and prejudices; as a result, students do not get used to reading their peers' work on a regular basis and generally view their writing as "right" or "wrong," to be judged by an external objective force rather than a collaborative discourse community. In a study of student writing for two different audiences—the teacher (graded writing) and distant peers—Cohen and Riel (1989) found that writing quality was higher when there was an anticipated peer reader, reinforcing the significance of an actual responsive audience in shaping students' sense of the importance of their own work.

Several scholars in composition have similarly argued that student writing improves when they expect their work to be read by fellow students, both because the process compels students to think through how they would respond not only to others' writing but, by extension, to their own, and, to an even greater extent, because of an embodied sense of audience (Cooper, 1986; Ede & Lunsford, 1984); when the feedback they receive is seen as part of a communal conversation rather than a measuring device, students are both more invested in their own ideas and more attentive to their means of presenting them (Anson, 1985; Olbert & Ring, 1993; Reynolds, 1987; Ziv, 1982). Students not only see teachers and their fellow students as performing different tasks and serving different purposes in giving feedback to the papers they've written; they understand themselves in entirely different contexts in relation to this feedback. With peer critique, students see themselves in a horizontal relationship, a conversation between mutually engaged partners and often rise to the expectations of that feedback community; with teacher feedback, students see themselves in a hierarchical relationship that operates more as a testing situation rather than a conversation. In this "testing" mode, student attention to audience often focuses at best on "what the teacher expects" (e.g., grammatical issues) rather than on what helps readers understand and get interested in the paper's discussion. Once students have a concrete sense of audience, regardless of

Copyright © 2006, Idea Group Inc. Copying or distributing in print or electronic forms without written permission of Idea Group Inc. is prohibited.

whether the course is online or in a classroom, their attention to and concern with audience often translates into improved quality in their papers (Greene, 1995).

Peer feedback is not without its problems, however. In a study of the peer feedback process, post-graduate students reported the process took a lot of time and was not within their comfort zone, although it did improve the quality of their work (Topping, Smith, Swanson, & Elliot, 2000). Sengupta (1998) found that students are reluctant to participate in peer feedback activities because they consider providing feedback to be a teacher activity, not a student activity. Even here, however, a sense of responsibility toward a community can improve student performance. DiGiovanni and Nagaswami (2001), for example, conducted a comparative study of live vs. online peer feedback in two ESL classes and found that, while students preferences for feedback format varied, online feedback partners were more likely to remain on task.

Further, Sengupta's (1998) study underscores the need for peer feedback earlier in writing instruction to counteract the sense that feedback is the teacher's turf; when students are not conditioned into this attitude, they can more quickly and effectively develop a sense of authority and empowerment as both writers and readers. Students are socialized in our educational system to look to the instructor for knowledge and guidance; peer contributions typically are not considered as valuable. In a traditional class, an instructor often maintains control of the viewpoint not necessarily to control the perspective presented in the course material, but rather to exert social and organizational control over the class. In an online course, social and organizational control are manifested in very different ways, and an instructor can open discussion to sharing viewpoints freely without completely handing over the reins. The shift of interest from instructor opinions to peer opinions increases motivation (Turoff, 2000); students want to participate when they feel that they can make valid contributions. Accordingly, this presentation in part proposes means toward creating a successful environment for peer critiquing that avoids these problems—for example, enabling students to feel more comfortable with the peer feedback process and to view it as a student (as well as teacher) activity, but one that elevates the role and responsibility of students within the class toward a more complex and engaged understanding of the writing and reading process.

Research Questions

This study sought to determine the effects of an online peer feedback activity on student writing in the preassessment stage. Some of the questions we hoped to answer include:

Copyright © 2006, Idea Group Inc. Copying or distributing in print or electronic forms without written permission of Idea Group Inc. is prohibited.

- Did the students improve from initial draft to revised draft?

- Did the students feel that providing feedback online in writing was more useful than providing it orally in class?

- Were the students more comfortable providing and receiving feedback online in writing, and was it more useful than providing it orally in class?

- Were the students satisfied with the feedback they received?

- Did the students feel that they had learned through the act of providing feedback?

Methodology

This study uses a mixed-method case-study approach to examine how online peer feedback was used as a formative learning and assessment activity in a required, university-level composition course. Case studies are useful for providing a descriptive account of the events that transpired during a particular educational activity. Their major limitation is generalizability, although one may readily examine the local knowledge generated by a case study and make his or her own "petite generalizations" (Stake, 1995). Petite generalizations, based on the themes and context of a case and how it relates to the reader's own context, can then be used to inform others' educational practice and research.

Participants

Two sections of a required composition class were studied. Students enrolled in the classes (n=48) were upperclassmen at a large public university who had either not passed a required writing examination or who had elected to take the course in lieu of the exam. They represented a wide variety of majors and included nonnative English speakers.

Description of Course and Activity

Both sections of the course were taught by the same instructor and used the same syllabus, assignments, and course activities. These classes were taught during a 6-week intensive summer session, meeting face-to-face 4 days a week and using Blackboard as a course communication tool to help share course materials, discuss and practice course concepts, and facilitate the peer-assessment process.

Copyright © 2006, Idea Group Inc. Copying or distributing in print or electronic forms without written permission of Idea Group Inc. is prohibited.

The instructional objectives of the course focused on developing basic writing skills for argumentative essays. Students completed three major units of instruction designed to increase student mastery of basic writing components such as introductions, problem, claims, and conclusions. These topics were introduced in the first unit and were continuously referred to and refined throughout the course. Each unit was 2 weeks long and was assessed by an essay. The online components of the class focused on two areas: The first part was an ongoing practice of argumentation skills, in which students critiqued an article each week; the second part was a peer feedback activity, which is the topic of this study.

Study Design

This study examines the results of the peer feedback activity for Unit 2 of the course. Unit 2 was chosen because the students had already had a chance to become familiar with how to use Blackboard and the instructor's expectations during Unit 1 and were not yet at the point of exhaustion that often overtakes students and affects their participation in an intensive summer course.

For this activity, each class was divided evenly into three groups of eight students each for a total of six groups across the two classes. Groups were formed by dividing the course roster, which was alphabetical by last name, into three even parts. Table 1 presents the breakdown of groups by gender and class standing.

Each group was given its own group discussion board in Blackboard and received the following directions:

By Monday at noon, post the first three paragraphs of your paper draft to the discussion forum in a new thread. By Tuesday at noon, provide feedback to AT LEAST three of your group members following the feedback instructions listed on the syllabus. By Thursday at noon, respond to your critiques by posting a revised draft. By Friday at noon, review the revised drafts of group members whose work you initially critiqued and let them know if you think it has improved.

Table 1. Composition of groups

Group	Class	Male	Female	Juniors	Seniors
1	A	3	5	1	7
2	A	4	4	3	5
3	A	6	2	2	6
4	B	5	3	4	4
5	B	5	3	2	6
6	B	3	5	0	8

Copyright © 2006, Idea Group Inc. Copying or distributing in print or electronic forms without written permission of Idea Group Inc. is prohibited.

The activity began during the second week of the unit, giving students the first week to choose a paper topic and to begin developing their drafts. Only the first three paragraphs of their papers were used for critique to keep the workload manageable for the students. The instructor felt that three paragraphs were a sufficient writing sample to help diagnose habitual writing problems without putting anyone in the position of editing a classmate's full paper. Indeed, students were not supposed to edit each other's papers, but were instead asked to point out areas in which the paper was not clear. The feedback model that students were asked to use is as follows:

When you provide peer feedback on a paper draft, try to address the following issues:

In terms of writing mechanics: Does it begin with a clear topic sentence? Does the first paragraph clearly state what the paper will be about? Are the characters and actions as concrete as possible? Are there any troublesome nominalizations? Does the writer use connectors to help make segues between thoughts? Is the information flow consistently old information to new information?

In terms of argumentation: What are the writer's claims and warrants? Are they as clear as they might be? Does anything detract from the argument? Is there anything that would strengthen the argument?

In terms of logistics, students copied and pasted their paragraphs directly into messages on the discussion board. Feedback was given in subsequent threaded messages. Students were told to either refer to paragraph numbers in their critiques or to provide quotes of the original work as needed to ensure the recipients of their feedback understood the segments to which a particular comment pertained. Participation in the activity was counted as part of the overall holistic course participation grade, including both online and in-class participation, and was worth 20% of the students' final course grades.

Data Collection Methods

Data were collected using a variety of methods. The archived peer feedback activity for each of the six groups, comprised of all student messages posted to the group discussion board for Unit 2, was downloaded in its entirety. For students who participated in the activity, this included both an initial and revised draft of the first three paragraphs of their Unit 2 papers.

Copyright © 2006, Idea Group Inc. Copying or distributing in print or electronic forms without written permission of Idea Group Inc. is prohibited.

Student demographic data (e.g., gender, class standing) were collected from the course roster. Additional demographic data were not deemed relevant to this study, although the instructor provided some contextual information about students in both classes.

Students completed a questionnaire at the end of Unit 2 at the time they turned in their papers. This questionnaire was administered on paper, at the end of a face-to-face class session, to help increase the response rate. Given the low online participation of some students, it was feared that an online survey would have a similarly low participation rate. For this study, we wanted to be sure to hear from all students, both those who were comfortable and likely to participate in online activities and those who were not.

Additionally, the instructor was interviewed after the Unit 2 papers were graded and returned to students. This timing was chosen both to help ensure that questions from the researchers did not influence the instructor's grading process and to allow the researchers to ask the instructor about any perceived influence the activity might have had on the quality of student work. The instructor also was asked to share his impressions of how smoothly the activity ran, why the groups had different results, and how useful the activity was for the students.

Data Analysis

The activity archives were reviewed in multiple ways to determine how the peer feedback activity affected student writing from initial to revised draft. A qualitative analysis was conducted to help develop an overall sense of flow and context for each group. Each message was then scored. The course instructor assisted in this process, developing a scoring rubric that could be used to rate the quality of both critique posts on a scale of 1 to 10. The rubric reflected the degree to which students were able to follow the feedback model. From these ratings we could compare overall quality levels across groups and measure individual student improvements.

Student surveys were analyzed using measures of central tendency, and the instructor interview was used to help provide context and to triangulate data from other sources.

Findings

The activity groups differed in terms of how much feedback they provided, as well as in the quality of that feedback. Table 2 summarizes the quantity of posts

Copyright © 2006, Idea Group Inc. Copying or distributing in print or electronic forms without written permission of Idea Group Inc. is prohibited.

Table 2. Quantity of posts

Group	Class	Mean number of critique posts	Median number of critique posts
1	A	6.13	6.0
2	A	6.13	6.0
3	A	2.63	2.5
4	B	5.88	6.0
5	B	3.63	3.5
6	B	1.63	2.0

for each group. Groups 1, 2, and 6 each had a high level of peer dialogue. The median number of critique posts for students in each of these groups was 6, exceeding the basic requirements of the assignment. In these groups, students tended to post feedback to each of their peers rather than just doing the minimum required. The other three groups had medians closer to the minimum requirements of the assignment (3 critique posts). Not everyone in these groups participated fully, and in one group there were two students who failed to participate at all.

On the questionnaire, students were asked why they did or did not participate in the activity. Overwhelmingly, the students who had been active posters cited reasons like "I knew it was supposed to help improve my grade," and "Because it was a course requirement." One student, who also posted rather high-quality critiques, commented "It helped me to see other people making mistakes because then I knew what the mistakes looked like and could avoid them myself." Conversely, the two students who did not participate at all stated "I didn't see the point," and "I was afraid I wuold [sic] look dumb." Other students whose participation was less than the minimum required made similar comments.

In looking at the quality of student posts, there also were great differences across the groups (See Table 3). Generally speaking, the groups with lower levels of participation had lower quality, too. However, these mean scores should not be viewed outside the context of the actual posts themselves. Indeed, two phenomena were observed in the holistic review of discourse in each group. Groups 1, 2, and 4 all had students who wrote strong critique posts, but not all posts by these strong students were rated highly. This in part appears to be due to the high number of critique posts written in these groups (most students in these groups received feedback from five or more peers). The first few critiques of a particular draft seemed to be the most detailed, answering most of the prompted critique questions, with subsequent ones more concerned with contributing to and developing the discussion and less focused on the original prompt. This strategy of transitioning from the prompt to more of a discourse-oriented type of message (e.g., commenting on others' critiques, elaborating on or questioning points

Copyright © 2006, Idea Group Inc. Copying or distributing in print or electronic forms without written permission of Idea Group Inc. is prohibited.

already made) reflected that the students were actually reading each others' contributions and building on them, not that they were letting quality of work drop off as they got deeper into the activity.

From initial to revised draft, some improvement was seen with almost all of the students. The instructor commented on this, stating:

I felt like the stronger students in the class were actually learning from the critique process. By that I mean that they learned how to improve their own papers by identifying weaknesses in others. In many cases I saw them rework part of the draft on which they did not receive feedback, making it stronger.

The weaker students in the class, on the other hand, had a tendency to treat the feedback process more mechanically. Their improvements tended to involve adopting the feedback comments they could implement literally (e.g., "I would change the character from 'The owner of the business's way of thinking' to 'business owner's thought process'"). They were unlikely to do much about in response to more conceptual feedback (e.g., "The characters in this paragraph are too abstract.").

When asked whether the activity had been helpful to them, 41 (85%) of the students indicated that getting feedback had been helpful, 26 (54%) felt that providing the feedback had been helpful, and 43 (90%) indicated that they had used the feedback they received to improve their drafts. All 46 students who participated in the activity indicated that they felt their revised draft was better than their initial draft. The seven students who indicated that the activity was not helpful were asked to elaborate on why it was not helpful. Four of them essentially responded that they thought it was busy-work, one said he does not type well enough, and the other two declined to respond.

Students also were asked to share their feelings about their confidence in the feedback that they received. Twenty-eight (58%) of the students felt that their

Table 3. Quality of posts

Group	Class	Mean quality of critique posts (1-10)
1	A	5.32
2	A	5.44
3	A	3.85
4	B	5.68
5	B	3.72
6	B	4.23

Copyright © 2006, Idea Group Inc. Copying or distributing in print or electronic forms without written permission of Idea Group Inc. is prohibited.

peers were able to provide appropriate feedback, and 30 (63%) felt that they themselves were able to do so. This response is not surprising given that students typically put their trust in the instructor, as the keeper and disseminator of knowledge, rather than their classmates.

When asked about how online feedback compared to in-class feedback, 31 students (65%) said they preferred online feedback. In open-ended responses, the students who preferred the online format most often cited preferences for having their feedback in writing to review as needed (14), having the time to think of what they wanted to say (12), and the general sense of anonymity or not having anyone watch them while they gave the feedback (6). Students who preferred in-class feedback most often stated that it was easier (7) and it took less time (6).

Discussion and Conclusion

The data from this study show that the effectiveness of online peer-feedback activities depends on several factors, including the amount of effort students put in, their own beliefs about self and peer efficacy, the value of their peers' contributions, the quantity and quality of feedback the students received, and the student's own level of knowledge and preparation for the activity.

There are five major points that are indicated by these findings. First, a student's level of engagement in the activity is related to their learning gains. Students who followed the instructor's prompts and posted more critique messages felt more positive about the learning activity and performed better than their peers who were less active in the peer-feedback forum. To some extent, this may have been a self-fulfilling prophecy, with students who believed they would learn from the activity (or that participation in it would help their grade) achieving the desired result and students who were less active not knowing the difference.

Second, one must value the concept of peer feedback in order to be fully engaged and benefit from it. Students who posted little peer feedback generally indicated that they did not value the process (e.g., they thought it likely that their peers would be wrong or did not think their peers' opinions were important) or they felt vulnerable because of their (self-assessed) low writing abilities. Looking at the messages these students posted, one can readily see their perfunctory nature.

Third, the feedback process actually helped some students become more confident about their own mastery of the subject matter. Students who found receiving critiques of their own work valuable generally also thought that the act of providing critique was helpful. Some provided comments to that effect, as well. This is not surprising, since it can be a rather affirming experience to look at someone else's work and find instances of a course concept either well- or ill-

Copyright © 2006, Idea Group Inc. Copying or distributing in print or electronic forms without written permission of Idea Group Inc. is prohibited.

conceived in practice. Knowing how to critique is clearly related to knowing how to apply the concept, and the online written format gave students the time to think and reflect as they engaged in asynchronous critique and provided permanent documentation of their efforts so they could see how critiquing helped their writing.

Fourth, interpersonal dynamics certainly had an effect on the liveliness of a peer-critique group. As few as two students starting a written exchange of messages could set the tone for a group in terms of depth of critique. Looking at the messages written within each critique group chronologically, it is clear that the first few items posted tended to set the bar for what was to follow. As a result, we need to think not only in terms of instructors setting a clear model for student interaction online but also of the effects of peer modeling, even if unintentional. Instructors might consider making mention of particularly good student messages so others know where to look for a model.

Finally, the idea of performing a critique in writing can initially be intimidating to some students. Written feedback is more challenging to provide than verbal critique and students often worry about how their words will be perceived by others. However, students preferred to receive written rather than verbal critique because they could read and reread it, engaging in reflective processes as they developed their written drafts.

In closing, using an online peer critique activity provided benefits for this class, although not all students were poised or prepared to take advantage of the potential learning opportunity. Clearly student values and fears need to be taken into account when requiring students to engage in these processes in an online environment where their words linger on through space and time and their absence of comments will be readily noted by an instructor. Providing structure, such as a prompt, can be a useful way of helping students understand what is expected of them and setting an overall tone, although an instructor should be watchful of early student contributions since those also have a tendency to serve as models for later peer feedback contributions.

References

Anson, C. M. (1985). The peer-group conference: Rediscovering a forgotten audience. *NEATE Journal, 84*(1), 18-23.

Bateman, C., & Benson, C. (1999). Using computer conferencing to extend the bounds of the writing curriculum or, how I quit the symphony and joined a jazz band. In T. Howard & C. Benson (Eds.), *Electronic networks: Crossing boundaries/creating communities*. Portsmouth, NH: Boynton/Cook.

Copyright © 2006, Idea Group Inc. Copying or distributing in print or electronic forms without written permission of Idea Group Inc. is prohibited.

Bonk, C. J., Kirkley, J., Hara, N., & Dennen, V. (2001). Finding the instructor in post-secondary online learning: Pedagogical, social, managerial, and technological locations. In J. Stephenson (Ed.), *Teaching and learning online: New pedagogies for new technologies*. London: Kogan Page.

Cohen, M., & Riel, M. (1989). The effect of distant audiences on student writing. *American Educational Research Journal, 26*(2), 143-159.

Cooper, M. M. (1986). The ecology of writing. *College English, 48*(4), 364-375.

DiGiovanni, E., & Nagaswami, G. (2001). Online peer review: An alternative to face-to-face? *ELT Journal, 55*(3), 263-272.

Ede, L., & Lunsford, A. (1984). Audience addressed/audience invoked: The role of audience in composition theory and pedagogy. *College Composition and Communication, 35*(2), 155-171.

Flanagan, M., & Egert, C. (2000). Courseware quality and the collaborative classroom: Implementing IOS courseware to generate seminar-style interactions. *Interactive Multimedia Electronic Journal of Computer-Enhanced Learning, 1*(6). Retrieved February 26, 2001, from http://imej.wfu.edu/articles/2000/1/06/index.asp

Greene, S. (1995). Making sense of my own ideas: The problems of authorship in a beginning writing classroom. *Written Communication, 12*(2), 186-218.

Olbert, S., & Ring, K. (1993). Scoring peers' papers: Teaching audience awareness and generating enthusiasm. *Teaching English in the Two-Year College, 20*(4).

Reynolds, J. F. (1987). *The effect of collaborative peer revision groups on audience-consciousness in the writing of college freshmen*. Unpublished doctoral dissertation, University of Oklahoma, Norman.

Sengupta, S. (1998). Peer evaluation: "I am not the teacher." *ELT Journal, 52*(2), 19-28.

Stake, R. E. (1995). *The art of case study research*. Thousand Oaks, CA: Sage.

Topping K. J., Smith E. F., Swanson I., & Elliot A. (2000). Formative peer assessment of academic writing between postgraduate students. *Assessment & Evaluation in Higher Education, 25*(2), 149-169.

Turoff, M. (2000). An end to student segregation: No more separation between distance learning and regular courses. *On the Horizon, 8*(1), 1.

Ziv, N. D. (1982). Using peer groups in the composition classroom. (ERIC Document Reproduction Service No. ED229799)

Copyright © 2006, Idea Group Inc. Copying or distributing in print or electronic forms without written permission of Idea Group Inc. is prohibited.

Chapter XI

Interpersonal Assessment:
Evaluating Others in Online Learning Environments

Aditya Johri
Stanford University, USA

Abstract

This chapter introduces and discusses the concept of interpersonal assessment. *Interpersonal assessment refers to the act of assessing what other participants in an online learning environment know and how they behave. Interpersonal assessment is critical for successful learning outcomes, especially in collaborative groups, since students need to know what others in a group know and how they act to be able to work them. Moreover, knowledge about participants has implications for self, peer, and group assessment. Although interpersonal assessment is important for both online and traditional learning environments, it is often more difficult to assess others in online learning environments due to the lack of face-to-face interaction, mediated cues, and unshared contexts. In this chapter, I review the literature to support this thesis theoretically and look at evidence from preliminary data analysis of an online class. I also suggest future directions for research and practice.*

Copyright © 2006, Idea Group Inc. Copying or distributing in print or electronic forms without written permission of Idea Group Inc. is prohibited.

Interpersonal Assessment:
Assessing What Others Know
and How They Behave

In this chapter I introduce and discuss a critical aspect of assessment that is often overlooked in online learning environments research and design—*assessment of other participants' knowledge and behavior*. Assessment has traditionally been understood and used as a method directed at evaluating the product of an educational exercise or the producer. In education and learning literature, assessment usually refers to assessing student learning. The title of a recent National Research Council (2001) report sums it up: "Knowing what students know." But over the last decade, the concept of assessment has evolved with the change in educational practice (Dochy, Segers, & Sluijsmans, 1999). We have started to move away form a teacher-centered perspective on education to one that involves more peer interaction and group activities, and assessment practices are also changing in part to reflect the change in educational practice, although such a move is not without its problems (Broadfoot & Black, 2004; Segers & Dochy, 2001). Group assessment, peer assessment, and self assessment are increasingly becoming a part of educational practice leading to a need to examine the social aspects of such arrangements (Meldrum, 2002; Reynolds & Trehan, 2000). In such a scenario the concept of interpersonal assessment assumes significance as its study is yet underrepresented in the literature. And even though assessment in e-learning is not fundamentally different than traditional face-to-face environments (Macdonald, 2004), there are some differences such as increased student reflexivity (Lea, 2001). Mediation by technology for communication changes the nature of social interaction in online environments and has the potential to affect assessment.

Interpersonal assessment refers specifically to the perceptions participants have about what others know and how they behave. This knowledge can range from information about how competent a peer is at a particular task to how helpful she is to others. Knowledge about other participants in a learning environment has several benefits. Information about other students can help in forming groups, facilitating teamwork, and increasing overall interest and participation levels in a course. Interpersonal knowledge is particularly important in classes where students have to work on group projects. In such instances, knowledge of what others in the group know and how they behave determines the success of group members to work together and to learn.

In traditional face-to-face learning environments, students and teachers come to know about each other as they interact over time. Through one-on-one interaction, observations, and conversations with each other, in class and out of class,

Copyright © 2006, Idea Group Inc. Copying or distributing in print or electronic forms without written permission of Idea Group Inc. is prohibited.

teachers and students gain interpersonal knowledge about other people in the class. Participants gain information through cues such as age, experience, and grades. Interpersonal knowledge about behavior develops through *interactions* that the peers have with each other. In an online environment this interpersonal knowledge is either absent or present in a mediated form, which is often harder to assess, and most online courseware provides minimal explicit support for such signals. Therefore, informal assessment of fellow students, teachers, and other participants is diminished in an online environment.

Interpersonal assessment has not been addressed so far in the literature of online learning but it is critical to gain an understanding of it for research as well as design of online learning environments as learning is a social process and collaboration among participants is essential for learning to take place (Brown & Duguid, 2000; Lave & Wenger, 1991; Wenger, 1998). Moreover, in online classes, communication, and hence interpersonal assessment, is mediated by technology. Therefore, it is important to understand the role of technology in the interpersonal assessment process. In the rest of this chapter, I attempt to provide a comprehensive introduction to this topic by synthesizing literature from different research streams. I will focus primarily on learning situations that involve group work since interpersonal assessment is most critical for such situations. In addition, I will provide preliminary evidence from a research study that I undertook. Finally, I will discuss research and design implications of the proposed framework and make some recommendations.

The Benefits of Group Work and the Importance of Knowing Others in a Group

The advantages of working in a group are well-documented in the literature. Research across disciplines has demonstrated the benefits of students working together, such as higher levels of achievement (Slavin, 1996), higher-order thinking (Cohen, 1994), improved communication and conflict management (Johnson & Johnson, 1994), and strategic problem-solving skills (Barron, 2000). In addition, small-group student collaboration has also been shown to positively enhance intrinsic motivation to learn, greater long-term maintenance of skills, prosocial behaviors, and persistence in courses and programs (Bruffee, 1999; Cohen; Ede & Lunsford, 1990; Johnson & Johnson; Roschelle & Clancey, 1992). Economic and technological changes in the work place require employees to work in teams, and real-world benefits of students gaining experience with small-group collaboration are clear. Several recent studies (Bransford, Brown, &

Copyright © 2006, Idea Group Inc. Copying or distributing in print or electronic forms without written permission of Idea Group Inc. is prohibited.

Cocking, 1999) underscore the importance of people working collaboratively and sharing expertise in the workplace (National Research Council, 2001, p. 17).

But for groups to be successful, recent studies show it is equally important that for participants to know each other. Research on *transactive memory systems* emphasizes the importance of understanding "who knows what" at the dyadic as well as team levels. Transactive memory refers to group memory systems that come into place as members of a group learn who knows what in a group, especially who is an expert on what (Wegner, 1987). Wegner studied relationships among intimate couples and found that transactive memory keeps one or the other member of the couple responsible for information at all times. Liang, Moreland, & Argote (1995) showed that training group members together, rather than apart, improves the performance of their groups, and that this change is due to the development of transactive memory systems (also see Moreland, 1999). Hollingshead (2000) expanded these findings to a dyadic level using a sample of clerical workers in a laboratory setting and found that people learn and recall more information in their own area of expertise when their partner has different, rather than similar, work–related experience, and that this effect reverses for recall of information outside work-related expertise. Taken together, studies on transactive memory emphasize the importance of knowing what a group member knows, especially knowing who has what expertise. Sharing of knowledge is critical for the success of teams and knowledge sharing takes place through the everyday interaction of people and the relationships that individuals form with one another (Cross et al., 2001). Moreover, our perception of others determines whether we ask them for information or not, and whether we share information with them or not. In a recent study, Cross et al. asked 40 managers to reflect on a recent project and indicate where they obtained information critical to their projects. Over 80% of the managers reported that they got this information from other people. They indicated that there were four features that made a relationship effective: (1) knowing what another person knows and thus when to turn to them; (2) being able to gain timely access to that person; (3) willingness of the person sought to engage in problem-solving rather than to dump information; and (4) a degree of safety in the relationship that promoted learning and creativity. In a separate quantitative study, the authors found that these dimensions are consistent even after controlling for education, age similarity, physical proximity, tenure in an organization, and formal position in the organization. These findings suggest that not only is knowledge about the nature of expertise of a coworker important to coworkers but also whether that person is accessible and willing to share knowledge. All four dimensions identified in the previous study indicate the importance of interpersonal assessment. Whether to identify what the other person knows, to find out if they are accessible, to gauge how they engage in knowledge-sharing, or how safe your relationship with them is, the prerequisite is that somehow you get that information about them. Given

Copyright © 2006, Idea Group Inc. Copying or distributing in print or electronic forms without written permission of Idea Group Inc. is prohibited.

the importance of knowing others in a group, it is important to understand how that understanding develops. Impression formation is the primary process by which people develop an understanding of each other.

Assessing Others by Forming Impressions of Them

Social psychologists have been studying impression formation for almost half a century starting with Asch (1946), who proposed the gestalt approach to impression formation; according to the gestalt approach, the impressions people form of others are holistic in nature, that is, we assign a particular category to a person, rather than different traits, and our actions are guided by the way we categorize a person. On the other hand, the piecemeal view of impression formation proposed that people form an impression of a target by averaging various isolated features of the target (Anderson, 1981). Bridging the gap between Gestalt and piecemeal views of impression formation, Fiske and Neuberg (1990) proposed a continuum model of impression formation. According to the continuum model, people do both: they form holistic as well as individuated impressions depending on the extent to which they use a target's particular attributes. Towards one end of the continuum are *category-based processes* that use a target's category membership (e.g., race and gender) and exclude individual attributes, and on the other end are *individuating processes* that include a target's particular attribute (e.g., jovial or sarcastic) and exclude category membership. Furthermore, Fiske and Neuberg's continuum model proposes four stages in the impression-formation process: initial categorization, confirmatory categorization, recategorization, and piecemeal integration. Of these, the process a perceiver follows depends on the *information* available to the perceiver and his or her *motivation* to form an impression. Only in high-motivation and high-information scenarios does piecemeal integration occur, and pure piecemeal integration is highly uncommon. Another important aspect of this model is the attention paid by a perceiver to attributes and the manner in which attributes are interpreted. Therefore, information and motivation affect impression formation by determining whether a perceiver pays attention to a cue, and if she or he does, then the cue is interpreted. Overall, the continuum model of impression formation (Fiske, Lin, & Neuberg, 1999; Fiske & Neuberg, 1990) suggests that to study the impression-formation process, it is important to look at the information a perceiver has about a target and the motivation she or he has for forming an impression. In addition, it is important to understand how much attention a perceiver pays to different cues about a target and how the cues are

Copyright © 2006, Idea Group Inc. Copying or distributing in print or electronic forms without written permission of Idea Group Inc. is prohibited.

interpreted. Therefore, to understand how people form impressions of each other in online classes, it is important to look at the information students have about each other and their motivations for forming impressions. It can be argued that motivations to form impressions do not differ substantially between online and face-to-face environments since students working in a group are motivated by the same factors to learn about each other Therefore, I will focus on the effect of technology-mediation on the information that participants have about each other.

Interpersonal Assessment in Online Environments

Online environments by their very nature are technology-based, and participants interact with each other via technology. Moreover, online classes often have no offline component and this precludes face-to-face interaction among participants. This means that whatever cues participants get about their peers are primarily technology-mediated. Mediation by technology changes the information participants have about each other, often in both quantity and quality, and this has the potential to result in impressions that are different from those formed in face-to-face interaction (Fiske & Neuberg, 1990). This conclusion is supported by several studies on impression formation in computer-mediated communication (CMC), which show that although impressions do form when people interact via communication technology the resultant impressions have characteristics that are different from those formed in face-to-face interactions.

Studies in the field of CMC suggest that people form interpersonal impressions of each other regardless of the medium of communication, but the process of impression formation in CMC takes more time than it does in face-to-face interactions (Walther, 2002). Hancock and Dunham (2001) found that, in CMC, impressions are more intense than they would be in face-to-face communication but there is less breadth in the impression, that is, the impressions one forms are strong but simple, unlike face-to-face impressions, which are often complex. Tidwell and Walther also found that, although impressions take longer to form in CMC, they reach the same intensity as those in face-to-face communication, and often they are more intense. Moreover, since participants interact within a similar context, they keep recategorizing their initial impression such that it confirms with the initial categorization, and their impression of a peer does not change with time.

Copyright © 2006, Idea Group Inc. Copying or distributing in print or electronic forms without written permission of Idea Group Inc. is prohibited.

Studies that directly compared the effect of medium and others' evaluations also show that the communication medium has an effect on how people evaluate each other. In a study to test the effects of communication media, Straus, Miles, and Levesque (2001) compared the effects of face-to-face, telephone, and videoconferencing on judgments in job interviews. Fifty-nine MBA students took part in mock interviews face-to-face and either through videoconference or telephone. Their results show that interviewers evaluated applicants more favorably over the telephone versus face-to-face. Interviewers also reported more difficulty regulating and understanding through videoconferencing but did not evaluate applicants less favorably. Hinds (1999) ran a series of studies to explore the relationship between communication media, cognitive load, and impression formation. She found that compared to audio only interaction, participants interacting over an audio-video system formed impressions biased towards a primed trait. The author attributed this finding to the additional cognitive load required to process information over an audio-video system as compared to the audio-only system (Hinds, 1999). Weisband and Atwater (1999) ran a study to understand how performance evaluations of self and others that are based on electronic interaction compare with evaluations that are based on face-to-face interaction. The authors found that the medium of communication made a difference and group members liked each other more when communicating face-to-face than electronically and liking accounted for significant variance in ratings of others in face-to-face groups but not in electronic groups. Moreover, actual contributions accounted for significant variance in ratings of others in electronic groups, but not in face-to-face groups, and the total variance accounted for by liking and actual performance was higher in the face-to-face condition than in the electronic condition (Weisband & Atwater, 1999). These studies show that in settings that use technology-mediated communication media have an effect on processing of interpersonal information, and therefore it is important to understand the use of communication technology within online learning settings. However, since CMC does not necessarily mean distributed or distance learning, we have to be cautious in assuming that the results from CMC studies will carry over to e-learning settings. Most CMC research draws conclusions from studies where participants meet for the first time in the lab, take part in the study, and then leave. In real-world settings, participants often interact face-to-face over a longer period and have the opportunity to interact in different contexts and situations, suggesting that different factors might be at play here, as compared to a solely CMC condition; this is can be determined empirically, and we need a lot more research in real-world settings to fully understand the effects of communication technology on interpersonal assessment.

Copyright © 2006, Idea Group Inc. Copying or distributing in print or electronic forms without written permission of Idea Group Inc. is prohibited.

Interpersonal Peer Assessment in the Global Classroom Project

This section presents preliminary results from an ethnographic study of an online learning environment. The data analysis from this study shows that students do engage in interpersonal assessment of their peers, especially when they are working in a group, and that there is a need to support interpersonal assessment.

The Global Classroom Project

The Global Classroom Project (GCP) is a technology-based class that has both face-to-face and online components. It connects students from the United States with students from Russia, Sweden, and other European countries. The learning philosophy behind the GCP is *experiential learning*—students learn best by personal experience. The class uses a discussion-board-based software called WebBoard as the primary tool for interaction among students from different countries in addition to face-to-face classes held at each location. The purpose of the class is two-fold: to teach students technical communication skills such as resume, proposal, and project-report writing and to teach them the skills needed to work in a crosscultural, online environment. The European students are typically graduate students enrolled in the social sciences, whereas the American students are either undergraduates or graduates and range from liberal arts to engineering majors. The major assignment for the class is a group project to be submitted at the end of the semester (Herrington & Tretyakov, 2005).

Research Methodology and Data Collection

The setting for this study is a large technological institute located in the southeastern United States. The research was designed as an ethnographic case study (Yin, 1994) using multiple data-collection methods to ensure data triangulation. In-depth interviews (45 to 90 minutes) were conducted with a total of 15 participants, including students and instructors. The primary participants for the interviews were American students. The researcher also participated as a team member of a group of six students for a period of 8 weeks and worked on their class project with them, in addition to observing the class overtly. Other data-gathering methods included open-ended surveys and informal communication between students and the instructor. Detailed analysis of online WebBoard transcripts provided valuable data about participation by the Russian and American students, and more data on the Russian perspective was gathered

Copyright © 2006, Idea Group Inc. Copying or distributing in print or electronic forms without written permission of Idea Group Inc. is prohibited.

from the Russian instructor via e-mail over several months. The total data-collection period lasted around 3 months. Data was analyzed using an inductive coding and categorization process, following a grounded-theory approach (Strauss & Corbin, 1990). One group was analyzed in-depth to understand the interpersonal-assessment process at different levels. This group consisted of American and Russian students who were assigned an open-ended topic to research in order to write a proposal for their final project. The topic given to the students was "analysis of propaganda." As part of their group project, students also compiled an annotated bibliography that they used for their project. They were also given a list of readings that were discussed electronically on the WebBoard and sometimes in the face-to-face classes (Johri, 2005).

Findings

During the interview, most American students expressed a desire to know more about the Russian students. Amy, one of the more enthusiastic students in the class, said:

I wish the Russian students would make a page with their pictures and profiles and interests, we know they are there, and we see them posting, so we don't know them very well, so they are kind of just there.

American students also mentioned the advantages of face-to-face interaction. Sarah, an American student, mentioned that her American group bonded when they met for lunch after a class:

We met for lunch, that was pretty neat, because we became friends actually. It was important to ease tension. Later, we were in the computer lab for 6-7 hours and we came to know each other pretty well and everyone was friendly.

She also expressed a desire to have known the Russian students better. When I asked her how well she knew the Russian students in her group, she said:

Not all that well, I would say. There were introductions online where we talked a little about our interests. The main thing was that we learned a lot more about their personalities from their posts, like they put a smiley face or a wink after everything, it was pretty cute, in their emails and stuff.

Copyright © 2006, Idea Group Inc. Copying or distributing in print or electronic forms without written permission of Idea Group Inc. is prohibited.

Moreover, she suggested that personal emails would have made it more fun and added, "We saw their photos towards the very end, that was kind of cool, we could put a face to a name, earlier, although it didn't make not that much of a difference then." Another student said that, "What would have helped me more, have them tell me about themselves. It was integral part of the process that I missed out on, in the long run it would have helped." As these responses suggest, American students had a desire to know more about their Russian colleagues as they thought it would have helped them in their group work and also made it easier for them to understand their counterparts. Moreover, in the absence of explicit information about their peers, American students tried to pick clues from whatever resources where available to them—primarily the messages posted by the Russian students on WebBoard. One student, Jennifer, narrated her learning experiences from the class:

One very important thing I learned, was the manner they posted, the method they are using to post, gotta understand the cultural differences, pick up posting styles, it took me to figure out why they posted one single post, you have to confirm to their way to get your message across other things- just being attentive, being flexible, being open to ideas, given, making sure that you clearly illustrate with an example.

The key way in which American students made use of interpersonal knowledge about their peers was in distributing tasks for the group project. Amy noted that one of the advantages of knowing about others was for doing group work, "I think so you know what kind of interests they have and you can go from there." "The four of us, we and Susie worked on content, Jason on web design, and the other guy what is his name, lets call him Mark, he worked on the computer languages, java part" says Sarah. Jason says that although he remembers the selection to be random, it was definitely done skill-wise to make best use of available resources, "Programming guys were all split up so each group would have one each." In addition to the major of the student, American students also made use of which year the students were in to distribute their work. Students who were more senior in terms of their years in school took on greater responsibilities. Through their interaction, American students came to know about the class schedules of their group members, which helped them in scheduling meetings. One group made use of the knowledge of whether students lived on or off campus to schedule meetings and to nominate members to submit assignments. Another kind of implicit contextual knowledge that American students used was their knowledge of technology use, and access to technology, by their peers. American students assumed that their peers in the United States had similar access to technology, which meant high bandwidth and frequent use of the

Copyright © 2006, Idea Group Inc. Copying or distributing in print or electronic forms without written permission of Idea Group Inc. is prohibited.

Internet. This meant that they were used to getting fast replies to their emails from their peers, and they also used technology such as instant messaging (IM) for communication. Although at face value this looks like a simple fact, similar assumption on their part for the Russian students played a big role in leading to a breakdown in communication between American and Russian students.

Several problems were created by the lack of interpersonal and contextual knowledge between American and Russian students. One problem mentioned by several American students was that the Russian students would misunderstand the messages send by the American students, and reply rudely to them. In reality, most American students later realized that their characterization of Russian students was wrong and that the Russian students were just being straightforward and not intentionally rude. But the damage was often done by the time American students realized this, and several of them stopped communicating with the Russian students. This shows that lack of contextual and cultural knowledge about ways of communicating can adversely affect communication. Another problem that puzzled American students was the tendency of Russian students to reply as a group to individual messages posted by American students on WebBoard. American students were frustrated by the lack of personal responses to their messages. Even after the end of the semester the American students had no idea as to why the Russian students posted as a group. Every American student I interviewed confirmed this observation. During the interviews, several American students also complained that they have no, or very little, idea of what goes on in the Russian class. To complicate matters further, Russian students expected American students to respond as a group to their messages. Another thing that stood out was the large amount of interaction among the different Russian groups, which influenced their group work and even their interaction with the Americans. The Russian students were talking to other students in their class who were in different groups to make sure that their topics did not overlap. From my interviews and participation in the class I observed that there was very little or almost no interaction among different American groups. One obvious reason for this is that American students did not meet face-to-face every class period as did the Russians students. This meant that American students had little idea of what other students in their class were working on, and the Russian students complained to them that they were not making any progress since their topic kept overlapping with other groups.

Discussion

As we can see, there is some evidence that interpersonal knowledge made a difference in how students interacted in the GCP. In the absence of information about how students communicate, how groups are formed, how they interact

Copyright © 2006, Idea Group Inc. Copying or distributing in print or electronic forms without written permission of Idea Group Inc. is prohibited.

within groups, and who people are as individuals, American students made more personal misattributions, and as a consequence, their interaction with the Russian students suffered. This analysis is a first attempt at trying to delineate some of the ways in which interpersonal assessment might influence online collaboration and learning. Although the data analysis in the previous section is preliminary, it suggests three things: First, students want and need interpersonal information about others to assess them; second, they utilize this knowledge to shape their interaction with other students; and third, lack of interpersonal knowledge leads to breakdowns in communication and collaboration, which results in breakdowns in learning. One important lesson from the in-depth analysis is that even though groups often realize that they are having problems communicating with others, they are not able to improve their situation when they lack interpersonal information. This is because even though they realize they have problems, they are often not able to recognize what gave rise to those problems. They are not able to ascertain whether it is because of the behavior of an individual, his or her lack of understanding of something, or simply because of situational factors beyond their control.

The findings from the study also point to the kind of information that students look for in each other. People essentially look for information about how other people behave, especially in a particular context, and also what people know or their expertise. Moreover, often these two characteristics go hand-in-hand (Faraj & Sproull, 2000; Sonnentag, 2000). Expertise without the ability to share it and without other people having access to it is of not much use for collaboration. Overall, the behavioral information about peers helps people in describing their peers, predicting their actions, and explaining the reasons for the actions (Berger & Bradac, 1982). There is another element that stands out from this analysis and which has also been reported in the literature: contextual knowledge about peers. Contextual knowledge refers to the information that peers have about each other's context: the places they live and study in, and the tools they use. Interpersonal knowledge is linked to contextual knowledge, since how and what we think about others is linked to what we know about their circumstances. Lack of contextual knowledge leads to lack of shared context, and lack of shared context has been recognized as a common problem in distributed teams, leading to misattribution (Cramton, 2001). Misattribution occurs when perceivers misinterpret a piece of information, and attribute something to people, rather than the situation. For instance, if someone is late for a team meeting because his or her car broke down, we are more likely to attribute lateness to the person as opposed to the event of the car breaking down, if we do not know the reason. Cramton suggests that people are more likely to make personal rather than situational attribution concerning their remote partners, because of a "failure to share and remember information about remote situations and contexts, an uneven distribution of information" (p. 365) which basically means that remote partners often

Copyright © 2006, Idea Group Inc. Copying or distributing in print or electronic forms without written permission of Idea Group Inc. is prohibited.

lack information to make situational attributions, in keeping with the attribution literature. She also suggests that when people work under heavy cognitive load, they become more likely to make personal rather situational attributions, since information processing limitations amount to blaming individuals for problems that may have broader causes. Moreover, in the absence of situational information, they are likely to make negative attributions concerning the dispositions of the remote partners. Gibson and Cohen (2003) also argue that when distributed team members find it difficult to form impressions of their teammates, "virtual team members often err on the side of dispositional attributions, assuming behavior was caused by personality, because they lack situational information and are overloaded, and this may make them less likely to try and modify problematic situations." In a study of distributed groups, Walther, Boos, and Jonas (2002), arrived at a similar conclusion. According to them, when distributed group members are unable to adapt to each other, group members are more prone to make attributional judgments about distant partners, rather than consider their own adjustment difficulties. They also suggest, that by redirecting participants' attention to situational issues in local, rather than distributed interaction scenarios, participants become more effective when they later encounter distributed environments. These studies also hint that technology might change one's perceptions of what is important in a peer with whom one must work. Therefore, communication skills using technology might become more important for distributed learners, as opposed to colocated learners. Also, in the absence of personal interactions the process of getting interpersonal information might change. Distributed learners might be more inclined to use electronic resources to find information, as they might not have access to people who know about their peers.

Implications

Research Implications

A lot more research needs to be done to understand interpersonal assessment in educational settings, especially online environments. Given advances in technology and the increase in the number of online classes and courses, it is critical to understand how people actually work and learn together in technology-mediated environments. This is not a new concern. Researchers have been studying the impact of technology on learning for some time. This study is important because it emphasizes an understanding not just of the technology but the process by which people come to know each other once the technology is in place. The main

Copyright © 2006, Idea Group Inc. Copying or distributing in print or electronic forms without written permission of Idea Group Inc. is prohibited.

premise is that whether mediated or not, or mediated by technology or not, we do form impressions of each other and this has implications for how we interact with each other. The next step that this study calls for is a focus on in-depth understanding of how impression formation processes occur in real world technology-mediated learning environments. If we understand these processes better, we might be able to design the technology or the interactions among participants in a manner that increases interpersonal assessment of participants.

Design Implications: Increasing Opportunities for Interpersonal Assessment

Although interpersonal assessment in online environments is difficult, its affects can be facilitated using a combination of technological and non-technological measures. Face-to-face interaction among participants has often been suggested as a way to increase participants' interpersonal knowledge. Face-to-face interaction, in addition to providing facial and physical cues, provides students the opportunity to interact in situations other than class. This leads to more complex impression of others (Welbourne, 2001) and hence leads to more interpersonal knowledge about others. Face-to-face interaction among learners has consistently been shown to be beneficial and several distance-learning classes have successfully integrated a face-to-face component into their programs (Haythornthwaite & Kazmer, 2004). However, often it is not possible for learners to meet face-to-face, and there are other possibilities that might be helpful in such a scenario.

Electronic resources can be used to store and share knowledge about participants in an online community but for this to happen they need to be designed with an explicit focus on the social aspects of learning. The technological solution does not require technical sophistication, but it should be able to augment everyday learning behavior of participants. Learners should be exposed to interpersonal information while searching or browsing and be able to access information about other participants. As one student, John, suggested when asked what he would want in a custom software:

For one thing, some thing that would have a backend database with more information on the students, we get responses from students we have virtually no personal information on, and some kind of personal database students will be required to fill out, it will also be useful to have more control for the moderators, fro example, it is always difficult to get the American students to interact, some kind of automated system that would keep track of who is posting with what kind of frequency, send some kind of reminder, something that would allow more control over the interaction and be able to enforce people to participate.

Copyright © 2006, Idea Group Inc. Copying or distributing in print or electronic forms without written permission of Idea Group Inc. is prohibited.

The solution can be as simple as a Web page for each learner. For instance, Bly, Cook, Bickmore, Churchill, and Sullivan (1998) studied the role of personal home pages in the workplace. They found that workers used the pages primarily for project information, but authors took advantage of the opportunity to personalize them. Even readers read the pages because they reflected the authors. Furthermore, they argued, that regardless of organizational culture, project tasks or difficulties of implementation, people personalized their work and their presentation of self, in ways that were meaningful both to themselves and their readers and that the emergence of personal Web pages at work suggests that Web technologies can play a useful role in the ways in which employees further their self presentation in the organization.

Another way in which computing resources can be used is to represent participants' interaction in an online community. Although not necessarily linked to interpersonal knowledge, these representations can go a long way in increasing participants' contextual knowledge about each other, especially their knowledge about how their peers are participating in an online community. VisOC (Avery, Civjan, & Johri, 2005), a digital assessment tool, was created specifically to allow visual analysis of student communication and learning outcomes in the GCP. VisOC's goal was to provide participants in the learning community with a versatile automated process for building interactive graphical representations that compare aspects of student profiles with performance patterns and analyze their role in contributing to the overall learning goals of the classroom. Awareness systems are yet another visualization technique that can be used (Gerosa, Fuks, & Lucena, 2003).

Conclusion

The chapter started out with the aim of putting forward and discussing an alternate view of assessment—interpersonal assessment. Although this view is not necessarily in line with the conventional view of assessment, it nonetheless sheds light on a very important part of assessment that goes on informally in an educational setting. Peers often make informal assessments of each other to determine what others know and how they are to work with. These assessments are particularly salient when students have to work with other students on a group project. In an online environment, cues to make such assessments are either lost or are mediated by communication technology, making it difficult for students to assess each other. Therefore, there is a need to study and understand how interpersonal assessment takes place in online environments to design successful e-learning environments. Although not discussed directly, interper-

Copyright © 2006, Idea Group Inc. Copying or distributing in print or electronic forms without written permission of Idea Group Inc. is prohibited.

sonal assessment also has implications for peer assessment in the conventional sense. Peer assessment may be biased by lack of contextual knowledge or by biased personal impressions of peers (Magin, 2001) therefore it is critical to understand how biases develop in technology-mediated learning environments.

I have discussed several studies on CMC to illustrate how technology-mediated communication might influence the information peers have about each other and consequently their impressions of each other. Although we stand to gain a lot from studies on CMC, it is important to keep in mind that most CMC studies have been conducted in lab settings and we still know very little about how interpersonal assessment takes place in real-world online learning environments. As a first step, through a preliminary data analysis from a study on a distributed online class I show that students do make use of interpersonal and contextual knowledge in their interactions with each other especially for group work. Lack of interpersonal and contextual knowledge between American and Russian students was shown to lead to a breakdown in communication, with adverse consequences for learning.

As we design online classes, one important design consideration is the social affordances of any technological environment (Volet & Wosnitza, 2004). What kind of social interaction does the environment allow? As this chapter shows, one key element is affordances for students to be able to share information about each other. This should not only be possible, but also encouraged, not only by the teachers, but by the design of the environment itself. When someone becomes a member or joins a class, information can be collected about him or her that can later be shared among peers. Students can be encouraged to post information about new students or to make their Web pages. In the same way that interactions are designed within physical spaces, it is essential that we foresee and design interactions in electronic spaces as well. Hopefully, this chapter will provide momentum for educators, teachers, and designers to work towards a better design of online learning environments to foster greater interpersonal assessment. Of course, this needs to be supported by researchers developing a better understanding of how interpersonal assessment happens in online learning environments.

References

Anderson, N. H. (1981). *Foundations of information integration theory.* New York: Academic Press.

Asch, S. E. (1946). Forming impressions of personality. *Journal of Abnormal and Social Psychology, 41,* 1230-1240.

Copyright © 2006, Idea Group Inc. Copying or distributing in print or electronic forms without written permission of Idea Group Inc. is prohibited.

Avery, C., Civjan, J., & Johri, A. (2005). Assessing student interaction in the Global Classroom Project: Visualizing communication and collaboration patterns using online transcripts. In K. C. Cook & K. Grant-Davie (Eds.), *Online education: Global questions, local answers.* Baywood.

Barron, B. (2000). Achieving coordination in collaborative problem-solving groups. *The Journal of the Learning Sciences, 9*(4), 403-436.

Berger, C. R., & Bradac, J. J. (1982). *Language and social knowledge: Uncertainty in interpersonal relations.* London: Edward Arnold.

Bly, S., Cook, L., Bickmore, T., Churchill, E., & Sullivan, J. W. (1998). The rise of personal Web pages at work. *Proceedings of Computer Human-Interaction* (pp. 313-314).

Bransford, J. D., Brown, A. L., & Cocking, R. R. (Eds.). (1999). *How people learn: Brain, mind, experience, and school.* Washington, DC: National Academy Press.

Broadfoot, P., & Black, P. (2004). The first ten years of assessment in education. *Assessment in Education, 11*(1), 7-26.

Brown, J. S. & Duguid, P. (2000). *The social life of information.* Cambridge, UK: Cambridge University Press.

Bruffee, K. A. (1999). *Collaborative learning: Higher education, interdependence, and the authority of knowledge* (2nd ed.). Baltimore: The Johns Hopkins University Press.

Cohen, E. (1994). Restructuring the classroom: Conditions for productive small groups. *Review of Educational Research.*

Cramton, C. D. (2001). The mutual knowledge problem and its consequences for dispersed collaboration. *Organization Science, 12*(3), 346-371.

Cross, R., Parker, A., Prusak, L., & Borgatti, S. P. (2001). Knowing what we know: Supporting knowledge creation and sharing in social networks. *Organizational Dynamics, 30*(2), 100-120.

Dochy, F., Segers, M., & Sluijsmans, D. (1999). The use of self-, peer and co-assessment in higher education: A review. *Studies in Higher Education, 24*(3), 331-350.

Ede, L. S., & Lunsford, A. A. (1990). *Singular texts/plural authors: Perspectives on collaborative writing.* Carbondale: Southern Illinois University Press.

Faraj, S. & Sproull, L. (2000). Coordinating expertise in software development teams. *Management Science, 46*(12), 1554-1568.

Fiske, S. T., Lin, M. H., & Neuberg, S. L. (1999). The continuum model: Ten years later. In S. Chaiken & Y. Trope (Eds.), *Dual process theories in social psychology* (pp. 231-254). New York: Guilford.

Copyright © 2006, Idea Group Inc. Copying or distributing in print or electronic forms without written permission of Idea Group Inc. is prohibited.

Fiske, S. T., & Neuberg, S. L. (1990). A continuum of impression formation, from category-based to individuating processes: Influences of information and motivation on attention and interpretation. *Advances in Experimental Social Psychology, 23,* 1-73.

Gerosa, M. A., Fuks, H., & Lucena, C. (2003). Analysis and design of awareness elements in collaborative digital environments: A case study in the AulaNet learning environment. *Journal of Interactive Learning Research, 14*(3), 315-332.

Gibson, C. B., & Cohen, S. G. (Eds.). (2003). *Virtual teams that work: Creating conditions for virtual team effectiveness.* Jossey-Bass.

Hancock, J. T., & Dunham, P. J. (2001). Impression formation in computer-mediated communication revisited: An analysis of the breadth and intensity of impressions. *Communication Research, 28,* 325-347.

Haythornthwaite, C., & Kazmer, M. M. (Eds.). (2004). *Learning, culture and community in online education: Research and practice.* Peter Lang Publishers.

Herrington, T. & Tretyakov, Y. (2005). The Global Classroom Project: Troublemaking and troubleshooting. In K. C. Cook & K. Grant-Davie (Eds.), *Online education: Global questions, local answers.* Baywood.

Hinds, P. J. (1999). The cognitive and interpersonal costs of video. *Media Psychology, 1,* 283-311.

Hollingshead, A. B. (2000). Perceptions of expertise and transactive memory in work relationships. *Group Processes and Intergroup Relations, 3*(3), 257-267.

Jarvenpaa, S., & Leidner, D. (1999, Winter). Communication and trust in global virtual teams. *Organization Science, 10*(6), 791-815.

Johnson, D. W., & Johnson, R. T. (1994). *Learning together and alone: Cooperative, competitive, and individualistic learning* (4th ed.). Edina, MN: Interaction Book Company.

Johri, A. (2005). Online, offline, and in-between: Analyzing mediated-action among American and Russian students in an online class. In T. S. Roberts (Ed.), *Computer-supported collaborative learning in higher education.* Hershey, PA: Idea Group Publishing.

Lave, J., & Wenger, E. (1991). *Situated learning: Legitimate peripheral participation.* Cambridge, UK: Cambridge University Press.

Lea, M. (2001). Computer conferencing and assessment: New ways of writing in higher education. *Studies in Higher Education, 26*(2), 163-181.

Liang, D., Moreland, R., & Argote, L. (1995). Group versus individual training and group performance: The mediating role of transactive memory. *Personality and Social Psychology Bulletin, 21,* 384-393.

Copyright © 2006, Idea Group Inc. Copying or distributing in print or electronic forms without written permission of Idea Group Inc. is prohibited.

Macdonald, J. (2004) Developing competent e-learners: The role of assessment. *Assessment & Evaluation in Higher Education, 29*(2), 215-226.

Magin, D. (2001). Reciprocity as a source of bias in multiple peer assessment of group work. *Studies in Higher Education, 26*(1), 53-63.

Meldrum, R. (2002, August). *The student experience of peer- and self assessment as a social relation.* Paper presented at the Learning Communities and Assessment Cultures Conference organised by the EARLI Special Interest Group on Assessment and Evaluation, University of Northumbria.

Moreland, R. (1999). Transactive memory: Learning who knows what in work groups and *organizations.* In L. Thompson, J. Levine, & D. Messick (Eds.), *Shared cognition on organizations* (pp. 3-31). Lawrence Erlbaum Associates.

National Research Council (2001). *Knowing what students know: The science and design of educational assessments* (J. Pellegrino, N. Chudowsky, & R. Glaser, Eds.). Washington, DC: National Academy Press.

Reynolds, M., and Trehan, K. (2000). Assessment: A critical perspective. *Studies in Higher Education, 25*(3), 267-278.

Roschelle, J., & Clancey, W. J. (1992). Learning as social and neural. *Educational Psychologist, 27,* 435-445.

Segers, M., & Dochy, F. (2001). New assessment forms in problem-based learning: The value-added of the students' perspective. *Studies in Higher Education, 26*(3), 327-343.

Slavin, R. E. (1996). Research on cooperative learning and achievement: What we know, what we need to know. *Contemporary Educational Psychology, (21),* 43-69.

Sonnentag, S. (2000). Excellent performance: The role of communication and cooperation processes. *Applied Psychology, 49*(3), 583-497.

Straus, S., Miles, J., and Levesque, L. (2001). The effects of videoconference, telephone and face-to-face media on interviewer and applicant judgments in employment interviews. *Journal of Management, 27,* 363-381.

Strauss, A., & Corbin, J (1990). *Basics of qualitative research: Grounded theory, procedures, and techniques.* Newbury Park, CA: Sage Publications.

Tidwell, L. C., & Walther, J. B. (2002). Computer-mediated communication effects on disclosure, impressions, and interpersonal evaluations: Getting to know one another a bit at a time. *Human Communication Research, 28,* 317-348.

Copyright © 2006, Idea Group Inc. Copying or distributing in print or electronic forms without written permission of Idea Group Inc. is prohibited.

Volet, S. E., & Wosnitza, M. (2004). Social affordances and students' engagement in cross-national online learning: An exploratory study. *Journal of Research in International Education, 3*(1), 5-29.

Walther, J. B., Boos, M., & Jonas, K. (2002). Misattribution and attributional redirection in distributed virtual groups. *Proceedings of the 35ᵗʰ Hawaii International Conference on System Sciences.*

Walther, J. D. (2002). Time effects in computer-mediated groups: Past, present and future. In P. J. Hinds & S. Kiesler (Eds.), *Distributed work.* Cambridge, MA: MIT Press.

Weisband, S., & Atwater, L. (1999). Evaluating self and others in electronic and face-to-face groups. *Journal of Applied Psychology, 84*(4), 632-639.

Welbourne, J. L. (2001, September). Changes in impression complexity over time and across situations. *Personality and Social Psychology Bulletin, 27*(9).

Wegner, D. (1987). Transactive memory: A contemporary analysis of the group mind. In B. Mullen & G. Goethals (Eds.), *Theories of group behavior* (pp. 185-208). New York: Springer-Verlag.

Wenger, E. (1998). *Communities of practice: Learning, meaning, and identity.* Cambridge, UK: Cambridge University Press.

Yin, R. K. (1994). *Case study research: Design and methods* (Rev. ed.). Beverly Hills, CA: Sage Publications.

Copyright © 2006, Idea Group Inc. Copying or distributing in print or electronic forms without written permission of Idea Group Inc. is prohibited.

Chapter XII

A Framework for Assessing Self, Peer, and Group Performance in E-Learning

Thanasis Daradoumis
Open University of Catalonia, Barcelona, Spain

Fatos Xhafa
Open University of Catalonia, Barcelona, Spain

Ángel Alejandro Juan Pérez
Open University of Catalonia, Barcelona, Spain

Abstract

In this chapter, we propose a framework that supports the analysis and assessment of collaborative learning of online groups of students working on a complex task (software project, or case study) in a real Web-based, distance-learning context. On the one hand, our approach is based on principled evaluation criteria that involve and measure a variety of elements and factors as well as on a combination of a basic qualitative process and a quantitative method that provide a grounded and holistic

Copyright © 2006, Idea Group Inc. Copying or distributing in print or electronic forms without written permission of Idea Group Inc. is prohibited.

framework to analyze and assess group and individual performance more effectively and objectively. On the other hand, the approach has been fully implemented and tested on an asynchronous collaboration platform. All in all, the aim of our work is to provide a better understanding of group interaction and determine how to best support the collaborative learning process.

Introduction

Computer-supported collaborative learning (CSCL) is one of the most influential research paradigms dedicated to improving teaching and learning with the help of modern information and communication technology (Dillenbourg, 1999). Collaborative or group learning refers to instructional methods where students are encouraged to work together on learning tasks. Collaborating in small groups may constitute a powerful means for promoting and enhancing learning and social interaction. However, the effectiveness and success of a group of learners depends on a variety of issues during its lifecycle (Pipek & Wulf, 1999). Furthermore, during task realization, students learning via CSCL technology and methods need guidance and support in order to collaborate effectively and achieve their learning goals successfully. This fact is especially critical when it has to do with collaborative learning practices that are carried out virtually, over a long period of time, mainly asynchronously, involving a significant number of tutors and students who have to work together to solve a complex real problem and participate in a variety of activities (Cameron, Barrows, & Crooks, 1999; Dobson & McCracken, 1997; Kiesler & Sproull, 1987; Thomas, 2000).

From the evaluator's point of view, a critical issue in the groups' lifecycle is how to assess self, peer, and group performance through efficient and functional assessment techniques (Barros & Verdejo, 2000; Martínez, Dimitriadis, Rubia, Gómez, & de la Fuente, 2003; Reiser, 2002; Soller, 2001). Most of the existing learning systems still have limitations when used by students in real settings. Some of the limitations are attributed to the fact that students have difficulties in developing metacognition on their own actions and processes or to self estimating the appropriateness of their participation in a collaborative group or a wider learning community. Students seem to need information (in a literal or visual form) on their own actions, that could support awareness, metacognition and thereby self regulation of their learning activity (Dimitracopoulou, 2004).

Interaction analysis is a core function for supporting both students' self regulation and evaluation in CSCL environments. On the one hand, both processes rely on the same basic functionalities (Jermann, Soller, & Muehlenbrock, 2001) and

Copyright © 2006, Idea Group Inc. Copying or distributing in print or electronic forms without written permission of Idea Group Inc. is prohibited.

their distinction depends on the roles assigned to the different participants (e.g., teacher, student) and the particular functions and needs assumed by each. On the other hand, they rely on information captured from the actions performed by the participants during the collaborative process (Martínez et al., 2003). The efficient processing of this information and the knowledge extracted from the analysis sets the basis for greatly enhancing both awareness and feedback (Zumbach, Hillers, & Reimann, 2003) as crucial aspects to achieving a successful learning process in collaborative environments.

CSCL applications for online collaborative learning are characterized by a high degree of user-user and user-system interaction, and hence generate a huge amount of event information. This information is an important data source for supporting group activity with relevant information as well as for understanding, explaining and predicting patterns of group behavior. Thus, it needs to be easily collected, appropriately structured and represented, as well as automatically processed by computational models in order to extract essential knowledge about the collaborative process.

The success of collaborative learning practices depends, to a great extent, on our capability to process information and knowledge of group activity and use it to achieve a more effective group modelling. For this reason, this issue has attracted the attention of researchers and developers of applications both from the CSCL domain (Greif, 1998; Krange, Fjuk, Larsen, & Ludvigsen, 2002) and knowledge building environments (Scardamalia & Bereiter, 2003). In the literature, however, a holistic and well-grounded approach that provides an efficient management of event information and knowledge regarding group activity has been, to the best of our knowledge, hardly investigated. An initial approach (Zumbach et al., 2003) considers the use of feedback in online learning and its effects on group activity in general. To that end, some types of information generated by the group interaction are considered as knowledge to be communicated to the group members for feedback purposes, but the process of how to collect the information, analyze it, and extract the desired knowledge is not provided.

As a consequence, our approach provides a principled framework that allows studying and analyzing the collaborative behaviour of online learning teams, enables a better understanding of group interaction, and determines how to best assess self, peer, and group performance and support the collaborative learning process. In particular, we propose a solution that consists of classifying information by means of three generic group-activity parameters, namely *collaborative learning product*, *group functioning*, and *scaffolding* (social support and task or group functioning help-oriented services), which represent high-level collaborative learning processes.

The chapter is organized as follows. First, we describe the case study on which our analysis method was carried out. Then, we present a process that builds a

Copyright © 2006, Idea Group Inc. Copying or distributing in print or electronic forms without written permission of Idea Group Inc. is prohibited.

conceptual model for data analysis that ideally captures, defines, and classifies four main types of information generated in group activity, by means of potential indicators of effective collaboration. These indicators can be measured by both qualitative and quantitative methods in order to extract the desired knowledge about self, peer and group interaction behavior. Taking into account the interaction analysis process, we ultimately discuss and argue about the different means that can be employed to provide different support functionalities to students involved in online collaborative learning activities. Finally, we conclude with outlining and making reference to ongoing and further work.

Case Study Description

This study was based on real collaborative learning experiences that were carried out in the scope of online (distance) learning, undergraduate, interdisciplinary courses, such as Case Studies in Information Systems Management or Software Development Techniques. Both experiences usually run over a period of 14 weeks and involve at least 10 tutors and more than 500 students distributed into more than 90 online groups of five to six members. In the first experience, students have to collaborate and work out a case study that simulates a real project in a business or organization. The second experience is based on the project-based collaborative learning paradigm.

The methodology design behind each collaborative learning practice consists of five well-differentiated and structured subproblems (phases): problem specification and planning, product design, implementation, testing, and documentation and product delivery. In each phase, students should be assessed both for their individual and group contribution, so even though students work together to achieve a learning goal and submit a common product, they are evaluated by means of their particular contributions as they impact the product and the collaborative process itself. Individual assessment also depends on the specific role a student plays at a particular phase. Roles are switched among group members as they pass from one phase to another, so a student plays a different role in each phase. Here, we explain the methodology design of the "Information Systems Management" experience; as for the second one, see Daradoumis and Xhafa (2004) for more details.

The case resolution consists of a set of target goals (phases) that are realized collaboratively (except the first one which aims at studying and understanding the case presented). The instructional design of each target goal includes several learning tasks, adequately linked to one other, that students should carry out individually (e.g., readings) or collaboratively (e.g., activities and exercises) in

Copyright © 2006, Idea Group Inc. Copying or distributing in print or electronic forms without written permission of Idea Group Inc. is prohibited.

order to achieve the goal. In addition, the design of some target goals also dictates the realization of specific debates at group and class level aiming at decision-making on specific questions set. Finally, in the beginning of the course, a document explains to students the process of group work and learning that should be followed in order to carry out the case study successfully.

An aspect, which is of particular interest of our design and analysis purposes, is the *coordinator role* that a member assumes during the realisation of a target goal. To that end, we assess the degree of success of this role by examining whether the following tasks, which a coordinator should carry out, are accomplished:

- Planning, assignment, and management of the target-goal activities.

- Setting and monitoring of virtual meetings.

- Workspace organization and maintenance.

- Monitor the completion of task planning by notifying group members for any eventual delay or failure to fulfil a given task.

- Mediate and provide support to the group members when needed.

- Prepare the definite version of the product that has to be delivered at the end of the phase, watching for its robustness and coherence.

- Deliver the collaborative product and the group functioning report; the latter is elaborated by all members and describes how they collaborated as a team to develop the product, including all significant matters or problems that took place during the collaborative learning process.

The whole project was carried out mostly asynchronously; synchronous interaction occurred in a few specific cases of decision-making. All asynchronous collaborative interactions took place on the basic support for cooperative work (BSCW) system, a groupware tool that enables asynchronous and synchronous collaboration over the Web (Bentley et al., 1997). BSCW offers shared workspaces that groups can use to store, manage, jointly edit and share documents, realize threaded discussions, and so on.

To structure the whole Web-based collaborative learning process, we set two particularized shared workspaces in the BSCW system. The first one is a general workspace, which can be accessed by all students of the online class. The main purpose of this workspace is to let the students interact with each other in order to form the online learning groups. In addition, it is used to effectuate specific debates, which form part of the project requirements and involve all students, as well as to share important information about the project among tutors and students. The other workspace type is a private space designated to house each

Copyright © 2006, Idea Group Inc. Copying or distributing in print or electronic forms without written permission of Idea Group Inc. is prohibited.

online group, that is to record and structure the interaction of its members that aims to achieve the project-target goals through the resolution of the specific tasks and problems of which the project consists.

Our analysis was carried out at the general and the private group spaces, using specific evaluation criteria as parameters to measure the real effectiveness of self, peer and group learning and collaborative skills. Indeed, the successful realization of these experiences (as well as of others that we carried out in subsequent semesters) provided us with a large volume of interaction data that constituted a valuable source for our analysis. Our approach first builds a conceptual model of analysis of Web-based interactions that relies on theoretical principles and indicators of effective collaboration, as explained in the next section.

A Conceptual Model for Analyzing and Assessing Self, Peer, and Group Performance

Collaborative distance learning involves a variety of elements and factors that have to be considered and measured in order to analyse and assess group and individual performance effectively and objectively. We need an approach that, on the one hand, integrates different data sources, tools and techniques in order to support the students' self regulation, the evaluation of their peers, and the group they belong to; and, on the other hand, allows the tutor to supervise, guide, and evaluate the collaborative learning process.

In principle, analysis data may come from different sources such as the group-activity log files maintained in the collaborative learning system. Log files capture the actions performed by the group participants on the shared workspaces. Other important sources are the content of these actions and of the collaborative activity products and group and individual self evaluation reports, as well as questionnaires aimed at extracting specific information from the participants related to task achievement (i.e., the activity product), the learning processes, and the quality of the collaboration itself.

Moreover, secific (custom-designed) software tools may also need to be used as supporting means for the filtering and processing of the previously mentioned data as well as for the visualization of the information and knowledge derived from the interaction analysis.

Finally, analysis or evaluation techniques may involve several qualitative, quantitative, or other approaches that should be combined appropriately to produce an effective study and assessment of the collaborative learning interac-

Copyright © 2006, Idea Group Inc. Copying or distributing in print or electronic forms without written permission of Idea Group Inc. is prohibited.

tion. The implementation and testing of this approach is explained in more detail in Daradoumis, Martínez, and Xhafa (2004) and Daradoumis, Xhafa, and Marquès (2003b).

The proposed framework tries to give an answer to issues of self, peer and group assessment by defining principled evaluation criteria (or indicators), a basic qualitative evaluation process and a multivariate statistical model supported by a specific tool for data extraction and filtering of the event information contained in the log files.

To that end, our study showed that the evaluation of a real collaborative learning situation is a very complex task, since one has to take a variety of factors into account (Daradoumis, Xhafa, & Marquès, 2003a). For this reason it is very important to identify adequate group activity indicators (and their estimated weights) that capture and describe group interaction and performance sufficiently in the context where group work and learning is situated. Based on theoretical principles and indicators of effective collaboration (McGrath, 1991; Sfard, 1998; Soller, 2001; Webb, 1992), we specify four important levels or aspects of collaborative learning analysis: *task performance*, *group functioning* (i.e., participation/interaction behaviour), *social support*, and *help services* (i.e., task/process scaffolding). All four of these high-level indicators are related to the qualification mark assigned to the learning outcomes achieved by the group and the individual members.

Consequently, the application of different techniques is essential to measure and satisfy all the identified indicators and thus to unfold the group's internal workings and achieve a more objective interpretation of each member's attitude and competence. Indeed, it is important for an analysis method to enable the student to distinguish particular cases of insufficient contribution or interaction behaviour about him or herself, and allow the student to infer correct conclusions for the performance and competence of each group member. By doing so, the student will be able to self regulate his or her activity and apply appropriate corrections in order to improve learning outcomes as well as the functioning of the group.

Table 1 shows the top level of the conceptual model we propose for the analysis of individual and group activity. It specifies the four previously mentioned high-level collaborative learning processes that constitute the first steps toward the classification of the many different variables that characterize collaborative interaction as well as identification and measurement of these variables in terms of the user- and system-specific events (or actions).

On the one hand, this provides a principled and effective manner to classify the information generated from group interaction; on the other hand, it facilitates the processing and analysis of this information and knowledge extraction. Each indicator is also assigned a specific weight. This is an important feature of our

Copyright © 2006, Idea Group Inc. Copying or distributing in print or electronic forms without written permission of Idea Group Inc. is prohibited.

Table 1. Description of the high-level indicators defined for each one of the aspects of the collaborative learning analysis

Collaborative Indicators		Weight
Task performance		**50%**
TP1	The students' individual and group problem-solving capabilities and learning outcomes (*acquisition* metaphor)	40%
TP2	The students' contributing behaviour during task realisation (e.g., production function and use of active learning skills)	40%
TP3	The students' individual and group ongoing (and final) performance in terms of self-evaluation	20%
Group functioning		**20%**
GF1	Active participation behaviour	30%
GF2	Social grounding (e.g., well-balanced contributions and role playing)	20%
GF3	Active interaction or processing skills that monitor and facilitate the group's well-being function	30%
GF4	Group processing (i.e., examine whether each member learnt how to interact and collaborate more effectively with his or her team mates)	20%
Social support		**15%**
SS1	Members' commitment toward collaboration, joint learning, and accomplishment of the common group goal	30%
SS2	Level of peer involvement and its influential contribution to the involvement of the others	30%
SS3	Members' contribution to the achievement of mutual trust	10%
SS4	Members' motivational and emotional support to their peers	20%
SS5	Participation and contribution to conflict resolution	10%
Help services		**15%**
HS1	Help is timely.	25%
HS2	Help is relevant to the student's needs.	10%
HS3	Help is qualitative.	30%
HS4	The student understands help.	25%
HS5	Help can be readily applied by the student	10%
Note. Each indicator is assigned a specific weight that it may have in the analysis process.		

approach since it determines not only the importance of each indicator but also the way the different indicators can be combined in the analysis and evaluation process. The weight assigned to each indicator depends on premises, such as the learning and evaluation goals, the context or situation surrounding the collaborative learning experience and its specific tasks, as well as the available analysis techniques and data sources. Our approach shows a specific way to set weights for the analysis and assessment of our particular case study. Both the indicators and the assigned weights are presented in Table 1. We now turn to discuss each generic indicator in more detail.

Copyright © 2006, Idea Group Inc. Copying or distributing in print or electronic forms without written permission of Idea Group Inc. is prohibited.

Task Performance (or Collaborative Learning Product)

This is the first top-level activity parameter featuring the production function and task performance of online groups. It is characterized by the type of events that capture and describe the functional knowledge, cognitive processes, and skills of the students and the group as a whole in solving problems and producing learning outcomes in a collaborative learning practice. It is used to analyze and evaluate the individual and group effectiveness as far as task-achievement concerns. It can be measured as a qualitative and quantitative parameter by the type of user task-based actions that represent contributions that express basic and supporting active learning skills as well as perception skills.

Table 2 shows the mid- and low-level indicators in the form of the skills and subskills that should characterize the students who participate in a Web-based collaborative situation in order to achieve effective group and individual performance of the task and thus obtain a successful learning outcome. To measure each indicator, we associated it with the actions that students perform and which represent each indicator in the best possible manner. Though we employed the terminology used in the BSCW system to refer to the actions that can be carried out, these terms are general enough to represent all the typical and basic actions encountered in every Web-based groupware platform.

Group Functioning

This is the second top-level activity parameter and is made up of the type of events that represent and are used to measure and analyze individual and group

Table 2. Indicators that model task performance

Skills	Sub-skills (learning outcome contribution)	Actions (&objects) involved
Basic active learning skills	Knowledge/info generation	Create doc/note
Supporting active learning skills	Knowledge/info refinement	Edit doc
	Knowledge/info elaboration	Version/Replace doc
	Knowledge/info revision	Revise/Branch doc
	Knowledge/info reinforcement	Create_Noteboard doc/URL /Notes (attach a note to a document, url or debate)
Information processing (perception) skills	Knowledge/info acknowledge	Read event

Copyright © 2006, Idea Group Inc. Copying or distributing in print or electronic forms without written permission of Idea Group Inc. is prohibited.

effectiveness regarding participation and interaction behavior that facilitate the group's *well-being function* (McGrath, 1991). As a quantitative parameter, it enables us to measure important participant contributions (in terms of specific types of user actions) which indicate skills related to: active or passive participation, well-balanced contributions and role playing, participation quality and communication flow among group members, as well as the necessary skills that facilitate and enhance group interaction, namely *active processing skills* (e.g., task-, workspace- and communication-processing skills). In addition, interaction behavior can also be measured as a qualitative parameter by *group reflection* (i.e., group and individual self evaluation).

Table 3 shows the mid- and low-level indicators in the form of the skills and subskills that students should exhibit in order to enhance participation, promote

Table 3. Indicators that model group functioning

Skills	Sub-skills (Group functioning contribution)	Actions (&objects) involved
Active participation behavior and peer involvement skills	Participation in managing (generating, expanding and processing) info	Create Event, Change Event, Read Event
Social grounding skills	Well-balanced contributions, adequate reaction attitudes, and role playing	Create Event, Change Event, Read Event, Move Event
Task processing skills	Task planning	Create/Link Appointment Create/ChangeAccess WSCalendar
	Task (and knowledge) management	Create Folder Create Notes (create a debate space)
Workspace processing skills	Workspace organisation and maintenance	Move event (cut, drop, copy, delete, forget)
Communication processing skills	Clarification	Change Description/ Change Event doc Change Description url
	Evaluation	Rate document/url
	Description (illustration)	Edit/Change Description Folder Change Description Notes
	Communication improvement	Edit Note Chvinfo/Chvno/Checkin/Checkout doc Rename Folder/Notes/doc/url/ Appointment/WSCalendar
	Meeting accommodation	ChangeDesc/ChangeDate /ChangeLocation Appointment

Copyright © 2006, Idea Group Inc. Copying or distributing in print or electronic forms without written permission of Idea Group Inc. is prohibited.

better communication and coordination, and thus achieve effective interaction and functioning of the group in a Web-based collaborative situation. Again, to measure each indicator, we associated it with the specific student actions that best describe each skill to be accomplished.

Scaffolding (Social Support and Help Services)

These two last top-level activity parameters are specified by the type of events that refer to *social support* among members as well as to *task- or group functioning-oriented help* provided to a participant who is not quite able or ready to achieve a task on his or her own. For the former, we look at event information that includes actions that support and promote group cohesion, such as motivational and emotional support, conflict resolution, and so on. For the latter, we focus on those specific actions designated to provide effective help to peers when they need it during the collaborative learning activities. The participants' actions aimed at getting or providing help are classified and measured according to whether they refer to the task or group functioning.

Table 1 shows the different types of social support and help services (Webb, 1992) that have been identified and accounted for in our model. Scaffolding can be provided explicitly if a member asks for it, or implicitly when a specific need or problem is detected. The latter is achieved through awareness and feedback. More specifically, once the groupcohesion, task-performance, and group-functioning parameters have been measured and analyzed, the group participants (including the mediator) or the system itself (by means of an intelligent agent) can be aware of what is happening during the group activity. Thereafter, they can decide to provide the participants an adequate scaffold associated to social support (e.g., motivation, encouragement, conflict resolution, etc.) or supply them with a specific help service related to the task itself or group functioning (e.g., member participation).

Interaction-Analysis Levels that Support Different Roles and Functions

Based on the interaction analysis process followed, one has to take into account different interaction-analysis levels that cover the needs of different types of users, thus providing diverse functionalities. On the one hand, we should consider interaction-analysis means that provide support to different cognitive systems involved in collaborative learning settings; that is, they should allow self

Copyright © 2006, Idea Group Inc. Copying or distributing in print or electronic forms without written permission of Idea Group Inc. is prohibited.

regulation and classroom monitoring, facilitate peer and group evaluation, and help the teachers themselves to control and assess the collaborative activity and learning more effectively. On the other hand, they should account for and measure the different roles and functions assumed by the participants in a collaborative learning experience.

The problem would consist of identifying the needs of each learner and other potential actors (including the teacher) at every moment and being able to decide what information is required to be provided, in which granularity, and how to present it. For example, the data obtained from the interaction analysis should be tailored in such a way that the support provided for self regulation or peer assessment is adapted to the role the learner plays at a particular moment. In that way, scaffolding information would be different for a learner playing a coordinator role from one that plays a software-designer role. Moreover, the format used to present the information could vary from case to case.

In general, we distinguish three interaction-analysis levels that provide different functionalities:

- **Awareness Level:** At this level, there is a need for techniques and tools that inform participants about what is going on in their shared workspace, providing information about their own actions or the actions of their peers, or presenting a view of the group interaction, behavior and performance. They usually display plane indicator values that show the state and specific aspect of the collaborative-learning interaction and processes that take place. The information presented to the learner can support him or her at a metacognitive level.

- **Assessment Level:** At this level, there is a need to provide data and elements to assess the collaborative activity, so the indicators used are associated with specific weights that measure the significance of each indicator in the assessment process, as showed in Table 1. As in the previous case, the information provided by assessment means acts at a metacognitive level, giving the actors the possibility to evaluate their own actions and behavior as well as the performance of their peers and the group as a whole.

- **Guiding Level:** At this level, we need means that produce information aimed at guiding, orienting, and supporting students in their activity. They help students to diagnose problematic situations and self estimate the appropriateness of their participation in a collaborative activity as well as to counsel their peers whenever insufficient collaboration is detected.

Copyright © 2006, Idea Group Inc. Copying or distributing in print or electronic forms without written permission of Idea Group Inc. is prohibited.

In addition, interaction analysis should take into account different types and profiles of users. In particular, given the case study that online groups should elaborate, students take on different roles at each phase. The main roles assigned are coordinator and subsystem developer). These roles are preestablished since they are assigned to the students before the beginning of a collaborative phase. Besides, these roles are also dynamic since they are switched among peers in each phase.

Moreover, students may come from different backgrounds (e.g., different interdisciplinary groups) and thus have different cognitive and metacognitive skills, needs, interests, motivations, time availability, contexts, or conditions of learning.

Thus, considering the cognitive systems (individuals, peers, group, classroom, and teachers), our approach aims at defining specific interaction-analysis indicators and adapting the analysis techniques so that the form and details of the information derived from the interaction analysis conforms to and accounts for each cognitive system appropriately.

Another issue to be considered was that the roles taken on by students within their group (i.e., intragroup interactions) should not continue to be the same in intergroup interactions (within the classroom). In that case, the indicators should be modified adequately so that they can measure student activity and contribution accurately.

Furthermore, consideration of the different types and profiles of users in the groups requires a particularization of each indicator for each case. Given a specific type of user, our approach refines the previously mentioned indicators into more specific ones, so that we can measure and evaluate different aspects of the user's collaborative interaction and performance, more specifically the degree of success of the role assumed by the user. Given the nature of dynamic roles, in order to obtain a better judgment and evaluation of the users' functions, we need to define the indicators and values that describe the shift from one role to another and how this affects individual and group performances. This issue is being studied.

Finally, another question we faced is what kinds of indicators are more appropriate and how they could measure and support users with various expertise; specific needs and interests; and different motivations, contexts, or conditions of learning. This question is quite complex and is still under investigation.

In any case, interaction analysis has shown that it helps to describe and measure user roles; more importantly, it provides the means for a student to self estimate his or her role, evaluate the role that peers play in the group, and thus apply corrections to any deviations of the functions associated with the role.

Copyright © 2006, Idea Group Inc. Copying or distributing in print or electronic forms without written permission of Idea Group Inc. is prohibited.

Conclusions and Ongoing Work

In this work, we have presented a framework to be used by students and evaluators of group interaction in order to set and assess the activity and performance of online learning groups effectively, especially in the case of real, complex, and long-term collaborative learning experiences. Our approach is based on an analysis of the collaborative-learning interaction by means of a principled evaluation methodology, that is, on theoretical principles, potential indicators of effective collaborative learning behaviour, and an adequate integration of different assessment techniques. Special attention has also been given to interaction-analysis tools that support different roles and functions. All in all, interaction analysis has proved to be an efficient approach for self, peer and group assessment in real settings.

This chapter has presented important findings of an ongoing research project that aims at developing a holistic, well-grounded computational framework of interaction analysis that allows different types of users to evaluate the activity, role, and performance of themselves, their peers, the group, and the classroom as a whole. An in-depth treatment of the whole problem requires a more comprehensive multivariate interaction-analysis model as well as better automated tools that assist users of different profiles to intervene online or off-line.

Acknowledgments

We would like to thank the tutors, as well as all the students, of the Open University of Catalonia who eagerly participated in this experience. This work has been partially supported by Spanish MCYT project TIC2002-04258-C03-03.

References

Barros, M., & Verdejo, M. (2000). Analysing student interaction processes in order to improve collaboration. The DEGREE approach. *International Journal of Artificial Intelligence in Education, 11,* 221-241.

Bentley, R., Appelt, W., Busbach, U., Hinrichs, E., Kerr, D., Sikkel, S., Trevor, J., & Woetzel, G. (1997). Basic support for cooperative work on the World Wide Web. *International Journal of Human-Computer Studies, 46*(6), 827-846.

Copyright © 2006, Idea Group Inc. Copying or distributing in print or electronic forms without written permission of Idea Group Inc. is prohibited.

Cameron, T., Barrows, H. S., & Crooks, S. M. (1999). Distributed problem-based learning at Southern Illinois University School of Medicine. In C. Hoadley & J. Roschelle (Eds.), *Computer support for collaborative learning: Designing new media for a new millenium: Collaborative technology for learning, education, and training* (pp. 86-94). Palo Alto, CA: Stanford University.

Daradoumis, T., Martínez, A., & Xhafa, F. (2004). An integrated approach for analysing and assessing the performance of virtual learning groups. In *Proceedings of the 10th International Workshop on Groupware* (pp. 589-304). Berlin, Germany: Springer.

Daradoumis T., & Xhafa, F. (2004). Problems and opportunities of learning together in a virtual learning environment. In *Computer-supported collaborative learning in higher education*. Hershey, PA: Idea Group Publishing.

Daradoumis, T., Xhafa, F., & Marquès J. M. (2003a). Evaluating collaborative learning practices in a virtual groupware environment. In *Proceedings of the International Conference on Computers and Advanced Technology in Education* (pp. 438-443). ACTA Press.

Daradoumis, T., Xhafa, F., & Marquès J. M. (2003b). Exploring interaction behaviour and performance of online collaborative learning teams. In *Proceedings of the 9th International Workshop on Groupware* (pp. 203-221). Berlin, Germany: Springer.

Dillenbourg, P. (1999). *Collaborative learning: Cognitive and computational approaches*. Oxford, UK: Elsevier Science.

Dimitracopoulou, A. (2004, October), Designing advanced collaborative learning environments: Current trends and future research agenda. In *CSCL SIG Symposium*, Lausanne.

Dobson, M., & McCracken, J. (1997). Problem based learning: A means to evaluate multimedia courseware in science & technology in society. In T. Muldner & T. C. Reeves (Eds.), *Educational multimedia & hypermedia*. Calgary, Canada: AACE.

Greif, I. (1998). Everyone is talking about knowledge management. In *Proceedings of ACM 1998 Conference on Computer-Supported Cooperative Work* (pp. 405-406). Seattle, WA: ACM Press.

Jermann, P., Soller, A., & Muehlenbrock, M. (2001). From mirroring to guiding: A review of the state of the art technology or supporting collaborative learning. In *Proceedings of the European Conference of Computer Support Collaborative Learning*, Maastricht, The Netherlands (pp. 324-331).

Copyright © 2006, Idea Group Inc. Copying or distributing in print or electronic forms without written permission of Idea Group Inc. is prohibited.

Kiesler, S., & Sproull, L. (1987). *Computing and change on campus*. New York: Cambridge University Press.

Krange, I., Fjuk, A., Larsen, A., & Ludvigsen, S. (2002). Describing construction of knowledge through identification of collaboration patterns in 3D learning environments. In G. Stahl (Ed.), *Proceedings of the Computer Support for Collaborative Learning Conference* (pp. 82-91).

Martínez, A., Dimitriadis,Y., Rubia, B., Gómez, E., & de la Fuente, P. (2003). Combining qualitative and social network analysis for the study of social aspects of collaborative learning. *Computers and Education, 41*(4), 353-368.

McGrath, J. E. (1991). Time, interaction and performance (TIP): A theory of groups. *Small Group Research, 22*, 147-174.

Pipek, V., & Wulf, V. (1999). A groupware's life. In S. Bødker, M. Kyng, and K. Schmidt (Eds.), *Proceedings of the 6th European Conference on Computer-Supported Cooperative Work* (pp. 199-218). Copenhagen, Denmark: Kluwer Academic Publishers.

Reiser, B. (2002). Why scaffolding should sometimes make tasks more difficult for learners. In G. Stahl (Ed.), *Computer support for collaborative learning: Foundations for a CSCL community* (pp. 255-264). Hillsdale, NJ: Erlbaum.

Scardamalia, M., & Bereiter, C. (2003). Knowledge building. In *Encyclopedia of education* (2nd ed.) (pp. 1370-1373). New York: Macmillan Reference.

Sfard, A. (1998). On two metaphors for learning and the dangers of choosing just one. *Educational Researcher, 27*(2), 4-13.

Soller, A. (2001). Supporting social interaction in an intelligent collaborative learning system. *International Journal of Artificial Intelligence in Education, 12*, 40-62.

Thomas, R. (2000). Evaluating the effectiveness of the Internet for the delivery of an MBA programme. *Innovations in Education and Training International, 37*(2), 97-102.

Webb, N. (1992). Testing a theoretical model of student interaction and learning in small groups. In R. Hertz-Lazarowitz & N. Miller (Eds.), *Interaction in cooperative groups: The theoretical anatomy of group learning* (pp. 102-119). New York: Cambridge University Press.

Zumbach, J., Hillers, A., & Reimann, P. (2003). Supporting distributed problem-based learning: The use of feedback in online learning. In T. S. Roberts (Ed.), *Online collaborative learning: Theory and practice* (pp. 86-103). Hershey, PA: InfoSci.

Copyright © 2006, Idea Group Inc. Copying or distributing in print or electronic forms without written permission of Idea Group Inc. is prohibited.

Chapter XIII

E-Assessment:
The Demise of Exams and the Rise of Generic Attribute Assessment for Improved Student Learning

Darrall Thompson
University of Technology, Sydney, Australia

Abstract

This chapter explores five reasons for a reduced focus on exams by questioning their value and sustainability in the assessment of student learning. It suggests that exam grades cannot provide accruing developmental information about the students' attributes and qualities vital for a changing world and workplace. It then argues for the integrated assessment of generic attributes (including those developed through exams) and describes two e-assessment tools developed by the author to facilitate this approach. These tools are based on the concept that assessment criteria should encompass the complete range of attributes and qualities that institutions proclaim their students will acquire. Given that assessment drives learning, explicit alignment between assessment tasks and criteria is essential. It is proposed by this chapter that the development of formative criteria (numerically valued) together with expert-derived criteria groups can facilitate students' development of important qualities, or generic attributes at both school and tertiary levels of education.

Copyright © 2006, Idea Group Inc. Copying or distributing in print or electronic forms without written permission of Idea Group Inc. is prohibited.

Introduction

The term *generic attributes* used in this chapter (sometimes referred to as *graduate attributes*) is intended to incorporate a broad range of qualities that are often claimed by educational institutions describing those who complete their courses of study. It is broader than the terms *key skills*, *generic skills,* and *key competencies* often interchangeably used in this research area.

The reader may well ask why a senior lecturer teaching visual communication is writing about e-assessment and educational research. It may be wise to slip into first person for a paragraph at the beginning of this introduction to contextualize and validate the contribution that this chapter is attempting to make.

On entering university teaching, my knowledge of educational research was limited to a 1-year postgraduate teaching certificate. A 6-month secondment to the University of Technology, Sydney (UTS), Centre for Learning and Teaching initiated my focus on research in this area. The realization that my background in information design and visual communication had something to bring to the design of learning environments led eventually to a research master's in design education and the design and development of online assessment systems described in this chapter. I do not teach on an exam-based course but have worked for 15 years with colleagues that do so. It is not my intention here to present an in-depth study of exams as an assessment strategy but rather to provide powerful reasons and supporting references that may encourage greater questioning of the value and sustainability of exams in educational contexts. My reasons for encouraging the assessment of graduate attributes are based on a long association with criteria-based assessment. I believe that—in a rapidly changing world and workplace—students, staff, and employers need much more feedback about the development of graduate attributes. These are hidden or simply not assessed by exam-based summative approaches.

The first part of this chapter explores five reasons to question the value and sustainability of exams in formal educational contexts. The references used include educational research, a recent United States patent granted to Microsoft®, and studies on youth suicide.

The second part explores five reasons for the explicit integration of graduate attributes in curricula and assessment processes. The Australian government's concern with the fact that graduate attributes publicized by universities were often not explicit in curricula or assessed in practice led them to initiate an independent Graduate Skills Assessment (GSA) test. This out-of-context approach is diametrically opposed to the integrated systems proposed in this chapter. A brief analysis of the GSA in this text concludes that whilst a great deal

Copyright © 2006, Idea Group Inc. Copying or distributing in print or electronic forms without written permission of Idea Group Inc. is prohibited.

of work has been put into it, there are flaws in both the approach and the questions themselves.

The third part describes an e-assessment system developed by the author (Re:View) and how knowledge and skills usually assessed by exams can be integrated with graduate attribute descriptive assessment that exams fail to address. This is done using assessment criteria for marking and formative feedback for learning tasks. These criteria are categorized in groups of attributes that accrue summative percentage marks in a secure online database. Students can visually monitor their development during a course of study in each category over a range of tasks (including exams assessed with criteria grouped under the same categories). Through research and experience in using this system, five optimal groups of attributes have emerged: creativity and innovation, communication skills, attitudes and values, professional skills, critical thinking, and research.

The second e-assessment system developed by the author in collaboration with other academic colleagues at UTS is called the Self and Peer Assessment Resource Kit (SPARK). It is used for the assessment of group projects using online self and peer ratings of group-performance criteria by students. These ratings produce a "factor," which when multiplied by the group mark produces individual marks for each group member.

The last part of the chapter illustrates the use of these two systems in an undergraduate program. The examples from case studies outlined are from a 4-year university undergraduate honors degree course and are included to provide evidence of graduate attribute development facilitated by these online systems.

The Demise of Exams: Five Reasons to Question Their Value and Sustainability

- Exams encourage "rote learned" responses and reliance on factual memory.
- Exams encourage surface approaches to learning.
- Exams viability will soon be challenged by the availability of memory-enhancing drugs and emerging technologies.
- Exams facilitate the "fee for degree" commercialization of education.
- Exams cause physical illness, depression, and youth suicide.

The first two reasons are different but related reasons and will be considered together.

Copyright © 2006, Idea Group Inc. Copying or distributing in print or electronic forms without written permission of Idea Group Inc. is prohibited.

Considering the first two reasons as they operate in a highly competitive environment the extensive use of practice exams and the study of answers to past exam papers can dominate the learning environment to the exclusion of more innovative strategies. The rote learning of facts and the one-off extrinsic motivation to succeed in exams is also known to encourage surface approaches, minimal retention of facts and poor knowledge transferability to other contexts. Thorough research on the effects and consequences of surface/atomistic approaches and deep/holistic approaches to learning are readily available in many published works by Marton, Hounsell, and Entwistle (1984), Ramsden (1992), Ramsden and Entwistle (1981), and others:

Surface approach and the motive of fulfilling demands raised by others (i.e., [sic] extrinsic motivation) seem to go together. (Marton & Saljo in Marton, et al., 1984, p. 51).

The following quote from a student in a study by Ramsden in the same book *The Experience of Learning* is just one from hundreds of similar studies:

I hate to say it, but what you've got to do is have a list of the "facts"; you write down ten important points and memorize those, then you'll do alright in the test.... If you can give a bit of factual information—so and so did that, and concluded that—for two sides of writing, then you'll get a good mark. (Ramsden in Marton et al., 1984, p. 144)

This quote from Ramsden's research is a student who received a first-class honors degree (ironically) in Psychology, and reveals a surface approach to learning even though they "hate to say it." It implies they are uncomfortable with achieving success through a memory-based formulaic approach that gives them good marks every time.

The highly complex issue of what is actually being assessed in the psychology student's essay is not addressed here, but new approaches to the assessment of essays online continue to be onerous and problematic (Shermis, Mzumara, Olson, & Harrington, 2001). It could be argued for example, that the psychology student is actually showing a certain degree of synthesis. However the point being made here is that the assessment method itself is adversely affecting the students' approach to their study, and this impact is supported in many specific researches, for example Biggs (1995), Marton and Saljo (1976), Ramsden and Entwistle (1981), and Sternberg (1997).

Apart from essay exam questions, there has been a large increase in the popularity of multiple-choice questions (MCQs), easily ported to online Web

Copyright © 2006, Idea Group Inc. Copying or distributing in print or electronic forms without written permission of Idea Group Inc. is prohibited.

sites and with the added advantage of automatic marking. These have been criticized for their bias toward memory testing and the design of these exams has been identified as a major area for concern by educational researchers. It is apparently very difficult to provide MCQs that do not cause the selection of the correct answer to be too easy, too difficult or just plain ambiguous (Pritchett, 1999).

The main issue centres upon the institutions' and lecturers' responsibility to design courses that encourage deep student engagement and their development of qualities and attributes essential for lifelong learning and continuing employment.

Exam's viability will soon be challenged by the availability of memory-enhancing drugs and emerging technologies. As early as February 2000 an article appeared in the Times Educational Supplement, titled "Spectre of Exam Drug Test Looms", that showed successful results with mice and reporting that "according to scientists brain-boosting drugs may soon hit students" (Bunting, 2000, p. 3). By 2004, the economic potential for pharmaceutical companies had expanded the drive for further research and development:

At least 40 potential cognitive enhancers are currently in clinical development, says Harry Tracy, publisher of NeuroInvestment, an industry newsletter based in Rye, New Hampshire... The interest in such drugs will not stop there, predicts James McGaugh, who directs the Centre for the Neurobiology of Learning and Memory at the University of California at Irvine. Next in line could be executives who want to keep the names of customers at the tips of their tongues, or students cramming for exams. (Economist, 2004, p. 27)

Apart from the problems associated with these advances in drug development, there are also the rapid advances in communication and computing technology. The integrity of exam submissions will be unverifiable due to the miniaturization of digital technology and wireless communication systems. To highlight the extent of this problem with regard to cheating in exams it might be worth considering the following extract from US patent no. 6,754,472 applied for on April 27, 2000, and granted to *Microsoft*® on June 22, 2004.

The human body is used as a conductive medium, e.g., a bus, over which power and/or data is distributed. Power is distributed by coupling a power source to the human body via a first set of electrodes. One or more device

Copyright © 2006, Idea Group Inc. Copying or distributing in print or electronic forms without written permission of Idea Group Inc. is prohibited.

to be powered, e.g., peripheral devices, are also coupled to the human body via additional sets of electrodes. (Williams, Vablais, & Bathiche, 2004)

Whilst there may be concern about health issues arising from electronic data transfer using the human body, the recent history of technological development has shown that the rate of technology adoption has been exponential and inevitable. Devices that transmit and receive data using human skin conductivity and human eardrums instead of headphones may soon become the technology that makes all information invisibly and undetectably available.

If the only educational challenge for young people at school or university is to pass an exam, Microsoft® and the drug companies are about to sell students the means to overcome that challenge, unless of course examinees are all drug tested, strip-searched and conducted to a specially designed radiation-proof room. Perhaps it would be better, and much less expensive, to encourage them to have a deep approach to their own learning and personal development using assessment processes that encourage and facilitate that approach.

Exams facilitate the "fee for degree" commercialization of education. It is conceded that the idea of the demise of exams is counter to current education and e-learning trends. Massachusetts Institute of Technology (MIT) and other North American universities have put their course content free online but charge large fees to take the exam. Given the focus on short-term memory and problems of invigilation already mentioned, is not this rather a dangerous direction? Does it fulfil the developmental needs of young people for survival in this new millennium, or just rely on the fact that those who can afford the fee are likely to have backgrounds that guarantee survival anyway?

The Australian government is making strong statements about the professionalism and quality of teaching in higher education, but whilst pressing for an increase in quality teaching, the government is reducing funding and encouraging commercialization:

Most importantly, teaching needs to be accorded a much higher status in universities. It is necessary to take a broader conception of academic work and the validation of alternative career paths to improve the status of teaching. The quality of teaching is absolutely central to the learning experience. There needs to be a renewed focus on scholarship in teaching and a professionalisation of teaching practice. (Department of Education, Science and Training, 2002, p. 10)

The demand for financial viability means that a focus on quality teaching is unlikely to happen with this economic pressure. Any attempt to improve the

Copyright © 2006, Idea Group Inc. Copying or distributing in print or electronic forms without written permission of Idea Group Inc. is prohibited.

quality of teaching through teacher development is expensive and accrues no direct financial benefit. Gaining research grants and collecting exam fees are far more profitable strategies. Equivalent financial support for teaching and learning is unlikely to be forthcoming unless governments are prepared to invest in providing resources.

Requiring fees for exams may also be a strategy that only the high profile "brand name" universities can apply. If all universities try to follow this approach, will education become like the car industry, where 50 smaller manufacturers have now been replaced by 4 massive ones? The early signs of this are already occurring in Australia, and with the advent of the US free trade agreement, this is likely to gather momentum. In 1999, evidence was emerging in the media:

Large for-profit corporations like Jones International University and the University of Phoenix have entered the huge and growing "virtual university" market to claim their share... indications are that virtual higher education will surely become a large enterprise. According to John Chambers, CEO of Cisco Systems, the company that makes routers that direct traffic on the Internet, education is the next big "killer application." Chambers believes that "Education over the Internet is going to be so big it is going to make e-mail usage look like a rounding error!" Chambers warns, "Schools and countries that ignore this will suffer the same fate as big department stores that thought e-commerce was overrated." (New York Times, 1999)

In October 2004, the South Australian government announced that Carnegie Mellon will be opening a new university in Adelaide in 2006, offering American undergraduate and postgraduate degrees with private students receiving government loans on the same basis as local students.

Whilst the media makes no mention of free content and fee for exam models, the potential for this development is clearly evident. This further commodification of education in Australia may reduce the emphasis on, and encouragement of, good teaching and effective assessment of high quality learning outcomes.

Exams cause physical illness, depression, and youth suicide. This is perhaps the most tragic reason for reducing the focus on exam-based systems.

New South Wales (NSW) in Australia has a Higher School Certificate (HSC) exam, which is used to determine a University Admission Index (UAI).

A report commissioned by the NSW Commission for Children and Young People (Sankey & Lawrence, 2003) studied the population of all deaths of children and young people in NSW by suicide or risk-taking, over a 5-year period (January

Copyright © 2006, Idea Group Inc. Copying or distributing in print or electronic forms without written permission of Idea Group Inc. is prohibited.

1996 to December 2000). The upper age limit for this study was 17 years 11 months, which suggests that its findings could be an underestimate of the number of HSC-related deaths, as many taking the exam were over 18. From 187 young people committing suicide in this period, 38 students were reported to have committed suicide as a result of school-related problems. Ten of these were directly related to HSC stress, and a further eight from related learning difficulties.

Previous research had not documented a link between HSC stress and suicide in NSW, however Smith and Sinclair (2000) found that more than 40% of Year 12 (HSC) students in their study reported symptoms of depression, anxiety, and stress that fell outside normal ranges.

In considering the university age range, the alarming increase in youth suicide (particularly males aged 15-24) prompted the Australian government in 1997 to allocate $31 million to the National Youth Suicide Prevention Strategy aimed at reducing youth suicides in this age range by June 1999 (Australian Government Publishing Service, 1997).

Although the following extracts are from a specific study, my brief research into reports from Japan and the United States shows that they are typical of extracts from studies in other countries with exam-based systems.

Report Extracts (Sankey & Lawrence, 2003):

The young people whose records indicated significant stress levels associated with their impending HSC exams all appear to have suicided in a state of acute stress and in close proximity to an event relating to their exams. (p. 67)

Of the 8 young people experiencing learning difficulties... When Chris told his father that he was at the bottom of his year, his father said that he didn't mind, he just wanted him to complete his HSC. A few weeks prior to his death, Chris told a friend that he felt "dumb" and was finding it very difficult to cope with this. He further said that he would rather be dead, in heaven where it was more peaceful. (p. 57)

Of the 10 young people who experienced significant levels of HSC-related stress, all died by suicide. As a group, these were successful students, with records indicating that they set high standards for themselves and worked extremely hard. Documentation also showed that the period leading up to their deaths was typically characterised by feelings of overwhelming pressure to succeed, coupled with an intense fear of failure. (p. 55)

Copyright © 2006, Idea Group Inc. Copying or distributing in print or electronic forms without written permission of Idea Group Inc. is prohibited.

The finding of an association between HSC stress and suicide warrants urgent investigation of how to support young people during this stressful period and how to work with parents and the community to provide realistic guidance to students. The Child Death Review Team (CDRT) considers that there is a need for the Strategy to address this important issue. (p. 114)

Dr. Anthony Kidman, director of the UTS Health Psychology Unit, conducted a study in 2004 in which an average of two out of five teenagers believed that the HSC exams would affect the rest of their lives. In an article about the study he said, "There is significant anecdotal evidence to suggest burn-out in a large number of students as well as sleeplessness, suicidal ideas and anxiety" (*Sydney Morning Herald*, 2004).

Dr.Gary Galambos in the same article commented, "You have to take that really seriously in a student population because the risk of suicide in teenagers is very high in Australia" (*Sydney Morning Herald*, 2004).

Dr. Kidman and his team are taking a very positive approach to the situation and have designed a "psycho-educational" program for teenagers studying the HSC. The program is called "Taking Charge! A Guide for Teenagers, practical ways to overcome stress, hassles and other upsetting emotions."

The pressure exerted on students by themselves, parents, relatives, peers, and the institutions involved, to achieve good exam results is clearly intense. It has become common practice for students to be advised to choose particular subjects to gain high university entrance scores. This extrinsic motivation overrides the intrinsic motivation to follow a natural inclination or interest.

Few would argue that stresses have not increased, even in the last 5 years; and burgeoning plagiarism and cheating in exams have become major concerns for many educators. *Test anxiety* and *exam stress* are now common terms and inevitably some students who cannot cope with these pressures can become reliant on prescribed antidepressant drugs. Selective serotonin reuptake inhibitors (SSRIs), are the new popular group of drugs that are supposed to have fewer side effects than previous tricyclic drugs.

Speaking at the 11th Annual Suicide Prevention Australia National Conference in October 2004 in Sydney, director of the Australian Institute for Suicide Research and Prevention, Professor Diego De Leo warned that SSRIs may not be a cure-all for depressed kids. He reported that prescriptions for the drugs were increasing, with some given to children presenting signs of suicidality as young as 10 or 11 years old. His concern was that no studies have been done with children in Australia, but recent investigations in the United States urged extreme caution in the prescribing of these inhibitors.

Copyright © 2006, Idea Group Inc. Copying or distributing in print or electronic forms without written permission of Idea Group Inc. is prohibited.

There has also been a link made between physical illness and exam stress:

The psychological stress of school exams can increase the severity of asthma by increasing airway inflammation response, said Dr. Lin Ying Liu and associates at the University of Wisconsin, Madison. In a study of 20 college students with mild allergic asthma, the percentage of sputum eosinophils was 10.5% at 6 hours and 11.3% at 24 hours following an antigen challenge during final exam week—significantly higher than the 7% level during a periods of low stress. (Ying Liu, 2002, p. 15)

It is clear from these studies that young people do not need an assessment strategy that adds aggravation and stress to the other sociocultural pressures during these important developmental periods. Is there a better and more developmental approach to the assessment of knowledge, skills, and attributes, instead of what has proved to be a stressful hurdle biased towards those who can cope and/or cleverly regurgitate?

For all the reasons mentioned in the first part of this chapter, exams have been reasoned to be an indefensible strategy for assessment. Their retention is not inevitable as there are viable alternatives that improve student learning and reduce aggravation and stress for both staff and students.

The following part of this chapter outlines the reasons for the assessment and development of graduate attributes, followed by a description of the effective application of e-assessment systems to enable this process.

The Rise of Generic Attributes: Five Reasons to Encourage Their Explicit Integration in Curricula and Assessment

- Australian Universities Quality Agency (AUQA) audits identify graduate attributes as a problem area.
- Universities need to validate their attribute statements through assessment.
- Schools and universities are responsible for student employability not just accreditation.
- Students actually need these attributes to cope with a changing world.
- Well-designed learning tasks can develop a very broad range of generic attributes.

Copyright © 2006, Idea Group Inc. Copying or distributing in print or electronic forms without written permission of Idea Group Inc. is prohibited.

AUQA audits identify graduate attributes as a problem area. Graduate attributes are referred to in the United Kingdom as key skills and other terms include generic attributes (Wright, 1995), *key competences* (Mayer, 1992) or *transferable skills* (Assiter, 1995). In addition to discipline knowledge, and skills, graduate attributes include, for example: problem solving, interpersonal understanding, critical thinking, written communication, and teamwork skills. Statements of graduate attributes can be found in one form or another on the Web sites and in the documentation of most universities in Australia. However, the statements appear to have minimal implementation in curricula. In a report on the 2002 AUQA audits, this was identified as a major problem:

The audit sampling process picks out the teaching of generic skills or graduate attributes for particular attention. Reflecting the policies of an earlier incarnation of the Department of Education, Science and Training, most of the institutions have some formal statement about the skills they aim to instill but are labouring to devise a means of ensuring that this occurs. One institution was commended for its explicit attention to graduate attributes; at least three institutions were seen to be fumbling the implementation of their policies. (Martin, 2003, p. 15)

It is interesting to note that perhaps thirty years ago "a university education" was assumed to instil implicit attributes in its graduates through traditions, social events, field activities, sports, and so on. This was clearly the case with Oxford and Cambridge whose graduates were considered to have the "moral fibre" and high standards suitable for service in the government or the church. The reduction of traditional socialization could be considered a backward step, but the explicit statements are more appropriate in a deregulated context where a university education is now ubiquitous. However, universities should perhaps be less forthright in the boldness of their graduate-attribute claims in an increasingly litigious society. AUQA's audit and open-publishing process may well provide public assurance of the improvements needed in this area. Their mission reads: "By means of quality audits of universities and accrediting agencies, and otherwise, AUQA will provide public assurance of the quality of Australia's universities and other institutions of HE, and will assist in improving the academic quality of these institutions" (Australian Universities Quality Agency, 2004, p. 2).

Universities need to validate their attribute statements through assessment. In order for universities to ensure their graduates' achievement in the qualities in attribute statements, they must initiate methods of assessing and monitoring attribute development in students.

Copyright © 2006, Idea Group Inc. Copying or distributing in print or electronic forms without written permission of Idea Group Inc. is prohibited.

In 1999, the Australian government decided to test the efficacy of universities' graduate attribute development by commissioning the Australian Centre for Educational Research (ACER) to develop the GSA test. This is completed voluntarily by students at entry, and again at graduation from the university sector, in order to compare results. Whilst the government's concerns are justified by recent AUQA audits, the test does not assess attributes in context and the questions are unrelated to the students' course of study. The test consists of a 2-hour multiple-choice exam and 1-hour essay, but to date has not been received favorably by universities or students. However, a brief analysis is included here, because the thrust of this chapter is diametrically opposed to this external examination method by which the development of graduate attributes or qualities can be measured.

The Australian GSA Test

Graduate Skills Assessment: GSA Introduction

ACER was commissioned by DETYA, in 1999, under the Higher Education Innovation Program to develop a new Graduate Skills Assessment test. The test has been designed to assess generic skills of students when they begin at university and just before they graduate. The four areas currently included in the test are: Critical Thinking, Problem Solving, Interpersonal Understandings, and Written Communication. Many universities have identified these skills as important and are included in their graduate attributes or capabilities statements. The test consists of a multiple-choice test and two writing tasks. The multiple-choice test is currently two hours long and the writing test is sixty minutes long. (Australian Council for Education Research, 2001, p. 1)

This is a very long test by normal standards, and if implemented by all universities will need a large resource in adjudication and benchmarking processes to achieve consistency. The practical implications are enormous in regard to the storage, translation, and analysis of information, and the marking of a massive amount of essay material. The data would also have to be stored for a minimum of four years for comparison to be made with exit scores, and no mention is made of the institutions that will have access to it, the privacy issues involved, equity and language issues, and so on.

The GSA claims to test a range of graduate attributes such as problem-solving and interpersonal skills. For example, Unit 1, Question 1 from the sample questions on Problem Solving, asks the student to work out the scheduling of

Copyright © 2006, Idea Group Inc. Copying or distributing in print or electronic forms without written permission of Idea Group Inc. is prohibited.

netball teams to meet, whilst avoiding their regular training sessions that are listed. It then shows drawings of four sample schedules from which to select, in a multiple-choice list. This task involved simply matching gaps in times listed on pairs of charts. The answer to this question does not require problem-solving skills but the ability to match diagrams with lists, and is clearly below university level.

The following question is a sample from the **Interpersonal Understandings** section of the GSA: UNIT 11 Question 23:

23   A job interviewer asks an applicant the following question:

"How would you persuade a person working with you in a team to follow your suggestions when that person is reluctant to do so?"

Which one of the following responses by the applicant most strongly suggests an ability to work well in a team?

A :   I would do the work myself. At least that way I know it would be done properly.

B :   I would make it very clear that I was more experienced in these matters than him/her.

C :   I would find out more about the person's concerns and then discuss these with him/her.

D :   I would follow his/her suggestions rather than mine to show the person they are wrong.

E :   I would point out that in a team there has to be some give-and-take, and that he/she should listen to me this time. (Australian Council for Education Research, 2002, p. 14)

Firstly, the question is contextualized, as though it is being asked in a job interview rather than a real group situation. It is possible that this is to trick the examinee (and the applicant) into a preset persuasive position, which they would need to avoid to answer the question correctly. This convoluted context is asking a young person to make a judgement from the position of an employer asking a trick question of an illusory applicant. How this is related to the examinees natural response when immersed in a group context is hard to fathom. Secondly, there are perhaps more appropriate responses, such as: F: I would apologize for trying to impose my suggestions through persuasion!; G: I would suggest we have a look

Copyright © 2006, Idea Group Inc. Copying or distributing in print or electronic forms without written permission of Idea Group Inc. is prohibited.

at the criteria against which the project will be assessed; or H: I would suggest we have a brief discussion about why we are doing the project and what we want to get out of it.

MCQs are unlikely (even with clever design) to test higher-level learning or attributes because of forced choice options (Pritchett, 1999). Given all the reasons discussed in the first part of this chapter, it would clearly be preferable not to add yet another onerous exam (for staff and students alike).

This chapter proposes that the solution is to ensure that the educational experiences in which students engage encourage the development of graduate attributes and that universities monitor the development of them throughout a student's course of study. The facilitation of this process is addressed by the database-driven Web applications described in this chapter.

Schools and universities are responsible for student employability not just accreditation. Business organizations rely on universities to stay ahead of changing requirements and to provide graduates with appropriate attributes and skills. However, because of their own increasingly pressured environment, employers are becoming more vocal in what they expect the university environment to deliver.

Graduate attributes have been identified as vital qualities for successful employment and lifelong learning. A number of employer studies have identified serious flaws in graduates' attributes. For example a study of design engineering graduates and their employers in the United Kingdom (Garner & Duckworth, 2000, p. 208) revealed a deep dissatisfaction with current graduate profiles. In their study, the employers' criticisms of graduates included the following points:

- They need greater ability to take other people's ideas on board.
- They have a lack of resilience to criticism.
- They have a weak ability to muster a reasoned defence of their contribution.
- They need to improve listening skills.
- They need higher-quality written, graphic, and verbal communication.
- They need to be able to be critical of their own work and contributions.

The following quote from the summary of their study resonates with a need for versatility and diversity in employees and lays a huge expectation at the doors of the university learning environment:

Copyright © 2006, Idea Group Inc. Copying or distributing in print or electronic forms without written permission of Idea Group Inc. is prohibited.

A breadth of skills and knowledge seems vital—as one manager put it, "we can't afford specialists". The desired profile seems a broad one: creative and analytical; practical and academic; numerate and literate; able to exploit both divergent and convergent thought processes; sensitive and strong! (Garner & Duckworth, 2000, p. 211)

Salchow (1994) in his critical writing on "employer-driven" responses in the educational provision for professional graphic designers suggests a more balanced view by suggesting that: "We should not attempt to give the provincial employer everything he expects of an applicant if it contradicts the needs of our students, society, and the profession" (p. 221).

However, a graduate fulfilling the attributes described in Garner and Duckworth's (2000) summary, could hardly fail to satisfy Salchow, the students, society, or the professions.

Students actually need these attributes to cope with a changing world. The exponential changes outlined in the first part of this chapter require graduates to have a broad range of attributes, including the versatility with which to apply them. Toffler (1980) goes further in his prophetic work: "The illiterate of the 21st century will not be those who cannot read and write, but those who cannot learn, unlearn, and relearn" (p. 12).

It is ironic, in my view, that the educational focus on the examination of reading and writing in children, often ignores, and perhaps even stifles, their natural curiosity and desire for learning. The ability to cope with, and adapt to change, is also hinted at in Toffler's (1980) definition of literacy for the 21st century. It is interesting to note that these abilities or qualities are supported in literature by those studying the natural worlds. Suzuki (1998) in his book *Earth Time* suggests that the two most important qualities of a sustainable life form are versatility and diversity. He also implies that these qualities may equally be necessary for the sustainability of business organizations and individuals in society. The knowledge and skills fundamental to an undergraduate degree are likely to be less important than the acquisition of these generic attributes for survival in a changing world and workplace.

Well-designed learning tasks can develop a very broad range of attributes. It is clear that the development of the broad range of generic attributes promoted in university statements can never be exclusively due to their educational experiences and may develop as a result of engagement external to the university. The lack of teaching and assessment of these attributes has been a cause for government concern in recent university audits by AUQA mentioned

Copyright © 2006, Idea Group Inc. Copying or distributing in print or electronic forms without written permission of Idea Group Inc. is prohibited.

earlier. However, well-designed learning environments offer a unique opportunity for the development of this broad range of attributes. The reasons for a mismatch in attribute statements and actual outcomes identified in AUQA audits are difficult to define. If graduate attributes are to be achieved through learning experiences they ought to be fundamental to the design of learning tasks and the basis for assessment criteria.

The following part of this chapter outlines two e-assessment systems developed by the author at UTS for the assessment of graduate attributes as part of an integrated approach, incorporating other knowledge and skills criteria.

E-Assessment for the Development of Generic Attributes Through Individual Tasks and Group Work

It ought never to be said that software of any kind is a solution, and later parts of this chapter propose that any assessment system needs to be carefully integrated at all stages of the learning design.

It is clear that exam grades do not provide the range of information about a graduate attributes necessary for a changing world and workplace. Written reporting does not accrue summatively to clearly indicate development in key areas. So how can software assist in this context?

In the first instance, the designers of exams need to develop criteria that actually make explicit what an exam is measuring or testing. For example, if an exam is testing the memorizing of facts, then this should contribute to a student's development of memory skills. If it is testing whether they can reference an academic document correctly then that should contribute to the students' development of research skills. If it is testing their ability to communicate rather than remember a concept, then the assessment should be adding to the students' ongoing development of communication skills. If they are asked to apply a concept innovatively, then assessment should be adding to their ongoing development of creativity and innovation; and if they are asked to analyze a text, the assessment should add to their ongoing development of critical thinking skills... and so on. If these criteria are made explicit and each one graded rather than all this information being hidden in a single grade, then the software can ascribe a value to each and store the numbers under different criteria categories.

If the exams are marked using criteria in this way, then other tasks throughout a course of study that also contribute to these criteria categories (including group

Copyright © 2006, Idea Group Inc. Copying or distributing in print or electronic forms without written permission of Idea Group Inc. is prohibited.

projects) can be added giving ongoing feedback about the students' development within these categories of attributes.

There is an obvious advantage in using systems that can combine the assessment of graduate attributes that are impossible to assess with exams, with criteria-based measurement of discipline knowledge and skills, which is normally assessed summatively.

The two software systems described in the following sections have been used in a university context, where the development of assessment criteria in various attribute categories has gradually occurred over a number of years.

- **Re:View—Online Criteria-Based Assessment.** A database-driven Web system for integrating graduate-attribute assessment with other criteria, and enabling students to monitor their progress in graduate attributes across a range of subjects.
- **Self and Peer Assessment Resource Kit (SPARK).** An online assessment system to enable self and peer ratings against group-work criteria, to be used in calculating individual marks for a group project.

Both these systems have been designed, at a grass-roots level, by academics attempting to solve problems related to assessment and feedback. As such, they have both been very successful and continue to develop and refine through pilot schemes in various educational contexts.

It is generally accepted in educational literature that to try to teach graduate attributes as separate subjects is not a successful strategy, and that attributes need to be embedded in curricula but made explicit in assessments. The Re:View

Figure 1. Logotype designed by the author for the Re:View Web-service assessment system

Figure 2. Logotype designed by the author for the SPARK Web-based group-work assessment system

Copyright © 2006, Idea Group Inc. Copying or distributing in print or electronic forms without written permission of Idea Group Inc. is prohibited.

Figure 3. Lecturer's view of assessment and feedback marking screen

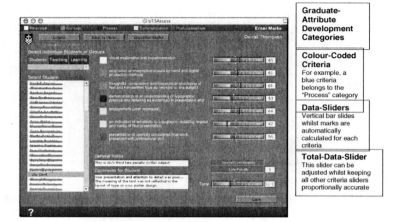

system is designed to facilitate this assessment within normal learning tasks and alongside other more content-focused discipline knowledge and skills criteria. SPARK is designed to bring group work into mainstream summative assessment using criteria to feed back to students about their development of group skills through self and peer assessment ratings that modify group marks into individual marks for each student.

A Description of the Re:View–Online Criteria-Based Assessment System

One of the major problems in criteria based assessment is that percentage marks allocated to particular criteria are rarely presented to the students as an additive progression contributing to important strands of learning. By categorizing criteria under graduate attribute development categories, the Re:View system can gather and accrue ongoing "profiles" showing progress in each category over time and across many different subject assessments.

Another problem is the difficulty of delivering private individual assessment and feedback to students other than by laboriously copying and pasting to online grade books or to e-mail addresses that are often out of date. With this system the student can log on at anytime from anywhere via the Web and see assessment and feedback the moment the assessing lecturer clicks the "publish marks" button.

Copyright © 2006, Idea Group Inc. Copying or distributing in print or electronic forms without written permission of Idea Group Inc. is prohibited.

Figure 4. Student view of assessment-feedback screen

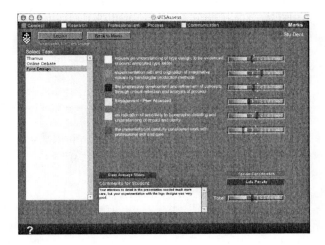

Figure 5. Feedback against an early set of graduate attribute categories based on an interpretation of the visual design process

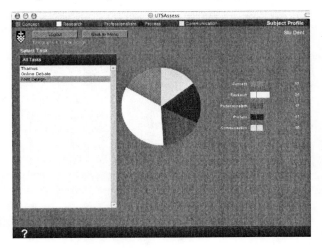

In the development of this e-assessment system, the criteria categories and individual criteria had to be written and refined. One side effect of entering these into the database system was that curriculum developers and staff were able to see a progressive overview of learning objectives reflected in assessment criteria across a broad range of subjects. There can be a great deal of hidden repetition in a course where individual lecturers are left to design their own

Copyright © 2006, Idea Group Inc. Copying or distributing in print or electronic forms without written permission of Idea Group Inc. is prohibited.

assignments independently. The Re:View system reduces the effect of this on assessment by displaying visual pie and bar charts of criteria categories, to illustrate the attribute development intended through different subject areas and during the progressive years of a course. It also displays students' achievement in those by individual, group, subject, year, and so on.

A Description of SPARK

This has also been a successful e-assessment tool aimed at the development of graduate attributes related to working in groups. It enables students' engagement in criteria-based reflection on their own and their peers' contributions (anonymously), through a Web interface. One of the factors produced by the system is then used to calculate an individual mark based on these self and peer ratings.

It is normally important to ensure that group work does not constitute the majority of a subjects' learning tasks, however, with the SPARK system, problems associated with all group members receiving the same mark are removed because individual marks are generated through the self and peer ratings process. I have successfully used SPARK for up to 70% of a subject's assessment.

Figure 6. Students view of group rating screen against sample criteria

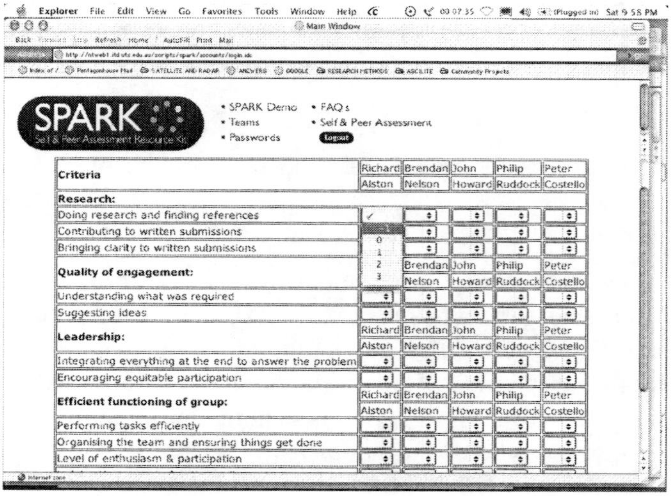

Copyright © 2006, Idea Group Inc. Copying or distributing in print or electronic forms without written permission of Idea Group Inc. is prohibited.

Case Study Outline Using SPARK and Re:View

The figures reproduced for this case study were from a design history assignment traditionally assessed using exams and allocated 20% of the total assessment for the subject. The learning task was designed as a group-based online debate project ending in a live debate in the lecture theatre.

First semester, 2nd-year students were randomly formed into 18 learning groups of 5 students each for the task at the beginning of semester, as a method for managing tutorial and studio sessions throughout the 13-week period.

The *Online Debate* ran whilst the other two tasks were being undertaken and spanned a period of 6 weeks in the middle of the semester. There were two online submission deadlines on Sundays at midnight to stimulate online activity and also to avoid other interim deadlines within the subject.

An extract from the briefing document shows the briefing explanation students received:

Scenario:

Imagine we have just been joined on our UTSOnline website by 18 famous typographers/artists/designers. They represent strong views about both the expressive and functional approaches to typography and design.

Some of them are in disagreement and want to have a discussion/argument about their approaches.

However quite a few of them are dead and the others not here in Australia so we have arranged for this to happen using your learning groups as champions of their points of view and philosophy."

The students were encouraged to "become" the typographer or designer using three devices: (a) a photograph of each learning group posted online with their new persona's name, at the time when they needed to challenge their opposing debate partner; (b) an instruction that all online written submissions, and the live debate at the end, were to be written or spoken in first-person; and (c) group research of a given persona through five holistic research questions, which I designed, to broaden the information which forms the basis for the debate submissions:

Copyright © 2006, Idea Group Inc. Copying or distributing in print or electronic forms without written permission of Idea Group Inc. is prohibited.

1.   **Propositions:** What did they believe and what were they trying to do?

2.   **Influences and connections:** Where did they draw their influences from and who were they connected to, for example, artistic movements, and so on?

3.   **Principles and ways of working:** How did they go about their work, and what did they consider important in the way it was done?

4.   **Character/Personality:** What were they like as a person and why do you think they did what they did?

5.   **Facts and Figures:** What interesting facts can you find as well as the usual birth/death/education that is available?

Students were encouraged, through video clips of a previous iteration of the project, to be creative in costume and drama, in making their points in the live debate at the end of the task.

The debate, both online and live was structured to reveal the positions of the individuals from history (or living) in reference to a spectrum—from functional, problem-solving design at one end, to expressive, artistic approaches at the other. Students were instructed that they would have to position their persona on a spectrum line as part of the live debate session. They were also asked to reflect on their own position with regard to this spectrum both prior to and after the project.

Functional <—> Expressive

As this learning task was only a 20% part of the subject assessment it was specifically targeted to develop two basic attributes in the context of an online group engagement. The two assessment criteria used to cover all three parts of the task (*Opening Statements, Challenging Statements* and *Live Debate*) related to subject-outline learning objectives in the attribute groups of research skills and process skills:

*   **Research:** Depth of research in substantiating the points of view, and
*   **Process:** The cogency with which arguments and rebuttals were developed.

The development of ability to work in teams was also part of the learning objectives of this task but the second online system, SPARK, was used for this purpose.

Copyright © 2006, Idea Group Inc. Copying or distributing in print or electronic forms without written permission of Idea Group Inc. is prohibited.

The Re:View software was used by the lecturer to mark and give feedback on this task (and the other tasks in this subject). Students logged on to see their group's assessment and feedback online. The staff members involved in the subject were keen to use the software, albeit at pilot stage, due to the timesavings they had experienced in both marking and then publishing grades and feedback online.

The live debate was videoed and both stills and clips from the video were put online as a reminder of the process, whilst group members had 10 days within which to rate each other and themselves using SPARK.

The factors produced from SPARK ratings were then used to modify the group marks to individual marks, based on the self and peer ratings against nine criteria (these were explained and agreed to by the students, with opportunity for comment and amendment, at a session introducing the learning task):

Category	Criteria
Online Submissions	Contributing to the cogency of written submissions
Online Submissions	Doing research and finding references
Efficient functioning	Helping the group to function well as a team
Efficient functioning	Level of participation in the online debate project
Efficient functioning	Performing tasks efficiently
Quality of engagement	Suggesting ideas
Quality of engagement	Understanding what was required
Leadership	Helping decide who does what and when
Leadership	Bringing things together for a good team result

Self assessment (SA) and peer assessment (PA) was new for these first-semester second-year students but categorized, criteria-based assessment had been experienced in other subjects.

There were two different factors produced by SPARK from these ratings, revealing some interesting aspects of this self and peer reflective assessment process. The first is a factor produced from the average of SA as a ratio to the PA. If this factor is less than 1.0, then the student underrated their own performance in comparison with their group members' ratings of them. The second is the SPA factor, which is a combination of the average of self and peer ratings and is the factor used to calculate individual marks through multiplication with the group mark given by the lecturer. The method for SPARK and the formulas for the calculation of factors were based on educational research (Thompson, 2002).

Copyright © 2006, Idea Group Inc. Copying or distributing in print or electronic forms without written permission of Idea Group Inc. is prohibited.

The analysis of overall ratings shown in this table reveals a very responsible approach to rating, in that the -1 rating was only used 12 times and 0 was used only 45 out of 2986 ratings. These ratings are used by SPARK to calculate the factors mentioned and the effect on individuals' marks when multiplying their factor by the group mark can be significant as seen in Table 2.

This table shows an example of the two factors generated by SPARK in the ratings process. If the SPA (Self + Peer Assessment) factor was *1.0* then the group member received the same mark that the group was given by the lecturer (e.g., 62% multiplied by 1.0 = 62%). The SPA factor is the one used to modify the group mark, so that if a student has a factor of 0.9 they would only receive 90% of the group mark given for the group task (e.g., 62% multiplied by 0.9 = 55.8%). Therefore, as previously shown in the case of Student 2, the group mark was 75.5 and the student received .86 of that, that is 64.9%.

The SA/PA factors show significant underrating by individuals of their own performance. It is interesting that both factors for Student 1 show that the group rated this team member's performance much more highly than they rated

Table 1. Total numbers of case study ratings for each rating level

Rating	Total
-1 (detrimental contribution)	12
0 (no contribution)	45
1 (below average contribution)	370
2 (average contribution)	838
3 (above average contribution)	1631
All ratings	2986

Table 2. SPARK factors showing effects on students' individual mark compared with the group mark given by the lecturer

SA/PA		SPA	Group Mark Given by lecture	Individual Mark: GrpMark x SPA
Student 1:	0.82	1.05	80.5%	84.5%
Student 2	0.83	0.86	75.5%	64.9%
0.84		1.04	73.5%	76.4%
0.84		0.84	76%	63.8%
0.86		1	62%	62.0%
0.86		0.97	86%	83.4%
0.87		0.86	71.5%	61.5%
0.88		0.99	75.5%	74.7%
0.88		0.99	75.5%	74.7%
0.89		1.01	75	75.8
0.89		0.99	86	85.1
0.9		0.96	62	59.5

Copyright © 2006, Idea Group Inc. Copying or distributing in print or electronic forms without written permission of Idea Group Inc. is prohibited.

themselves, and their individual mark shifted from a Distinction to a High Distinction (High Distinction is the grade given in the Australian New South Wales banding system when a mark is 85% or above). SPA factors for Student 2 show that the group agreed with this student's low ratings of their own contribution and their individual mark was reduced by 11% from a Distinction (75-84%) to a Borderline Credit (65-74%).

Overall from this group of 90 students, 24 underrated themselves (as in the example of Student 1) with varying degrees of agreement from their peers.

Students reflected that they felt the SPARK process was fair, and that they could relax into group work knowing that individual contributions would be taken into account in the final individual mark. The criteria for the group project were simple, but thought to be appropriate for a task worth 20% and anonymous feedback against teamwork criteria was added to their ongoing profile under the five strands of development: research, concept, communication, process, and professionalism.

Conclusion

The argument for reducing the focus on exams becomes clear in the light of research surrounding the two sets of reasons explored in the first two parts of this chapter:

- Consistent educational research identifies assessment as a powerful driver in directing student learning.

- Exams appear to drive learning down pathways that no educator would support, with deadly side effects and the prospect of "invigilation" costs rising exponentially.

- Graduate attributes are a range of qualities that students need to develop in order for them to survive in a rapidly changing world, whilst contributing positively to it.

- The qualities that are consistently part of graduate-attribute statements therefore must become the core focus of our mainstream assessment systems.

Educational literature poses an important question underpinning assessment: What do we want students to learn and how does our assessment encourage that learning? Given that part of necessary student learning is that learning itself is

Copyright © 2006, Idea Group Inc. Copying or distributing in print or electronic forms without written permission of Idea Group Inc. is prohibited.

a developmental lifelong process, our assessment processes should themselves give developmental feedback over time.

The two assessment systems described in this chapter are designed to bring the development of generic attributes into mainstream assessment processes, integrated with other more content-focused criteria. However, the introduction of e-assessment systems is not viable without delivering time and flexibility benefits to teaching staff. Change relies on the genuine reflection by curriculum developers and teaching staff, about the real impacts of their assessments on young people. An important rider to the changes suggested in this chapter is that the thorough explanation and careful introduction of an e-assessment system (to both staff and students), is an essential ingredient in its success.

Through early pilot schemes introducing the two systems, one of the most interesting aspects was the opening of a dialogue about assessment processes between lecturers and students. The lecturers have had to explain the reasons for these processes and be far more explicit in the definition of criteria used in the marking of work. The students, on the other hand, have had to relinquish surface approaches through discussing criteria and exercising responsibility in rating their own and their peers' contributions. The benefit of students of developmental feedback across subject boundaries was not studied in this research although the benefits of formative assessment with accruing summative marks was positively noted by teachers.

It is hoped that the reasons and references relating to the use of exams will assist in their gradual demise as a dominant feature of the assessment landscape, and that the case studies and descriptions provided will encourage a serious attempt to implement less stressful and more useful assessment processes.

References

Assiter, A. (Ed.). (1995). *Transferable skills in higher education.* London: Kogan Page.

Australian Council for Education Research (2001). Higher Education Innovation program. *Graduate Skills Assessment test.* DETYA. Canberra, Australian Capital Territory: Author.

Australian Council for Education Research (2002). GSA report. Canberra, Australian Capital Territory: Author.

Australian Government Publishing Service (1997). *Youth suicide in Australia: A background monograph* (2nd ed.). Author.

Copyright © 2006, Idea Group Inc. Copying or distributing in print or electronic forms without written permission of Idea Group Inc. is prohibited.

Australian Universities Quality Agency (2004). *Annual report 2003*. Retrieved January 1, 2005, from http://www.auqa.edu.au

Biggs, J. B. (1995). Learning in the classroom. In J. Biggs & D. Watkins (Eds.), *Classroom learning: Educational psychology for the Asian teacher* (pp. 147-166). Singapore: Prentice-Hall.

Bunting, C. (2000, February 18). Spectre of exam drug tests looms. *Times Educational Supplement, 4364,* 3.

Department of Education, Science, and Training (2002). *Striving for quality: Teaching, learning and scholarship* (Vol. 6891, HERC02A). Canberra, Australia Capital Territory: Author.

Economist. (2004, September 18). Supercharging the brain. *Economist, 372*(8393).

Garner, S., & Duckworth, A. (2000). In C. Swann & E. Young (Eds.), *Re-inventing design education in the university* (pp. 206-212). Perth, West Australia: Curtin University of Technology.

Martin, A. (2003). *2002 institutional audit reports: Analysis and comment.* Retrieved January 13, 2005, from Australian Universities Quality Agency Web site: http://www.auqa.edu.au/qualityenhancement/occasional publications/

Marton, F., Hounsell, D., & Entwistle, N. (Eds.). (1984). *The experience of learning.* Edinburgh, Scotland: Scottish Academic Press.

Marton, F., & Saljo, R. (1976). On qualitative differences in learning, II— Outcome as a function of the learner's conception of the task. *British Journal of Educational Psychology, 46,* 115-127.

Mayer, E. (1992). Canberra, Australian Capital Territory: Australian Government Publishing Service.

New York Times (1999, November 17). NYT Education Supplement.

Pritchett, N. (1999). Effective question design. In S. Brown et al. (Eds.), *Computer-assisted assessment in higher education.* London: Kogan Page.

Ramsden, P. (1992). *Learning to teach in higher education.* London: Routledge.

Ramsden, P., & Entwistle, N. J. (1981). Effects of academic departments on students' approaches to studying. *British Journal of Educational Psychology, 51,* 368-383.

Salchow, G. (1994). In M. Bierut (Ed.), *Looking closer 1: Critical writings on graphic design.* New York: Ailsworth Press.

Sankey, M., & Lawrence, R. (2003). *Suicide and risk-taking deaths of children and young people.* Sydney: New South Wales Commission for

Copyright © 2006, Idea Group Inc. Copying or distributing in print or electronic forms without written permission of Idea Group Inc. is prohibited.

Children and Young People, Child Death Review Team, & Centre for Mental Health.

Shermis, M., Mzumara, H., Olson, J., & Harrington S. (2001). Online grading of student essays: PEG goes on the World Wide Web. *Assessment & Evaluation in Higher Education, 26*(3), 247-259.

Smith, L., & Sinclair, K. E. (2000). Transforming the HSC: Affective implications. *Change: Transformations in Education, 3*(2), 67-79.

Sternberg, R. J. (1997). *Thinking styles.* New York: Cambridge University Press.

Suzuki, D. (1998). *Earth time.* Toronto, Canada: Stoddart Publishing Company Ltd.

Sydney Morning Herald (2004, October 28). Stress put to the test. Australia.

Thompson, D. (2002). In A. Davies (Ed.), *Enhancing curricula: Exploring effective curriculum practices in art, design and communication in higher education* (pp. 360-392). London: Centre for Learning and Teaching in Art and Design.

Toffler, A. (1980). *The third wave.* New York: William Morrow.

Williams, L., Vablais, W., & Bathiche, S. (2004). *U.S. Patent No. 559746.* Washington, DC: U.S. Patent and Trademark Office.

Wright, P. (1995). Canberra, Ausralian Capital Territory: The Higher Education Quality Council, Quality Enhancement Group.

Ying Liu, L. (2002, August 1). In *Family Practice News, 32*(15).

Copyright © 2006, Idea Group Inc. Copying or distributing in print or electronic forms without written permission of Idea Group Inc. is prohibited.

About the Authors

Tim S. Roberts (t.roberts@cqu.edu.au) is a senior lecturer with the Faculty of Informatics and Communication at the Bundaberg campus of Central Queensland University, Bundaberg, Australia. He has taught a variety of computer science subjects, including courses to more than 1,000 students located throughout Australia and overseas, many of them entirely online. In 2001, together with others, he developed the Online Collaborative Learning in Higher Education Web site at http://clp.cqu.edu.au, and in 2003 the Assessment in Higher Education Web site at http://ahe.cqu.edu.au. He has previously edited two books, *Online Collaborative Learning: Theory and Practice* (Information Science Publishing, 2003) and *Computer-Supported Collaborative Learning in Higher Education* (Idea Group Publishing, 2004).

*   *   *

Rozz Albon is director of teaching and learning at Curtin University of Technology, Miri Campus, in Sarawak, Malaysia. She has been teaching in higher education institutions for 15 years following a short career in primary education and the NSW Technical Education Sector. Her interests in continuous education, adult education, child and adolescent development, approaches to learning, assessment, motivation, self-regulated learning, and gifted education have impacted on her current interest in e-learning and the role of social constructivism in online learning, particularly in a multicultural context. Mediated

Copyright © 2006, Idea Group Inc. Copying or distributing in print or electronic forms without written permission of Idea Group Inc. is prohibited.

learning, informal mentoring, evaluation of online learning, and the role of assessment to drive learning reflect her current research interests.

Pamela L. Anderson-Mejías has taught English as a second language and prepared teachers to do the same at the University of Texas - Pan American, USA, National University of Tucumán (Argentina), University of Hawaii, Southern Illinois University, and Indiana University. She has published language-related work in the *Foreign Language Annals, International Journal of Sociology of Language, Hispania,* the *Southwest Journal of Linguistics,* as well as teacher training and online delivery of instruction in *TESL Online Journal* and *Technology Source*, among others. She resides in the multicultural and multilingual Rio Grande Valley of South Texas.

Thanasis Daradoumis (adaradoumis@uoc.edu) has a PhD in information sciences from the Polytechnic University of Catalonia-Spain, a master's degree in computer science from the University of Illinois, and a bachelor's degree in mathematics from the University of Thessaloniki-Greece. Since 1984, he has been an assistant professor at several universities in the U.S., Greece, and Spain, teaching a variety of courses in mathematics and computer science. Since 1998, he has been working as a professor in the Department of Information Sciences at the Open University of Catalonia, Spain, where he coordinates several online courses as well as the development of teaching materials appropriate for virtual learning. His research focuses on e-learning and learning technologies, ontologies and Semantic Web, distributed learning, CSCL, CSCW, interaction analysis, and grid technologies.

Vanessa Paz Dennen is an assistant professor of educational psychology and learning systems at Florida State University, USA, where she teaches courses on instructional design, computer courseware, and evaluation. She teaches both traditional and distance-education courses, with extensive use of Web-based conferencing, collaborative learning, and problem-based learning in both formats. Dr. Dennen earned a PhD in instructional systems technology from Indiana University. Her research examines the design and facilitation issues facing instructors using online learning technologies.

Anne Dragemark holds a teaching degree from McGill University, as well as a Swedish teaching diploma from Göteborg University, Sweden. Presently a PhD student in language education, she also lectures in teacher education at Göteborg University. Her professional background includes teaching Swedish and English at both secondary and upper-secondary levels. She has extensive

Copyright © 2006, Idea Group Inc. Copying or distributing in print or electronic forms without written permission of Idea Group Inc. is prohibited.

experience in the field of language testing through working with the Swedish National Testing Programme and was responsible for the development of the Swedish Self-assessment Material. In addition, she has been active in several language projects that concern assessment, for example, the Swedish Research Council project *Self-Assessment of Language Learning* and the European Union language projects *Teaching English for Technical Purposes* and *Learning English for Technical Purposes.*

Eric Ellis is director of information support services at Treasure Valley Community College, USA. Having recently completed a master's degree in education technology, where his work centered on the issue of trust and access to institutional information, he is currently pursuing his doctorate at Pepperdine University.

Aditya Johri is a doctoral candidate in the Learning Sciences and Technology Design program at the School of Education, Stanford University, USA. He is interested in psychological and sociological aspects of communication and technology pertaining to electronic knowledge communities and computer-supported collaboration issues. For his dissertation, he is investigating the role of interpersonal knowledge in facilitating expertise sharing and learning in technology-mediated communities. For more information, please visit http://www.stanford.edu/~ajohri/.

Gabriel Jones is in the doctoral program in the Department of Literature at the University of California, San Diego and teaches rhetoric, composition, and cultural studies at San Diego State University, USA.

Bernarda Kosel (bernarda.kosel@fs.uni-lj.si) (MA, English; BA, French) has been involved in teaching English to adults and students for more than 20 years. Presently, she teaches ESP courses at the Faculty of Mechanical Engineering, University of Ljubljana, in Slovenia. She wrote several course books of English for mechanical engineering for university students. She has recently been involved in two European projects dealing with innovative teaching methods in ESP with the aim to develop teaching English across the curriculum using the problem-based learning model. In the year 2000, she attended a training program, Testing and Evaluation at the Language Studies Unit, University of Aston, with the aim to develop forms of assessment appropriate for problem-based learning.

Paul Lam is a postdoctoral fellow in the Centre for Learning Enhancement and Research at The Chinese University of Hong Kong. He has extensive experi-

Copyright © 2006, Idea Group Inc. Copying or distributing in print or electronic forms without written permission of Idea Group Inc. is prohibited.

ence in English-language teaching at the school level, and this education experience has been applied in several education-development projects in Hong Kong universities. Paul's current focus is on the design, development, and evaluation of Web-assisted teaching and learning.

Carmel McNaught is a professor of learning enhancement in the Centre for Learning Enhancement And Research (CLEAR) at The Chinese University of Hong Kong. McNaught has had more than 30 years experience in teaching and research in higher education and has had appointments in eight universities in Australasia and southern Africa in the discipline areas of chemistry, science education, second-language learning, e-learning, and higher-education curriculum and policy matters. Current research interests include evaluation of innovation in higher education, strategies for embedding learning support into the curriculum, and understanding the broader implementation of the use of technology in higher education.

Mary Panko has a variety of experiences in the tertiary education sector, and, although her original background was zoology, over the last decade she has specialized in adult education. She is currently programme director of a professional tertiary teaching qualification and earned a master's of education at Unitec in New Zealand. Her primary research interests are online education and the e-moderation of discussion forums where she has investigated the impacts of teacher beliefs on practice. Panko is currently carrying out collaborative research projects into topics ranging from evaluating professional tertiary training programs to exploring learning styles in the construction industry.

Ángel Alejandro Juan Pérez (angel.alejandro.juan@upc.edu) has a PhD in applied mathematics from the UNED (Spain) and a master's degree in information technologies from the Open University of Catalonia (Spain). Since 2000, he has been working as a consulting professor at the Open University of Catalonia; and, since 2002, he has been working as a lecturer in the Department of Applied Mathematics at the Technical University of Catalonia. His research areas are computer simulation and e-learning.

Pedro C. C. Pimenta graduated in chemical engineering from the University of Porto and finished his PhD at this university on process control in 1997. He is currently an auxiliary professor at the Department of Information Systems, University of Minho, Portugal and his research is aimed at the role of information

Copyright © 2006, Idea Group Inc. Copying or distributing in print or electronic forms without written permission of Idea Group Inc. is prohibited.

systems in formal learning processes in higher education from a technical—as well as a pedagogical, organizational, and sociopolitical—perspective.

James Rhoads is currently the Web designer for Citrus College, USA. His research interests are identity and learning in virtual environments. He has recently completed his master's degree and is currently pursuing his doctorate in educational technology at Pepperdine University.

Margaret Riel is a senior researcher at the Center for Technology in Learning, SRI, International, and a visiting instructor at Pepperdine University, USA, teaching action research. Her interest in online teaching and learning arises from decades of research and development in the area of communication technology and education. Currently, she is engaged in two projects—one to evaluate social-network analysis as a way to explore social capital for school reform and the other to investigate adaptive expertise in the reasoning process of science teachers—both funded by the National Science Foundation. Her work is available at gsep.pepperdine.edu/~mriel/office.

Darrall Thompson had an early scientific education with a switch to the arts, followed by 15 years as a professional designer and lecturer in London. A family-led move to Australia in 1989 was supported by consultancies with major companies and involvement in the development of online systems. Thompson's current design practice and teaching in interface design together with a research master's in design education has led to a focus on e-assessment systems and curriculum development. He is currently full-time senior lecturer in the Faculty of Design, Architecture, and Building at the University of Technology, Sydney, Australia, and Conjoint Senior Lecturer in the Faculty of Science and IT at the University of Newcastle.

Natascha van Hattum-Janssen holds a master's degree in educational science and technology at the University of Twente, The Netherlands. Her specialization area is curriculum development. In 2004, she finished her PhD at the University of Minho in Portugal on peer and self-assessment in engineering education. She currently works as an educational specialist at the Council of Engineering Courses of the University of Minho on various assessment projects for first-year engineering courses and supports teachers who implement new assessment methods. She is also involved in staff development on assessment methods.

Fatos Xhafa (fatos@lsi.upc.edu) has a PhD in computer sciences from the Polytechnic University of Catalonia in Barcelona, Spain. Since 1996, he has been

Copyright © 2006, Idea Group Inc. Copying or distributing in print or electronic forms without written permission of Idea Group Inc. is prohibited.

working as a lecturer in the Department of Languages and Informatics Systems at the Polytechnic University of Catalonia and, since 1999, as a consulting professor at the Open University of Catalonia. Dr. Xhafa has participated in several research projects funded by the European Community.

Copyright © 2006, Idea Group Inc. Copying or distributing in print or electronic forms without written permission of Idea Group Inc. is prohibited.

Index

Copyright © 2006, Idea Group Inc. Copying or distributing in print or electronic forms without written permission of Idea Group Inc. is prohibited.

Copyright © 2006, Idea Group Inc. Copying or distributing in print or electronic forms without written
permission of Idea Group Inc. is prohibited.

Copyright © 2006, Idea Group Inc. Copying or distributing in print or electronic forms without written permission of Idea Group Inc. is prohibited.

Copyright © 2006, Idea Group Inc. Copying or distributing in print or electronic forms without written permission of Idea Group Inc. is prohibited.

Copyright © 2006, Idea Group Inc. Copying or distributing in print or electronic forms without written permission of Idea Group Inc. is prohibited.

Experience the latest full-text research in the fields
of Information Science, Technology & Management

InfoSci-Online

InfoSci-Online is available to libraries to help keep students,
faculty and researchers up-to-date with the latest research in
the ever-growing field of information science, technology, and
management.

The InfoSci-Online collection includes:
- Scholarly and scientific book chapters
- Peer-reviewed journal articles
- Comprehensive teaching cases
- Conference proceeding papers
- All entries have abstracts and citation information
- The full text of every entry is downloadable in .pdf format

**InfoSci-Online
features:**
- Easy-to-use
- 6,000+ full-text
  entries
- Aggregated
- Multi-user access

Some topics covered:
- Business Management
- Computer Science
- Education Technologies
- Electronic Commerce
- Environmental IS
- Healthcare Information Systems
- Information Systems
- Library Science
- Multimedia Information Systems
- Public Information Systems
- Social Science and Technologies

*"...The theoretical bent
of many of the titles
covered, and the ease
of adding chapters to
reading lists, makes it
particularly good for
institutions with strong
information science
curricula."*
— Issues in Science and
Technology Librarianship

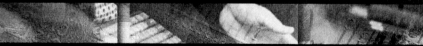

To receive your free 30-day trial access subscription contact:
Andrew Bundy
Email: abundy@idea-group.com • Phone: 717/533-8845 x29
Web Address: www.infosci-online.com

InfoSci Online
Full Text · Cutting Edge · Easy Access

A PRODUCT OF IDEA GROUP INC.
Publishers of Idea Group Publishing, Information Science Publishing, CyberTech Publishing, and IRM Press

infosci-online.com

Single Journal Articles and Case Studies Are Now Right at Your Fingertips!

Purchase any single journal article or teaching case for only $18.00!

Idea Group Publishing offers an extensive collection of research articles and teaching cases that are available for electronic purchase by visiting www.idea-group.com/articles. You will find over 980 journal articles and over 275 case studies from over 20 journals available for only $18.00. The website also offers a new capability of searching journal articles and case studies by category. To take advantage of this new feature, please use the link above to search within these available categories:

- ◆ Business Process Reengineering
- ◆ Distance Learning
- ◆ Emerging and Innovative Technologies
- ◆ Healthcare
- ◆ Information Resource Management
- ◆ IS/IT Planning
- ◆ IT Management
- ◆ Organization Politics and Culture
- ◆ Systems Planning
- ◆ Telecommunication and Networking
- ◆ Client Server Technology

- ◆ Data and Database Management
- ◆ E-commerce
- ◆ End User Computing
- ◆ Human Side of IT
- ◆ Internet-Based Technologies
- ◆ IT Education
- ◆ Knowledge Management
- ◆ Software Engineering Tools
- ◆ Decision Support Systems
- ◆ Virtual Offices
- ◆ Strategic Information Systems Design, Implementation

You can now view the table of contents for each journal so it is easier to locate and purchase one specific article from the journal of your choice.

Case studies are also available through XanEdu, to start building your perfect coursepack, please visit www.xanedu.com.

For more information, contact cust@idea-group.com or 717-533-8845 ext. 10.

www.idea-group.com

IDEA GROUP INC.

New Releases from Idea Group Reference

Idea Group REFERENCE

The Premier Reference Source for Information Science and Technology Research

ENCYCLOPEDIA OF
DATA WAREHOUSING AND MINING

Edited by: John Wang,
Montclair State University, USA

Two-Volume Set • April 2005 • 1700 pp
ISBN: 1-59140-557-2; US $495.00 h/c
Pre-Publication Price: US $425.00*
*Pre-pub price is good through one month
after the publication date

- Provides a comprehensive, critical and descriptive examination of concepts, issues, trends, and challenges in this
rapidly expanding field of data warehousing and mining

- A single source of knowledge and latest discoveries in the
field, consisting of more than 350 contributors from 32
countries

- Offers in-depth coverage of evolutions, theories, method-
ologies, functionalities, and applications of DWM in such
interdisciplinary industries as healthcare informatics, artificial intelligence, financial modeling, and applied statistics

- Supplies over 1,300 terms and definitions, and more than
3,200 references

ENCYCLOPEDIA OF
DISTANCE LEARNING

Four-Volume Set • April 2005 • 2500+ pp
ISBN: 1-59140-555-6; US $995.00 h/c
Pre-Pub Price: US $850.00*
*Pre-pub price is good through one
month after the publication date

- More than 450 international contributors provide extensive coverage of topics such as workforce training,
accessing education, digital divide, and the evolution of
distance and online education into a multibillion dollar
enterprise

- Offers over 3,000 terms and definitions and more than
6,000 references in the field of distance learning

- Excellent source of comprehensive knowledge and literature on the topic of distance learning programs

- Provides the most comprehensive coverage of the issues,
concepts, trends, and technologies of distance learning

ENCYCLOPEDIA OF
INFORMATION SCIENCE AND TECHNOLOGY
AVAILABLE NOW!

Five-Volume Set • January 2005 • 3807 pp
ISBN: 1-59140-553-X; US $1125.00 h/c

ENCYCLOPEDIA OF
DATABASE TECHNOLOGIES AND APPLICATIONS

April 2005 • 650 pp
ISBN: 1-59140-560-2; US $275.00 h/c
Pre-Publication Price: US $235.00*
*Pre-publication price good through
one month after publication date

ENCYCLOPEDIA OF
MULTIMEDIA TECHNOLOGY AND NETWORKING

April 2005 • 650 pp
ISBN: 1-59140-561-0; US $275.00 h/c
Pre-Publication Price: US $235.00*
*Pre-pub price is good through
one month after publication date

www.idea-group-ref.com

Idea Group Reference is pleased to offer complimentary access to the electronic version
for the life of edition when your library purchases a print copy of an encyclopedia

For a complete catalog of our new & upcoming encyclopedias, please contact:
701 E. Chocolate Ave., Suite 200 • Hershey PA 17033, USA • 1-866-342-6657 (toll free) • cust@idea-group.com